Managing Visitor Attractions

Second Edition

This book is dedicated to

Alan Fyall to Lise, Alix and Elliot
Brian Garrod to Alison, Lydia, Drew and Nick
Anna Leask to Malcolm and Euan
Stephen Wanhill to Eluned

Managing Visitor Attractions

Second Edition

Alan Fyall
Brian Garrod
Anna Leask
Stephen Wanhill

AMSTERDAM • BOSTON • HEIDELBERG • LONDON • NEW YORK
OXFORD • PARIS • SAN DIEGO • SAN FRANCISCO • SYDNEY • TOKYO
Butterworth-Heinemann is an imprint of Elsevier

Butterworth-Heinemann is an imprint of Elsevier
The Boulevard, Langford Lane, Kidlington, Oxford, OX5 1GB
30 Corporate Drive, Suite 400, Burlington, MA 01803, USA

First edition 2008
Reprinted 2008

British Library Cataloguing in Publication Data
A catalogue record for this book is available from the British Library

Library of Congress Cataloging-in-Publication Data
A catalog record for this book is available from the Library of Congress

ISBN: 978-0-7506-8545-0

For information on all Butterworth-Heinemann publications
visit our website at www.elsevierdirect.com

Printed and bound in *Great Britain*

08 09 10 10 9 8 7 6 5 4 3 2

Contents

Contents

List of Figures

List of Tables

Editors and Contributors

Editors

Alan Fyall is Deputy Dean, Research & Enterprise, in the School of Services Management, Bournemouth University, UK. He has published widely with his particular areas of expertise spanning the management of attractions, heritage tourism and destination management. Alan has co-edited *Managing World Heritage Sites* published by Elsevier Butterworth-Heinemann and has co-authored *Tourism Marketing: A Collaborative Approach* and the third edition of *Tourism Principles and Practice* published by Channel View and Pearson Education, respectively. Alan sits on the editorial boards of the *Annals of Tourism Research*, the *International Journal of Tourism Research* and the *Journal of Heritage Tourism* and is Book Reviews Editor for *Anatolia*. He has conducted projects for a number of major clients across the UK and Europe in addition to undertaking projects in the Middle East, the Caribbean, Southern Africa and Central Asia. Alan is currently serving as an adviser to the Commonwealth Tourism Centre, based in Kuala Lumpur, and is a Board Member of the Bournemouth Tourism Management Board.

Brian Garrod is Senior Lecturer in Tourism at the Institute of Rural Sciences, University of Wales, Aberystwyth, UK. He lectures in tourism and economics, specializing in sustainable tourism and ecotourism. His work has been published in a wide range of academic journals, both tourism-related and non-tourism. He is co-editor of *Marine Ecotourism: Issues and Experiences* and co-author of *Tourism Marketing: A Collaborative Approach*, both published by Channel View Publications. He has also recently co-edited a volume entitled *New Frontiers in Marine Tourism: Diving Experiences, Sustainability, Management* for Elsevier. He is Book Reviews Editor of the *Journal of Heritage Tourism*, Associate Editor of the *Journal of Ecotourism* and sits on the editorial boards of

Tourism in Marine Environments and the *International Journal of Sustainable Development*. Brian has twice been retained by the World Tourism Organization as an expert adviser on the subject of sustainable tourism. He has also worked for the OECD as a consultant in the area of corporate environmental strategy.

Anna Leask is Senior Lecturer in tourism management at Napier University, Edinburgh, UK. Her teaching and research interests combine and lie principally in the areas of heritage visitor attraction management, visitor attraction pricing and general conference management. She has also co-edited *Managing World Heritage Sites* (2006) with Alan Fyall and *Heritage Visitor Attractions: An Operations Management Perspective* (1999) with Ian Yeoman. Anna has presented and published extensively in the field of visitor attraction management in both UK and international contexts. She currently leads research in the School of Marketing, Tourism and Languages and the Centre for Festival and Event Management at Napier University, Edinburgh.

Stephen Wanhill is Professor of Tourism Economics, University of Limerick and Emeritus Professor of Tourism Research, Bournemouth University and Visiting Professor at the Universities, Nottingham and Swansea. He is Director of Global Tourism Solutions (UK) and his principal research interests are in the field of tourism destination development. To this extent he has acted as a tourism consultant to a number of UK Planning and Management Consulting firms, and has undertaken a wide range of tourism development strategies, tourism impact assessments, lecture programmes and project studies from airports to attractions in over 50 countries. He has acted as tourism policy adviser to the Select Committee on Welsh Affairs for a period of five years in the House of Commons and has been a Board Member of the Wales Tourist Board with responsibilities for the development and research divisions. He is the Editor of *Tourism Economics* and an Editorial Board Member of the *Acta Touristica*, the *Service Industries Journal, Tourism Management*, the *European Journal of Tourism Research*, the *International Journal of Tourism Research*, and the *Journal of Travel Research*.

Contributors

Roy Ballantyne is Research Professor in the School of Tourism, University of Queensland, Australia.

Stephen W. Boyd is Professor of Tourism at the University of Ulster, UK.

Bradley M. Braun is Associate Dean in the College of Business Administration, University of Central Florida, USA.

Neil Carr is Senior Lecturer in the Department of Tourism, University of Otago, New Zealand.

Chris Cooper is Foundation Professor of Tourism Management and Head of the School of Tourism, University of Queensland, Australia.

Janet Dickinson is Senior Lecturer in Leisure and Tourism, School of Services Management, Bournemouth University, UK.

Jonathan Edwards is Reader in Tourism in the School of Services Management, Bournemouth University, UK.

Philip Feifan Xie is Assistant Professor in the School of Human Movement, Sport and Leisure Studies, Bowling Green State University, USA.

Dorothy Fox is a PhD Student in the School of Services Management, Bournemouth University, UK.

Philip Goulding is Senior Lecturer in Tourism, Sheffield Hallam University, UK.

C. Michael Hall is Professor of Marketing in the Department of Management at the University of Canterbury, New Zealand.

Joan C. Henderson is Associate Professor at Nanyang Technological University, Singapore.

Martin McCracken is Lecturer in Organisation Behaviour, University of Ulster, UK.

Gianna Moscardo is Associate Professor in Business Studies in the School of Business, James Cook University, Australia.

Bruce Prideaux is Professor in Tourism Management and Marketing in the School of Business, James Cook University, Australia.

Steven Richards is Senior Lecturer in Tourism Management in the School of Services Management, Bournemouth University, UK.

Brent W. Ritchie is Senior Lecturer in Tourism, Director of the Centre for Tourism Research and ACT Network Coordinator for the Sustainable Tourism CRC, University of Canberra, ACT, Australia.

Derek Robbins is Senior Lecturer in Tourism in the School of Services Management, Bournemouth University, UK.

Myra Shackley is Professor of Culture Resource Management and Head of the Centre for Tourism and Visitor Management, Nottingham Trent University, UK.

Mark D. Soskin is Associate Professor of Economics in the Department of Economics, University of Central Florida, USA.

Terry Stevens is Managing Director of Stevens & Associates, Swansea, UK and Visiting Professor at Bournemouth University, UK.

Richard Voase is Senior Lecturer at the Lincoln Campus of the University of Lincoln, UK.

Geoffrey Wall is Associate Dean, Graduate Studies and Research, at the University of Waterloo, Ontario, Canada.

Sandra Watson is Head of the School of Management and Law, Napier University, UK.

Keith Wilkes is Deputy Dean, Education, in the School of Services Management, Bournemouth University, UK.

Foreword

When invited to write the foreword to the first edition, I said that while I was naturally pleased to accept, I loathed the words 'visitor attraction'. Although this may sound contradictory, I believe that the world has moved on from the time when the term held meaning. It is now an umbrella term, covering such a wide range of activities, interests and ambitions that new descriptive phrases will have to evolve.

What has changed since 2002, when I first wrote, is that many visitor attractions have opened and failed and many have gone into a decline. Only a minority have increased their visitor numbers and it might be informative to ask why. It is understandable that the great Lottery projects, opened with a fanfare and then left to fend for themselves, have reached a peak and then declined slowly to reach a steady state. The successes might include the Bankside Tate, Kew's Wakehurst Place Seed Bank, the Deep in Hull, Dynamic Earth in Edinburgh and the London Eye for example. All have declined but are performing well. The real champions for sustained growth, I would suggest, are Chester Zoo, Kew and the National Trust as a whole. They have all transformed themselves into relevant, personal organizations that have strengthened their storytelling ability beyond recognition over the last few years and who, as a result, have engaged with their loyal supporters who believe, rightly, that these organizations are actively going somewhere. The list of failures is as long as your arm, with many being propped up by emergency refinancing measures or, worse, being allowed to go bust.

They all share visitors; but what has changed more quickly than could have been anticipated five years ago is the motivation behind many of the visits. My experience may be of interest. I began by undertaking a garden restoration which was to open to the public under the name, 'The Lost Gardens of Heligan'. We opened while the restoration was in its early stages and we found that people took real ownership over what we were doing and returned time and again and told their friends about us to the point that Heligan became the most-visited private garden in Britain. I then became involved with the creation of the Eden Project, the largest conservatories in the world, the home to a new scientific foundation and an educational and entertaining visitor destination which has attracted more than eight million visitors over the six years of its being open and, like the earlier successful examples, began with a high of 1.8 million visitors and then reached steady state three years ago, since when we have held to a constant 1.2 million. Our secret? Return visits. From a second year 17 per cent, we now receive more than 50 per cent of our visitors as returnees. This is a sign of health. Those projects that fail do not get the loyalty.

What makes Heligan and Eden successful? They are both physically beautiful and of a status that has guaranteed them miles of newsprint and television coverage; but the secret of their continuing success comes from two things. First is a recognition that most people are to a lesser or greater degree lonely (how many couples or families do you entertain who seem to have lost the art of conversation?). They want to have their attention engaged, but they actually desire something deeper – a connectedness that links to their lives either actually or wishfully. This may sound pretentious but it is not. The great visitor attractions understand this and are selling what they do in terms of lifestyle choices, not passive entertainment and a great day out. The eye for detail, the curious, the talking point are the seducers of conversation and they are often fired up by the second factor, staff. We employ massively more people than an MBA manual would advise (400+ full time and a further 200 seasonal as of March 2007). We do this because visitors like nothing more than to talk to someone who is enthusiastic about what they are doing for a place that is 'authentic'. People love people who love people, and they return time after time to enjoy the experience. This is only a truth that everyone reading this book knows in their heart, but most do not translate it into their businesses. If you would love to go to the place you work at you are probably not doing much wrong; if you would not pay to go there – fire yourself. The best form of marketing is word of mouth and the best ambassadors are your visitors.

Tim Smit
The Eden Project
6 April 2007

Preface

While the idea for this book originally arose out of an informal discussion over coffee in a wet-and-windy Edinburgh in November 1999, this second edition began with a very relaxed discussion among the editorial team in the heat of Guildford while attending a conference at the University of Surrey in June 2006. The success of the first edition, to the pleasant surprise of the original three editors, clearly served as a catalyst for this second edition; as did the highly supportive comments and considerable enthusiasm shown for the project by Sally North and Tim Goodfellow at Elsevier. Their support, in addition to the many positive comments that each of the editors has received over the past few years, made the decision to proceed with a second edition relatively straightforward, although as with everything else, finding time was never going to be easy! In this regard, Professor Stephen Wanhill kindly accepted an invitation to join the editorial team. With many years of professional and academic experience behind him, Steve's appointment was welcomed by everybody and helped bring to the fore a number of viewpoints and issues to make what we consider very real improvements to the first edition.

Despite the above, however, what is perhaps a little disappointing is the extent to which many of the problems and challenges identified in the first edition remain. While the sector has moved on from the surge of activity in the early months of the new millennium, both in the UK and in other countries around the world the aftermath of the 'millennium exuberance' phase in visitor attraction development continues to demonstrate the need for a much greater understanding of the visitor attraction domain. For example, we still need to understand more fully what visitor attractions actually are, what forces drive their development, who visits them and why, how they are funded and what the numerous day-to-day challenges are in respect of their management, marketing and, perhaps most importantly, their long-term viability.

The paucity of reliable research data, particularly of a comparable nature, and the general lack of published work available in the field of visitor attractions, somewhat disappointingly continues to make answering the above questions difficult. Unlike other sectors of the tourism industry where there is a continual supply of new academic and practitioner-focused sources of information and analysis becoming available, it still remains a mystery that so little has been published on visitor attractions. After all, they represent the very aspect of tourism that acts as the principal tourist draw to so many destinations around the world. The first edition of this book apart, a sector-wide focus on visitor attractions has been conspicuous by its absence. One of the possible explanations for such a vacuum lies in the fact that visitor attraction sectors around the world are often typified by a very large number of small, geographically fragmented and resource-poor attractions trying to meet a multitude of objectives for a diverse set of owners. This can be demonstrated by the fact that historic monuments, castles and battlefields, zoos, theme parks, industrial attractions, museums and galleries, visitor centres, churches and cathedrals and, increasingly, retail sites and sporting arenas, to name but a few, can all to varying degrees legitimately be classified as visitor attractions. Addressing the sector in its entirety is therefore a challenging proposition, and continues to raise the question as to how worthwhile such an endeavour is in the first place.

Back in 1972, in his seminal work *Vacationscape*, Gunn refers to visitor attractions as '… the first power, lodestones for pleasure and the real energizer of tourism in a region … without attractions there would be no need for other tourism services' (Gunn, 1972). This viewpoint continues to gain our unequivocal support. Visitor attractions as a sector sometimes may lack the glamour of international airlines, the diversity and appeal of destinations or the political and critical challenge of tourism policy. Individually and collectively, however, they represent the catalytic focus for the development of tourism infrastructure and services. For this reason alone they continue to warrant academic attention and deserve a research-base equivalent to, or even better than, other much more talked-about and researched sectors of the wider tourism industry. Visitor attractions represent a complex sector of the tourism industry and are genuinely not very well understood. It is thus the principal aim of this book to generate greater interest and discussion of visitor attractions, to stimulate critical debate and to provide a foundation for a much greater research contribution from both the academic and practitioner communities.

As with the first edition, the issues discussed in this book were selected carefully to address the areas considered to be of the utmost importance to the future direction of the management of visitor attractions. With the book divided into four parts, focusing on the *role and nature* of visitor attractions, and their *development, management, marketing*, an attempt has been made to identify and address thematic issues that connect a variety of seemingly disparate elements in the visitor attraction sector. Issues explored in the book include the nature and role of visitor attractions, interpretations of the development of the visitor attraction product, factors impacting on attraction failure and success, economic aspects of their development, issues pertaining to the development of visitor attractions on the geographic periphery, visitor attraction development in East Asia and the integrated role of transport to visitor attractions.

Management issues covered include discussion on the authentication of ethnic visitor attractions, meeting the needs of the 'new' visitor, the management of visitor impacts and seasonality, school excursion tourism and the appropriate management of attractions and the management challenges for garden and religion-based attractions. In addition, the importance of recruiting and managing an effective human resource-base for attractions is explored as is the relationship between interpretation and attractions. The book also examines a number of marketing issues relating to heritage attractions, the marketing and management of attractions over time, competitive strategies for theme parks and the emergence of a more collaborative approach to the marketing of visitor attractions. As with the first edition, no doubt this list omits many other issues considered to be of great significance. What the list does represent, however, is a genuine attempt to bring together issues that are important to both academics and practitioners, and are likely to be of real value to students of this dynamic sector of tourism.

Of great significance to all of the above is the role and experience of the visitor at attractions. Without visitor attractions, one could argue there is no basis for tourism; yet, without visitors there is clearly no market for visitor attractions. Tim Smit stressed the importance of the visitor, and especially the repeat visitor, in his foreword to the book and there is no doubt that this principle cannot be emphasized enough. Despite the slowdown in visitor demand in many markets, visitors are still frequenting attractions in very large numbers indeed. However, the nature of their visits, their motivations and expectations, their experiences and perceived 'value for money', their willingness and readiness to act as ambassadors for attractions and their readiness to return are likely to change over time and be influenced by the vast array of alternative 'things to do' in their leisure time. Visitor attractions are not only competing for visitors with other attractions, they are in the market for 'people's time'. Time is continually at a premium for many people around the world. Visitor attractions need to understand their visitors, understand what draws them to attractions in the first instance and understand what satisfies their thirst for fun, education or whatever it is that the visitor of the future is searching for.

In putting this book together, the editors are in considerable debt to the efforts of all the contributors for their acceptance of initial interest and readiness to participate in the project, and for their hard work and valued contribution with regard to subject matter and ideas. All contributors are either recognized academic experts in their field or well-respected and highly experienced practitioners in the visitor attraction sector. In view of the busy schedules of everyone concerned, the prompt response to invitations for contributions, the speed with which ideas were forthcoming and the efficiency with which deadlines were met, all contributors are worthy of praise. In particular, we are delighted with the geographic coverage of both our contributors and their chosen themes and case material. Contributions span all corners of the UK, Australia, Singapore, Canada, New Zealand and the United States. In addition, we wish to offer our deepest thanks to Sally North who has always been a great believer in our ideas and projects, past and present.

Sally is not only a highly professional colleague but she is also a great friend, so thank you Sally!

In closing this preface, it is important to refer back to the first edition of the book and its original ambition to advance 'new directions' in the management of visitor attractions rather than merely to report the *status quo*. Although much time has passed since the first edition was published, it is our collective view that many of the new directions advanced back in 2003 remain 'work in progress'. With this in mind, it is hoped that this new edition develops further many of the ideas, themes and issues introduced in the first edition, as well as bringing to the fore many new thoughts and cases of contemporary interest. What perhaps is still lacking, however, is the necessary research-base upon which to compare and contrast international best practice, to provide a national or international benchmark of visitor attraction quality or to provide a foundation for the advancement of some of the issues discussed in this book beyond national boundaries. It is hoped that this second edition of *Managing Visitor Attractions* will serve as a catalyst for change and help raise the study of visitor attractions to a higher level.

Alan Fyall
Bournemouth University, UK

Brian Garrod
University of Wales, Aberystwyth, UK

Anna Leask
Napier University, UK

Stephen Wanhill
Bournemouth University, UK

28 June 2007

Reference

Gunn, C. (1972). *Vacationscape: Designing Tourist Regions*. Bureau of Business Research, University of Texas, Austin, TX.

Introduction: The Role and Nature of Visitor Attractions

Part One of this book explores the broad context within which visitor attractions operate and provides an historical overview of how the visitor attraction product has developed over time. While the overall focus of the book is on the role of visitor attractions as a major component of the tourism system, it is important to recognize that visitor attractions operate within a number of interrelated internal and external environments. For example, many visitor attractions play a vital role in conserving and protecting the natural and built historic heritage. Others have an explicit educational function or are important in helping to maintain specific cultural identities and practices. As a result, the management of visitor attractions is influenced by a range of complex issues in addition to those arising out of their role as tourism resources. The key themes identified in the first part of this book therefore cover a broad range of issues relating to the context in which visitor attractions are managed.

After providing an introduction to the variety and scope of visitor attractions, Chapter 1, by Anna Leask, considers how visitor attractions may best be defined and categorized. Definitions of visitor attractions vary significantly around the world, as does the basis for the categorization of different types of visitor attraction within a certain definition. This gives rise to a major dilemma for the conduct of research into the management of visitor attractions. On the one hand, the lack of a common definition of what constitutes a visitor attraction can frustrate efforts to compare management concepts and identify best practice across different categories of visitor attraction, as well as across the visitor attraction sectors of different countries. On the other hand, the existence of a wide diversity of visitor attractions may call into question the necessity and desirability of a common definition. Indeed, visitor attraction sectors around the world are often characterized by a very large number of small attractions that have poor access to resources and are diffuse in spatial terms, yet are trying to meet a wide range of objectives set by a multitude of stakeholders. This chapter attempts to clarify the role and nature of the visitor attraction product and the context within which they operate.

Chapter 1 then goes on to explore how visitor attractions fit into the overall tourism product and system. Visitor attractions are clearly only one part of a complex network of tourism service providers. Leask considers the main interrelationships and interdependencies between visitor attractions and the wider tourism industry. Visitor attractions are then discussed in relation to the wider political and sociocultural environment. The degree to which the focus of analysis should be at the level of the individual attraction, at the destination level or at the national level is also explored. This, in turn, raises the question of whether the focus of analysis should be on the management of the attraction as a whole or on particular management functions, such as marketing or human resource management. This book has adopted an inclusive and flexible approach to the questions of definition, categorization and analytical focus, in a deliberate attempt to stimulate debate and discussion. The collective thoughts of the editors can be found in the concluding section of this book. From the beginning of the writing process, contributors were encouraged to sow the seeds of thought and question the existing *status quo* within the visitor attraction sector. The contributors responded enthusiastically, particularly so in the case of the contribution of Stephen Wanhill, who in Chapter 2 introduces the concept of the market–imagescape mix. He then goes on to use a framework based on the market–imagescape concept to suggest a revised classification of attractions which, he argues, will contribute to the better understanding and management of both individual visitor attraction products and the wider visitor attraction sector.

The third major issue explored in Part One relates to the multiplicity of objectives arising from the wide range of stakeholder interests that is typically evident among visitor attractions. Despite the diversity of objectives in evidence around the world, increasingly competitive market conditions are serving as a catalyst for the adoption of more common approaches to attraction management. However, the current lack of commonality in objective setting continues to generate conflicting management pressures. It also continues to provide a diversity of challenges and impediments to the effective management of visitor attractions. The two opening chapters offer some valuable insights into the environment within which visitor attractions operate and how the challenges and impediments may best be addressed and ultimately overcome.

Finally, Part One considers the perceived economic benefits of visitor attractions and, in particular, the extent to which the development of visitor attractions represents a viable means of economic development and/or regeneration. In so doing, Chapter 2 offers some insights into the criteria that are likely to determine the success, or otherwise, of visitor attractions.

CHAPTER 1

The Nature and Role of Visitor Attractions

Anna Leask

Aims

The aims of this chapter are to:

- introduce the variety and scope of visitor attractions,
- discuss the basis for definitions and categories of visitor attractions, and
- identify the range of roles that visitor attractions play in international, national, regional and local environments.

Introduction

There can be no doubting the crucial role that visitor attractions have in the development and success of tourism destinations. At their most basic level they work to attract visitors to an area, while many also operate in a much broader sense as agents of change, social enablers and major income generators. Indeed, Boniface and Cooper (2001: 30) state that 'attractions are the *raison d'être* for tourism; they generate the visit, give rise to excursion circuits and create an industry of their own'.

The purpose of this chapter is to introduce the variety of visitor attractions, discuss the issues involved in establishing their definitions and identify their varying roles in differing destinations. This allows authors of later chapters to concentrate on the specific management issues as they relate to visitor attractions, without each needing to discuss the broad context within which they operate. While no fixed definition of visitor attractions is to be used for this book, the following discussion will allow for this multi-faceted sector to be explored, thus setting the broad parameters and international context of this area of interest. The chapter starts with an explanation of the huge variety of visitor attractions that exists around the world, followed by a brief discussion of the key working definitions currently in use. The chapter finishes with an assessment of the roles that visitor attractions may have within a range of tourism destinations.

The variety and scope of visitor attractions

Visitor attraction categorization

There have been many attempts to explain the multitude of forms in which visitor attractions may manifest themselves (Cooper *et al.*, 2005; Holloway, 1998; Smith, 1998), with classification generally being on the basis of the natural or built character of the resource. However, this appears to be a rather narrow, one-dimensional view of a sector which often has multiple stakeholder involvement in individual properties and consequently an extensive range of often-conflicting management objectives. Figure 1.1 attempts to outline the various approaches that could be considered in the classification of this dynamic sector of the tourism industry.

At the centre of Figure 1.1 is the core product offered by the visitor attraction, which focuses mainly on the resource that attracts the visitors to visit in

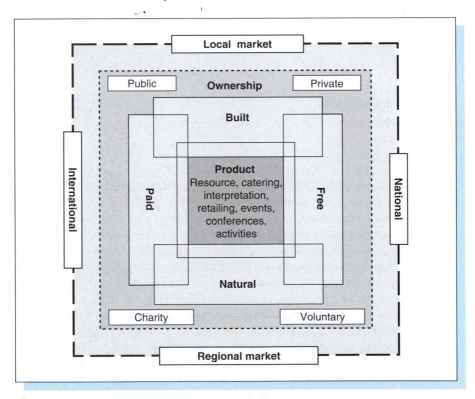

Figure 1.1
Classification of visitor attractions

the first instance. The increasing need to generate alternative revenue streams has led to expansion of the core activities in many new and existing attractions, with very few now opening without some element of retail or catering, and many others also investing in conference rooms for hire, various off-site activities to boost income or associated product development such as cookery schools to attract additional markets, such as at Glenturret Distillery in Scotland. As Bland (2001: 14) states, 'funding visitor attractions in the 21st Century is not an insoluble problem, but most will involve packaging with other less risky cash flows or with the generation of indirect benefits for investors'. It could be argued that the interpretation of the resource should, however, remain the key feature of the attraction visit, with increasing focus on meeting the needs of broader markets or more specific niche markets, since this is often the main motivation for the visit. The use of technology to enhance the presentation of the resource is currently a popular approach, with the development of hands-on interactive exhibits, virtual–reality shows and the development of augmented-reality systems, such as those in the ARCHEOGUIDE system in place at Olympia, Greece (Buhalis et al., 2006). While these developments may well cater for specific markets, often children, they are costly both to install and to maintain, and they may serve to exclude other markets that are not impressed with or predisposed to use this style of presentation. New trends in visitor attraction products have shown innovative uses of existing resources, which are developed into products accessible to visitors, for example the use of forests in the UK for 'Go Ape', high-rope adventure courses that offer the visitor the opportunity to access the tree canopy 60 feet (18 metres) up. New-built developments continue to focus on established themes but tend to be located within a broader leisure arena, for example Dickens World in Kent. It would appear that some of the policies outlined in visitor attraction reports a decade or more ago (CBI, 1998; ETC, 2000; Scottish Enterprise, 1997) have been put in place, with fewer new sites opening while existing sites are being redeveloped and revitalized.

The next stage in classification usually focuses on the nature of the resource itself, be it natural or built (Millar, 1999). The main reasons for this categorization result from the different approaches required for their management, with natural sites usually requiring fewer staff, incurring lower fixed costs and having a more open attitude towards access than in the case of built properties. This is not to say that natural sites require no management, but that the objectives of site management often focus on conservation issues and the management of visitors, rather than increasing visitor spend and entertainment. Built sites may also be subdivided into those built for the purposes of tourism, such as the Ngong Ping Cultural Village at the Skyrail on Lantau Island, Hong Kong, and those converted from other uses, such as Robben Island, the former prison of Nelson Mandela in South Africa. The significance of this is apparent when looking at the design and operation of these differing properties, where the conversions often have to compromise on operational issues in order to meet building conservation legislation. Additionally, the converted buildings often carry higher fixed costs, have fixed capacity and need to consider the needs of existing users, for example in religious buildings such as Rosslyn Chapel in Scotland, where worshippers stand next to increasingly large numbers of tourists attracted as a result of publications and movie involvement and promotion.

Visitor attraction classification

The other main approach to classification often centres on the pricing policy for access to the visitor attraction, that is, whether it is paid admission, free access or a combination in the form of free access to some areas, with a charge levied for temporary exhibits or specific areas or events. While government policy on this varies internationally, there is usually some provision for key national sites to offer free access to visitors on either a permanent or specific-day basis. This often overcomes the perception of local residents that the attractions are purely there for use by tourists, and meets the broader educational and social inclusion aims of many institutions. Additionally, some sites, such as Pompeii, offer free access to the under-18 age group for citizens of the European Union. There is some evidence to show sites varying their pricing throughout the year to encourage off-peak visitors and meet broader educational objectives, for example at Versailles, France, where prices vary by day and month of the year. In addition there has been development of pricing targeting local residents, such as the Florida Resident 'After 4' Pass that encourages visits at non-peak times of the day.

The management objectives of the managing body usually determine the admission-charging policy for the visitor attraction. One example of this is Historic Scotland, the executive agency responsible for many of Scotland's historic monuments, which charges admission at approximately 70 of their 330 sites in order that money raised at the revenue-generating sites can be used to support conservation work at less-visited sites. Additionally they offer free education visits in the shoulder months to help meet their broader educational objectives.

The ownership category and differing objectives of the visitor attractions will naturally impact on the management and operations of each site. Figure 1.1 separates these into private, public, charity and voluntary/trust categories. While the last two categories may seem similar, there is a distinction to be made here between large-scale operators, such as Edinburgh Zoo or the Glasgow Science Centre, which have charitable status, and National Trust or voluntary organizations, such as the Scottish Railway Preservation Society, that operate on a different basis in terms of staffing, use of funds and membership priorities. Quite different approaches to management issues such as pricing, visitor access, interpretation and marketing can be seen across the ownership categories across the world (Deloitte & Touche, 1997; Garrod et al., 2007), though an increasingly competitive market is encouraging more common approaches to be adopted, most noticeably in the areas of revenue generation, the use of technology for management purposes and associated product development.

The final point shown in Figure 1.1 is that the operating environment for visitor attractions will vary depending on the market or markets in which it exists. Some may cater mainly for the local market and require facilities that allow this, for example flexible use of space to allow community use, while others may cater more significantly for the international market, acting as key flagship attractions within a destination. The target market for an attraction may well determine the nature and management of the product offering, particularly in terms of pricing, visitor spend and interpretation. One evident implication of the market within which an attraction operates is the potential pool of visitors that might be attracted. Very few visitor attractions attract large numbers of visitors on an annual basis, while most, particularly in rural areas, rely on much smaller visitor throughput. This can be clearly seen in UK, where, for example, only 10 per cent of visitor attractions responding to a recent English annual attractions survey recorded visitor numbers above 200 000, while 50 per cent attracted fewer than 20 000 per annum (VisitBritain, 2006). Attempts to broaden an attraction's visitor appeal may entail increased collaboration and training, as will be discussed in Chapter 20.

The different ways of classifying visitor attractions suggested in Figure 1.1 are not exhaustive but serve to indicate the main features of classification used in various settings. Each national tourist board or attraction governing body has its own classification mechanisms appropriate to its own context. What it does do, however, is demonstrate the great diversity of visitor attractions that exists and offer some explanation of how this diversity has evolved over time. The variety of visitor attractions on offer around the world has developed significantly in the past 20 years (Scottish Enterprise, 2004; Stevens, 2000), no doubt influenced by the increased ability and propensity to travel. While more traditional museums and galleries have long attracted local markets, they can now also look to international audiences both in attracting actual visitors to their properties and in providing remote access via the use of advanced technology. Changes in funding structures often influence the available stock of facilities within a country, seen significantly since the introduction of National Lottery funding in the UK in the 1990s and the availability of European Union structural funding in countries previously unable to access these sources. Similarly, changes in access to public finance for ongoing revenue support or to capital funding priorities by enterprise companies can make vast differences in the development of and reinvestment in the visitor attraction product. Current trends indicate an increasing need for attractions to appeal to broader audiences and to generate increasing levels of external income, resulting in an increased mix of product offering and choice for the visitor. Changing patterns of leisure time and discretionary income are influencing the form of the attractions wanted by consumers, calling for products that meet their needs and quality expectations (CBI, 1998; Cooper et al., 2005; Phelps, 2002), rather than a decision taken by the attraction operators on the basis of what they feel the visitor wants. According to Stevens (2000: 64) 'attraction designers will innovate to create a new generation of all-inclusive, multi-faceted destination attractions capable of year-round operation, appealing to different markets and providing sound returns on large-scale investments'.

Defining visitor attractions

There is a temptation to aim to define visitor attractions for research and management purposes, although views on how they should best be defined and categorized vary around the world. This variety frustrates efforts to compare management concepts and management practices, but the question can be posed: is acceptance of a common definition necessary or even desirable?

Visitor attraction sectors around the world are often typified by a very large number of small, geographically fragmented, resource-poor members, trying to meet a multitude of objectives for a diverse range of owners. Although agreement of definitions can sometimes cause unnecessary delay in a research study, a universal definition of attractions is considered desirable in order to 'record, map and monitor attractions for information and statistical purposes' (ETC, 2000: 24). This having been said, once a definition is set and used for certain purposes, for example, annual visitor surveys, it is considered inadvisable to change it because doing so would compromise the comparability of results over time. This recognition has resulted in the continued use of basically the same definition for visitor attractions in the UK for a number of years, although this has been slightly amended from time to time. The current definition is:

> an attraction where it is feasible to charge admission for the sole purpose of sightseeing. The attraction must be a permanently established excursion destination, a primary purpose of which is to allow access for entertainment, interest, or education; rather than being primarily a retail outlet or a venue for sporting, theatrical, or film performances. It must be open to the public, without prior booking, for published periods each year, and should be capable of attracting day visitors or tourists as well as local residents. In addition, the attraction must be a single business, under a single management, so that it is capable of answering the economic questions on revenue, employment etc. (VisitBritain, 2006: 13)

Changing leisure patterns and product development have meant that the above definition, currently used by the UK national tourism bodies, has been brought into question. Although ostensibly inclusive, there are a number of weaknesses, both domestically and internationally, in using the VisitBritain definition for research purposes. The main reason for developing a definition is to allow national and international comparison between attractions and between comparable periods of performance, but with a new generation of 'destination' attractions emerging wherein consumers are offered a comprehensive range of services and facilities for entertainment, shopping, eating and drinking, and other aspects of leisure (Stevens, 2000), the above definition does not cater for these developments. Although not a permanent attraction, the much-derided Millennium Dome in London was typical of such developments. The ever-changing, dynamic market context in which visitor attractions operate thus makes a succinct definition both elusive and, it can be argued, increasingly irrelevant. This issue of definition is highly pertinent, as numerous retail and sporting attractions that are included in studies conducted in other countries, such as Canada, would be excluded if one were to adopt the VisitBritain definition. Likewise, the condition that to be considered an attraction for sightseeing purposes it should be possible (but not compulsory) to charge an admission fee for access would exclude many monuments and historic battlefields. One part of the definition that VisitBritain proposes changing is the element of the definition which relates to 'without prior booking', though no change has been implemented in this regard as yet.

Related to the question of definition are the issues of comparability and equivalence. In particular, such issues relate to the means by which visitor attractions are categorized in each country. As with any changes to the definition of an attraction between countries, data available for each category must be manageable, meaningful and usable. The incorporation of all attractions across all countries into standard visitor attraction categories would prove highly complex and not necessarily advantageous. For example, the National Historic Site category used in Canada does not correspond with any category used in other countries. From a marketing standpoint, the use of Wilderness, Thrill Zone, Heartland, Kiwi Spirit and Chill Out categorization of attractions in New Zealand in the early 2000s was highly pertinent and facilitated consumer choice. However, they served as obstacles to the researcher trying to achieve comparability and equivalence in international studies at that time (Garrod *et al.*, 2002). Although the broad classification of attractions as either natural or built, whether for tourism-specific reasons such as a museum or for other reasons such as a castle, does alleviate the problem, it does so somewhat artificially, as many sites will contain aspects of both. Perhaps even more challenging is the means by which the researcher classifies visitor attractions by ownership and whether or not a charge is levied on entry. In previous studies conducted on Scottish visitor attractions (Garrod *et al.*, 2007; Leask *et al.*, 2000), ownership category proved to be a key dependent variable with regard to determining the entire approach to attraction management. This is particularly the case for managing revenue and overall yield, visitor management strategies and the management of environmental impacts at attractions. Although there are similarities across many of the ownership categories used internationally, the use of the terms 'public', 'charity', 'trust' and 'society' on occasion makes for spurious accuracy of comparison. Equally challenging is the means by which the researcher defines an attraction which charges, or does not charge, for visitor entry. Although there is a large number which clearly charge for admission, there is a significant proportion of visitor attractions which rely on voluntary donations and alternative 'pricing' mechanisms. For example, many churches, historic properties and gardens in Scotland rely heavily on visitor donations, while in New Zealand the enormous number of wineries do not charge for visitor admission but set token prices for wine tasting. In this instance, the New Zealand winery is similar to the Scottish whisky distillery in that it serves both tourism and non-tourism objectives such as building brands and brand loyalty. Further anomalies exist in the number of 'free' access sites charging for temporary exhibitions or events, plus those which do not charge for admission but do levy a car-parking charge at the point of entry.

Thus, it is difficult to determine an internationally recognized definition for visitor attractions, mainly due to the variety of product offerings and scope as discussed above. For the purposes of this book, authors were invited to determine their own definitions and definitional parameters, within the generally accepted categories as discussed.

Researching visitor attractions

One of the challenges in researching visitor attractions is the lack of available data and material on which to base a project. Much of the data available to attraction operators is sourced via voluntary self-completion questionnaires and consultancy reports that often rely on a very small sample size, while academic research may focus specifically on one issue of interest or locality. This results in a limited pool of data for attraction operators and decision-makers to access, with serious questions being raised with regard to the reliability and comparability of the results. The very appeal of many attractions, their individuality or distinguishing features, results in issues of comparability, not least in defining and allocating them to categories of classifications (Leask and Fyall, 2006).

Where studies do exist on an annual basis, usually when commissioned by national tourism organizations, these tend to be volume and value based, with little investigation of factors that operators would like to know more about, for example motivations for visits and non-visitors. It is interesting to note that the flurry of research activity towards the end of the 1990s and early 2000s (CBI, 1998; Deloitte & Touche, 1997; ETC, 2000; Scottish Enterprise, 1997, 2004) in relation to the UK and European attractions has now stopped, with virtually no new reports other than a recent report by Keynote (2005). This may be the result of structural and priority changes in the public sector, where the UK visitor attraction monitors are no longer combined and are not available in any one UK-wide source and the remit of visitor attraction development falls into broader product development roles. These circumstances make it even more important that further research activity is directed towards this vital sector of tourism activity, to allow full recognition of the role of visitor attractions and their development opportunities.

The purpose and role of visitor attractions

As stated by Swarbrooke (2000: 267), 'visitor attractions are at the heart of the tourism industry, they are motivators that make people want to take a trip in the first place'. Richards (2001: 4) points out that while it can be argued that attractions do not always literally 'attract' visitors, they 'certainly do provide a focus for much tourist activity, and are an essential weapon in the arsenal of tourism destinations engaged in a competitive struggle for tourist business'.

The role of visitor attractions within a destination forms only one part of a complex network of tourism service providers within the broader tourism product. However, they are often used as key products in marketing activities. Examples of this are the use of images of iconic sites such as Uluru when marketing Australia or those of the British Airways London Eye in publications promoting England. The main interrelationships and interdependencies between visitor attractions and the wider tourism industry appear to focus on standard areas of mutual benefit, with an increasing move to develop more formal partnerships and collaboration being seen in recent years (Fyall *et al.*, 2001). Fluctuating visitor numbers in an environment of decreasing public capital and revenue funding have encouraged visitor attractions to expand their revenue streams into areas such as conference venues, events, new product developments and off-site activities. These all require attractions to work effectively with other tourism operators within a destination, such as accommodation providers, food and beverage suppliers, destination management companies and transport operators. One example of this is New Zealand Leading Attractions which is a group of independently owned operators working in collaboration with locations across New Zealand and in partnership with BP Connect Stores, Regency Tax and Duty Free and Air New Zealand.

The value of specific visitor attractions within a destination is that they can also be a key motivator in attracting business to the destination. Therefore, the quality and success of these interrelationships depends not only on the visitor attraction itself, but also on its contribution to the development of the critical mass of the destination product offering. Within the business tourism context, visitor attractions may also be an important part in the decision to return to a destination for a leisure visit, thus attracting those elusive repeat visitors. The ability of visitor attractions to respond quickly to visitor needs and wider external factors is also crucial within the destination context, as evidenced by the actions of Madame Tussauds in London immediately following the July 2005 terrorist bombings, where their management strategies and prompt actions helped to manage the immediate drop in visitor numbers to Central London (due to families and visitors not wanting to travel to central London for fear of further attacks), and how working in collaboration with other hospitality providers and government bodies aided relative business recovery. A European attractions report (Keynote, 2005: 1) asserts that 'attractions tourism will continue to grow despite disruptions by the types of terrorism and environmental disaster that occurred during 2005' and notes that there is evidence to suggest that tourists are 'becoming more resilient to threats and returning to popular destinations more quickly than they did in the 1990s'.

Visitor attractions may also play a crucial role in the revitalization of an area or destination, one example of this being the Guggenheim in Bilbao.

The creativity shown in the nature of the architecture of a building to house a key development may in itself elevate the role of the attraction to flagship proportions. Another classic example of this would be the success of the National Museum of New Zealand and its contribution to the development of Wellington as a destination. Flagship attractions can be used to pull visitors in, meet the needs of local residents and develop stronger tourism activities within the destination. While a destination rarely survives long term on the basis of one attraction, it can be the key 'pump-primer' in the sustainable development of a destination, for example the increased business opportunities now available within Cornwall that developed from one of the key objectives of the Eden Project – economic regeneration. Where possible, Eden buys from local suppliers, supports local businesses and farmers and has contributed £700 million (€1 billion) to the local economy to date (Smale, 2006).

The role of visitor attractions in this manner should form part of a general strategic tourism plan that may identify such opportunities to 'use' the attraction as a management tool within the destination, rather than leaving it to operate in isolation. Examples of this might include the location of some of the UK's most recently opened visitor attractions, such as the Royal Yacht Britannia in the Ocean Terminal complex in Leith, Edinburgh, the Spinnaker Tower in Portsmouth, and the Science Centre on Glasgow's abandoned waterfront. These ventures all offer continued opportunities to tackle management issues such as seasonality, economic benefit and the development of civic pride. One of the next such developments currently in the planning process is the Titanic Signature Project, Belfast, Northern Ireland. This £1.5 billion (€2 billion) waterfront development includes an 'iconic' tourist attraction aiming to attract in the region of 500 000 visitors per annum, hotels, restaurants, apartments and marina. Based on a brownfield site, it is due for completion in time for the centenary events in 2012 and aims to establish the Titanic Quarter as a major leisure and tourism destination.

In considering the role of visitor attractions within a destination, it is important to consider not just the views of visitors and how they might be attracted and catered for. The needs of the local population must also be met and may indeed play a more significant role in the success of an attraction, particularly in rural settings where their support for repeat visits, staffing, recommendation and participation may be vital. There is also the issue of social inclusion to be considered, to encourage cultural awareness within the local population and meet educational objectives. The maintenance of specific cultural identities and practices can often only be achieved through the involvement of those from the local population. This aspect rarely features in the key performance indicators for visitor attractions, which tend to focus on visitor numbers, but could form the basis of the measurement of success in a move to broaden the criteria to include aspects such as engagement with the local community through usage, membership and participation, or support and links with local businesses.

The multiplicity of stakeholders involved in the operation and use of visitor attractions can create difficulties in identifying the future practices of a development. Objectives may include revenue generation, enterprise, conservation, cultural issues or simply entertainment. The market might be local, national or international, resulting in differing needs and product offerings. It is unlikely that any one attraction can be compared directly to another in terms of its role and purpose within a setting, as these will vary considerably between destinations. However, certain policies can be set in place to encourage successful management of the visitor attractions that exist. While individual attractions may achieve certain levels of success according to their own set of objective criteria, it usually falls to national bodies and organizations to determine the parameters and structure for long-term success. It is important that these structures, be they strategic policies, funding principles or quality standards, take account of the variety of purposes that visitor attractions may have within their particular contexts. What might be considered appropriate in one area or country may not be in another. Much of this can be attributed to the fact that the focus of existing schemes can often reflect the organizer's particular interest or background, or the need to meet institutional administrative requirements. As with all issues pertaining to the definition of visitor attractions, there is also the need for a cross-sectoral benchmarking scheme that concentrates on visitor, marketing, commercial and quality aspects, and perhaps most importantly is in a format suitable to both large and small attractions (ETC, 2000). International benchmarking initiatives may well offer opportunities in this area and there is some evidence of their increased use in this sector in recent years (Scottish Enterprise, 2004). Continued international research work based on identifying and disseminating best practice is also required.

Conclusions

There is no doubt that the international visitor attractions sector is facing a challenging time ahead. Uncertainties over the continued growth of tourist movements in the light of terrorist activity, changing patterns of leisure time and use, the current oversupply of visitor attractions in some regions, and the potential product developments in the field of technology in particular, all create the need for new approaches to be developed in the way visitor attractions are managed. The multiple objectives of visitor attractions need to be clarified in order to determine the nature, role and resultant success of sites, but also to invite innovation and change. Meanwhile the wide range of stakeholder interests relating to an attraction, be they related to education, revenue generation or conservation, will inevitably lead to conflicting management pressures. The purpose of this book is to identify what the main challenges might be in the future and how they can be overcome to the benefit of all concerned.

References

Bland, N. (2001). *Leisure Review: A Digest of Corporate Financial Activity*, 2nd quarter. Deloitte & Touche.

Interpreting the Development of the Visitor Attraction Product

Stephen Wanhill

Aims

The aims of this chapter are to:

- show how the nature of the visitor attraction product has changed over time,
- explain the nature of visitor attraction development,
- explore the concept of the market–'imagescape' mix and present a way to evaluate attractions based on this dimension, and
- discuss the criteria which can determine the success or otherwise of visitor attractions.

Introduction

As a general definition, a visitor attraction is a focus for recreational and, increasingly, educational activity, undertaken by both day and stay visitors, and frequently shared with the domestic resident population (see Chapter 1 for more specific concepts). Within any society, the range of visitor attractions is extensive – every municipality and rural district boasts at least one attraction, adding to its appeal as a destination. They are often the reason for visiting a destination and provide activities and experiences, and, importantly for the visitor when he or she returns home, the visible signs of consumption. From a sociological perspective, visitor attractions are consumed through sightseeing and do not exist without this. There are numerous variations in respect of the product concept or creativity of the design and its appeal. This will be termed the 'imagescape' to match the use of the word 'imagineers' by the Disney Corporation when describing its designers (Kirsner, 1988). The concept is based on the fact that all attractions, in some part, measure their performance by the number of visitors, for which the output is the visitor experience. The object is to generate memorable mood benefits for the visitor, and in consequence attachment, leading to repeat visits and positive recommendations. To enhance the experience, the modern approach is to place tangible objects, say, a thrill ride or a collection of artefacts, within the context of a specific theme or image in a particular setting or environment; hence the word 'imagescape'.

It is possible to classify attractions along a number of different dimensions: ownership, capacity, market or catchment area, permanency and type. Classification by type is the common way in which countries collect attraction statistics, but here some form of permanency is required so that public access can be controlled and measured, which implies that even some iconic attractions (those featuring in destination marketing strategies) are never listed in official statistics, for example, the monument to Sibelius in Helsinki, although the music festivals, concert hall and museum in his honour are recorded. The simplest classification by type is to group attractions into those that are gifts of nature and those which are human-made. The former include the landscape, climate, vegetation, forests and wildlife, embodied in, say, country parks in Britain, lakes in Canada, mountains in Switzerland, the coast in Spain or game reserves in Africa. The latter are principally the products of the historical development of countries and civilizations, but also include artificially created entertainment complexes, that is, attractions designed almost exclusively for amusement and enjoyment, such as theme parks. Among the most well known of these are the Walt Disney parks, the imagescape originating in California (1955) but since reproduced in Florida, Tokyo, Paris and Hong Kong, with one further park due to open soon in Shanghai (see Chapter 6).

Going further, it will be appreciated that this basic classification may be sub-divided again into attractions which are site-specific because of the physical location of facilities and therefore act as a destination, and attractions which are temporary because they are events. International events that are regarded as world class normally stand alone as 'hallmark' activities, while others may be used to complement site-specific attractions. What is happening at the time is usually more important for events than their location, so mega-events, such as the Olympics, and exhibitions, for example world trade fairs, may move around the globe. However, some hallmark activities do evolve in and become specific to their location, so that they become branded by it. Thus, several of the most spectacular events in the form of parades or carnivals have become associated with major cities, for example, the Calgary Stampede in Alberta, the Lord Mayor's Show in London or the Rio Carnival. This is because towns and cities provide access to a large market and have the economic base and desire to support the increasing popularity of festivals arising from the growth in cultural tourism (Andersson and Getz, 2007).

Similarly, important religious festivals are often connected with locations that are considered the foundations of the faith, such as Mecca and Jerusalem.

Complementarity may be achieved, for example, by staging a festival of the countryside to enhance the appeal of a country park, or markets and fairs in towns and villages of historic interest. Similar benefits may be achieved by staging a performance of a Shakespeare tragedy in the courtyard of a historic castle. Janiskee (1996) examines three event models as suitable attractions for historic houses – community festivals, stand-alone tours and living history portrayals – and deduces that the latter, which include holiday celebrations, ceremonies, rituals and parties, historic re-enactment and the learning of vernacular skills, crafts and household 'chores', are best suited to such venues

Attraction product

In the post-industrial society that Pine and Gilmore (1999) label the 'Experience Economy', it is argued that the production system should be re-engineered to add value through marketing experiences. This implies producing services with attached goods rather than the traditional mass production process in which commodities are uniformly produced and sold on price. In this way, customers are able to receive a package that can be tailored to their needs. In fact, Pine and Gilmore draw many of the examples in their work from the leisure industry. Following this line of reasoning, Figure 2.1 presents an abstract construction of an attraction product where the core is the imagescape, the purpose of which is to convey the essence of the visitor experience to the potential market. Thus the intangible output of a constructed

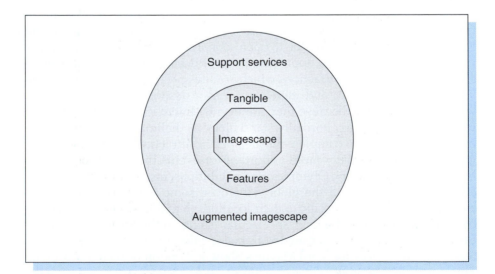

Figure 2.1
The attraction product

imagescape is central to the visitor experience. The core is surrounded by commodities and services, which are combined to add value or support the imagescape. The right imagescape portrays, through the functional aspect of theming, all four realms of the visitor experience, namely entertainment, education, aesthetics and escapism. These four aspects are embodied in all truly successful visitor attractions, be they theme parks in the private domain or heritage attractions in the non-commercial sector. As commercial operators well know, failure to distinguish between the core and peripherals designed to augment the imagescape, or lack of content control, as in the case of exhibitions that are made up of a variety of sponsors, or failure to communicate the imagescape to the market in terms of the product offer and how to consume it, will lead to under-performance and possible project failure.

When presenting the core, the diversity of imagescape themes for visitor attractions is beyond doubt extensive, as indicated in Table 2.1. But in essence, there is very little new in what draws visitors. The main attractions are still the wonders of the natural and physical world and the endeavours of human society, including, albeit to a much smaller extent, dark subjects that deal with what are considered to be behaviour inversions, such as the grim consequences of war, crime and punishment, and the unusual, for example catastrophes and the erotic.

While the broad themes indicated in Table 2.1 may be globally enduring, their presentation within the context of an imagescape may not be. The

Table 2.1   Imagescapes

Armed forces	Industry
Art and media	Miscellaneous
Built environment	Myths and fantasy
Childhood	Natural world
Civilizations	Physical world
Dark subjects	Politics
Entertainment	Religion
Famous and notorious	Retailing
Food and drink	Science and discovery
Future	Society and culture
History and heritage	Sport
Hobbies and pastimes	Transport
Human body	War and conflict

acceptance of the content and style of production of the imagescape is determined by fashion, which has its own dynamic that is born out of the spirit of
enquiry and competition within society to alter its patterns of consumption
and value systems. Thus, animals in captivity in the form of zoos or safari
parks are no longer acceptable to many people and there is a marked decline
of interest in static attractions and object-oriented museums, unless they are
national collections (Swarbrooke, 2002) or they are best presented in this way,
as for example jewellery. Despite the intrinsic value of historic buildings and
collections, presentation, interpretation and good support facilities have
become increasingly important. On the other hand, historical tableaux (which
have developed from static wax museums to animatronic figures and even
fantasy presentations), the performing arts, sporting events and thrill rides
seem to have universal appeal. To complete the attraction product, the core
imagescape in Figure 2.1 is supported by facilities such as retailing, catering,
cloakrooms, first aid, special needs access, internal transport and car parking,
as well as an augmented imagescape designed to ensure that all customer
experiential requirements are met, for example, visitor orientation, queue
entertainment, complaints handling, puppet characters, shows, presentations, and so on.

A significant aspect of the core of the attraction product, which is sadly
lacking in many visitor attractions, is the encouragement of repeat visits. This
is a necessary requirement for long-term success, unless the market for the
experience is global, which therefore provides a catchment population that is
to all intents and purposes infinite in size, since it is continually being replen-
ished. This, of course, may not be an issue with public attractions that are free,
depending on whether or not visitor numbers are used as a performance indicator. Entertainment attractions, such as cinemas and theatres are able to survive on one-time-only purchases of the experience, because they continually
change the core attraction (the film or show). Meanwhile, theme parks
embody thrill rides for which there is a repetitive demand that they reinforce
with a rolling programme of replacement and re-theming to persuade their
customers to return. Leisure shopping facilities continually replace their merchandise in line with fashion, but for the majority of visitor attractions that
were not built for such purposes, their ability to maintain attendances is functionally related to the size and dynamics of their market, as well as their
capacity to alter the core imagescape and supplement it by special events
(giving animation to object-oriented attractions such as museums) and other
supporting features. To this extent, national museums are at a considerable
advantage because the size of their collections enables them to change the
imagescape. For example, the Victoria and Albert Museum in London has
only about 3 per cent of more than 4 million objects on public display,
although more are accessible in its reading, study and print rooms. On the
other hand, small attractions that are exhibiting collections, whether they are
in the public or private domain, need to change their displays by, say, borrowing objects and works from elsewhere, or to stage events in order to tempt visitors to return. Looking at the revenue side, a local residents' privilege card,

season tickets and promotions such as allowing the local community free access if they bring a guest, are all ways of encouraging attendance.

Attraction development

Within different subject disciplines, the development of new commodities and services in the marketplace is termed 'innovation' in economics, 'new product development' in marketing and management and 'design' in engineering. In order to give a historic context, the term 'innovation' will be used here to encompass all these notions, but it is acknowledged as a very wide term that has been used to describe a concept, a process or the product of the process. This leads to the seminal work of Schumpeter (1934), wherein the key concept is the linking of long-wave business cycles to innovational change. This arises because, as Schumpeter observed, major innovations (whether they are new products, markets, sources of supply or organizational changes leading to increased market power) are not spread evenly in time but tend to come in swarms and are therefore discontinuous in their occurrence. Invention may take place at any time, but innovation, that is putting a new product to the market, comes about in the upswing of the cycle when the economic climate looks favourable. The essence of Schumpeter's theory is that the vehicle of economic growth is 'creative destruction' through innovation that disrupts existing technologies and creates new markets, collapsing old ones.

The above is, however, rather a special case, for transcribing what has been said so far across the landscape of natural and man-made attractions serves to show that commerciality and consumer choice are rather modern concepts, in the sense that the majority of today's attractions have not been brought into existence for visitor purposes. The innovation process in terms of imagescape creation is therefore a gradation from a situation of no adaptation (but rather controlled management) to visitor attractions that are fashioned for purpose, which is very different from the stereotypical image of monumental change as understood by Schumpeter's theory. More recent literature recognizes a much greater variety in the nature and classification of innovations (Booz, Allen and Hamilton, 1982; Hjalager, 1994), although these are not necessarily relevant to many attraction developments because of the degree of adaptation permitted. This is because alterations in the cultural capital stock (by which it meant tangible or intangible assets that hold cultural value, irrespective of any economic value they may possess) are, in the main, irreversible. The actuality of having a spectrum of innovations with regard to visitor attractions is reflected also in the pattern of ownership, as shown in Table 2.2. Here the public sector is more likely to take on a stewardship role of what are considered to be national assets, where innovation is constrained, while private-sector firms may be much more innovative because of the need to maintain contact with consumers and their position in the marketplace. Observed ownership models indicate that most attractions are non-corporate, which absolves them of public shareholding constraints, while many are in the

Table 2.2 Agencies owning attractions

Public
Central government
Government agencies
Local authorities
State industries

Voluntary organizations
Charitable trusts (incorporated)
Private clubs and associations

Private
Individuals and partnerships
Private companies
Corporations

non-profit sector (public or voluntary) and so have a myriad of objectives (often conflicting), and mixed funding and operating methods arising from different ideals. Essentially, the mission statement rather than the financial bottom line holds sway, which makes performance measures, particularly financial ones, hard to achieve and assess.

Development process

From a commercial standpoint, to paraphrase the famous dictum about hotels that has been attributed to Conrad Hilton: 'There are only three things you need to know about attractions: visitors, visitors and visitors!'. No better example of this principle can be found in the Millennium Dome at Greenwich, in London. It was designed as a celebration for the Year 2000, but was judged by the press as a commercial attraction, so that the out-turn of 6.5 million visitors for the year as against a forecast of 12 million was declared a financial 'disaster' in the media and the political arena, and an embarrass-ment to the government.

Once paying visitors are introduced to attractions in the public and volun-tary sectors, then pressure builds up for the visitor experience, in support of admissions, to become the marketed output, as in the commercial sector. This has its own dynamic in terms of fashion and tastes, and so creates a momen-tum for change in the nature of the imagescape and perhaps the presentation of the overall product. This is something that is often resisted by the curator-ial side of these attractions, who are rightly concerned about the authenticity of the visitor experience. For example, in the 1980s, the Victoria and Albert Museum was heavily criticized for using the marketing strapline 'Ace café with a rather nice museum attached!' to stimulate a re-appraisal of the museum by the public; a marketing strategy that would be considered quite acceptable today. But although these changes bring the public and voluntary sectors closer to the market, their mixture of ideological objectives such as conservation, authenticity and education, along with their charitable status and sunk capital costs, implies that they cannot be matched completely with commercially established visitor attractions. This is because the latter are seeking a return on capital invested and attempting to maintain a strong, if not dominant, position in their marketplace.

Key features

The key aspects to consider in developing an attraction from a demand perspective are indicated in Figure 2.2. Ideally the system is sequential, which begs the question of the running order. Commercial logic dictates that the optimum path is Market → Imagescape → Location, but given the fact that most attraction developments are limited by their type, conditions of ownership and location, this only applies to what are termed 'footloose' attractions that have flexibility across all three aspects in order to ensure economic success. Sea-Life Centres provide a good example: they are modern aquariums (a subject that has an enduring interest), are not too sophisticated and require relatively small visitor numbers to succeed. They may therefore be found in many coastal locations. The instances of theme and ride parks, which are also seeking to maximize their visitor potential, are discussed in Chapter 4. In comparison, there are limited adjustments that can be made to the imagescape of a country park because the location is fixed and it has fairly unalterable intrinsic

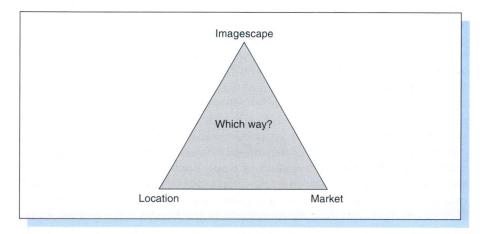

Figure 2.2
The development process

elements. This means that change is restricted to adding support facilities to augment the imagescape, such as a visitor centre. Similarly, a mining museum, that has a mine visit as part of the attraction, is tied by its location (Wanhill, 2000). What is important here is to recognize that location, market assessment and imagescape are bound up with one another. Thus, if site selection becomes at most a second-best choice, this throws greater weight onto the market–imagescape mix in order to achieve visitor numbers commensurate with notions of the economic viability of the attraction. But precisely how these factors are balanced depends on the objectives of the attraction. Thus a botanical garden has other aims than simply maximizing visitor numbers. Similarly, wildlife sanctuaries and other natural attractions do not want to be swamped by visitors. This brings the debate back to ownership patterns and the organization's objectives, because once the commercial pathway to development is abandoned, financial viability may be difficult to attain.

Regeneration

The regeneration and property development model typically follows a reverse pathway, Location → Imagescape → Market. In such cases, where old industrial buildings, disused market halls, railway stations and docks are located close to urban centres, it is fairly widespread to find public-sector intervention, both at national and international levels, to convert them into tourist zones, which serve both visitors and residents alike. Since leisure shopping is an increasingly important visitor and resident activity, there has been a focus on speciality shopping – as in Covent Garden, London – intermingled with hotels, leisure attractions and also business facilities. Such facilities can include a convention centre, an exhibition hall or trade centre and offices in order to attract commercial developers. In this way, tourism has replaced manufacturing and distribution industries, which have left the inner core for more spacious and cheaper locations on the outskirts of the city. Thus tourism has been recognized as a feasible economic option and catalyst for community regeneration. The development of Baltimore's Inner Harbor from the 1960s, for example, became an inspiration for revitalization of decaying industrial waterfronts in other parts of the world (such as the Albert Dock in Liverpool, Darling Harbour in Sydney, the Victoria and Alfred Wharf in Cape Town). In this way, tourism can become the 'glue' that holds the area together, particularly where there is little else the local authority can do with such assets and when the object is to stabilize economic 'shrinkage' by raising place image in order to attract private investment. An example of this can be seen in the long-term regeneration of Cape Breton Island, Canada (Brown and Geddes, 2007). Ownership of regeneration development is mixed, frequently resulting from a private–public sector partnership in which the revenue-earning activities are commonly in the hands of the private sector and the rationale for public participation is vested in the wider economic, social and environmental benefits that are bestowed. Even for commercially desirable urban sites, there is usually a proportion, of around 15–20 per cent, devoted to leisure in order to obtain planning permission. However, the leisure development may be drawn from the local authority's 'wish list' of amenities for local residents and could be unsuitable for tourism purposes. On the other hand, the trend in modern retail malls is to provide an entertainment experience for the whole family through adding themed areas, health clubs, cinemas, performance venues, restaurants and bars to traditional shopping facilities in an enclosed space that can be open all year round. Such developments, which have become increasingly commonplace in North America and Europe (for example, West Edmonton Mall in Canada and the Mall of America in Minneapolis), have become noted visitor attractions in their own right, with high levels of repeat visitation giving attendance levels in tens of millions that match those of destinations.

From a pure attraction (as opposed to a mixed development) standpoint, the reverse pathway of regeneration strategies may carry a high degree of risk, in that they can result in an 'outside-in' project and/or project inflation. The former is used to describe an investment that goes from the physical structure to the imagescape, as opposed to an 'inside-out' project that takes as its starting point the imagescape and then creates the structure around it. The latter is the case of most visitor attractions that appear to be flourishing. For example, the structure of the Millennium Dome in London was finalized long before the content was known, so it had to be designed to give maximum exhibition space. The creativity of the imagescapes, and how they linked together, were not effectively communicated to the general public and allowed the media to satirize the project as ersatz and of no substance, even though the satisfaction rating amongst those who had visited the Dome was well over 80 per cent (NAO, 2000).

Where public authorities are involved, there is always the danger of project inflation in response to civic pride and the vainglory of local politicians. This results in an exaggeration of employment creation to obtain development grants, increased complexity, which boosts consultants' fees, and substantial capital structures to the benefit of the architects. Several millennium projects sponsored by the Heritage Lottery Fund in the UK have gone this way. Some have had to be closed, for example the National Centre for Popular Music in Sheffield, the Centre for the Visual Arts in Cardiff and the Earth Centre near Doncaster. The lesson for the UK Millennium Commission from these examples is straightforward. Major capital projects should not be undertaken unless their market function is clear, visitor displacement from other attractions has been considered, and a 'proper' feasibility study has been carried out so that the nature of the risks involved is thoroughly understood and accepted.

Industrial developments

Industrial visitor attractions tend to pursue a path, Location → Market → Imagescape. In the first instance, natural association with the place of production dictates the location, as for example, Cadbury World, Bourneville, near Birmingham, UK (opened in 1990), Tetley's Brewery Wharf, Leeds, UK (opened in 1994), Universal Studios, Hollywood (opened in 1964), Ford at Dearborn, USA (opened in 1999), and Glenturret Whisky, Crieff in Perthshire, Scotland (opened in 1980). Almost all of these attractions have developed from capitalizing on the demands of consumers to visit the factory, brewery, studio or distillery. Not all are successful. Tetley's Brewery Wharf was closed in 2000 due to visitor numbers falling away. The imagescape of the attraction is built on consumer interest in the product and its history, and may be regarded as brand stretching or brand extension, so as to associate the attraction with the merchandise of the organization and distinguish it from its competitors (Grant, 1999). Legally registering a brand, be it a name, logo or design, protects the organization's right to use it exclusively and enables the business to harvest the benefits of customer loyalty, reduced sensitivity to price and added value. Many industrial businesses go further than brand extension, as has, for example, the LEGO Corporation (for which there is a case study in Chapter 4). LEGO sees the primary role of its parks as one of brand support. Similarly, the Anheuser Busch brewing corporation entered the leisure entertainment arena to provide a showcase for its beer interests, Budweiser being the best known of its brands.

Market–imagescape mix

The great array of imagescapes has already been noted, but it is significant that they are inextricably bound up with assessment of the market, as indicated by the classifications given in Figure 2.3, and vice versa. Thus, while there is a clear demand for entertainment attractions, success is related to the creativity of the design and its appeal. Both axes are defined from the stance of a developer of a new attraction project, whether in the commercial or not-for-profit sector or in some private–public partnership. The development is taken to be the establishment of a new business, a new activity in a current attraction or a reformulation of an existing attraction. In the last two

Market	Image	
	Current	**New**
Current	Q I 'Me too' attraction	Q II 'Grand inspiration' attraction
New	Q III 'New version' attraction	Q IV 'Wonder' attraction

Figure 2.3
The attraction market–imagescape mix

instances, it should be appreciated that there are likely to be more limitations on the development of the imagescape, either because it has to be in keeping with the overall branding of the attraction product, or it is constrained by the nature of available resources. For example, cultural events and heritage attractions yield both cultural as well as economic values, but there is no *a priori* reason for these values to move in the same direction, and changes in the stock or nature of cultural assets will usually lead to the loss of that which is authentic through irreversibility. This limits the scope of what is possible in the creativity of the imagescape, as in the case of the traditional performing arts such as orchestral music, ballet and opera (Wanhill, 2006). The economics of classical works are dictated by a long-gone composer and there is little today's artistic director can do about it. Hence considerable public subsidy is necessary if these art forms are to survive in their original format. What is also important is scale, thus small attractions may offer only a single imagescape, often proscribed by the resource base, while created attractions like theme parks promote multiple imagescapes structured around different rides and features in order to achieve the required market penetration rates.

'Me too' attractions

The common attraction experience is linked to the first quadrant of Figure 2.3, since this involves least risk, which in turn has implications for finance and operational viability. It involves the least risk because it is possible to look at parallel projects (tried-and-tested imagescapes) to see whether or not they are successful. It should also be possible to obtain reliable data to be combined with overall market trends to see what the market absorption capacity is likely to be. Where there is public-sector involvement, the danger to guard against is 'me tooism' on the part of local politicians who see a political opportunity arising from the location of the project in their area. An example of this can be seen in the development of coal mining museums/heritage centres in the valleys of South Wales during the late 1980s, following the closure of the collieries (Wanhill, 2000). A number of developments went ahead in spite of survey evidence which suggested that only about 7 per cent of visitors were likely to visit more than one mining attraction in the area. Politically, 'me too' projects can always be justified on the basis of need, but whether it is possible to turn need into demand at a price which will make the project financially or economically viable is another question. From the perspective of the economy at large, such projects should not go ahead until questions over displacement of visitors from other attractions have been considered, since oversupply can result in a series of non-viable attractions that end up wasting resources. Commercial feasibility studies often do not take sufficient account of this aspect when looking at the competition for market share, or the irreversibility of most attraction investments. The innovation process at this stage is usually minor since it is based on followership, but it can have a cumulative impact over time from a series of adaptive improvements that raise visitor throughput and enhance the experience. There is no disruption to existing imagescape delivery and markets. Innovative changes simply strengthen the dominant design and its appeal, in clear contrast to the Schumpeter's position stated earlier.

'Grand inspiration' attractions

One of the difficulties of evaluating attraction investments in this quadrant is weighing up whether the 'grand inspiration', in terms of the imagescape, will work in relation to the market or whether it is simply the sole brainwave approach to project development. The latter could be an indulgence that is unnecessarily or unrealistically costly in the context of what the market can afford. To counter this, major players now have whole sections devoted towards creativity, with the opportunity to bring in design consultants. This is not to undermine the importance of the single genius such as Walt Disney, whose personal inspiration was the creation of Disneyland in 1955. On the public-sector side, the North of England Open Air Museum at Beamish was the personal inspiration of Frank Atkinson, a local museum curator, who had to 'drive' the project for 14 years before it finally opened in 1972 (Johnson and Thomas, 1992).

In terms of assessment, a common strategy in this area is to try to reverse the project evaluation sequence by estimating the volume of visitors needed to make the project both feasible and viable at a price the market is prepared to pay. Even if this hurdle is passed, however, delivering projects in this quadrant is very much dependent on the track record of its proposers, so that it is possible to raise the necessary finance and to obtain various planning consents. The latter is a 'minefield' of issues in the developed world, as most important sites are under local authority control and local government culture is not noted for being receptive to new ideas or being able to think in 10–15-year trends. Equally, many developers have experienced and recognized the ability of local pressure groups to 'kill off' sound project proposals.

The innovation process in this quadrant should make the existing imagescape delivery style obsolete and is therefore radical in approach (corresponding to Schumpeter's view of innovation as carrying out new combinations or ways of doing things), yet it deals with existing market structures. While it may build competitive advantage and take market share from others, it does not destroy the competition, which may, in any case, have the opportunity to copy the new ideas.

'New version' attractions

The innovation process here involves the opening up of new market opportunities while preserving the existing imagescape in content and format, having the effect of rejuvenating the existing attraction because the current public has become too familiar with the product or the market has moved on. Spatial division of markets can be important, thus old concepts can work in new destinations, while new concepts are needed to move forward in established destinations. An example of the former is the gradual movement of Disney overseas, beginning with the establishment of Tokyo Disneyland (in 1983). Similarly, Universal Studios has sought to increase their global presence through park development. This innovation route is analogous to yield-management procedures, and heritage associations may partake of this by acquiring new properties and adapting them to visitors in areas where there is an under-supply of castles, palaces and stately homes open to the public. National museums and galleries have a public duty to display their collections and may open branches in different parts of their home country. Such developments are supply led, as they are generating demand in spatial terms where it has not been previously. This means that in order to attain visitor targets there is a need for substantial market research and forecasting to take account of both the short-term conditions (economy, financial climate and the political situation) and the longer term (demographics, social values and lifestyle, technology, climate and environment).

Clearly, product rejuvenation is a defensive strategy to retain existing attendances, requiring careful monitoring of key market trends affecting attractions. These currently include:

- continued growth in multiple, shorter vacations, so that main attractions are likely to receive the lion's share of any new growth, with the exception of visits that are repeats,
- the rise in the allocation of the household budget to 'quality' leisure time,
- increasing influence of children on the use of leisure time in families with both partners working,
- growth in concern for environmental issues and the recognition of the need for sustainable environmental management practices, and
- other leisure activity spending, namely in-home leisure, retailing and computer systems.

It is readily apparent that current markets in themselves are not static, so the key question for 'new version' attractions is whether, for example by their use of new technology for better visual interpretation, experiences and sales, they are leading the market or simply catching up in terms of product formulation, the communications proposition and the channels of communication. Meeting the needs of new and future markets may require a much greater leap forward in terms of imagescape development for the new version to be successful. This is something that was achieved by the opening in 2000 of the Tate Modern gallery in the old South Bank Power Station on the River Thames in London.

'Wonder' attractions

The term 'wonder' attraction is used here to describe those very large projects that have major economic impacts on their location and are eagerly sought after as 'flagship' enterprises. Maximum uncertainty holds in this quadrant because of the number of unknowns and often the scale of the project, which on the one hand deters competition but on the other increases financial exposure. However, this quadrant only applies to relatively few projects (examples being Disneyland in California, EPCOT (opened in 1982), the Sydney Opera House (opened in 1973), Baltimore's Inner Harbor and the Millennium Dome). This is because well over 90 per cent of all attractions are geared to fewer than 200 000 visitors, which minimizes the risk of scale in developed destinations. Governments, very large attraction operators or major corporations with a leisure interest, are the ones who fund projects of this kind.

Commercial operators are careful to limit their financial exposure, so 'usually proceed with public-sector support, both in terms of kind (usually land) and cash, so as to spread the risks and help draw in external finance. The downfall of 'wonder' projects on the financial side has commonly come from:

- Too large a capital cost, making the project unfundable from the standpoint of raising equity to match debt. Examples include the proposed theme parks in the UK of Wonderworld near Corby in Northamptonshire and the Battersea Project in London that came forward to the City of London for finance during the 1980s.
- Delays in building or underestimation of construction costs which lead to serious cost overruns and the need for refinancing, as in the case of the Sydney Opera House in the 1960s, which was completed 10 years late and more than 14 times its original budget.
- Ignoring funders' demands by bringing them in at the end of all the feasibility work, when it would have been more appropriate to have them in at the beginning.
- Changing project specification some way into its development, thus incurring step changes in costs and therefore overruns against the original budget, as in the Millennium Dome which was intended to be completed by October 1999 for opening on 31 December 1999. First impressions count, so it is customary to have a 'soft' opening some weeks or months before any official launch to iron out 'teething' problems. This was not to be, so the Dome's glitches had to be dealt with in the full gaze of the media and paying visitors.
- In response to political enthusiasm, the project is oversold by inflating revenues and economics benefits, and underestimating costs, and social and environmental impacts, in the knowledge that the construction phase is irreversible. Once development has started it has to be completed, as failure will lead to a loss of political and commercial credibility. For example, within one year of winning the bid in 2005, the budget for the London Olympics in 2012 rose from £2.4 billion to £9.3 billion, but it is seen as a major regeneration project for East London.

Alternatively, money may come solely from public or quasi-public funds. The spate of 'millennium vision' attractions sponsored by the Heritage Lottery Fund in the UK fell into this category, though not necessarily, as noted earlier, to good effect. In Europe, many large projects have been initiated through the European Regional Development Fund and most members of the European Union offer some form of investment support to new tourism projects. Such funding is in addition to the many other ways where the public sector has tried to set the 'right climate' for tourism development.

For 'wonder' attractions, the innovation process can be one that departs from established imagescape delivery systems and sets down a new marketing agenda and communication strategy, which then becomes an inspiration for subsequent development. Projects of this kind lay down a new structure for the industry (Abernathy and Clark, 1985) and the new framework in which competition will occur and develop, setting future standards for some time to come. Market assessment for such unique attractions is notoriously difficult. For example, the estimates of visitor numbers for the Millennium Dome ranged from 8 to 17 million (NAO, 2000). Twelve million was the figure that the Government was prepared to accept and budget for, on the basis that it was meant to be a public festival, so that everyone who might want to come should be able to do so. In these circumstances, there is a need to build up a large database of market trends in different leisure activities, make future change assumptions (predictions) and consider the project in a 'with and without' situation. Developing project scenarios so as to give a thorough understanding of what is being proposed and the risks involved is more important than the actual projections, though the latter are required to give dimensions to the project and to assess its impact on the economy.

Successful attractions

With visitor attractions covering such a wide setting and mixture of ownership, it is a moot point as to whether anything can be concluded as to what constitutes successful innovation and development. But on the supposition that attendances (and in certain circumstances membership) are a performance target, then critical to the prospects of new attraction investments, whether they are low-risk 'me too' developments or high-risk 'wonder' projects, is how the creativity of the imagescape connects to the market. The imagescape does not have to be revolutionary, as in the Schumpeterian concept of innovation. In fact few are, but the imagescape needs to be flexible if the attraction has to rely on repeat visits to meet its performance targets.

The creation of imagescapes suggests that in those sectors of the economy where the marketed output is experiences, the transformation of invention to innovation cannot be compared to the processes seen in manufacturing. It appears that some of the winning attractions are those that have followed a reverse product development cycle to that normally understood in the production of commodities (Barras, 1986). For commodities, development starts with the invention and introduction of the product, then qualitative process innovation, which is the setting up of the manufacturing systems (capital widening), and finally quantitative process innovation that takes the form of improvements and rationalization of the production system for mass supply (capital deepening).

In the case of the majority of attractions, the reverse appears to be true. Products either exist in the natural world or in the physical environment, or they are at the end of the supply chain where they have been developed for other purposes and in other economic sectors. They are then adapted to provide a visitor experience with the aid of new communication techniques. In the latter case, public monuments, buildings and infrastructure are obvious examples. Even in the commercial sector, however, it may be observed that the Disney characters were well known in the entertainment industry and as toys before the development at Anaheim. Similarly, Asterix the Gaul was widely read in several languages as a cartoon character before the opening of Parc Asterix in 1989. It is now fashionable for companies to go down this 'post-Fordist' road of building on their customers' association with their products to stretch their brands into visitor attractions. The point here is that leisure is an experiential activity that has to do with a style of living, but key to success is to identify the product within that style of living. Brand extension enables this, because there is product identity. Museums and galleries also follow this formula by presenting objects and works in ever more stimulating ways. Many of these works and artefacts already have a high intrinsic value and association in the public's mind, so that the desire to consume the product is already high, which makes it much simpler to form a communications proposition.

In essence, the reverse product development cycle, when applied to visitor attractions, is trying to minimize the risks of failure through building imagescapes around already well-received environments, artefacts, commodities or services, so as to call to mind positive images or happenings and then communicating these to the market. These may be termed 'reproductive' imagescapes. For many cultural resources, monuments and works of art, which are now venerated by certain segments of the visitor market, this was not always so. Thus one of the best-loved of Verdi's operas, *La Traviata*, was not that well received when it was first performed, there was fierce opposition to the Eiffel Tower, and Van Gogh only ever sold one painting in his lifetime. This was because the audience had no prior perceptual experience of the creativity put before them and acknowledgement, which can come from experts in the field, as to its acceptability. This supports the view that an 'avant-garde' or 'anticipatory' imagescape is difficult to evaluate in the marketplace, thus separating cultural value from economic value because there is no recognition at large of its worth, so that acknowledgement as to its acceptability has to come from experts in the field. Such imagescapes run the risk, as in the case of the Millennium Dome, of being lampooned in the media as the 'emperor's new clothes', or causing public outrage when it runs counter to what is currently accepted as 'good' taste. When the decision was made to go ahead with the Dome in June 1997, it was a great leap of faith and it was realized that the political 'fallout' from a cynical press would be risky. Highly damning reviews of the project in the press severely affected the desire to visit.

By way of contrast to the Millennium Dome, another millennium project in the UK that has been generally regarded as very successful is the London Eye, a giant Ferris wheel on the southern bank of the Thames, near to the Houses of Parliament. It is selling a tried-and-tested product (reproductive imagescape) in a setting of superb quality. The media are also capable of taking unknown attractions and developing them as reproductive imagescapes through their use as backdrops for films and television programmes, though Beeton (2006) warns about excessive media hype in these situations. It seems therefore that creating a reproductive imagescape is a sufficient condition for attraction success with the public, but not a necessary condition for all attractions. So for example, the Sydney Opera House became an immediately popular symbol once the financial embarrassment was put aside.

While imagescape association can be seen as a significant ingredient in the popularity of an attraction, there is also the question of fashion and taste. Fashion exists and is encouraged in the branding of everything that is purchased, resulting in the obsolescence of commodities and service provision long before their use value is exhausted. Thus, as noted earlier, object-oriented museums are, by and large, no longer considered fashionable. Taste balances the desire to conform to the established fashion against the desire to be different and so, while all attractions aim to achieve an element of surprise, it is important for public acceptance that the content of imagescapes conforms to styles that are characteristic of the time so as not to exceed the bounds of taste. There are some commercial attractions, such as the London Dungeon (a macabre exposition of medieval crime and punishment), which are designed to shock and appeal to the voyeur and those who love the bizarre. They have a particular target market and their style of presentation would not on the whole be acceptable in the public and voluntary sectors.

Conclusion

When dealing with visitor attractions it will be readily appreciated that the number of permutations to do with the variety of imagescapes (Table 2.1), organizations (Table 2.2) and ways of classifying attractions are immense. From an innovation perspective, a useful classification is to place attractions on a scale that has at one end those that have been built or designed for visitor purposes, which are in the minority, and at the other, resources and facilities that are neither for visitors nor can be adapted for them. The bulk of attractions would then be spread out between these two poles. This, in turn, is linked to the pattern of ownership and the multiple objectives that beset different ownership structures. Once attractions have been adapted for visitors, then pressure builds up to interpret success in terms of the quality of the experience, visitor numbers (to capture the spill-over benefits of visitor expenditure) and, where admission is charged, some level of financial viability. The latter brings the non-profit sector closer to the workings of commercial operators.

On the presumption that visitor numbers are a performance target, key attraction demand concepts – the market, imagescape and location – and their linkages have been identified, noting that for the majority of attractions their location is already proscribed by circumstances. This in itself has inherent dangers to do with being able to reach out to the market, which in turn throws greater weight on the market–imagescape mix (Figure 2.3), the degree of uncertainty associated with the level of innovation and the need to develop an imagescape, at whatever level of the attraction, for which demand is more or less continuous through the universality of its popularity. While this is readily accepted in the case of entertainment attractions, in the museum world the commitment to popularizing the product has raised concerns about overstaging the experience, in the sense of being too technologically driven, overemphasizing the media rather than the message embodied in the resource base.

Within the commercial sector, attractions that are flourishing are, as a rule, those that have followed the reverse product development sequence, namely the creation of reproductive imagescapes from products designed for other purposes and in other industries. Similarly, in the not-for-profit sector, the reverse product development model supports the observation that award-winning museums are those that have good collections and use technology to add value to the experience. To take the technology route alone is to embark on a fashion cycle that may be unsustainable in the longer term, though this route is not to be confused with major museums that sequentially update or renew their various departments as a matter of course. A sufficient condition for successful innovation in attraction development concerns the creation of imagescapes that have strong associations, are different (but not too different) and are flexible enough to encourage visitors to return. Avant-garde or anticipatory imagescapes have a high probability of economic failure, although they may be judged to have significant cultural values. This implies that non-market models of resource allocation are needed for many such attraction developments to occur, as can be seen in the various funding arrangements for the performing arts.

References

Abernathy, W. and Clark, K. (1985). Innovation: mapping the winds of creative destruction. *Research Policy*, **14**, 3–22.

Andersson, T. and Getz, D. (2007). Resource dependency, costs and revenues of a street festival. *Tourism Economics*, **13**, 143–166.

Barras, R. (1986). Towards a theory of innovation in services. *Research Policy*, **15**, 161–173.

Beeton, S. (2006). Understanding film-induced tourism. *Tourism Analysis*, **11**, 181–188.

Booz, Allen and Hamilton (1982). *New Products Management for the 1980s*. Booz, Allen and Hamilton.

Brown, K. and Geddes, R. (2007). Resorts, culture, and music: the Cape Breton tourism cluster. *Tourism Economics*, **13**, 129–141.

Grant, A. (1999). *Marketing Opportunities: The Growing Phenomenon of Brand Extension and Industrial Tourism*. Grant Leisure Group.

Hjalager, A.-M. (1994). Dynamic innovation in the tourist industry. In *Progress in Tourism, Recreation and Hospitality Management* (C. Cooper and A. Lockwood, eds), pp. 197–224. Wiley.

Janiskee, R. (1996). Historic houses and special events. *Annals of Tourism Research*, **23**, 398–414.

Johnson, P. and Thomas, B. (1992). *Tourism, Museums and the Local Economy*. Edward Elgar.

Kirsner, S. (1988). Hack the magic: the exclusive underground tour of Disney World. *Wired*, (March), 162–168, 186–189.

NAO – National Audit Office (2000). *The Millennium Dome*. National Audit Office, The Stationery Office.

Pine II, B. and Gilmore, J. (1999). *The Experience Economy*. Harvard Business School Press.

Schumpeter, J. (1934). *The Theory of Economic Development*. Harvard University Press.

Swarbrooke, J. (2002). *The Development and Management of Visitor Attractions*, 2nd edn. Butterworth-Heinemann.

Wanhill, S. (2000). Mines: a tourist attraction – coal mining in industrial South Wales. *Journal of Travel Research*, **39**, 60–69.

Wanhill, S. (2006). Some economics of staging festivals: the case of opera festivals. *Tourism, Culture & Communication*, **6**, 137–149.

Part Two

Developing Visitor Attraction Provision

The wide variety of different types of visitor attraction arguably explains, at least in part, why no unified theoretical framework currently exists to explain and guide the development of either individual attractions or the visitor attraction sector as a whole. Part Two takes four different approaches to examining the development of visitor attractions: a resource-based approach, a geographical approach, a geopolitical approach and a broadly strategy-based approach.

The mobilization and effective use of resources are crucial to their success of attractions, both in terms of their planning and with respect to their operational aspects. In Chapter 3, Steven Richards and Keith Wilkes consider the small business aspects that apply to most attractions, particularly the turbulence caused by survival rates, and examine the criteria for success and, by indication, failure. They go on look at three UK case studies: the National Centre for Popular Music (NCPM), the Earth Centre and the Shugborough Estate. These give insight into how these criteria interact to meet the objectives of the enterprise for good or ill.

In Chapter 4, Stephen Wanhill continues to address resource-based issues, particularly those of an economic and financial nature. Obtaining funding is problematic for most visitor attractions, not only in terms of the initial capital investment required to develop the visitor attraction but also in relation to the day-to-day financing of the attraction once it has come into operation. After outlining the historical development of amusement parks to the point of their establishment as themed entertainment attractions by Walt Disney in 1955, Wanhill goes on to classify theme parks according to their principal economic characteristics. He then goes on to consider some important aspects of their planning and development, exploring the key that arise and how they are dealt with. Examples are provided throughout Chapter 4 to demonstrate the economic and financial aspects of theme park development, which also have some general applicability to the attraction sector as a whole. A detailed, 'true-to-life' case study of the LEGO Company is also provided. The historical context of the development of the company is presented in order to help enhance understanding of the Legoland parks, from their inception to their sale to the Merlin Entertainments Group. As with some of the examples used elsewhere in the chapter, the LEGO case study emphasizes the importance of scale, ownership and location on funding decisions. Chapter 4 concludes by identifying the current trends followed by major operators of theme parks, both in the US and UK, the impact of 9/11, and the growth of other types of themed entertainment attractions.

While focusing on the same theme of visitor attraction development, Chapter 5 adopts a geographical rather than a resource-based approach to the development of visitor attractions. After defining the meaning of peripherality as it applies to visitor attractions and identifying a range of factors, particularly transport, that affect the success of attractions in the periphery, Bruce Prideaux discusses the development process using the farming community of Gatton in Queensland, Australia, as a case example. This explores the vital contribution that the development of visitor attractions can make in meeting the challenges faced by peripheral locations. The main case study, based on Alice Springs in Australia, illustrates the importance of tourism product infrastructure in addition to physical infrastructure in the establishment of a successful group of complementary tourism attractions in a remote periphery.

By way of contrast, Chapter 6 selects two heavily urbanized locations, namely Hong Kong and Singapore, to explain and illustrate the tendency for visitor attractions to be used as instruments of local, regional, national and international political agendas. In this chapter, Joan Henderson explores the political drivers and implications for the development of visitor attractions in East Asia. Although sharing similar urban characteristics, the different political backgrounds of the two countries provide an interesting contrast of how notions of culture, nationhood and ethnicity can be incorporated into the development of modern visitor attractions and manifest themselves in traditional, predominantly heritage-based attractions. Hong Kong and Singapore are responding to the challenges of tourism expansion in the region by pursuing comparable strategies in terms of product enhancement, innovation and marketing which are directed at almost identical objectives of pre-eminence as an Asian city destination, with similar types of attractions. Case studies on the Hong Kong Disneyland, and Marina Bay and the island of Sentosa are then used to illustrate this process.

The final chapter in Part Two adopts a broadly strategy-based approach to the development of visitor attractions by addressing a variety of transport-related issues and their impact on attraction development. In many countries, the majority of visitor attractions rely on the private car as the principal means of transport for their visitors. Derek Robbins and Janet Dickinson examine the major implications of this by exploring the relationships between private and public transport in developing effective access strategies. Thereafter, Chapter 7 analyses the impact of tourism transport on the environment and the case for sustainable transport policies. It then evaluates the success criteria of integrated transport policies. This is demonstrated in the case study on the Eden Project, which shows the limitations of attractions in bringing about modal change when acting in isolation.

Attraction Failure and Success

Steven Richards and Keith Wilkes

Aims

The purpose of this chapter is to:

- review the state of the UK visitor attraction sector,
- discuss the literature pertaining to business failure and success,
- identify potential success criteria for visitor attractions, and
- discuss specific case examples of recent failure and success in the sector.

Introduction

> Visitor attractions are one of the great glories of English tourism, spanning a huge range, from high culture to pure fun. There are blockbuster attractions, but the majority is small businesses – over half receive fewer than 20 000 visitors a year. (ETC, 2000: 1)

Although there were regional and sectoral variations, 2005 visit figures in England showed little change in visitor admissions, with an average sector decrease of −0.5 per cent, following a slight increase in 2004 (+1 per cent). The trend for visits to migrate away from the smaller attractions continued. Attractions with fewer than 20 000 visits reported a 2 per cent decline, following two years of lower growth compared with larger competitor attractions (VisitBritain, 2006).

The small business focus also emerges in terms of employment and gross revenue trends. In 2002, employment data submitted by 1854 attractions in the UK revealed that of the 111 550 employees, 50 per cent were unpaid volunteers, 23 per cent were paid, permanent full-time employees, and 8 per cent were paid, permanent part-time employees. Seasonal employees completed the workforce. The average number of paid employees in UK attractions was 20, a figure which can be further broken down to 23 in England, 15 in Wales, 14 in Scotland and 12 in Northern Ireland (VisitBritain, 2003). Leisure/theme parks were the only attraction category to record an average number of paid employees in excess of 100.

The gross revenue trend for 2004–2005 varied by sector (from +14 per cent for country parks to +4 per cent for places of worship and workplaces) and attractions across all size bands reported average revenue increases. However, attractions with over 100 000 visits recorded a higher proportion of attractions with revenue increase than attractions with fewer than 50 000 visits, as was the case in 2003 and 2004 (VisitBritain, 2006).

Visitor attractions operate in a very competitive environment and the predominance of the small business sector is important. This chapter examines critical factors in the success or otherwise of the visitor attraction sector.

What makes a successful attraction?

Since the 1980s, the visitor attraction sector has experienced many spectacular successes and equally spectacular failures. Equally, a contemporary view was that 'rather more facilities limp along from year to year, continually short of funds for day-to-day promotion and operation, as well as to invest in improvements in facilities for the future' (Martin and Mason, 1993: 34). Martin and Mason identified three key elements in the successful operation of attractions:

- how to draw new visitors and repeat business,
- setting standards of performance and monitoring how the business is doing, and
- being prepared for future changes in visitor needs and expectations.

In 1998, the Confederation of British Industry (CBI) organized a conference 'Visitor Attractions in the New Millennium: The Challenges and Opportunities' to focus attention on the key issues facing the sector. These were considered to be:

- The domestic market, which provides most visitors to smaller attractions, is now largely compared of those on day trips or short breaks with shifting demographics and changing fashions.
- The importance of day visitors to attractions means that they are in effect competing directly for consumer leisure spend. Competition for this spend is becoming increasingly fierce, with the growth of shopping as a leisure

activity, more eating out and the revival of indoor leisure activities such as multiplex cinemas and bowling alleys.
- The large number of new and planned attractions funded by the Lottery or European Union may put existing private-sector attractions at a competitive disadvantage.
- Privately owned attractions continue to experience the displacement effects of the policy of free admission to the national museums and galleries.

These challenges were seen to impact heavily on the quality of the visitor experience and would determine the long-run survival of existing and new attractions, most evidently those in the private sector. Success would only come by 'competing through customer focus', this involving a focus on:

- *Product*: attractions failing to make the most of their 'product', including catering and retail opportunities (what is on offer?).
- *People*: smaller attractions, like smaller businesses in general, face difficulties in developing and using staff to full effect (how are staff recruited, managed and trained?).
- *Pricing*: a lack of competitive benchmarking and competition from free-admission attractions leading to some underpricing (how are price structures set?).
- *Marketing*: limited innovation (how does the attraction try to reach potential customers?).

The conference encouraged the production of *Action for Attractions* (ETC, 2000), offering a *Framework for Action* with a comprehensive set of strategic objectives and recommendations for the visitor attractions sector in England. Key areas were identified for attention, comprising: market measurement, increasing visitor satisfaction, improving attraction management skills, benchmarking, quality, funding and investment, taxation, and development and planning.

Camp (2001) suggested that leisure is about fun and learning – for the visitors – but for Europe's visitor attraction operators, fun was in short supply and tough lessons needed to be learned. He noted that European attractions receive millions of visits each year, and while a great deal of publicity is centred on the big sites, the reality is that there are thousands of attractions struggling to make ends meet. In the UK around 6000 attractions were attracting 400 million visits each year. While both figures had been growing, growth in attractions had exceeded growth in visits.

In the UK, visits per capita reported a 4.8 per cent annual growth in total attendance during the 1990s, this being driven largely by growth in international tourist numbers. More recently, visitor numbers to the UK attractions were static. Camp (2001) suggested that in such situations, operators must take stock of:

- What is it that the attraction offers?
- Is it unique?

- Is it offering something special?
- What are the fundamental aspects of the operation and what is superfluous?
- Is the catering operation actually contributing to the business?
- Is all the space required?
- Are there cuts that can legitimately be made without harming the offer?
- Is the operator kidding itself that attendance figures will rise back up to historic levels without major investment?

Possible solutions include looking at new business areas or expansion. However, while corporate hospitality and off-site retailing might increase revenues, if the facility or brand is not up to it such activities will cost money. Many attractions are physically incapable of operating commercially. Many museums and historic buildings will continue to require subsidy. For all attractions operating close to break-even, or operating at a profit, the key thing is to remain alive to changing market factors and plan for them rather than react to them – an easier thing to say than do. In every case, the key considerations are the marketplace and market conditions. Most problems arise from attractions not designed for the marketplace or that have been overtaken by changes in supply or market conditions.

Five years later, at 'VAC 2006', the Third National Conference for Visitor Attractions Conference in London, a questionnaire was sent to all delegates to identify current issues and factors influencing the sector. The main results are shown in Table 3.1. The list of factors identified by delegates was both lengthy and familiar, confirming that the visitor attractions sector still needs to adopt a more strategic approach to managing its activities in order to ensure a lasting

---

Table 3.1 'Sharing your views' (VAC 2006)

How best can we improve demand?
- Regularly refresh the product, with new features and displays – reasons to re-visit
- Tell the public through targeted marketing
- Act to improve word-of-mouth recommendations
- Use a more contemporary image
- Increase capacity at peak times
- Improve educational facilities
- Make changes to increase value for money
- Re-present our content in ways that appeal to potential visitors
- Focus, above all, on customer satisfaction (applies from theme parks ... to churches)

What currently stops you acting to improve demand?
- Budget constraints
- Constricted and inadequate premises

Continued

Table 3.1   (Continued)

- Poor recognition of need by decision-makers (e.g., trustees)
- Too small to afford the exhibit improvements – the 'arms race'
- Rules, regulations and bureaucracy (e.g., inadequate road signage)
- Lack of ideas!

Positive factors that increased demand in the last two years?
- Special-events programmes
- Temporary exhibitions
- New permanent features
- Suitable weather
- Comparatively strong domestic economy (domestic visits)
- Improved links with other attractions

Negative factors that reduced demand in the last two years?
- The World Cup
- Terrorist acts and fears
- More competition for leisure spend
- Road congestion and travel costs
- Unsuitable weather
- Strong pound (fewer inbound visits; more UK residents going abroad)
- Cheap short-haul flight availability
- Financial constraints
- Declining domestic tourism numbers

Positive factors that are expected to increase demand in the next 10 years?
- Create new facilities
- Refocus on core assets/theme and identity
- New distribution channels and related incentives, vouchers, e-commerce
- Trend towards pre-booking
- Relative decline in value of pound – more UK residents stay home, more inbound
- Involve more volunteers
- Diversify to overcome limitations that threaten viability

Negative factors expected to reduce demand in the next 10 years?
- More competition for leisure spend and time
- Inability to effect improvements
- Lack of investment
- Terrorism acts and fears
- Global warming – weather
- More competition for leisure spend
- Road congestion and travel costs
- Un-level playing field between private- and public/charity-sector attractions
- Government/Tourist Board bureaucracy
- Olympic distractions
- Increased energy costs; lower profits for reinvestment
- Aviation restrictions, limiting tourism
- Older working age – reducing volunteers

future. With the continued slowdown in visitor demand and an acknowledged oversupply of attractions, visitor attractions generally across the UK, and smaller attractions in particular, face a challenging future.

Reasons for business failure

Due to the limited research into tourism business failures and attractions in particular, this section starts by providing an overview of generic causal factors. Berryman (1983) focused more on the managerial causes of small business failure identifying 25 causes under six headings:

- *Accounting*: accounting problems such as debtor and stock control or inadequate records.
- *Marketing*: these can be many and various, from a lack of understanding of customer needs or identification of target customers to poor selling skills.
- *Finance*: financing a firm that is failing is bound to be a problem. Cash flow will be poor and further finance may be unavailable. However, this is simply an obvious symptom of the problem, rather than a root cause. Nevertheless, as many firms have found, undercapitalization at start-up can be a significant factor in subsequent failure. Firms that are highly successful almost from start-up can face the danger of overtrading if they are undercapitalized.
- *Other internal factors*: for example excessive drawings, nepotism or negligence.
- *Behaviour of owner–manager*: personal problems such as an inability to delegate, reluctance to seek help, excessive optimism, unawareness of the environment, inability to adapt to change and thinness of management talent as reasons for failure.
- *External factors*: the effects of the economic environment or changes in the industry or market.

Berryman (1983) notes that conclusions are difficult because of the lack of homogeneity of small firms and because many of the items are symptoms rather than causes of failure. These he categorized together as 'poor management' and concluded that this combines with the personality traits of the owner–manager and external factors to cause decline. However, there is no discussion of the process of failure and, therefore, how it might be avoided.

The literature on business failure can be divided into that which focuses on the corporate sector, the small business sector and business start-ups. As business start-ups aim to become small-medium enterprises, of which some will grow to become large corporations, it is expected that there is some commonality in reasons given for business failure within the different literature, and these will now be explored in more detail.

Poor management may result from autocratic control, where the leader is not receptive to new ideas and not willing to change, referred to as 'top management blindness' (Richardson *et al.*, 1994: 5); an ineffective board where the necessary skills (e.g., finance, marketing, human resources, operational skills, etc) are not balanced and directors do not participate fully in discussions and communication is limited; and situations where managers focus on internal operations rather than responding to changes in the business environment, resulting in strategic drift (Richardson *et al.*, 1994). Inadequate financial control refers to the inadequacy or even lack of systems in place to monitor financial indicators, control budgets and forecast cash-flows, resulting in a weak information base upon which to act (Slatter and Lovett, 1999).

Failed start-ups have also attracted attention in the literature. Richardson *et al.* (1994) identified the following reasons for failed business start-ups:

- Over-optimistic assumptions during the planning stage, including assumptions about levels of sales and prices, the growth of sales, operational costs, profits and cash, support from external stakeholders and the ability of management to implement the planned development.
- Lack of contingency planning.

Slatter and Lovett (1999) conducted research into corporate failures and identified 13 causes of business decline and failure. Internal factors included poor management, inadequate financial control, high costs, lack of marketing effort and organizational inertia. These were often aggravated by external changes in market demand and competition. Some entrepreneurs focus more on coming up with new ideas rather than making sure developments are a long-term success. These are called 'serial entrepreneurs' by Stokes and Blackburn (2002).

There have been few studies into the reasons for tourism business failures. However, similar reasons for business failure emerge. A study of tourism and hospitality businesses in Cornwall by Shaw and Williams (1990) found that businesses struggled due to lack of capital and weak management. Management were typically resistant to change and unwilling to accept advice. Other reasons for failure within the small-business sector noted by Getz *et al.* (2004) were undercapitalization and a lack of working capital, a problem that is exacerbated where demand is seasonal.

Leiper (2003) provides a case study of a failed attraction in Australia, the Big Banana. This was developed into a theme park in 1989, but failed within six months with losses of AU$30 million. Originally, a transit stop with a stall, parking and toilets, sited next to a 15-m high model of a banana. It was sold in 1988 to a large horticultural company which wanted to diversify into tourism and develop a theme park based around horticultural displays. Consultants prepared a feasibility study and forecasted demand of 1.1 million visitors by 1993/94. Half of the development funds were raised from the banking sector; however income was not enough to cover interest payments and the park was placed into receivership in 1990, eventually being sold in 1992. Suggested reasons for the park's failure were:

- visitor numbers were over-estimated within the feasibility study,
- the park did not meet the needs of the previous target market (transit visitors), who did not want to spend time and money visiting a theme park,
- over-optimistic forecasts in feasibility study based upon high penetration rates,
- the location meant there were few local residents to ensure repeat business and day trippers, and
- lenders held a boosterist attitude towards tourism and did not question assumptions made in the business plan.

The Millennium Dome in London has attracted much attention as a case study of a failed tourism attraction. A report by the Comptroller and Auditor General (2000) highlighted the following factors which contributed to its underperformance and ultimate failure:

- over-optimistic visitor projections of 12 million visitors were used to develop the business plan,
- the management company lacked experience in operating visitor attractions,
- the marketing budget was set too low and the marketing strategy relied heavily on free media exposure, and
- weak financial management.

This discussion has highlighted a number of internal and external reasons for business failure. It is most likely that several factors will combine to cause business failure. Business failure is considered to be dependent upon both the characteristics of the business and the owners (Beaver, 2003; Headd, 2003).

Reasons for attraction success and failure

The easiest way to define business failure is as the opposite of success. If success is defined as 'the attainment of certain predefined objectives that can satisfy stakeholder aspirations' (Beaver, 2003: 119), then failure can be seen as the inability to attain these predefined objectives. These objectives will vary, depending on the type of organization and the stakeholders involved.

Stakeholders may be internal or external to the organization. For most attractions, the key stakeholder will be the owner/manager, and different owners will have different objectives for developing their business. Entrepreneurial owners will set business growth and profit maximization as their main objectives. However, many small attractions are started to provide the owner–managers with a degree of independence and an acceptable level of income. Attractions in the public and voluntary sector have many and varied objectives.

External stakeholders will also have their own definition of business success and failure, which may include wider social, economic and environmental objectives. Given these wider and potentially conflicting objectives, it will be difficult for an attraction to meet everyone's definitions of success or failure, and indeed it may be judged as both a success and a failure by different groups, depending on their particular objectives (Beaver, 2003).

It should also be noted that, for the economy as a whole, individual business failure may be a good thing. Research conducted for the Small Business Service (SBS, 2007) shows that high levels of 'business churning' (Anyadike-Danes et al., 2005: 276), where high failure rates are combined with high start-up rates, actually leads to improvements in productivity and economic growth. As such, higher failure rates are not necessarily a bad thing, as they allow resources to be reallocated in a more 'socially optimal' manner (Cressy, 2006: 114).

Measuring survival and failure rates

The most common way to measure failure rates is to use business closure as a surrogate for business failure (Watson and Everett, 1999). Although this method is adopted here, this approach does have its weaknesses. Indeed, not all businesses that close are necessarily considered to be a failure by stakeholders. Research in the USA has shown that around a third of businesses which closed were actually considered to be a success by their owners (Headd, 2003). Research has also shown that the majority of owners of failed businesses return to start new businesses, having learned from the experience. Measuring business closure does not measure the number of failing owners (Stokes and Blackburn, 2002).

In the UK, VAT registrations and de-registrations are often used as a proxy for business start-ups and failure (SBS, 2007) and are used here to show failure rates within the sector. There are additional issues related to the use of VAT data, as businesses do not need to register if their turnover is less than the compulsory VAT threshold. This was £58 000 at the start of 2005, when only 1.8 million of the estimated 4.3 million businesses in the UK were registered (SBS, 2007). Furthermore, if turnover falls below the threshold, a business may de-register without closing, resulting in an overestimate of failure rates (SBS, 2007). Given this threshold, VAT data excludes changes within the smaller (micro-) business sector.

For all businesses registering in 2002, 7.9 per cent failed within the first year and 28.7 per cent had failed by 2004. Within the 'Other Services' sector, which includes visitor attractions, the one- and three-year failure rates were 7.9 and 27.6 per cent, respectively. These failure rates are comparable with those for all businesses, but it must be noted that Other Services includes a number of public administration organizations (SBS, 2007).

Cressy (2006) suggests that failure rates may be higher than this data suggest, with around half of all new businesses closing within two and a half

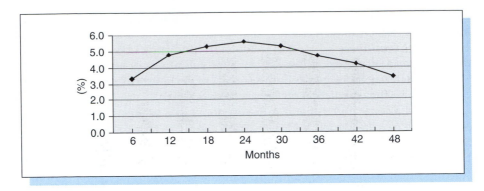

Figure 3.1
Failure rates of UK registered enterprises: 'Other Services' (SBS, 2007)

Table 3.2   Failure rates by SIC code

SIC	2000 (%)	2001 (%)	2002 (%)	2003 (%)	2004 (%)	2005 (%)
923: Other entertainment activities	8.0	7.6	7.5	7.8	7.8	7.5
925: Library, archives, museums and other cultural activities	3.8	4.6	3.7	5.3	4.9	5.2
927: Other recreational activities	10.4	8.8	8.5	9.0	9.6	7.6
Total	8.1	7.6	7.5	7.9	7.9	7.4

Source: SBS (2007).

years of opening. It was also found that failure rates rise to a peak at around 18–24 months, after which they tail off. This pattern is also evident in the failure curve for the 'Other Services' sector (Figure 3.1).

One of the reasons suggested for this rise in the failure rate is the exhaustion of financial resources, which may be used in the short term to cover trading losses (Cressy, 2006). To get a clearer understanding of the level of business churn within the visitor attraction sector, and in particular the levels of failure, VAT registrations and de-registrations for relevant SIC codes have been analysed (Table 3.2). These classes do include other sub-classes which are not of relevance to the sector; however, data are not published beyond the 3-digit level.

Since the beginning of the new millennium, failure rates for the sector have remained relatively steady, varying between 8.1 per cent in 2000 and 7.4 per cent in 2005. Higher failure rates tend to be experienced within the 'Other

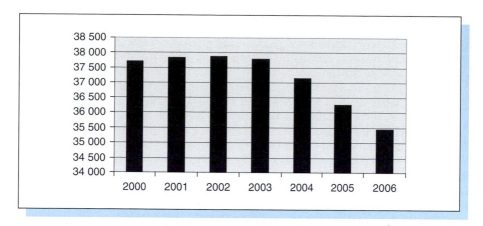

Figure 3.2
Stock of VAT-registered enterprises, UK, 2000–2006

Recreational Activities' category, reaching 10.4 per cent in 2000. However, these figures have fallen in recent years. Failure rates tend to be lower in the 'Library, Archives, Museums and Other Cultural Activities' category. Taking into account new registrations as well as these failure rates, the impact on the total number of businesses within this sector is shown in Figure 3.2.

Overall, since 2000 there have been more de-registrations than registrations. This has led to a 6 per cent decrease in the number of registered businesses since 2000. The number of 'Other Entertainment and Recreational Activities' fell by 5 and 15 per cent, respectively; however, the number of 'Library, Archives, Museums and Other Cultural Activities' actually increased slightly, from 1175 in 2000 to 1255 in 2006, up by 6 per cent.

Case Studies: Mixed fortunes

The three case studies presented here display characteristics encountered frequently in the visitor attractions sector, such as undercapitalization, over-optimistic visitor projections and poorly defined attraction objectives, combined with limited project and operations management experience. The significance of location cannot be ignored. The first two attractions – The NCPM and The Earth Centre – both failed. The third case study offers greater optimism and confirms the importance of a clear and coherent strategy and strong leadership and management.

The National Centre for Popular Music

The NCPM took the theme of world popular music (Comptroller and Auditor General, 2003) and was developed as an interactive arts and education centre. It was designed as a technology-based attraction, explaining the technology of music using information technology, video, laser and interactive exhibits, thereby differentiating itself from other music attractions with a memorabilia focus (Williamson,

1999). The NCPM was housed in an iconic new building designed to look like four giant steel drums (Watson-Smyth, 2000). Each drum was themed differently, with the first drum showing how music impacts upon daily lives, The second drum enabled visitors to make music, by allowing them to play different instruments and mix their own record. The third drum (called 'turning points') displaying films on a video wall, while the final drum contained a 200-seat arena within a 360-degree 'soundscape'. There was also a shop, a café, an exhibition space, an educational area, an outdoor public performance area and a bar used as a music venue in the evenings (Comptroller and Auditor General, 2003; Sturges, 1999).

Sheffield was chosen as the location for the £15.2 million attraction and a lottery grant of £11.085 million was awarded by the Arts Council England, with the remainder raised through partnership funding (Comptroller and Auditor General, 2003; Williamson, 1999). The eventual cost of the development reached £16.9 million, 11.2 per cent above budget (Comptroller and Auditor General, 2003). The Centre opened in March 1999, but soon ran into financial difficulties, amassing debts of over £1 million (Ashworth, 2000). In order to continue trading, an agreement was reached with creditors, who accepted part-payment of 10 pence in the pound in the hope that they would get more if the venture was turned around (Herbert, 1999).

With the appointment of a new CEO with experience of managing London's Rock Circus, the Centre attempted to reposition itself to appeal more to the local market and attract a wider audience. New exhibits were introduced, displaying more traditional items of rock memorabilia, admission prices were reduced and the new management team set about trying to attract high-profile concerts. A supplementary grant of £290 000 was awarded in March 2000 to help fund the re-design and development of the contents (Comptroller and Auditor General, 2003), and a new visitor target of 150 000 was set (Herbert, 2000).

An additional £900 000 was earmarked by the Arts Council England (The Times, 2003) to fund improvements to the public facilities and exhibitions and to add more interactive content. However, to avoid further losses to its creditors and risk personal liability, the Centre decided to cease operations as a visitor attraction in June 2000 (Comptroller and Auditor General, 2003). The Centre did reopen briefly as a music venue before closing to the public in 2002. It eventually reopened again in 2005 as a student union (student social centre), after being sold for £1.85 million to Sheffield Hallam University.

Reasons for failure identified include:

(i) *Over-optimistic visitor projections*: The original visitor target for the Centre was 400 000 visitors per annum. To be a viable operation, the Centre had to attract almost 8000 visitors per week (Watson-Smyth, 2000). However, only 66 000 came in the first six months of operation (Comptroller and Auditor General, 2003). The over-optimistic visitor projections were highlighted as a problem by the insolvency practitioners (Ward and O'Hara, 1999). As the Chairman of the Arts Council England noted, they were told by consultants that 'because hundreds of thousands of people go to rock concerts, a museum would get very good attendance figures. They were wrong: people who go to rock concerts do not go to museums' (Frayling, cited in Rowan, 2006: 43).

(ii) *Content*: Content was seen as a problem, with the architect concerned about the lack of memorabilia (Niesewand, 1999), the limited hands-on approach (Williamson,

1999) and a lack of educational content (Jury, 1999). The Deputy Director noted that 'the exhibitions aren't interesting, there is not enough "live" music and it's not plugged into the local community' (Ashworth, 2000: 31).

(iii) *Location*: The Centre's location has also been highlighted as a reason for its failure, as Sheffield is not on the international tourist's map – 'you have to remember that this is in Sheffield – it's the fourth largest city in the UK, but it is not a top tourist attraction' (Ward and O'Hara, 1999: 9). The Deputy Director asked 'would any attraction in Sheffield attract 400 000 people?' (Ashworth, 2000: 31). It was hoped that such a development would help develop the image of Sheffield as a tourist destination, but some felt that there was a lack of cultural fit as the city is not renowned for its pop culture. Since Sheffield is not seen as a top tourist destination, it meant that the attraction needed to focus more on the domestic market and hold a wider appeal for the local community.

(iv) *Project management*: Issues relating to the development and construction phase of the Centre may have contributed to its ultimate failure. An exhibition consultant involved in the early stage of the project's development considered the project team to be enthusiastic but inexperienced, with a lack of effective business planning from the start (Higgins, 2006). The Select Committee on Public Accounts also found that the construction of the Centre had not been suf-ficiently regulated by the Arts Council England's independent building monitor and this may have contributed to the cost overruns noted above.

The Earth Centre

The Earth Centre was designed to be a 'museum of the earth', based on the theme of sustainability in order to increase awareness of environmental issues and sustainable development (McKinney *et al.*, 2004: 61). Originally, a site was sought in London, but land prices were too high and in 1990 a site in South Yorkshire, which was to be reclaimed from two disused collieries, was selected (Johnson, 2004). Doncaster Council supported the development and provided funding to undertake initial research and further funds were secured to conduct a feasibility study for the development (Epstein, 2000).

This study proposed a £120 million project covering a 400-acre site, to include buildings, exhibitions, gardens and accommodation. In 1995, the Millennium Commission agreed to offer a grant of 50 per cent funding up to £50 million. The initial project was scaled down to £100, and match funding was secured from sources including the European Regional Development Fund (£9 million) and English Partnerships (£5.4 million). However, funding came in more slowly and in much smaller amounts than expected, which meant development had to be phased (Epstein, 2000; McKinney *et al.*, 2004).

Phase One began in 1997 and focused on the reclamation and landscaping of the site. Some features and facilities were developed, including galleries and a café at the site entrance (Epstein, 2000). However, the required infrastructure works took up most of the available funds (House of Commons, 2000), meaning there was little money left to develop the content.

The Earth Centre opened in the Spring of 1999, and planning and fund-raising for Phase Two then began (McKinney *et al.*, 2004). This second phase focused on improving the visitor product, as it was felt that the public perception of sustainable development was limited, and more attention needed to be paid to the content of the attraction (House of Commons, 2000). It also aimed at developing facilities to generate additional income streams, including business tourism and environmental consultancy services (Epstein, 2000).

The site closed in Autumn 1999 to allow for the construction of Phase Two, which included additional galleries and exhibition space, a new conference centre and an accommodation block (Epstein, 2000; European Academy of the Urban Environment, 2001). However, due to difficulties in securing match funding and the overrun in construction work, the Centre did not reopen until July 2001 (McKinney *et al.*, 2004).

Due to lower-than-expected visitor numbers, the Centre ran into financial difficulties in Spring 2003, and a new CEO was appointed in June 2003. The new management team focused on widening the appeal of the Centre by introducing new attractions including a road train, an indoor play area, miniature golf and a children's play galleon. These changes did have an impact on attendance, the Centre attracting 150 000 visitors in 2003. However, despite this increase, the Centre was still operating at a loss, amounting to £140 000 for the year, with further debts of £60 000 accruing in the first six months of 2004 (Stokes, 2004). The Centre could not afford to continue operating at a loss, and it closed in October 2004 and was wound up in April 2005 after a buyer could not be found.

Problems identified include:

(i) *Undercapitalization*: A major problem the Earth Centre faced was raising capital to fund the project, in particular, the 50 per cent match funding required by the Millennium Commission (McKinney *et al.*, 2004). Initially there was a £40 million shortfall (Johnson, 2004), which led to phased development. The need to reclaim the site meant that the development of the visitor attraction product was delayed, thereby reducing revenue streams and leading to further financial difficulties. The problem was exacerbated by initial financial projections including only capital expenditure and overlooking the need for revenue costs to operate and maintain the large site during the extended development period (McKinney *et al.*, 2004).

(ii) *Over-optimistic visitor projections*: It was anticipated that the Centre would attract 500 000 visitors per annum; however only 80 000 came in the first year (Johnson, 2004). A former CEO is quoted as saying that the Millennium Commission originally projected one million visitors in the first year of operation, and this figure seems to have been 'pulled out of thin air' (McKinney *et al.*, 2004: 63).

(iii) *Attraction objectives*: The lower-than-expected visitor numbers highlights another issue the Earth Centre faced. The Earth Centre always sought to be more than a visitor attraction, aiming to be (Epstein, 2000: 28):

- a place of and for education,
- a research and demonstration resource,

- a standard setter in sustainability design, construction and operation,
- an ecological park,
- a catalyst for sustainable regeneration,
- a resource for the promotion of sustainable technologies, processes and produces, and
- a place for exhibitions, events and shows.

This broad mix of aims shows the ambition of the founders to provide a 'major public resource for sustainability' (Epstein, 2000: 28), rather than purely a commercial visitor attraction. As stated by David Copeland from the Millennium Commission, 'it wasn't intended to be and will never be a popular visitor attraction' (McKinney *et al.*, 2004: 63).

(iv) *Management experience*: The management team that developed the concept had no attraction management experience. Their lack of operational experience was highlighted by the Millennium Commission, which criticized, for example, their decision to place the restaurant and shop after the paypoint. In order to revive the operation, the 'visionaries' (McKinney *et al.*, 2004: 63) were removed from the Board and replaced by a management team with previous attraction operation experience.

(v) *Location*: Site selection was also seen as a problem by some. Although located in the centre of the country with good transport links and a large catchment area with 17 million potential visitors within two hours' journey time, the local travel to work area was one of the poorest areas in Europe (Epstein, 2000). The site itself was in need of reclamation, which added to the overall cost of the project. Again, this links back to the aim of the development to be more than just an attraction, as reclamation and regeneration were seen as key benefits of the Centre.

Shugborough

After two examples of attraction failure which confirm the difficulties of developing and operating visitor attractions in the UK, it is appropriate to complete the trio of case studies with positive evidence about the possible transformation of an attraction from struggle to optimism.

The Shugborough Estate comprises a set of mid-eighteenth century Greek revival garden monuments, set in 900 acres of open parkland, along with a number of functional buildings, most dating from the early nineteenth century onwards. Having passed to the National Trust on a 99-year lease, it is operated as a visitor attraction by Staffordshire County Council where, in 2003, the senior management decided that Shugborough should aim to become a commercially viable estate. In spite of the unique and high-quality presentations at Shugborough, unlike many UK museums and stately homes there was no commercial exploitation. Shugborough remained a regional attraction, free (or at very little charge) for the taxpayers of Staffordshire.

Managing this change demanded the co-operation of the National Trust, the County Council, the Earl of Lichfield, the villagers and the long-serving County Council employees who staffed the estate. A new General Manager from the private sector (Richard Kemp, who contributed fully to this case study) was appointed with an open brief to realize the commercial potential of Shugborough and to make the site financially independent of the public purse (Kemp, 2006).

What made change possible?

Despite the development of new income streams since the 1980s – shows, fairs and events which dominated the site both physically and in terms of its profile – by the start of the twenty-first century Shugborough's visitor base was a very low-spending, small, mainly local or sub-regional audience, supplemented by National Trust members from further afield. The gardens (shops, restaurant, toilets, etc.) were accessed by many visitors for free due to an open-access policy. Whilst local access might not be seen as detrimental (apart from damage to monuments and gardens), tourists from the nearby Trent and Mersey Canal were enjoying a free day out at the taxpayers' expense. Day visitor spend per head was low, paying day-visitor numbers were in decline and physical damage to the gardens was frequent. The attraction was held in low esteem amongst councillors, frustrated at the apparent inability of the attraction to compete in a commercial marketplace and requiring permanent financial support.

The following changes were made:

(i) *Business direction*: Shugborough had at least two incompatible functions: day visitors and special events. The process of establishing the business direction for the site involved the definition of core assets and intrinsic qualities and how they could be best interpreted and accessed. While single component of the estate was in itself unique, the rare survival of an entire complex of interdependent, historic, working buildings, full of relevant working artefacts, made the site special and possibly unique in the UK. It was decided to address the nascent day-visitor market and feature a whole-site approach to interpretation. Other ancillary income streams (such as events) would only be maintained if they did not interfere or impair the day-visitor experience.

(ii) *Communications*: The name 'Shugborough' was well known locally, but for the wrong reasons. In terms of wider marketing, the name meant nothing: no brand existed. There was a much undeveloped communications strategy based within the County Council. It was decided to use the term 'Shugborough: The Complete Working Historic Estate', designed to convey the 'USP' of a vibrantly presented complex of inter-dependent historic buildings in a readily digestible form, and indeed to act as 'the brand'. A new Shugborough website was created with no County Council linkages. Visits to the website increased by 400 per cent. The site now emerges top in a search for 'Shugborough' on all major search engines, whereas it had been fifth or sixth previously.

(iii) *Physical access*: The site's road layout and car parks generated a fragmented feel, confusing first-time visitors but also, of more concern, not being conducive to providing a rounded view of the entire estate in which the house could be viewed in the context of a complex of working buildings. Access infrastructure denied the relevance and the historical, educational and architectural importance of the ancillary estate buildings. The solution was to create a new approach to the site and a single new ticket office. The visitor route was then designed to incorporate all major facets of the estate. Early public concern over the provision of transport for those unable to walk the distances between car park, farm and house was resolved with a range of solutions.

(iv) *Intellectual access*: An essential element of the estate's development was to combine all elements of the estate into a single unit – 'The Complete Working Historic Estate' – providing an opportunity to present a unique, estate-wide interpretation of a stately home. The stately home sector of the UK visitor attractions market has existed for at least 50 years. However, the rationale for the original construction of these magnificent palaces was as an extension of each family's prestige and wealth: an overt way, through contemporary design, fashion, the sheer size of buildings and the richness of its contents of impressing ones contemporaries. The National Trust runs a great many historic properties, most of them of high status, but their portfolio also includes the utilitarian. Properties like workhouses (Southwell in Nottinghamshire) or ordinary houses (Birmingham's 'back to backs') are amongst the public's favourites in the National Trust stable.

The decision to present Shugborough not simply as a house but as a whole estate thus places it in a category of its own. The addition of a working, historic walled garden as the new start of the visit, followed by a working, historic farm and working, historic servants' quarters, gives the visitor an initial view of the support networks that were required to maintain the big house. The house may be seen as the ultimate architectural achievement, and repository of the family wealth, but, following a visit to Shugborough, one cannot fail to understand that this splendour was won on the toil of an army of servants in what was undoubtedly a mutually beneficial, symbiotic relationship with the family. In a related, natural extension of this shift towards the ordinary, contextual aspects of the stately home, it was decided to tell its stories (where appropriate) largely from a servant's personal 'first-person' point of view.

(v) *Culture change*: A parallel culture change amongst the staff, in their attitudes towards the site, what it was worth and what customers might expect, was required. A similar challenge was the change required of local attitudes, particularly amongst those who had known and used (and abused in some very limited cases) the site.

Staff had fundamentally ceased to believe in the site's viability as a visitor attraction. The biggest challenge was to persuade the staff of the confidence they should have in the site as a 'day out' and as a quality educational experience. This lack of confidence manifested itself in many ways, but prices were the focus of attention and perhaps the most tangible way that this lack of confidence manifested itself. Amongst the earliest move was a measure that sought actively to sell the whole site as the only way to look at Shugborough. This was promoted as being intellectually sound and commercially advantageous, through increased spend per head, length of stay and satisfaction levels. This was done through on-site signage, advertising and, most importantly, through active selling at the point of entry.

Results so far?

Enhanced optimism is evident with this extract from the North Staffordshire Tourism Strategy:

> Star attractions such as Shugborough continue to bring in significant numbers of visitors, and also play host an increasing number of profile-raising events.
>
> (Locum Destination Consulting, 2004: 8)

Shugborough is now in the midst of a 10-year business plan, and is successfully delivering the income levels and the visitor numbers it needs to become financially self-sufficient in that time (Staffordshire County Council, 2006). The site has a growing reputation nationally for delivering what is called 'living history'. New business levels (people coming to the site for the first time) have increased from 1 per cent in 2003 to 43 per cent in 2005. The average length of stay has increased from two hours to three hours (and it will increase inevitably with the new access arrangements); spend per head has increased nearly 60 per cent; and the numbers of real visitors (i.e., those who have paid to access the attraction) has increased by 19 per cent between the 2004 and 2005 season. Locals buying the Season Pass in 2006 have increased 73 per cent from the 2005 levels when the scheme was launched. Whilst it is still too early to judge the wider public's reaction to change, the site is already being better cared for, is more appropriately presented, has a believable business direction, has the overwhelming support of The National Trust and the confidence of elected members, local media and politicians, and has already a more secure and stable future. To finish on an optimistic note, 2007 visitor numbers have increased by 50 per cent compared to the same period last year.

Conclusion

This chapter has examined visitor attraction success and failure with a focus on the increasingly difficult competitive environment in which many visitor attractions, especially small-medium enterprises, find themselves. Case studies examine two failures in the sector and the process of transformation at a heritage attraction to engender an optimistic tone. Accounting and finance, marketing, the behaviour of owners and managers, and the effects of the external economic and social environment, can all contribute to attraction success and failure. Recent figures released by ALVA (the Association of Leading Visitor Attractions) indicate that overall the visitor attraction sector 'has staying power and has managed to remain vibrant and to continue to be a significant contributor to the British economy' (Broke, 2007: 10). Whilst no simple recipe exists to guarantee the successful development and operation of a visitor attraction, this chapter has indicated many of the factors and issues affecting the sector in the first decade of the twenty-first century.

References

Anyadike-Danes, M., Hart, M. and O'Reilly, M. (2005). Watch that space! The county hierarchy in firm births and deaths in the UK, 1980–1999. *Small Business Economics*, **25**, 273–292.

Ashworth, J. (2000). Pop music centre hits low note. *The Times*, 4 February, p. 31.

Beaver, G. (2003). Small business: success and failure. *Strategic Change*, **12**, 115–122.

Berryman, J. (1983). Small business failure and bankruptcy: a survey of the literature. *European Small Business Journal*, **1**, 47–59.

Broke, R. (2007). Visitor attractions. *Tourism*, **131**, 10.

Camp, D. (2001). Welcome to reality. 10th Anniversary TiLE Conference 2001. London.

Comptroller and Auditor General (2000). *The Millennium Dome*. The Stationary Office.

Comptroller and Auditor General (2003). *Progress on 15 Major Capital Projects Funded by Arts Council England*. The Stationery Office.

Cressy, R. (2006). Why do most firms die young? *Small Business Economics*, **26**, 103–116.

Epstein, D. (2000). Earth Centre and global issues. *Sustainable Development International*, **3**, 27–31.

ETC (2000). *Action for Attractions*. English Tourism Council.

European Academy of the Urban Environment (2001). *Doncaster Earth Centre: An International Centre for Sustainable Development and Living*. European Academy of the Urban Environment.

Getz, D., Carlsen, J. and Morrison, A. (2004). *The Family Business in Tourism and Hospitality*. CABI.

Headd, B. (2003). Redefining business success: distinguishing between closure and failure *Small Business Economics*, **21**, 51–61.

Herbert, I. (1999). Creditors allow the troubled museum of pop music to live now and pay back later. *The Independent*, 3 November, p. 5.

Herbert, I. (2000). New director leaves stricken pop centre. *The Independent*, 12 January, p. 5.

Higgins, P. (2006). Up the albion. *The Observer*, 2 July, p. 11.

House of Commons (2000). *Culture, Media and Sport – Eighth Report*. House of Commons.

Johnson, A. (2004). Earth Centre runs out of time and cash. *The Independent on Sunday*, 7 November, p. 4.

Jury, L. (1999). The day the museum went pop: why the National Centre for Popular Music was just too much fun for its own good. *The Independent on Sunday*, 24 October, p. 20.

Kemp, R. (2006). Transformation of Heritage Attractions: Shugborough. VAC 2006. The 3rd National Conference of Visitor Attractions, London.

Leiper, N. (2003). *Tourism Management*, 2nd edn. Pearson Education.

Locum Destination Consulting (2004). *North Staffordshire Tourism Strategy 2004–2014.* Locum Destination Consulting.

Martin, B. and Mason, S. (1993). The future for attractions – meeting the needs of new consumers. *Tourism Management*, **14**, 34–40.

McKinney, R., Jones, D. and Kahn, H. (2004). *Lottery Funding and The UK Voluntary Sector: Capacity, Change and Sustainability.* Heriot-Watt University.

Niesewand, N. (1999). Architecture: 1999 – the year of the turkey. *The Independent*, 27 December, p. 9.

Richardson, B., Nwankwo, S. and Richardson, S. (1994). Understanding the causes of business failure crises. *Management Decision*, **32**, 9–22.

Rowan, D. (2006). Where did all your money go? *The Sunday Times*, 6 August, p. 43.

SBS – Small Business Service (2007). *Survival Rates of VAT-registered Enterprises.* Small Business Service.

Shaw, G. and Williams, A. (1990). *Progress in Tourism, Recreation and Hospitality Management.* Belhaven Press.

Slatter, S. and Lovett, D. (1999). *Corporate Turnaround: Managing Companies in Distress.* Penguin.

Staffordshire County Council (2006). Minutes of the Development Services Scrutiny and Performance Panel, 22nd November.

Stokes, D. and Blackburn, R. (2002). Learning the hard way: the lessons of owner–managers who have closed their businesses. *Journal of Small Business and Enterprise Development*, **9**, 17–27.

Stokes, P. (2004). Cash blow for Earth Centre. *The Daily Telegraph*, 15 November, p. 10.

Sturges, F. (1999). This is pop! No it isn't. Do the hi-tech displays at the National Centre for Popular Music tell us about rock, or are they just gizmos and gimmicks? *The Independent*, 16 June, p. 8.

The Times (2003). Two centres that shut after failing to attract enough visitors. *The Times*, 2 May, p. 10.

VisitBritain (2003). *Sightseeing in the UK 2002.* British Tourist Authority.

VisitBritain (2006). *Visit Attraction Trends in England 2005.* British Tourist Authority.

Ward, D. and O'Hara, K. (1999). Bankruptcy threatens pop music centre. *The Guardian*, 19 October, p. 9.

Watson, J. and Everett, J. (1999). Small business failure rates: choice of definition and industry effects. *International Small Business Journal*, **17**, 31–47.

Watson-Smyth, K. (2000). Pop goes the national music centre. *The Independent*, 29 July, p. 4.

Williamson, N. (1999). National Centre for Popular Music. *The Times*, 27 February, p. 29.

CHAPTER · · · · 4

Economic Aspects of Developing Theme Parks

Stephen Wanhill

Aims

The aims of this chapter are to:

- define a theme park,
- briefly assess the historical development of theme parks,
- examine the classification of theme parks,
- discuss key economic and financial aspects of developing theme parks, and
- demonstrate these issues using a contemporary case example of the LEGO Corporation.

Introduction

The early history of themed entertainment attractions, or theme parks in everyday understanding, was one of redirecting the concept of amusement parks and fairgrounds of former times into a fantasy-provoking atmosphere. But, as is well known, the Walt Disney Corporation (WDC) has moved beyond fantasy to encompass learning experiences as in the Experimental Prototype Community of Tomorrow (EPCOT) Center, so that fun is also educational, for which the word 'edutainment' has been coined. Nevertheless, the underlying principle of the theme park product remains: it is to provide a pleasurable day out for the family and is founded on resolving a long-established market research outcome, that families cannot stay together for more than two to three hours without bickering, unless a variety of distractions are provided (McClung, 1991). Today, such parks are the modern form of the travelling fairs of yesteryear that have been made obsolete by technology, laws on safety and duties of care to the public, and the increase in leisure expenditure that has reduced the need to travel from one market to another to capture limited spending power.

A suitable definition of a theme park is 'a family amusement complex oriented towards a range of subjects or historical periods, combining the continuity of costuming and architecture with edutainment through rides and other attractions, catering and merchandising, to provoke an experience for the imagination'. The Disney Corporation uses the term 'imagineers' to describe its designers and what they create are 'imagescapes' (see Chapter 2) through sophisticated 'audio-animatronics' tableaux that blend fantasy into reality around an activity in a spatial setting. Thus, the intangible output of a constructed imagescape is central to the visitor experience and success comes from having a clear idea of what this should be, proven management skills and knowledge of the market. Wong and Cheung (1999) undertook a brochure analysis to produce a classification of park imagescapes into seven storylines, namely adventure, futurism, international, nature, fantasy, history and culture, and the 'movies'.

As a rule, parks tend to have multiple imagescapes designated to zones or 'lands' (Richards, 2001), but some parks, as in the case of Warner Bros MovieWorld, Legoland or BonBon-Land (Wanhill, 2003), which began life as a chocolate factory in Næstved, Denmark in 1930, have one main image running through them. Imagescapes compress history and culture, and thus time and space, into marketable entertainment experiences that have been criticized as 'no place places' (Zukin, 1991). However, complex or scholarly themes have difficulty producing the emotional experiences necessary to attract family groups and have limited repeat-visit potential. This market wants easy access, fun rides and attractions, little waiting in queues, good weather and scenery, and a 'clean' family atmosphere.

Normally, such facilities have a pay-one-price (POP) admission charge and differ from traditional amusement parks in that they tend to be on open sites outside towns and cities, have high management standards and finish in a themed environment where everything is centrally owned as opposed to being made up of a large number of concessionaires. In the manner of long-established parks, they may offer 'optional' pricing in the form of free or low-cost entry general admission (GA) and a 'pay-as-you-go' system, or the opportunity to buy an all-inclusive ticket or book of tickets.

Historical development

The earliest amusement park, which still exists today, is the 'Bakken', 10 km north of Copenhagen, which dates from 1583. Thereafter, pleasure gardens began to appear in Europe during the late seventeenth century. For example, in 1661 Vauxhall Gardens was established in London at the time of Charles II, featuring music, entertainment, fireworks, games and even primitive rides. The first Tivoli amusement park was originally a rich man's 'folly', for which the name was created, and appeared in Paris in 1771. It was swept aside in the Revolution, as were the frivolous activities of the pleasure gardens, but the idea and name were copied elsewhere in Europe, the most notable being Copenhagen's Tivoli Gardens (1843), which draws in around 4 million visitors per year. As a result of their growth in popularity, Tivolis became somewhat commonplace and the public's appetite moved on, so that many disappeared in the 1850s, some to become dance halls.

The next major impetus to amusement park development came from the industrial revolution and the growth of urbanization. It enabled the harnessing of power, at first steam and then electricity, to build and regulate more powerful rides, while the railways brought the visitors to their destination. The impact in Europe took the form of building attractions at the growing coastal resorts (Blackpool Pleasure Beach was established in 1896) and at the ends of piers, particularly in Britain, where 78 were developed between 1860 and 1910. Very few piers were built on mainland Europe. At the same time, in USA the expansion of towns following the Civil War gave rise to 'Trolley Parks'. They came about because the utility companies charged the new electric traction (trolley) companies a monthly flat fee for the use of their electricity. As a result, to stimulate weekend use they created amusement parks, typically at the end of the line. The success of these parks caused them to spread across the US, though relatively few survive to this day. Of the 12 still operating, the most significant is Dorney Park that was opened in Allentown in 1884 and still averages around 1.5 million visitors.

It was at Chicago's Columbian Exposition in 1893 that a key 'architectural' innovation (Abernathy and Clark, 1985) took place, with the introduction of George Ferris's Giant Wheel and the Midway Plaisance with its wide array of rides and concessions. The success of the latter dictated amusement park design and the framework in which competition and linkages to consumers would occur and develop for the next 62 years, both at home and abroad. The industry in the States experienced strong growth over the next three decades or more, its heart remaining in Coney Island, but this was to end with the Wall Street Crash of 1929. Thereafter, the industry struggled to survive and apart from a short-lived post-Second World War boom, parks were now out of vogue as people in the TV age were looking for more sophisticated leisure than could be found in these old-fashioned and, in many instances, dilapidated parks.

To restore the fortunes of the US industry, a new architectural innovation was needed and this was created by Walt Disney in Anaheim, California in 1955. Built at a cost of some US$17 million, Disneyland was the largest park investment that had ever been made. Instead of the fairground style of a Midway Plaisance, with numerous concessionaires, Disneyland offered five distinct themed areas (Main Street USA, Adventureland, Frontierland, Fantasyland and Tomorrowland) that provided 'guests' with the fantasy of travel to different lands and times, all designed and managed by one organization. As often happens with new ideas, there were many sceptics who were unable to see how an amusement park without any of the traditional attractions, such as the Ferris Wheel or Tunnel of Love, could be successful. They listed a catalogue of perceived mistakes that would end in failure, for example, having only one entrance, which would cause excessive congestion for visitors, the lack of traditional revenue earners, and the amount of space devoted to non-revenue earning Main Street USA (Adams, 1991). In Europe, De Efteling in the Netherlands was created in 1951, with fairy tales as the central theme, and drew in 300 000 visitors in 1952, but it was Disneyland that set the agenda for the theme park developments that are so familiar around the world today. Confounding its critics, the park brought in 3.8 million visitors in its first year, a figure that reached 13.9 million by the millennium (now approaching 15 million) as the number of attractions grew from 17 to 61 and the area became a fully fledged resort. In the beginning, Anaheim only had seven motels with 87 guest rooms and it is now estimated that there are now some 50 000 guest rooms within the surrounding areas of the park.

Classifying theme parks

Table 4.1 draws out a broad classification of parks in modern terms, but it should be noted that over the years the boundaries have become increasingly blurred. Where the population catchment is small, and/or there are climatic limitations on the season, this has tended to restrict development to the refurbishment of existing parks, some of which have become 'classics' in their own right and are difficult to compare with any other, such as Copenhagen's Tivoli Gardens or the Liseberg, Gothenburg (1923). Many such parks have the added advantage of being able to capitalize on their prime sites that are now within city limits. Most have become hybrids with a mixture of attractions, themed areas and traditional fairground amusements, though the Bakken is still essentially a funfair drawing mainly on the 1.5 million population of Greater Copenhagen. It has some 60 concessionaires and entry is free, so visitor numbers of 2.5 million are only broad estimates (Wanhill, 2003).

Modern parks have also become hybrids, thus during the 1990s in the USA, water parks all began to introduce thrill rides to compete with dry parks. Similarly, dry parks have added water parks adjacent to them. In the Middle East, Korea and South East Asia many 'leisure parks' have been designed as indoor attractions, sometimes combined with shopping, whereas in Europe and the US large shopping complexes and malls have been introducing leisure entertainment into their portfolio of activities. For example, Knott's Camp Snoopy (1992) is an indoor park with free GA and depends on the 'footfall' within the Mall of America. Similarly, New Metroland (1996), UK, is within the Gateshead Metro Centre.

Destination parks normally belong to chains operators and are rare in Europe compared to the USA. This is because catchment areas are closer together and it is difficult to generate the required staying visitors to make them viable. The demand here is principally for regional parks. However, the major US brands (with the exception of Six Flags, which is a regional park

Table 4.1 Categories of themed entertainment attractions 2007 (US$ prices)

Product features	Destination park	Regional park	Traditional park	Water park
Concept	High theming/multiple imagescapes; Resort amenities and hotels; Major branded attraction	Rides and shows; Theming; Some branding	Rides and Fairground arcades; Individual theming; Concessionaires	Indoor/outdoor; Local and tourist appeal; Short stay
Nos. Europe	4+ million	1.0–2.0 million	0.5–1.0 million	0.4–0.8 million
Nos. US	6+ million	1.5–3.0 million	0.75–1.5 million	0.6–1.2 million
Season Europe	Year-round	180–220 days	120–190 days	Year-round/seasonal
Season US	Year-round	Year-round/180–220 days	180–220 days	Year-round/seasonal
Cost Europe	$450 million	$160–$270 million	$100–$160 million	$25–$65 million
Cost US	$600 million	$220–$350 million	$110–$180 million	$35–$75 million
Market	Tourist	Tourist/resident	Resident/tourist	Resident/tourist
Source markets	Regional/national/international	Regional tourist/resident	Two-hour resident/limited tourist	One-hour resident/tourist
Admission	High POP	Medium POP	Small/free GA/low POP	Medium-low POP
Competition	Low	Medium-low	High-medium	Medium
Site (1 hectare = 2.471 acres)	100–200 hectares	25–50 hectares	10–30 hectares	<10 hectares

Sources: Author and Amusement Business.

operator) have created super-destinations through park clustering in Southern California and Florida. An illustration of this can be seen in Table 4.2, which shows attendances at the Florida destination cluster.

Economic issues

Location

In a broad sense, the key economic aspects to consider in developing any attraction are the imagescape (or a number of imagescapes, thus giving a place within a place), the location and the market. Demand-oriented logic dictates that the optimum path is Market → Imagescape → Location. Theme parks are the most obvious examples of attractions that can follow this pathway, because they are seeking to maximize their level of attendance. Attendance is functionally related to the population catchment area within a specified drive time of up to two hours for cars and three to four hours for coach, bus or train. Opinions vary as to what is the appropriate catchment size. Thus Oliver (1989) argues, within a European context, for a location to be found

Table 4.2 US chains' Florida parks visitors (millions)

Corporation	2000	2001	2002	2003	2004	2005
Walt Disney attractions						
Magic Kingdom	15.40	14.78	14.04	14.04	15.17	16.16
EPCOT	10.60	9.01	8.29	8.62	9.40	9.92
D's/MGM Studios	8.90	8.37	8.03	7.87	8.26	8.67
D's Animal Kingdom	8.30	7.77	7.31	7.31	7.82	8.21
Blizzard Beach	1.95	1.83	1.72	1.60	1.75	1.78
Typhoon Lagoon	1.80	1.66	1.56	1.70	1.85	1.91
Universal Studios Recreation Group						
Universal Studios at Orlando	8.10	7.29	6.85	5.90	6.70	6.13
Islands of Adventure at Orlando	6.00	5.52	6.07	5.60	6.30	5.76
Wet'n Wild	1.30	1.33	1.33	1.25	1.34	1.34
Anheuser Busch Theme Parks						
Adventure Island Waterpark	0.50	0.56	0.60	0.60	0.58	0.62
Busch Gardens Tampa Bay	5.00	4.60	4.50	4.30	4.10	4.30
Discovery Cove	0.18	0.27	0.27	0.28	0.26	0.27
Sea World Florida	5.20	5.10	5.00	5.20	5.60	5.60

Sources: Author and Amusement Business.

within a population catchment of 15 million within 90 minutes drive by motorway or other rapid transit system. In the 1990s, the English Tourist Board proposed a standard of 12 million residents within two hours drive or approximately half that number when the location is close to a major resort. But whatever the particular norms that may apply, it is generally agreed that the two hours driving edge is critical, so that in North America, parks attracting up to 3 million visitors are located within this drive-time band from large cities. For example, Six Flags, as a regional park operator, is able to claim that its parks serve nine of the ten largest metropolitan areas in the USA and that about two-thirds of the US population is within a 150 mile radius of one of their parks (Six Flags, 2005).

In practice, the availability of large sites for land-extensive entertainment complexes is often limited. In America, the 1960s and 1970s saw the closure of large inner-city parks to be replaced by corporate-backed theme parks outside of cities. Parks in major cities are now more valued for their environmental benefits than being locations for amusement activities. Europe too can trace modern theme park development back to the 1970s, but at lower intensity than in the US, given the much richer tradition of alternative visitor attractions. Initially, European parks were concentrated in the north, where the highest levels of disposable income and car ownership were to be found. France experienced a building boom in the 1980s, and in recent years the concept has spread to Italy, Portugal and Spain. But both in Europe and North America, desirable sites near major cities are somewhat rare, unless they become available under an urban renewal programme. By and large, these sites are usually under the control of local governments or public development agencies, with strong environmental and physical planning controls that permit them to dictate terms. For example, it took Thorpe Park in Britain six years and 150 planning applications before it could open in 1979, and permission is still needed for every new attraction. Conversely the park site may become more valuable as a real estate development, which caused Six Flags to close down its 37-year-old under-performing Astroworld in Houston at the end of its 2005 operating season. However, where theme parks are currently spreading in Central and Southern America, Asia and the Pacific Rim, site provision is much easier.

Therefore, site availability may limit commercial attraction developers to a second-best pathway that runs Imagescape → Location → Market, which incurs the risk of 'talking up the market' to justify the location. This happened in the case of Disneyland Paris where the site was offered at 1971 agricultural prices as part of the French Government's regional policy, in spite of the fact that it had already been zoned for urban development. What is important to recognize here is that location, market assessment and imagescape are bound to each other, so that the sequential process may go through several iterations over the development period of the park. For example, once the site is selected then the development can come into place, but the further the location is away from the optimal market position, the more appealing and exciting the design content has to be in order to 'pull' visitors in. Alternatively, the market assessment may be changed, which in turn can affect the imagescape. Either way, the calculations for the feasibility study will need to be revised at this stage and most likely continuously during the time it takes to translate the imagescape from idea into practice, in order to keep abreast of market trends.

Development

Theme park planning is normally centred on the first and fifth years of operation, the latter being the design standard, when park operations should have settled and the future of the park is established. The market potential is made up of the resident population in the specified catchment area, visitors to the area and groups. The latter includes schools, company outings, clubs and associations. In the calculation of market penetration rates for the park to ascertain likely visitor numbers, account has to be taken of disposable income, accessibility, competing attractions, the appeal of the imagescape, and the level of capitalization required to ensure that visitors have a variety of activities to enjoy during their stay and want to return. The last of these is termed the 'warranted' level of investment.

The evidence indicates that to minimize the risks of failure, 'reproductive' imagescapes that evoke known products or events in the mind of the public are most suitable. Thus the Lego brick was well established as a toy, the Disney characters were well known in the entertainment industry and as toys, and Universal Studios was famed for its cinematography long before the creation of the parks. They are in fact 'branded' parks that have been established around the success of the core business. 'Anticipatory' or 'avant-garde' imagescapes, however, are difficult to evaluate in the marketplace, because there is no recognition at large of their value (see Chapter 2).

As theme parks are for the family, then the importance of the children's influence on the decision to visit, particularly with both partners working, must not be overlooked in the images that are portrayed (McClung, 1991). To balance this, an evening theme with shows and good restaurants will attract adults to the park. Generally speaking, US parks have a greater level of warranted investment and thus higher market penetration rates than European parks. In part, this can also be explained by closer proximity of parks to each other in Europe, which means greater competition through overlapping catchment areas. In addition, parks in the US have a larger percentage of admissions as groups than in Europe: established parks should generate 35–50 per cent of their market as groups.

Planning

Planning may best be understood by taking a simple numerical example, say, a theme park designed for 1.5 million visitors, with a catchment area of about 9 million people as presented in Table 4.3. The overall penetration rate is estimated at 9 per cent in the first year, dropping down in the second year after the celebratory phase of the launch year, but with market growth to the design level

Table 4.3 Design characteristics for a 1.5 million visitor theme park

Item	Year 1	Design year 5
Population catchment	13 300 000	13 300 000
Penetration rate	9%	11%
Visitor numbers	1 200 000	1 500 000
Peak month	216 000	270 000
Design day	12 558	15 698
Peak in ground	9419	11 773
Average entertainment units/hour	1.5	1.5
Total entertainment units/hour	14 128	17 660
Average ride throughput/hour	600	600
Mean number of attractions	24	29
Poisson (1.5, 1.5) at 75% coverage	28	35

in the fifth year of operation. The park is year-round, but has some seasonality, the peak month being August, with an anticipated 270 000 guests in the design year. There are eight weekend/holiday days in August and 23 weekdays, with attendance at weekend days being 2.5 times those of weekdays. From this it follows that the design day is 270 000 × 2.5/(2.5 × 8 + 23) = 15 698 guests, which is typically 10–20 per cent below peak numbers. As a rule, seasonal parks in the US may expect to have a design day of 1–1.2 per cent of annual attendances.

The design day is used to determine the time period in which the 'peak in ground' number would occur. The latter is arrived at by first recording likely hourly arrival numbers during opening hours and then deducting departure patterns, recorded on the same basis, from arrivals. Let this value be 75 per cent of the design day occurring late in the morning (though it can be as high as 85 per cent), giving a peak in-ground figure of 11 773 upon which the infrastructure, facilities and attractions in the park will be based. The industry standard is that, given queuing time, 'walk-around' time and miscellaneous activities, the average guest should participate in 1.5–2.5 entertainment units per hour, the lower figure being typical in dry parks with a higher figure being more appropriate for water parks. Taking 1.5 as the standard, then this park should have an hourly operating capacity of 1.5 × 11 773 = 17 660 entertainment units. Major roller coasters have ride throughputs that range from 1000 to 2000 entertainment units per hour (the Disney model is based on approximately 1600 per hour), but the simple provision of, say, 17 coasters is not the planning answer. While some park operations, such as Six Flags and Wet'n Wild, specialize in 'white-knuckle' rides (though health reasons do not allow them to go much above G-force 4.5), most provide a mix of rides and shows to entertain the whole family. This will reduce average hourly throughput, for while an average coaster ride may only last around two minutes (the larger ones lasting up to four minutes), a show can be up to half an hour in length. Applying an overall hourly throughput standard of 600 entertainment units indicates an 'adequate' provision of 29 attractions made up of, say, six key or 'anchor' rides that can be the focus for promotion, 16 medium-sized round rides, capacity-filling flat rides that appeal to young children, and seven live shows, play areas and film-based activities to round out the mix. The latter are continually improving, thus Futurescope, which was established at Poitiers in 1987, is made up entirely of 3D films, 360° cinema, simulators and other audio/visual attractions.

The figure of 29 attractions is stated only as 'adequate' because several judgmental factors need to be considered before placing the mix on an overall plan for the park, namely:

- Does this level of investment warrant the market penetration rates used at the proposed admission charges?
- Are there enough attractions to encourage sufficient repeat visits? In the best parks, repeat visit rates can run at 80 per cent and certainly should not be below 40 per cent for established parks.
- What will the queues be like for the principal rides?

The consequences of not achieving the right level of investment can be seen in these examples:

- undercapitalization was one amongst a number of reasons for Britannia Park in England opening and closing in 1985,
- in 1987, Zygofolis in Nice had serious cost over-runs, resulting in the 'skimping' of the theming, and
- also in 1987, Mirapolis in Paris had too small a number of attractions.

The outcome was that Zygofolis and Mirapolis both failed to meet their design standard and went into liquidation in 1991. Parks encourage repeat visits through events, re-theming old attractions and spending 5–10 per cent of their initial investment on launching new rides every few years. If such activities are not carried out, the catchment area simply becomes exhausted and attendances fall away.

It is becoming evident in the major parks that in spite of improvements in the design of queues as part of the fabric of the attraction, guests are becoming ever more irritated with paying high entrance fees, only to wait for hours for a two-minute ride. Traditional solutions have been to increase capacity and try to manage visitor flows around the park, but most recent direction has been the introduction of timed ticketing, such as Disney's Fast Pass, Universal's Express and Six Flags' Fast Lane, for the anchor rides. Given the variable movement of guests around the park, arrivals at the various attractions tend to exhibit a Poisson distribution, so the standard of 1.5 entertainment units would cover the activities of 68 per cent of the guests. On average, visitors can expect to spend about 25 per cent of their stay queuing, the exception being at peak times, so raising coverage to 75 per cent of peak in ground activities would add six attractions to the design level (Table 4.3), if overall throughput were not increased. It is a matter of economic judgement as to whether higher-capacity rides will be added so as to maintain the design level at 29, or whether some rides may be phased in as visitor numbers adjust to the park's design year, which tends to happen, or whether dealing solely with queuing at the anchor rides will be sufficient. It is to be noted that the benefits of reducing waiting times go beyond customer satisfaction, as more time is now available to spend in the restaurants and shops.

Once the number of rides has been agreed, they are evaluated for their place on the master layout, their suitability for the range of imagescapes proposed in the park and their contribution to the balance of the experience provided by each zone. A popular layout is the 'hub-and-spoke system', where the hub is a central facility offering restaurants, shopping, arcades, entertainment, conference rooms and other amenities (benefiting from economies of scale in infrastructure provision), while the spokes are the themed areas connecting the visitor experience. Locating refreshment points, souvenir sales and amenities appropriate to the imagescape in each themed zone is also necessary in order to create additional spending opportunities and allow flexibility of provision in accordance with the daily and seasonal fluctuations of visitor numbers. It is likely that the master layout will go through several iterations in refining the details, so as to optimize the park's creative appeal, effectiveness and affordability, and to ensure that no particular cultural habits are overlooked (for example, the tendency of the family to always lunch together in a fixed one-hour period, as in France). Of course, it is possible to over-design a park, so a normal tenet is that the 'soft' costs for professional services, pre-opening expenses and other incidental costs, should not exceed 30 per cent of the total investment.

Theming

Theming allows imagineers to give new meaning to attractions, park facilities and infrastructure, and can cost as much again or more than the attractions themselves. To be effective, the message is continually repeated in the imagescape of each zone so as to have the highest visitor impact and serving to solidify the entertainment value through the illusion and sense of role-play created by the use of different storylines and settings. Beyond this there are a number of other advantages:

- Park operators are in continual touch with the main ride and attraction manufacturers, so that there is a broad element of similarity in terms of what is on offer. Theming allows parks to develop a sense of individuality and product differentiation. It can also create competitive advantage if it is a popular and well-recognized imagescape.
- Creates a perception of quality.
- A memorable environment serves to increase the probability of return.

vents may be themed for certain target markets and times to raise attendances.

- The imagescapes provide passive entertainment for seniors and family members with young children who may not wish to participate in the anchor rides, but enjoy watching others, particularly members of their group, having a good time.
- Themed entertainment and waiting spots make queuing a less-frustrating experience.
- Well-themed areas, restaurants and shops can help in managing visitor flows by increasing walk-around time as well as raising secondary spend.
- Merchandise may be co-ordinated to themes to encourage purchase.

Finance

Table 4.4 draws up a pro forma income statement for the design year of the theme park used earlier as a numerical example. The park is estimated to cost US$250 million and is positioned to charge an adult entrance of US$45, which after-sales tax at 8 per cent and discounts for children and groups, gives an achieved rate of just under 70 per cent of the adult gate price. The POP admission system is generally regarded as advantageous for marketing, family budgeting and enjoyment, is cost-efficient and also serves to deter those who may want to come to the park and create a disturbance through rowdy behaviour. Ideally, parks try to achieve a secondary spend in the grounds equivalent to the revenue gained from admissions, but the former normally settles at 80 per cent or less of the latter. Income from sponsorship, corporate hospitality and the rental of facilities is often difficult to predict, so it is included as a separate category, 'Other Income'.

The largest item of Controllable Expenses is Payroll, but only about 30 per cent of this is for salaried staff, the remainder being for seasonal employees, whose numbers are variable in line with attendances. Marketing expenses account for 5–8 per cent of revenue in Europe but up to 10 per cent or more in US parks. Generally speaking, the operating expenses for theme parks are relatively low, yielding a high cash flow, which makes them attractive to multi-product firms or conglomerates, such as Universal and Anheuser–Busch (see Chapter 19 for an in-depth analysis of the major Florida parks). The latter owns Sea World, where the ability of the facility to contribute to the cash flow of the overall business and promote the product line (Budweiser) may be given a higher priority than return on capital. Production industries frequently have long lead times between incurring costs and receiving revenues. In these circumstances, the ownership of subsidiaries capable of generating ready cash inflows into the organization on a daily and weekly basis can contribute greatly to total financial stability. In the annual financial accounts, the equivalent of the cash flow listed in Table 4.4 would be earnings before interest, tax expense, depreciation and amortization (EBITDA), which is the measure used to allocate resources to the business. By convention, the industry values parks at acquisition between eight and ten times their EBITDA.

Table 4.4 Summary income statement for a 1.5 million visitor theme park

Item	Design Year 5 (US$)	Revenue percentages
Revenue		
Admissions[a]	47 125 000	55.6
Catering	18 850 000	22.2
Merchandising	14 137 500	16.7
Miscellaneous[b]	4 712 500	5.6
Total	84 825 000	100.0
Cost of sales		
Catering	7 540 000	8.9
Merchandise	7 068 750	8.3
Total	14 608 750	17.2
Gross profit	*70 216 250*	*82.8*
Other income[c]	*7 634 250*	*9.0*
Total income	*77 850 500*	*91.8*
Controllable expenses		
Payroll	27 483 300	32.4
Marketing	8 652 150	10.2
Admin. and general	3 664 440	4.3
Maintenance	2 646 540	3.1
Operating supplies	2 137 590	2.5
Utilities	3 664 440	4.3
Insurance	2 646 540	3.1
Total	50 895 000	60.0
Cash flow	*26 955 500*	*34.9*
Capital expenses		
Attraction replacement and renewals	12 500 000	14.7
Occupation costs[d]	4 875 000	5.7
Total	17 375 000	20.5
Net income before taxation	9 580 500	11.3

[a] Adult admission is US$45, giving an average discount (after sales tax) of 30.2 per cent.
[b] Includes rentals, arcades and vending machines.
[c] Sponsorship, corporate hospitality and rental of facilities.
[d] Rental provision for site and premises.

However, it is the capital expenses relating to site occupation costs (20–30 per cent of the initial investment) and the provision for the replacement and renewal of attractions that make inroads into long-run profitability, thus rendering parks as somewhat risky investments. To understand the nature of this risk, it is necessary to manipulate the data shown in Table 4.4. Let *N* stands for net income before taxes, R for revenue, I for other income, C^k and C^o for capital and operating expenses (cost of sales plus controllable expenses) respectively. Then the basic income model for this park is

$$N = R + I - C^o - C^k \qquad (4.1)$$

It may be seen from Table 4.4 that C^o constitutes 77.2 per cent of R, of which 40 per cent of R is estimated to be the variable component C_v^o and 37.2 per cent the fixed element C_f^o. From this it follows that the break-even revenue, say, R^*, when only fixed and variable operating costs are accounted for, is

$$
\begin{aligned}
R^* &= (C_f^o - I)(1 - C_v^o/R) \\
&= (37.2 - 9.0)/(1 - 40.0/100) \qquad (4.2) \\
&= 47.0\%
\end{aligned}
$$

This result corresponds to US\$39 899 167 of revenue and 705 556 visitors, respectively, and gives a substantial margin of safety (MS), defined as the excess of actual (or planned) revenue over break-even revenue, which in per-centage terms is

$$
\begin{aligned}
MS &= [(R - R^*) \times 100]/R \\
&= [(100 - 47.0) \times 100]/100 \qquad (4.3) \\
&= 53.0\%
\end{aligned}
$$

However, once C^k (the capital expenses total in Table 4.4) is introduced into equation (4.2), the situation changes, for now

$$
\begin{aligned}
R^* &= (C_f^o + C^k - I)/(1 - C_v^o/R) \\
&= (37.2 + 20.5 - 9.0)/(1 - 40.0/100) \qquad (4.4) \\
&= 81.2\%
\end{aligned}
$$

At this point, the park needs to earn US\$68 857 500 from 1 217 639 visitors to remain viable, and the margin of safety is reduced to 18.8 per cent.

The different situations are illustrated in Figure 4.1 in which C^oC^o is the operating cost line, giving rise to the first break-even point at V_1, representing 257 407 visitors. Beyond this point the theme park is said to be economically feasible in that $R + I$ is in excess of operating costs, but it is not viable until V_2 admissions are reached at 805 247 visitors. At this point, the park covers all costs, including capital expenses. The triangle ABD indicates the area on the graph where long-run losses occur if attendances fall below V_2 and clearly the gap between C and $R + I$ grows alarmingly as $V_2 \rightarrow V_1$. Thus, parks such as Zygofolis (design 900 000) and Mirapolis (design 2 million) mentioned above, quickly closed when attendances settled at 350 000 and 650 000, respectively. Thus the cost structure of theme parks makes them inherently risky projects, the financial term for this being 'a high operating leverage'. This means that parks generally have a high level of fixed costs in relation to variable costs, which makes them financially vulnerable to downturns in the market. As a

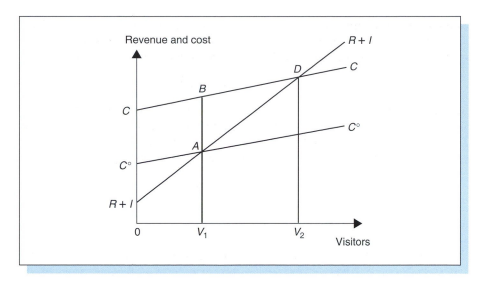

Figure 4.1
Theme park break-even chart

consequence, providing the capital funding package for theme parks is often difficult: banks will not usually lend more than 40 per cent of the required sum and so the rest has to be found from equity investors who carry the risks. Sponsorship of attractions also helps, but another important component has been public money. Because parks can generate significant 'spillover' benefits at the destination, many have been given government assistance, either through benefits in kind, such as site and infrastructure provision, or grant in aid. Support of this kind acts as substitute equity by reducing investment costs, but is likely to be no more than 25 per cent of the capital provision, with an absolute ceiling of 50 per cent for public funds made available from all sources.

Case Study: The LEGO company

The growth of LEGOLAND parks came under the Global Family Attractions division of the LEGO Company and, as they are branded parks, their history and development has been, and still is, very much bound up with the core business of the company, which is toy manufacturing. The company is wholly owned by a Danish family, the Kirk Christiansens, which is somewhat unusual for an organization of this size. Since the early 1960s, the company has become truly international: at its largest it had 57 subsidiaries spread around 30 countries, with worldwide sales of its product in over 130 nations, with some 8400 employees and a turnover well in excess of US$1 billion, prior to the virtual standstill of the toy market in 2003. The basis of the company's growth has been the eight-stud plastic brick that offers creative play to children in the form of a new toy every day. This may be appreciated when it is realised that the mathematics of combinations dictates that six bricks can be combined in 102 981 500 ways.

History

Understanding some of the history of the company is significant for compre-hending the development of the Legoland parks, as they are a cross between the usual themed ride park and the 'brand'. The story begins with Ole Kirk Christiansen establishing his joinery and carpentry business in Billund, Jutland, in 1916. But like most of Denmark, Billund was an agricultural area that suffered greatly during the inter-war depression and in order to find alternative employ-ment, since construction work had come to a halt, Ole started manufacturing wooden products in 1932, both household goods and toys. He saw particularly good prospects for the latter, since children will always need playthings. In 1934 he called both his toys and his company LEGO, which is an abbreviation for the Danish words *leg godt*, meaning 'play well'. He also inscribed his aim on a wooden sign in his workshop that read 'only the best is good enough', which has remained the motto of the company to this day.

The next major step took place in 1949 when, based on the ideas of an English inventor, Hillary Page, the company produced interlocking plastic bricks. In 1954 Ole's son, Godtfred, realized that the bricks could be worked into count-less combinations and developed the 'LEGO System of Play', which was intro-duced into the Danish market in 1955, using a town plan as the basis for building houses, shops and other buildings with small plastic bricks. But the breakthrough came in 1958, when the company patented a way to improve the clutching strength of the bricks (and therefore structural stability) by placing inner tubes inside the hollow underneath part. In 1960, the wooden toy workshop burnt down and the company decided to concentrate on a single product idea: the LEGO building bricks. This 'one-brand company' phase was to last until 1979, when Kjeld Kirk Christiansen (Godtfred's son) took over as managing director and developed the product along the following lines:

- Duplo – for the one- to three-year-olds
- LEGO System – for the three- to nine-year-olds
- LEGO Technic – for the nine- to sixteen-year-olds
- LEGO Dacta – for use in schools.

The parks

As shown in Table 4.5, there are currently four parks, one of which is still estab-lishing itself. The accepted thesis in the 'post-Fordist' society is that to retain mar-ket position, suppliers should no longer sell goods with attached services but rather sell services with attached goods to create experiences (Pine and Gilmore, 1999), so that each customer receives a bespoke package. It might be thought that the park at Billund, which is the home of LEGO, is an early develop-ment of this concept, but the reality was somewhat more indirect and personal, as it was born out of Godtfred's frustrations with disruptions caused by visitors to the factory and the desire to be rid of them. Its development came about from three sources of inspiration:

- Godtfred had seen a miniature park in Holland, which gave the idea for the 1:20 scale Miniland to be found in every park today.

- Godtfred was impressed with the Louisiana movement in modern art and hired its chief of exhibitions, Arnold Boutrup, to mastermind the development of the park.
- The creative ability of his cousin, Dagny Holm, in using the bricks to make outstanding models.

Table 4.5 LEGO global family attractions

Legoland	Opening year	Area (hectares)	Visitors 2002 (millions)	Visitors 2005 (millions)	Design standard (millions)
Billund, Denmark	1968	10	1.59	1.48	Site restricted
Windsor, UK	1996	60	1.45	1.42	1.40
Carlsbad, CA, USA	1999	52	1.31	1.33	1.80
Günzburg, Germany	2002	140	1.32	1.32	1.50

Nevertheless, it has turned out that the Billund park, unlike its replicates in Windsor and Carlsbad, which principally serve the domestic resident population, has become an iconic international tourist attraction that reaches sacralization status amongst LEGO enthusiasts, who may perhaps even be regarded as 'pilgrim tourists'. Replication has only served to elevate the standing of Billund (MacCannell, 1989), which is now suffering from too many visitors on peak days. This is, however, difficult to control through 'de-marketing' methods because they are tourists, many being international, who are hard to reach through normal communications channels such as local radio announcements telling listeners that the park is likely to be full early on that particular day.

The gap in theme park development is also explained upon personal lines, arising from the involvement of the company in a consortium to create the Hansa-Park in Germany during the late 1960s. This was not a success and LEGO withdrew from the venture, leaving Godtfred determined neither to cooperate with anyone in the park business nor undertake any park expansion outside Billund. At the beginning of the 1990s, under Kjeld's stewardship, the latter policy was changed and park development was seen as a way of growing the market for the core business. The planning for the Windsor project was started in 1990 and since opening it has been an undoubted accomplishment. The parks are planned along the following guidelines:

- The overall strategy is that their design and existence is to support the toy sales. Thus, for example, Castle Land/Hill is themed on the LEGO Castle Play System and the Dragon Ride contained within it tends to be the most popular activity.
- Prospective locations are in regions where sales are substantial and there is strong brand awareness.

- They are family parks for children aged two to thirteen years and the investment requires a resident catchment area of around 20 million, with about 50 per cent or more being target families.
- An established tourist area yielding a steady flow of visitors.
- Attractive rural surroundings, with planning permission for leisure development.
- Minimum site requirement of 40 hectares.
- Locally available support services in terms of suppliers and general tourist infrastructure.

In current terms the parks would cost about US$180–200 million each to build and the company financed them internally. The latter gives advantages in decision speed and ensuring minimal information leakages to competitors. For this money, taking Günzburg as an example, there will be more than 40 rides and attractions covering 12 hectares of land, with a further 20 hectares allocated for parking and the remainder of the site will be used for administration, park expansion, woodlands and other 'green' areas. Günzburg will have a full-year staff of about 120 and a seasonal workforce of around 600 employees. As a rule, branding with LEGO lifestyle goods and services enables the company to take as much money inside the parks as it does at the turnstiles. Sponsorship of attractions is accepted but there is no franchising. The company mimics Disney in quality and it sees this as being achievable only through complete control so that every day can be seen as 'fresh as springtime' by the visitors.

Given that LEGO toys have a worldwide distribution, the aim is to develop optimally each park, but in a way that specifically supports the brand. It follows therefore that the parks have a high degree of commonality in their imagescapes, save where local cultural adjustments are clearly necessary. Thus Legorado in Billund, which has a Wild West imagescape, is not suitable in Carlsbad in the light of current American cultural attitudes towards this period of their history. As a counterpoint to the company's strategy, it should be noted that a new line of toys can fail or have a short lifetime, while investment in a new rides in the parks are expensive and have to be depreciated over four to six years. The risk is therefore that the parks end up with rides that have no reference to the LEGO product portfolio. The hybrid nature of the parks also has consequences for performance measurement. For example, it is customary to measure capacity in theme parks by ride throughput, but the LEGO parks have a great deal of 'soft' capacity in the form of workshops where model-makers are on display and give advice to visitors. Similarly, Miniland is a passive visual activity that can absorb a variable number of visitors. Calculating the return on capital employed is also problematic, as the role of the parks in uplifting toy sales creates a longer payback time.

Strategic change

Towards the end of the 1990s, the company set itself the mission statement of being the strongest global brand amongst families with children by 2005. But although acclaimed as the toy of the last century and widely admired by developmental psychologists for the scope it offers for children's inventiveness and experimentation, and by parents for creativity and the quiet absorption that results, the brick has been a casualty of the advance of high-tech gadgetry (with instant action and gratification) for older age groups of children against the simpler toys (and in this case a 'make-and-create' toy) of yesteryear. This has seen sales growth fall back, forcing the company to trim its costs and embark on new developments. The company has fought back at different times with the introduction of robotics (LEGO Mindstorms), Bionicle (LEGO Technic), Clikits for girls, Quatro bricks, which were eight times the size of their Duplo equivalents, and licensing agreements with the WDC, Lucas Licensing Ltd (Star Wars) and Warner Bros (Harry Potter) to obtain characters. It will be readily appreciated that, from the perspective of the parks, the LEGO Company has no iconic children's characters as can be found in the theme parks of Disney or Universal Studios. However, these new products are fashion items, matching the achievement of the films as with the Harry Potter figures, and in 2003 with the turbulence in the toy market and no new films coming on stream, the company saw a significant fall in its global sales.

Plans were mooted for further parks in Japan and the USA (Florida being an obvious choice), but in 2004 the company decided to focus solely on its core business, which was the LEGO brick. The result was a substantial downsizing (arguably 'rightsizing') of its activities to adjust its costs and assets to a lower revenue base, so as to bring the organization into profit. As part of this rightsizing, the company's direct ownership and operation of the LEGOLAND parks were sold in July 2005 for a little under US$460 million to the Merlin Entertainments Group (owned by Blackstone Capital Partners) and replaced by a considerably smaller financial investment in the form of an ownership share of 15 per cent. Merlin already operated other leisure attractions such as the Sea Life centres, the Dungeons and the Earth Explorer, and in 2007 purchased the Tussauds Group from its owners, Dubai International Capital, for about US$1.8 billion, making Merlin the second largest operator of leisure attractions in the world. Apart from expanding existing parks, Merlin plans to open a fifth park within the next few years.

Conclusion

The architectural innovations created by Disney in 1955 spread outwards as they were adopted by the amusement park industry. By 1975, the top 30 parks drew in some 65 million visitors. Ten years later this number had risen to 95 million, reaching 160 million in 1995 and 200 million in 2005. Of the latter figure, 105.7 million attendances were attributable to Walt Disney attractions. As the market has matured, so the major US operators, such as Disney, Six Flags, Cedar Fair, Universal Studios, Paramount and Anheuser–Busch have used their economic 'muscle' and expertise to expand overseas normally through acquisition of independents (which simplifies planning issues) and joint ventures. The LEGO Corporation, as noted above, is exceptional in this instance, for by establishing a park in California it has bucked this trend. In the UK, the three parks of the Tussauds Group (Alton Towers, Chessington World of Adventures and Thorpe Park) were all obtained initially through acquisition. The economic downturn following 9/11 put a brake on these activities, forcing Six Flags to sell its European division in 2004 and put itself up for sale, but there were no bidders. However, the industry does now see itself in a period of recovery, after a period of consolidation, as discussed in Chapter 19 for the principal Florida parks.

The next radical innovation coming from imagineers is the combination of the physical and virtual worlds, producing an enhanced fantasy (4D) imagescape, though at much greater cost. Thus Universal Studios, in their Islands of Adventure at Orlando, has established a Spider-Man ride at the cost of US$200 million. Costs of this kind can only be endured in parks that are resort destinations, which further increases the competitive advantage of chains over independents. The ride matches 3D imagery with structured sets, as opposed to backdrops, and a motion simulator that culminates in a 400-foot sensory drop. In reality the 12-passenger vehicles never leave the ground and never travel more than a few miles per hour. Paramount's Tomb Raider at Kings Island park near Cincinnati, features a mammoth indoor spinning ride themed to the popular Lara Croft video game and the Angelina Jolie film. Smaller parks are able to afford the cheaper 4D simulator attraction, which combines 3D visuals and the other sensory elements, such as water misters and scent cannons, with theatre-style seats that are synchronized with the screened action.

In like manner, taking advantage of modern electronics, the new Disney Quest is an enclosed, interactive theme park covering five floors with virtual-reality video games that can be located in the downtown areas of cities. Moreover, the gambling city of Las Vegas has a history of creative imagescapes to match any of the parks: the Adventuredome at Circus Circus has some 4.4 million visitors and Paramount has developed and manages both *Star Trek: The Experience* at the Hilton and CBS Television City at the MGM Grand Hotel and Casino. Not to be outdone, production industries have also seen the benefits of creating experiences for their customers, notably the branded parks established by the motor car industry, for example, the Spirit of Ford at Dearborn, USA, and Volkswagen with Autostadt, and Opel with Opel Live in Germany.

References

Abernathy, W. and Clark, K. (1985). Innovation: mapping the winds of creative destruction. *Research Policy*, **14**, 3–22.

Adams, J. (1991). *The American Amusement Park Industry: A History of Technology and Thrills*. Twayne.

MacCannell, D. (1989). *The Tourist: A New Theory of the Leisure Class*, 2nd edn. Schocken Books.

McClung, G. (1991). Theme park selection: factors influencing selection. *Tourism Management*, **12**, 132–140.

Oliver, D. (1989). Leisure parks: present and future. *Tourism Management*, **10**, 233–234.

Pine II, B. and Gilmore, J. (1999). *The Experience Economy*. Harvard Business School Press.

Richards, G. (2001). Marketing China overseas: the role of theme parks and tourist attractions. *Journal of Vacation Marketing*, **8**, 28–38.

Six Flags. (2005). *Annual Report*. Six Flags Inc.

Wanhill, S. (2003). Creating themed entertainment attractions: a Nordic perspective. *Scandinavian Journal of Hospitality and Tourism*, **2**, 1–22.

Wong, K. and Cheung, P. (1999). Strategic theming in theme park marketing. *Journal of Vacation Marketing*, **5**, 319–332.

Zukin, S. (1991). *Landscape and Power: From Detroit to Disneyworld*. University of California Press.

C H A P T E R 5

The Role of Visitor Attractions in Peripheral Areas

Bruce Prideaux

Aims

The aims of this chapter are to:

- define the meaning of 'periphery' as it applies to visitor attractions,
- identify factors that affect the success of attractions in the periphery, and
- discuss the significance of these factors in the development of attractions in peripheral regions, using Alice Springs, Nothern Territory, Australia, as a case study.

Creating visitor attractions in peripheral areas

According to Richards (1996), attractions are an integral part of the tourism industry because they provide a focus for tourism activity and often influence travel decisions. The scale of attractions ranges from those that can be described as generally having only a limited local significance, to those that are iconic in nature, perhaps even having global appeal such as the pyramids. Irrespective of their level of significance, sites, places and events require the communication of their unique values to visitors through interpretation and promotion (MacCannell, 1976). The ability of the tourism industry to convert a potential site, place or event into an attraction is the essence of the industry's unique ability to create tourism resources to which visitors must travel, rather than a product that can be transported to customers for consumption.

This process lies at the core of developing a tourism industry and is responsible for the flows of visitors from generating regions to destination regions. At another level, the tourism industry exhibits a core–periphery relationship that explains many elements of the ability of the industry to attract tourists from a developed core to a periphery in search of unique attractions and novel experiences not available in the core. The volume of the tourism flows in this core–periphery relationship is a function of the significance of the site (or sites), technology of travel, cost of the experience, degree of hardship endured during travel to the attraction and conditions encountered in the locality of the attraction. Cities, towns and smaller localities located in periphery areas that are seeking to build a tourism industry must first overcome impediments associated with their location relative to the core by offering a tempting visitor experience built on the pulling power of their visitor attractions and supported by associated tourism infrastructure.

This chapter examines a number of aspects of the development of visitor attractions in peripheral areas and concludes with a case study. After discussing the concept of perpherality, the chapter identifies the importance of transport in facilitating travel to peripheries, the role of communities in developing successful attractions in areas of this nature and the desirability of having a group of attractions as a key selling point.

Many peripheral areas experiencing declining regional economic conditions have turned to tourism as a source of economic regeneration, often seeing tourism as a panacea to their deeper economic and social malaise. A common response in these circumstances is to look for the development of attractions that may provide the stimulus for increased visitation. The twentieth century witnessed a remarkable transformation of rural and urban landscapes caused by the migration of rural dwellers into urban enclaves in search of employment and services not available in the country. This has had a serious impact on rural areas including: depopulation; declining education, commercial and health services; deteriorating infrastructure; high living costs; and high business costs. Rapid transformation of the rural landscape through this process has generated significant social and economic problems for remaining rural residents creating a city–country dichotomy that can be described in terms of a core–periphery relationship. The search for new industries to revitalize the rural economy has often identified tourism as a potential candidate. Perhaps part of this interest in rural tourism may be more to do with city dwellers' attempts to harness postmodern nostalgic desires for returning to rural origins and values as a form of personal identity-building than with creating viable industries for rural residents. Yet, possession of an interesting landscape, old building, unique event or historic site is no guarantee that tourism will flourish in peripheral areas. Success lies beyond preservation of the past and its celebration. Success has much more to do with the decidedly un-nostalgic issues of marketing, pulling power, viability, sustainability and informed management.

Potential attractions in peripheral areas may include natural features such as wildlife, landscapes and unique ecosystems; built heritage, events and sites of historic interest. Attempting to exploit these resources for touristic purposes is not a simple matter, with complex problems including competition, presentation, community support and funding posing significant obstacles. As will be argued later in this chapter, the sense of periphery imposed by the time and length of travel from origin to destination, as well as access difficulties, further complicate attraction development in the periphery.

How far is peripheral? Defining peripheral areas

Contextualizing peripheral areas is difficult because the concept of distance is very much governed by spatial factors, human perceptions and the technology of transport. Distance and location have traditionally defined the degree or scale of isolation of the periphery from the core. New technologies have altered traditional perspectives of isolation by reducing travel times and bridging communication gaps. The core–periphery argument has attracted the attention of tourism researchers and has been interpreted in a number of ways, including an international core–periphery dynamic, an internal core–internal periphery dynamic (Weaver, 1998), the 'plantation tourism model' (Weaver, 1988) and the distinction between formal and informal tourism space (Oppermann, 1993). Weaver (1998: 292) argues that the core–periphery model '. . . provides a valuable and fundamentally geographical framework for contextualizing and comprehending spatial disparities in power and levels of development'. Wall (2000) takes a slightly different approach defining the core–periphery, or alternatively the centre–periphery relationship as the link between a powerful urban concentration of demand and distant less-powerful areas where the supply of tourism opportunities is dispersed. This chapter adopts the view that the periphery is defined by a number of factors including distance, accessibility, visitor perceptions and scale, which can be measured from slightly peripheral to very peripheral, or exhibit location characteristics which describe the periphery as near or far. Degrees of peripherality affect investment decisions, management practices and marketing strategies, leading to a co-dependent relationship involving the scale of an attraction and the degree of its remoteness. As remoteness increases, the scale of attractions must grow if they are to offer the inducement of uniqueness or 'differentness' needed to attract visitors who might otherwise confine their travel to less remote sites. Concurrently, attractions in the periphery need to attract investment in infrastructure and tourism products that collectively build an attractive tourism experience from the visitor's perspective. Importantly, the ability to market and periodically refresh these experiences is significant and related to the financial sustainability of the site or sites.

In most circumstances, access to the periphery declines as distance and the difficulty of travel increases. Peripheral areas are generally regarded as those located some distance from the centre of tourism activity. However, this need not always be the case as accessibility is also a determining factor in defining the periphery (Lew, 2000). A visitor attraction located a considerable distance from the centre of tourism activity, but offering easy access, may be described as a near-periphery according to access criteria, while a site located near a major centre, but that is difficult to access, may also be termed a medium-periphery based on access but not distance. To take an Australian example, Uluru (formerly known as Ayres Rock) is located almost in the middle of the continent but is easily accessible by air and may be regarded in one sense as located on the near-periphery if defined by access criteria, but the far-periphery if defined on distance criteria. Conversely, King Island located in Bass Strait is near Melbourne but difficult to access and therefore occupies a peripheral location based on access criteria but not necessarily distance. Access is a critical factor and a major potential barrier to travel (Prideaux, 2000). The cost of travel is also significant and influences consumers in their selection between substitute attractions. This concept is developed in greater detail later in this chapter.

Part of the answer to defining the periphery is provided by tourists who in many cases are attracted by uniqueness and novelty in the design of their holiday. Interesting attractions located far from major tourism transit routes usually fail to attract the number of visitors that a similar attraction would draw if it were located adjacent to a major tourism transit route, thereby indicating a measure of peripherality from the tourist's perspective. A further part of the question of definition is supplied by investors who must judge viability as major investment criteria because viability in the periphery may be more problematic than in the core for similar types of attractions.

The scale of uniqueness is therefore an important consideration, particularly for attractions located in peripheral areas. If an attraction is unique on a global-scale, its uniqueness is likely to overcome many of the constraints imposed by distance and cost of travel. If on the other hand the attraction's uniqueness is more limited, perhaps on a national scale, it may attract national visitors but have little interest to international visitors. In the Australian context, the Sydney Opera House, the Great Barrier Reef and Uluru exhibit global scale uniqueness, while historic streetscapes in regional centres exhibit only national uniqueness. Uniqueness is a major selling point and is reflected in the images of attractions used by National Tourism Offices and private firms in their marketing to international audiences.

Peripheral area tourism

The extraordinary interest in tourism development and the apparent panacea-like qualities ascribed to tourism's ability to save many rural areas otherwise in decline has clouded issues that should be considered part of any feasibility study into proposals for construction and ongoing operation of visitor attractions. Two orders of magnitude based on importance help explain the success of tourism in the periphery. The first order of magnitude is largely dependent on two factors: the presence of something worth visiting and the accessibility of the attraction. These factors are co-dependent. The manner in which such resources are developed, managed and marketed will be discussed later in this chapter. If hasty decisions to establish visitor attractions are made, there is a strong possibility that the fundamental economic axioms of demand and supply may be ignored, leading to projects that become financial drains on sponsoring communities. Second-order magnitude factors include community participation, local infrastructure and the willingness of the public sector to bear some of the costs of establishing tourism as an industry. In the latter case, costs may include provision of education and training opportunities in the community, upgrading infrastructure and offering financial support.

Visitor attractions

Visitor attractions comprise a complex sector of the tourism industry and are not well understood; yet they are one of the more important components of the industry (Lew, 2000; Swarbrooke, 1995). While a number of definitions have been suggested for attractions (Swarbrooke, 1995), the definition suggested by Walsh-Heron and Stevens (1990) appears the most comprehensive. According to this definition, a visitor attraction is a feature in an area that is a place, venue or focus of activities and does the following:

- sets out to attract visitors,
- is a fun and pleasurable experience and is developed to realize this potential,
- is managed as an attraction to provide satisfaction to its customers,
- provides appropriate facilities, and
- may or may not charge for admission.

Visitor attractions may range is size from very small to the enormous (Disneyland-sized theme parks), be free to enter (a national park) or expensive (some theme parks), and be based on natural features, built features or a combination of the two. Moreover, attractions may be grouped into clusters, be isolated, be located on a touring circuit, or be located in urban or rural settings. Lew (2000) suggests that attractions can also be classified into cognitive or perceptual categories including educational, recreational, authentic and adventurous. The presence of a visitor attraction acts as a lynchpin for the local tourism industry, providing the reason for the visit as well as the reason for parallel investment in associated infrastructure. Large, well-known attractions create visitor interest in an area and may constitute the primary driver for tourism visits. By increasing this pulling power, Bull (1991) argues that well-known attractions may create a degree of obligation on the part of tourists to visit the attraction as well as conferring bragging rights upon the tourist.

Swarbrooke (1995) has written extensively on the subject of visitor attractions and suggests that the factors which experience would suggest as being critical to the success of visitor attractions are: the organization and its resources, the product, the market, and the management of the attraction. Additional factors suggested in Leask and Yeoman (1999) include: quality, productivity, management of supply and demand, visitor management, and technology, although the categories listed by Swarbrooke are arguably sufficiently inclusive to encompass these factors. Surprisingly, community participation has largely been ignored, although this element of the social and economic environment in which attractions operate is important, particularly in small communities. Peripheral areas face a unique set of problems in firstly establishing and then successfully operating visitor attractions. Accordingly, guidelines that may apply to an attraction located in the vicinity of a large urban area do not necessarily apply in the periphery, irrespective of size.

Factors affecting success of attractions in peripheral areas

Of all first- and second-order magnitude factors, four that stand out as being critical for the ongoing success of attractions in peripheral areas are: location and access factors, community support, operating economies and management of the attraction, and supporting tourism infrastructure in the surrounding area.

Location and access factors

Rapid technological advancement in the transport industry has reduced the cost, discomfort and time of travel, bringing once peripheral destinations into or near the core. Air travel has removed the Caribbean from the distant periphery of European tourism in the 1940s and 1950s, into the near-periphery of the 1990s and 2000s. High-speed rail has achieved a similar reduction in the size of the periphery in Europe. Where automobiles remain the dominant form of transport, distance and travel times continue to define the location and scale of the periphery. Figure 5.1 examines the role of transport as one of the factors determining travel patterns, and thereby defining the scale of the periphery in terms of access and location.

In Figure 5.1, the vertical axis represents costs associated with travel while the horizontal axis represents the distance of travel. Point A represents a visitor origin point, a city for example, while points B, G and F represent attractions that are located at increasing distances away from the origin point. For the purposes of this chapter, B represents a coastal attraction, G a near-hinterland attraction and F represents an attraction located in the periphery. Travel is assumed to be on an overnight basis. Accommodation cost is represented by AD, DE represents discretionary expenditure and EC represents the cost of travel to the destination and is referred to in this chapter as 'transport access cost'. In reality, a tourist may substitute between these categories of expenditure, perhaps trading superior standard accommodation for more money to spend on tours or entertainment (discretionary expenditure). Transport costs (EC) can also be further dissected into three categories:

- time taken to travel from the origin to the attraction,
- the fare cost, and

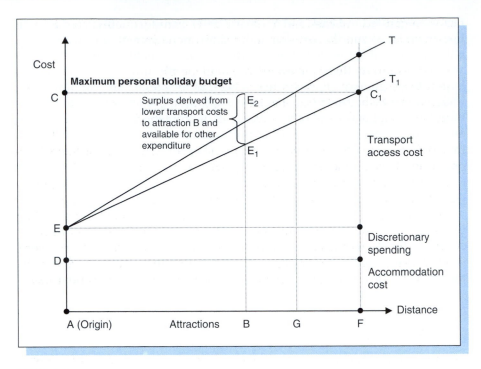

Figure 5.1
Impact of travel cost on demand for attractions in peripheral areas
Source: Adapted and modified from Prideaux (2000).

- the cost of comfort (an example in air travel is first class air versus economy seats).

Transport costs are treated as a variable because they increase with distance from the origin point. Figure 5.1 also assumes that travellers have a fixed personal holiday budget represented by CC_1 It is further assumed that travellers have a choice of transport modes, with ET being the most expensive and ET_1 being the least expensive (in this example ET may be air transport, while ET_1 may represent rail). Funds saved by changing the mode of transport can be reallocated to other classes of expenditure or used for travel to a more distant attraction. Figure 5.1 also illustrates the inverse relationship between transport and other costs using the location of Attraction B relative to Attractions G and F. Irrespective of which transport option is selected, travel to B is less expensive than to G or F. If, when travelling to B, transport option ET_1 is taken, the surplus (E_1E_2) will consist of the lower fare based on distance plus the lower cost of ET_1 relative to ET. Regardless of the transport option selected, a decision to visit B will generate a surplus from the original travel budget. The surplus is then available for other purposes. If the traveller opted to visit attraction F, the surplus E_1E_2 will be reduced to zero as transport costs rise with distance. In the case of attraction F, transport access cost ET will force travellers to choose between a series of alternatives:

- use transport mode ET_1 in preference to mode ET,
- reduce anticipated expenditure on discretionary items and/or accommodation if continuing to travel to F by transport mode ET, and
- amend travel plans and only travel as far as attraction G.

In peripheral areas, the impact of transport factors is critical and is likely to be one of the keys to success, particularly where the scale of the attraction is small or if it does not exhibit some level of iconic value. The type, frequency and cost of transport is also an important factor. As the distances from visitor origin points increase, attractions must exert a proportionately larger pulling power to overcome negative distance and access factors. This is unlikely to occur if attractions merely replicate similar attractions closer to the core. Uniqueness is likely to be the single most important factor in creating the degree of interest needed to overcome the problems of isolation and access.

The community

Community support is generally required for the success of visitor attractions, particularly where financial or in-kind assistance is required on an ongoing basis. Evidence by McKercher (2001) suggests that where public money is available to build an attraction, ill-conceived projects and hasty decision making may lead to financial disaster. Commenting on the Queensland Heritage Trails Network, Prideaux (2002) observed that some of the projects funded under the AUS$110 million programme were arbitrarily allocated funding in the absence of an initial request for funds, the absence of a Steering Committee and the absence of a specific project. A subsequent examination of the success of projects funded by the Queensland Heritage Trails Network found that many of the projects were struggling to achieve financial sustainability in the absence of recurrent public financial support. To overcome problems of this nature, Prideaux (2002) identified a seven-step approach to establishing a rural heritage attraction in Queensland, Australia, based on the experiences of the small farming community of Gatton attempting to develop a rural attraction as the cornerstone for local tourism development. The approach outlined in Figure 5.2 illustrates the process adopted by the farming community over the course of a rural heritage project that was considering building.

The strength of the approach outlined in Figure 5.2 is that it establishes the sponsoring community's willingness to support the project and verifies financial sustainability through independent consulting advice and subsequent review of that advice. A further important element of this process is the selection of a Steering Committee that will represent the interests of the community yet also includes the technical skills needed to accept, modify or reject consultancy

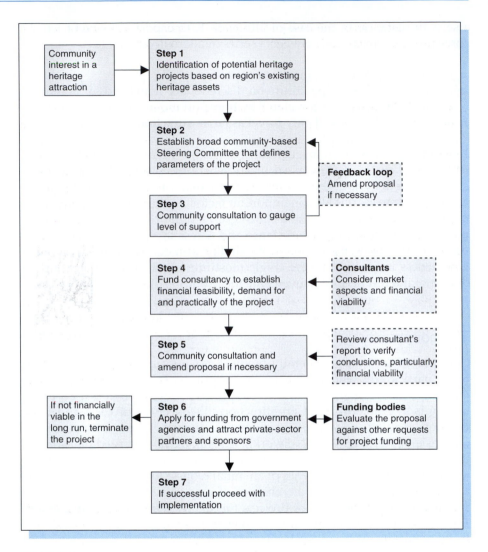

Figure 5.2
Seven-step approach to establishing a rural attraction
Source: Prideaux (2002).

advice and steer the project from inception to completion. A significant quality of the Steering Committee should be its possession of a capacity to connect with the community, build trust and represent community aspirations adequately. Where the rhetoric of self-interest expressed by community organizations and individual stakeholders is allowed to dominate, process objectivity may be lost and long-term viability jeopardized. In situations where the private sector is providing funding, a modified model of community consultation will be required. In the case of the rural heritage project under consideration by the Gatton community, it became apparent at Step 5 that the project would encounter difficulties achieving long-term financial sustainability in the absence of recurrent public support and the project was abandoned.

Operating economies of attractions located in the periphery

In a crowded tourism market where there is a growing supply of new attractions, careful consideration needs to be given to each new project to ensure that the additional supply created also has an ability to generate additional demand. This applies particularly in peripheral areas where the evidence (Ditton *et al.*, 1992) suggests that heritage visitors in peripheral area constitute a specialized subset of visitors described by Light *et al.* (1994) as belonging to the middle class, middle aged, no children, well-educated, on holiday away from home and having a prior knowledge of history.

If viability is doubtful, the likelihood of government subsidies must also be considered. Tools for assessment of viability include competition, demand, profitability, employment generation, estimation of net multiplier effects, cost recovery and the total community value of a tourism investment versus investment in other forms of infrastructure. Consideration of operating economies need not follow an economic rationalist approach because there are some community aspirations and needs that are not directly measurable and for which there is little common agreement on an implied or ascribed value. If cultural values are high but the chance of financial sustainability is small, there may be a case for requesting a government subsidy in the same way that governments are often petitioned to support the Arts. In some cases, where there is no commonality of agreement, decisions may have to be made arbitrarily by the responsible authorities.

Factors that may affect long-term financial viability include:

- scale or size,
- uniqueness,
- operating model of the attraction (e.g., volunteers often reduce costs in not-for-profit attractions that may include parks and heritage attractions),
- the attraction's ability to maintain visitor interest in the long term,
- the impact of competitors located either nearby or in other parts of the nation (Bull, 1991),
- the complexity of the range of tourism products that support the attraction,
- market segments that may be broad or narrow, and the potential to attract new generations of visitors,
- long-term marketing,
- size of investment relative to the income that may be generated by target visitors, and
- transport (Prideaux, 2000).

While the degree of significance of each of these factors may vary according to the size, location and cultural significance of the attraction, the combination of these factors will determine if the project is viable in its own right, requires external support from the government or sponsors, or is non-viable and is in need of restructuring or cancellation. A final consideration for long-term viability is the attraction's ability to reinvent itself periodically so as to attract repeat visitors and win new customers.

Supporting tourism infrastructure

Two types of physical infrastructure are required to support the establishment and nurturing of a tourism industry: physical infrastructure and tourism product infrastructure. Physical infrastructure includes hardware such as transport, communications, water, sewerage, health facilities, and services that include law and order, public health and education. Tourism product infrastructure is defined as the fabric of supporting tourism-orientated businesses that include visitor attractions, accommodation, food and beverage services, shopping, recreation, entertainment, festivals and sites of tourism interest. Without supporting tourism product infrastructure, attractions face a difficult task in attracting visitors, particularly where distance is a major consideration. However, the expense of providing both forms of infrastructure increases with distance from the core, driving up operating costs and creating a barrier that can only be surmounted either by passing additional costs onto the visitor or attracting public-sector subsidies. In the former case, the attraction is likely to suffer diminished competitiveness *vis-à-vis* attractions located near the core. The following case study based on Alice Springs in Australia illustrates the importance of tourism product infrastructure, in addition to physical infrastructure, in the establishment of a successful group of complementary tourism attractions in a remote periphery.

Case Study: Alice Springs, Northern Territory

Located in the heart of the continent and surrounded by vast areas of low-quality grazing land and deserts, Alice Springs has in recent decades emerged as a major centre for desert tourism. Its environment can be described as red desert with less than 300 mm of rainfall annually and an average summer daytime temperature of up to 38°C. In winter, the night-time temperature may fall to −5°C.

Established in 1871 as the site for a telegraph relay station on the transcontinental telegraph line that linked Australia with Europe, Alice Springs occupies a peripheral location relative to Australia's major population centres. Initially supplied by camel trains, the town's role as a supply and service base for the surrounding mining and pastoral industries grew and resulted in the opening of a railway line from South Australia in 1929. The bombing of Darwin to the north in 1942 by Japanese Imperial forces resulted in the relocation of the Northern Territory Administration to Alice Springs and a rapid growth in size as its importance as a military base and administrative centre grew. During this period, the road to Darwin was rebuilt and bituminised, although it was 1987 before the road south to Port Augusta was fully bituminised. The development of the north–south highway facilitated greatly enhanced access to Alice Springs and surrounding regions by drive tourism.

First settled by the Arrernte Aboriginal people, early settlers included German missionaries, Afghan camel drivers, pastoralist, miners and, as the town grew in the post-Second World War era, a more diverse group of migrants. The buildings, artefacts and stories of this diverse group of settlers today constitute the cultural and build heritage of the town.

While drive tourists are an important sector of the Australian tourism industry in general, the distance of Alice Springs from Australia's major population centres has always been a major disincentive for this group of tourists. The distances between home and Alice Springs for many self-drive tourists are too large, and the range and quality of attractions between coastal generating cities and the destination is too small to encourage large-scale drive tourism. Alice Spring's remoteness and the difficulty of travelling to it precluded its development as a major tourism centre until comparatively recently and only when road and, more importantly, air links were improved. Currently, Alice Springs has a population of approximately 25 000 persons, including a substantial Aboriginal population.

Aside from the opportunity to undertake a desert experience, Alice Springs' major natural attractions until relatively recently were Uluru and Kata Tjuta (the Olgas) located about 400 km to the south. Apart from a small number of drive tourists, tourists wanting to visit Uluru had to first fly to Alice Springs and then travel onwards by coach. In 1984, the establishment of a resort and opening of a jet airport at Uluru resulted in tourism numbers to Alice Springs reaching a plateau, prompting the community and the Northern Territory Government to look for other attractions to reinvigorate its tourism base which by then had become a key element of the town's prosperity.

Part of the solution had been provided by the establishment of an Australian/US joint defence satellite monitoring base as Pine Gap, 19 km south of Alice Springs. Employing up to 700 US and Australian service personnel and civilians, the facility was instrumental in broadening the range and quality of facilities, including a new airport, available in the city. The city's pioneering past and location in a desert environment were also used to build an attractions base that collectively offered visitors a unique desert experience. Although developments at Urulu deprived Alice Springs of a major attraction, the subsequent preservation of a number of important heritage sites and construction of a range of new attractions has built an attractions base that is now able to offer a set of experiences that are sufficiently robust to attract approximately 462 000 visitors in 2005. Tourism is estimated to contribute an estimated AUS$250 million to the local economy (Tourism NT Profile, 2006).

The attractions base comprises four sectors: the city's built heritage, its cultural heritage based on its indigenous population and their art, natural heritage based on surrounding desert landscapes, and built attractions that include a desert flora and fauna park and a casino. Together, these attractions offer visitors sufficient unique experiences to occupy them for an average of 4.0 days.

Part of the response to the redirecting of tourists away from Alice Springs by resort developments at Uluru has been the emergence of Alice Springs as a desert tourism centre where tourists can participate in a range of experiences within the city and in the nearby desert landscapes. For example, there are still a number of Uluru tours originating from Alice Springs, as well as tours to the nearby McDonald Ranges, a unique desert landscape ecosystem and geological structure. Many of the city's unique heritage buildings have been preserved and there is a heavy emphasis on indigenous culture particularly in the art galleries that have emerged within the city and in surrounding regions. The building of a casino and later construction of a convention centre were also designed to broaden the city's appeal and enhance its image as more than a dusty desert city. From an environmental tourism aspect, the development of the Desert Park Environmental Centre was a key element in featuring desert flora and fauna.

In terms of the core–periphery argument, Alice Springs occupies an interesting position, being able to be described according to a number of peripheral locations relative to its ease of access. From a geographic position, its location in the middle of a sparsely populated region serviced by only a singe north–south highway, qualifies its classification as a distant periphery both for domestic tourists and for international tourists. For drive tourists, who constitute the majority of Australian domestic tourists, Alice Springs does occupy a peripheral position. However, its accessibility by scheduled jet services has reduced the degree of prepherality to that of other destinations that lie at equal distances from Australia's major generating centres. For example, from Sydney, a major domestic generating region and Australia's largest international hub, Alice Springs is approximately three hours' flying time on a one-way ticket, that if booked well in advance on a no-refund basis will cost about AUS$250. Cairns, a major ecotourism centre located on the northeast coast of Australia, is three hours' flying time from Sydney, and a one-way ticket, if booked well in advance on a no-refund basis, will cost slightly less at AUS$190. Alice Springs is therefore competitive with other destinations in Australia based on flying distance and price. Both air and road classes of peripheries fit Weaver's (1998) notion of a domestic periphery. On an international scale, the city is located in the international periphery.

Its location in the desert and the composition of the city's tourism product based on a mix of natural and built attractions have exercised a significant influence on the character and structure of the city's tourism industry. The development of a range of attractions including several internationally unique attractions, and its ease of access by air has reduced the impact of perpherality for a significant number of tourists. Based on the total number of visitors and the revenue they generate, Alice Springs can be classed as a successful peripheral tourism attraction. The success of Alice Springs also demonstrates the need for strong community support and that resources allocated to developing an attraction must match the benefits that are derived from that investment. A key to the success of the tourism industry has been the creation of an attractions sector that has diversity and can offer a visitor a sufficient range of activities to attract their attention for an average of 4.0 days. In comparison, Uluru, while an internationally unique attraction, has a lower length of stay because of the narrowness of its attraction base.

It is apparent for this discussion that the success of attractions in distant peripheries is a function of their uniqueness on national and international scales and the development of a sufficiently diverse cluster of activities, including attractions, to provide a worthwhile visitor experience. Without a substantial attractions base able to provide visitors with unique experiences, the barriers of a peripheral location will continue to hamper tourism development in remote regions. The economic stimulus able to be delivered by tourism to communities in remote area will always be a function of the community's ability to provide visitors with an experience that is based on unique attractions and activities.

Conclusion

Creating viable visitor attractions in peripheral areas is a major task. Many challenges that need to be surmounted, include overcoming access factors, coping with competition, development of a cluster of activities and gaining local community support. As the isolation factor increases, the scale of the attraction becomes increasingly important, as does the attraction's ability to achieve and maintain viability. This chapter has highlighted many of the issues facing the supporters and managers of attractions in peripheral areas, demonstrating that problems can be overcome but also highlighting that if viability is an important criterion, the number of candidate attractions will decline as the degree of isolation increases. This was demonstrated by Alice Springs which, despite its geographic isolation, has created a sufficiently diverse cluster of activities and attractions that it is able to attract a large number of visitors.

Several areas for future research that would benefit communities and investors contemplating construction and operation of attractions in peripheral localities are the related issues of long-run viability and the creation of supporting tourism product infrastructure. If the countryside is not to be littered with increasing numbers of publicly funded but poorly conceived attractions, built to encourage rural tourism, the blowtorch of viability must first be applied. Moreover, tourists need to be encouraged to make the additional effort required to travel to the periphery by the provision of complementary attractions, visitor services and quality facilities that reward their efforts with unique experiences not found in the core.

References

Bull, A. (1991). *The Economics of Travel and Tourism*, Pitman.

Ditton, R., Loomis, D. and Choi, S. (1992). Recreation specialization: re-conceptualization from a social worlds perspective. *Journal of Leisure Research*, **24**, 33–51.

Leask, A. and Yeoman, I. (1999). *Heritage Visitor Attractions: An Operations Management Perspective*, Cassell.

Lew, A. (2000). Attractions. In *Encyclopaedia of Tourism* (J. Jafari, ed.), pp. 35–37, Routledge.

Light, D., Prentice, C., Ashworth, G. J. and Larkham, J. (1994). Who consumes the heritage product? Implications for European tourism. In *Building New Heritage: Tourism, Culture and Identity in the New Europe* (G. J. Ashworth and P. J. Larkham, eds), pp. 90–116, Routledge.

MacCannell, D. (1976). *The Tourist: A New Theory of the Leisure Class*, Schocken Books.

McKercher, B. (2001). Attitudes to a non-viable community owned heritage tourism attraction. *Journal of Sustainable Tourism*, **9**, 29–43.

Oppermann, M. (1993). Tourism space in developing countries. *Annals of Tourism Research*, **20**, 535–556.

Prideaux, B. (2000). The role of transport in destination development. *Tourism Management*, **21**, 53–64.

Prideaux, B. (2002). Creating rural heritage visitor attractions: the Queensland Heritage Trails Project. Unpublished research paper. The University of Queensland.

Richards, G. (1996). Production and consumption of European cultural tourism. *Annals of Tourism Research*, **23**, 261–283.

Swarbrooke, J. (1995). *The Development and Management of Visitor Attractions*, Butterworth-Heinemann.

Tourism NT (2006). *The Alice Springs Area Profile*. http://www.tourismnt.com.au/nt/system/galleries/download/NTTC_Research/Alice_Springs_Area_05.pdf.

Wall, G. (2000). Centre-periphery. In *Encyclopaedia of Tourism* (J. Jafari, ed.), p. 76, Routledge.

Walsh-Heron, J. and Stevens, T. (1990). *The Management of Visitor Attractions and Events*, Prentice-Hall.

Weaver, D. (1988). The evolution of a 'plantation' tourism landscape on the Caribbean Island of Antigua. *Tijdschrift voor Economische en Sociale Geografie*, **79**, 319–331.

Weaver, D. (1998). Peripheries of the periphery tourism in Tobago and Barbuda. *Annals of Tourism Research*, **25**, 292–313.

CHAPTER 6

Visitor Attraction Development in East Asia

Joan Henderson

Aims

The aims of this chapter are to:

- identify recent trends in the development of visitor attractions in East Asia,
- compare the tourism resource base of Hong Kong and Singapore with particular reference to heritage and more modern attractions, and
- illustrate the importance of both heritage and new-style attractions in the region.

Tourism in East Asia: an overview

The United Nations World Tourism Organization (UNWTO) defines Asia and the Pacific in terms of North East and South East Asia, South Asia and Oceania. Countries making up the East Asian regions exhibit some similarities and marked contrasts, both generally and as tourist destinations. The range in the scale of their tourism industries is indicated by the 2005 figures for international arrivals and earnings, which are shown in Table 6.1.

China dominates, although the statistics cover visits from the Special Administrative Regions (SARs) of Hong Kong and Macau, which might be deemed domestic tourism, and North East arrivals exceed those of the South East as a consequence. Provisional data for 2005 indicates that Asia and the Pacific as a whole increased its share of the international tourist market to 19.4 per cent in 2005, up from 9.5 per cent in 1985, and accounted for 20.4 per cent of total spending. Outbound travel too has expanded, with tourists from the region recording some of the highest global growth rates (UNWTO, 2006).

Table 6.1 International tourism in North East and South East Asia 2005

	Arrivals (thousands)	Earnings (US$ millions)
China	46 809	29 296
Hong Kong SAR	14 773	10 119
Japan	6728	12 440
South Korea	6022	5660
Macau	9014	5040
Taiwan	3378	4054[a]
Total North East Asia	87 569	NA
Brunei	815	NA
Cambodia	1422	NA
Indonesia	5002	4316
Laos	672	147
Malaysia	16 431	8543
Myanmar	232	NA
Philippines	2623	2130
Singapore	8942	5740
Thailand	11 737[a]	10 108
Vietnam	3468	NA
Total South East Asia	50 593	NA

[a]Figures for 2004.
Source: UNWTO (2006).

Much of this movement takes place within Asia and has been accompanied by greater participation in domestic tourism, made possible by economic advances and the emergence of an affluent middle class as well as the burgeoning of the budget airline sector.

The strong performance of many East Asian states reflects their popularity and the presence of attractions with considerable appeal. However, the comparatively low volumes of inbound tourism for several countries that have a wealth of resources suggest unexploited opportunities. In many instances there are serious barriers to overcome before such potential can be fully realized and progress depends upon changes in the economic, political and social environments (Hall and Page, 2000), which are likely to be part of a long-term process.

Trends in visitor attractions

Countries of East Asia, especially those of the South East, have traditionally been associated with natural and cultural heritage attractions. The former is represented by climate, beaches and islands, forest and mountain scenery, and plant and animal life. Cultural attractions include built heritage, historic sites, festivals, customs, traditional lifestyles, and arts and crafts. However, modern attributes such as shopping malls, events, theme parks and all-inclusive resorts are of significance, as well as sports and health treatments. The role of sex tourism in certain locations cannot be overlooked and food is another resource that is difficult to classify. Attractions are therefore diverse and not confined to coastal and rural areas and historic urban zones, but are to be found in specialized centres and the major metropolitan conurbations.

Theme parks have emerged as prominent attractions that are not geographically dependent and are characterized by their artificiality. They are part of a rapidly evolving entertainment industry driven by mounting regional demand for leisure services, with investment shifting from Europe and America to Asia and the Pacific Rim. Four of the top ten most-visited parks are now located in Asia compared to one in Europe and the remainder in the USA. Attendance at Asian theme parks is forecast to rise from 234 million in 2005 to 278 million by 2010, and revenue in mainland China is set to grow by over 7 per cent annually to reach US$1.8 million in the same period (PWC, 2006). The industry in Japan is already well established and Tokyo Disneyland dates from 1983. Universal Studios opened its first park outside the USA in Osaka in 2001, when a new Disney Sea park also began operation in Tokyo. South Korea currently has two of the world's busiest parks, and major investment is planned in China. Hong Kong Disneyland, described in one of the chapter case studies, is seen as a test of the Chinese market and has been watched closely by analysts since its 2005 opening.

In terms of other modern attractions, there is evidence in East Asia of the more universal shift towards 'inclusive, all-weather, mixed retail, entertainment and leisure developments' (Stevens, 2000: 68). Large purpose-built facilities, which often rely heavily on technology and possess a retail component, thus have an important place alongside more conventional attractions of nature, culture and heritage, and this trend is demonstrated by the integrated resort projects in Singapore that are the subject of the second chapter case study. The resorts incorporate a casino, and gaming tourism is another observable regional trend, many places hoping to emulate the example of Macau, which surpassed Las Vegas as a generator of gambling revenue in 2006.

East Asian destinations thus comprise a composite of attractions serving markets of excursionists, domestic tourists, and Asian and Western visitors, that each has their own needs and expectations. It must be noted that what constitutes an attraction is open to interpretation, and depends on individual and group perceptions. Cultural differences are probable and tourists from the West could be more interested in certain qualities than their Asian counterparts. Westerners might be expected to have more romantic and idealized notions of the Orient, which is presented to them as exotic and mysterious in the promotional materials disseminated by the tourism industry. Contrived and sophisticated attractions of a sort they can find at home may be of limited appeal, yet be capable of enticing local and regional tourists.

In order to take advantage of the multiplicity of markets and resources, differentiation has been adopted by many national tourism organizations that have moved from mass to niche marketing. Instances include Malaysia and Thailand, where an assortment of products such as food, shopping, health, heritage, sports, culture, nature and beach resorts are promoted to target markets. Other countries, like Cambodia, with a more restricted product range, have chosen to focus on particular attributes. Ecotourism, combining natural and social dimensions, is being widely pursued, as is heritage tourism.

Some characteristics of the region's tourism and wider trends are exhibited in the examples of Hong Kong and Singapore: leading Asian destinations that are very active in new product development and marketing. Cultural heritage has a prominence in current strategies and future plans, and the same comment applies to modern and new-style attractions, with some attention also devoted to natural heritage. A comparative study of the two locations forms the remainder of the chapter.

Hong Kong and Singapore compared

Tourism resources and marketing

Hong Kong and Singapore are successful, albeit mature, international tourist destinations (Mintel, 2005; Travel & Tourism Intelligence, 1999), both of which are seeking further growth. The Hong Kong Tourism Commission (HKTC), responsible for policy and planning, aims to maintain and enhance Hong Kong's position as 'Asia's premier international city' with a 'kaleidoscope of attractions' (HKTC, 2006). The Tourism 2015 strategy launched by the Singapore Tourism Board (STB) in 2005 is designed to double visitor arrivals in a decade, partly by 'developing tourism products and services to strengthen Singapore's appeal as a must-visit destination' (STB, 2005a: 3). The two aspire to be the principal Asian urban tourism destination and plans necessitate consolidating current strengths, devising innovative products, and widening market appeal by adding new attractions and upgrading those already in existence.

The locations have a history of exposure to outside influences and an ambivalent culture has emerged that is neither wholly Asian nor Western. Hong Kong became an SAR of the Communist People's Republic of China in 1997, after 150 years as a British colony, while Singapore too was formerly under British colonial rule and gained full independence in 1965. Singapore's population is multiracial, with a Chinese majority, whereas Hong Kong citizens are largely of Chinese ethnicity, and both groups of residents enjoy a comparatively high standard of living as a result of very rapid development. There are, however, divergences in economic and political systems, as well as in matters of society and geography. Hong Kong occupies a significantly larger area than Singapore and is less affected by space constraints outside the city.

Defining features are reflected in the tourism resource bases of the two destinations, which comprise attractions rooted in the past, present and future. In juxtaposition to heritage, facilities of ultra-modern hotels, retail centres and transport services are highlighted, and opportunities for shopping, fine dining and access to the arts and world-class events are advertised to leisure tourists. Family fun at theme parks is another selling point for Hong Kong, while Singapore markets the island of Sentosa as a holiday playground, consisting of a series of specially created attractions. Promotional images depict sophisticated cities where there is a fascinating, if somewhat clichéd, mix of East and West and old and new.

Marketing and promotion is the task of the Hong Kong Tourism Board (HKTB), which initiated a global branding exercise entitled 'Hong Kong – Live It, Love It!' in 2003. This was supplemented by the 2006 Discover Hong Kong Year that sought to capitalize on the newest attractions. The HKTB campaigns are intended to convey vibrancy and diversity, enriching the Hong Kong brand, which is conceptualized as a marriage of the traditional and contemporary (HKTB, 2005). The STB also paints a picture of a modern, progressive and cosmopolitan city-state, which is epitomized in the Uniquely Singapore brand introduced in 2004. The brand's attributes are cosmopolitan, modern, culturally diverse, efficient quality and blend of disparate things that co-exist comfortably. Brand personality traits are confidence, sophistication, elegance, colour and good humour (STB, 2004). There are clear parallels between the content and execution of the promotion undertaken by Hong Kong and Singapore, disclosing a long-standing degree of rivalry.

Heritage attractions

Heritage has a contribution to make to the realization of formal tourism goals and has been given a high priority in Hong Kong by the HKTC and HKTB. Buildings and historic and archaeological sites with tourism potential have been identified, and the survival of colourful traditions has been fostered by a Heritage Tourism Force. The allure of heritage and ancestral cultures is equally recognized in Singapore, where the development of clusters of heritage and cultural attractions has been encouraged. Tourism authorities in the two destinations are aware of the advantages of heritage as a marketable commodity, vigorously promoting it and becoming advocates of conservation as a consequence. Hong Kong's tourism literature refers to a range of built heritage from the Imperial Chinese and British colonial eras, museums, heritage trails and tours, customs, festivals and cultural appreciation classes (HKTB, 2006). Singapore also advertises its museums and galleries, and the physical heritage of monuments, buildings and miscellaneous venues. Many sites have their origins in colonial times, but indigenous architecture and manifestations of ethnic cultural heritage are showcased (STB, 2006a).

In addition to the appreciation of commercial gains, there are socio-political considerations to take into account, and official interest in heritage tourism can be partly attributed to political agendas. The colonial government in Hong Kong, acting through the Antiquities and Monuments Office, was especially busy in the years before the handover. Most listed monuments were approved by the Office in the 1980s and mid-1990s, and a Heritage Trust was formed in 1992 to raise awareness and aid community-organized heritage projects. The British regime also built the Hong Kong Cultural Centre in 1989, an arts venue of striking design on the waterfront, and was behind several new museums. These actions can be explained as an assertion of a separate Hong Kong identity and heritage to help assist the territory retain its individuality and remain intact within the larger Chinese entity.

The current government stance is one of the support for heritage, but there is evidence of a new emphasis on Hong Kong's long Chinese history linked to contemporary achievements and future ambitions. The Hong Kong Museum of History reopened at an enlarged site in 2000 when a Hong Kong Heritage Museum was also founded, along with a newly reconstructed Tang dynasty monastery that is devoted to the Chinese lineage of the Hong Kong people. Such attractions can be seen as an embodiment of the common origins and destiny of China and Hong Kong, strengthening ties and signifying the People's Republic as the motherland. Thus heritage sites are a way of delivering political and socio-cultural messages about formal constructions of identity, and the heritage from which it is derived, to audiences of residents and external publics, which also encompass tourists.

Singapore has been following a more conventional journey towards nationhood, and the nurturing of a sense of identity and purpose has been a principal objective of the People's Action Party, in power since the 1960s. This aim has been made more difficult by the presence of minorities formally classified as Malays, Indians and others besides the ethnic Chinese who make up over 75 per cent of the population. Originally, the government was concerned mainly with economic advancement and the satisfaction of material aspirations, but there was a subsequent acknowledgement that a nation is determined by its culture as well as economics. Attempts have thus been made to articulate and inculcate appreciation of a distinct Singaporean nationality, history and shared future. At the same time, the benefits of multiculturalism are promulgated and the official view is that the races should be free to celebrate their own cultures provided this does not disturb the *status quo* by provoking conflict or finding political expression.

These policies have infused attitudes to conservation of the built heritage and there was initially little regard for the past as Singapore moved at great speed from a colony to a modern state. Urbanization and industrialization transformed the island, with few people sympathetic towards saving old buildings, which were seen as an unproductive use of scarce land and a barrier to progress. Later, heritage was reassessed and accepted as a positive force in both nation building and tourism development. It is now seen to symbolize and transmit a unifying Singaporean spirit and character, transcending other allegiances (URA, 1991). Cultural heritage attractions also reinforce conceptions of an ethnically diverse community living in peace and harmonious multiculturalism, which is represented in tourist guides by the country's food, festivals and cultural events. Preserved monuments display a balance, with Chinese and Indian temples, Muslim mosques and Christian churches appearing in promotional material. The nineteenth-century ethnic enclaves of Chinatown and Little India, and the Malay quarter of Kampong

Glam, have been conserved in schemes that incorporate redevelopment and adaptive reuse, and are essential elements of most tour itineraries.

Many commentators have been critical of the exploitation of heritage by the tourism industry and authorities in pursuit of hegemonic interests, but tourism has also been praised as a guardian of heritage and a positive force for conservation. The debate is especially relevant in newly independent countries and former colonies, or during times of change and uncertainty, as illustrated by Hong Kong and Singapore where heritage attractions have been shown to have a function relating to pressing questions of national and cultural identity and government legitimacy. They have a value as political, social and economic capital that pertains more widely in the region. Certain states are struggling with the demands of nation building, and some regimes are striving to assert and retain control. These and almost all other governments make decisions that impinge on the interpretation and presentation of heritage, often employing tourist attractions to communicate preferred notions of history and contemporary circumstances.

Modern attractions

While heritage is a core pillar of tourism, modern attractions remain a central product in Hong Kong and Singapore. They are critical to future plans and exceed heritage in importance if measured by levels of current and proposed investment. Hong Kong has favoured large-scale facility and attraction projects such as an international performing arts venue and a multi-purpose stadium, and a new cruise terminal that will be operational in 2012. Recent innovations include Hong Kong Disneyland, the redevelopment of Ocean Park amusement park with a HK$500 million 'Adventure Bay' attraction, a cable car system connected to a culturally themed village on Lantau Island and the 'world's largest permanent light and sound show' at Victoria Harbour. Government commitment to such a type of development is confirmed by its backing of Hong Kong Disneyland which also provides an interesting example of Chinese political and cultural sensitivities over Westernization giving way to commercial imperatives.

Singapore, which had some ambitions to host Disney's first non-Japanese Asian theme park, has invested heavily in tourism infrastructure and superstructure. For example, the Esplanade – Theatres on the Bay performing arts complex was built at a cost of approximately S$600 million and opened in 2002. It is crucial to official efforts to turn Singapore into a global arts hub and there are attempts to draw world-class sporting competitions and other major events, again like Hong Kong, which portrays itself as the events capital of Asia. The integrated resorts are the newest multi-million dollar project, due to open in 2009, and much is expected of them.

Although several completed and proposed schemes are impressive, the approach has some limitations. It is not a realistic strategy for every nation, especially for those that are less advanced economically, and calls for substantial expenditure by the public and private sectors and expensive technical expertise. Within the specific context of Hong Kong and Singapore and their promises of an exciting fusion of West and East and old and new, there is perhaps a danger of an over-emphasis on international-style attractions and a loss of perceived and actual distinctiveness. Development may create a uniform tourism landscape of contrived attractions, promoted in a way that reinforces similarities. Problems arise of maintaining a balance between the past and present, and ensuring that aspects of heritage, such as the built environment and cultural traditions, are not overwhelmed by the race to modernize and globalize. Heritage assumes a vital role in this situation, whereby its conservation can help to maintain a unique sense of place and difference, which is a role that has intrinsic worth and commercial merit as a means to secure competitive advantage.

These arguments extend to natural heritage and nature-related tourism is another strand in strategic planning, exemplified by Hong Kong's Wetland Park at Mai Po Marshes, which opened in 2006 and is hailed as its 'first major green tourism facility' (HKTC, 2006). Similar resources include nature parks devoted to conservation and recreation that occupy 40 per cent of the total land area of 1097 km^2, almost double that of Singapore. They encompass parts of the rural hinterland of the New Territories, numerous small islands, beaches and upland scenery, which support a diversity of outdoor activities. Some of Singapore's offshore islands, besides Sentosa, have been designated for recreation and it has an unexpected array of nature sites. Its cleanness and greenness are constantly lauded in the images projected of a clean-and-green, tropical garden city. The fact that such assets are exploited for tourism purposes in destinations renowned for their urban attractions suggests the influence of the environmental movement on tourist tastes and the rise of ecotourism, in all its manifestations, as a marketable product. However, in contrast to some East Asian countries, more natural attractions are likely to be secondary as a motivator to visit Hong Kong and Singapore, and environmental problems should not be discounted. There have been objections about the pace of development on Lantau Island in Hong Kong, for example, which critics say is under threat.

Case Study: Hong Kong Disneyland

After lengthy negotiations, Disney selected Hong Kong as the location for its third theme park outside the USA in November 1999. The Hong Kong government and Walt Disney Company (WDC) formed a joint-venture company named Hong Kong International Theme Parks Ltd (HKITP) to build and operate the park.

The agreed funding package for the park was HK$14.1 billion, with a debt-to-equity ratio of approximately 60:40, in an attempt to avoid the financial problems faced by Disneyland Paris. The government took a 57 per cent equity share in HKITP, amounting to HK$3.25 billion, with WDC holding the remainder. Provision was made for both the government and WDC to sell down their shares at some future date, which is common practice in venture capital schemes. Disney is required to retain a minimum of 1.9 billion shares in the company, but the government is not restricted by such a provision. The debt structure was made up of HK$2.3 billion of commercial loans and a further HK$5.6 billion from the government, the latter to be repaid with interest over the 25 years after the park's opening. Interest is payable on a sliding scale of Prime rate less 1.75 per cent during construction and the first eight years after opening; Prime rate less 0.875 per cent for the next eight years; and then Prime rate for the remaining term of the loan. The reason for raising only one-third of the loan commercially was to better support the cash flow of HKITP in the early years of the park's development.

The Hong Kong government spent a further HK$13.6 billion on infrastructure such as roads, two ferry piers, police, fire and ambulance stations, drainage and sewage systems, and preparing the site. The authorities maintained that such heavy expenditure would have been necessary anyway, as the site had been earmarked for recreation development even if the Disney theme park was not built. Moreover, it was agreed that the government should receive HK$4 billion in subordinated shares as a land premium for the estimated pro-rata cost of land reclamation and site preparation in the first phase of development. These shares attract no dividend, but are convertible into ordinary shares at a progressive rate in accordance with operating performance. Share conversion can commence only after the park has been operating for five years and the amount is capped at 10 per cent in any one year to prevent other shareholders' equity from being adversely affected.

The park opened in September 2005 on reclaimed land at Penny's Bay on Lantau Island where the airport is situated. It is about 12 km from central Hong Kong and linked to the city by road, high-speed rail and ferry. Under Phase I, Disneyland and related hotel and catering, retailing and entertainment outlets occupy about 126 ha, which make it the smallest Disney park. There is a Phase II plan which would see an extension to 180 ha, subject to initial results, and a right-to-buy option for the enlarged site that is valid for 20 years after opening. The park is of traditional American Disney-style and Chinese influences are limited to food and official languages. Disney was said to have vetoed early government proposals for the infrastructure and periphery designs that sought to introduce a Chinese and Hong Kong flavour.

The projected attendance was 5.2 million visitors in the first year, most of these from mainland China, which would double after 15 years. Numbers would then rise to some 20 million at the end of 2024 after the implementation of Phase II. Of the Year 1 total, 3.4 million would be incoming tourists who would spend an additional HK$8.3 billion (1999 prices); by Year 15 these figures would have increased to 7.3 million and HK$16 8 billion, respectively. The net economic benefit of the project were estimated in 1999 prices to be HK$148 billion over 40 years, with 18 400 new jobs created directly or indirectly on opening and 35 800 over 20 years. More conservative scenarios put the net economic benefit in the range of HK$80–128 billion over the 40-year period and downgraded job creation accordingly.

Prior to opening, the government claimed that 'Hong Kong Disneyland will herald a new era for Hong Kong's tourism industry and enhance Hong Kong's image as a vibrant and cosmopolitan international city. Disney's choice of Hong Kong for its third international theme park is a vote of confidence in our city and our future by the world's best known and most prestigious theme park and entertainment corporation' (HKVAR, undated). There were some criticisms, however, which continue to be voiced about the extent of government commitment, over-optimistic forecasts and adverse environmental impacts. A recent example of the last point is pollution from the nightly fireworks.

Such criticisms were countered by reference to two environmental impact assessment studies aimed at ensuring that all environmental standards would be met by mitigating projects. It was also argued that the site was leased for 50 years, with the right of renewal for a further 50 years, and there was an option to buy. It was bound to be a concern that the government was committing itself to just over 80 per cent of the start-up costs, albeit with future payback arrangements. However, from a public relations perspective, both the government and WDC were anxious to avoid the difficulties encountered in Paris and hence it was important that the development should not be under-capitalized.

Although the park opened on schedule, the event was accompanied by negative publicity surrounding various news stories. These included the controversial decision to allow some hotels to serve shark's fin soup, later rescinded after an outcry by animal welfare groups, and labour disputes over working conditions. There were long queues on rehearsal days before the formal opening and crowding during the 2006 Lunar New Year holiday when the park reached its 30 000 capacity. The gates had to be closed, leaving large numbers of ticket holders outside clamouring to enter.

Management took steps to rectify problems and the company announced that it had attracted over five million visitors in the first year. However, the total was lower than its revised target of 5.6 million and it was not clear whether the figure covered the large numbers admitted for rehearsals and those with free or heavily discounted passes. Media reports also described how Hong Kong Disneyland would soon have to address the challenge posed by more Disney parks in China, not least the likelihood of a much larger and more expensive park in Shanghai

(China Online, 2000; HKVAR, undated; *The Wall Street Journal*, 2006).

Case Study: Singapore's integrated resorts

The legalization of casino gambling in Singapore had been raised on numerous occasions, but rejected by the government due to fears about the social repercussions. The stance was revised in the twenty-first century, when the nature and outcomes of casinos were subject to reappraisal. They had come to be viewed as one ingredient of larger and more diverse leisure complexes, with the power of drawing substantial numbers of international tourists, which merited official support. After some public discussion, it was announced in late 2004 that the Government would invite potential investors to present concept plans for the development and operation of an integrated resort (IR) that would incorporate gambling facilities; this was labelled a Request for Concepts (RFC). Two possible sites were identified, one of 12.2 ha in the new downtown area to be called Marina Bay and another of 47 ha on the small recreational island of Sentosa.

The Prime Minister stated in Parliament in April 2005 that the Cabinet had agreed to go ahead with the IR projects and would be asking selected companies and partnerships that had contributed to the RFC to take part in a Request for Proposals (RFP). According to the STB, the Marina Bay site was to be a 'large-scale iconic lifestyle destination with a compelling mix of convention and exhibition facilities, themed attractions, entertainment and performance venues, casino gaming, recreation facilities, hotels and retail uses' (STB, 2005b: 1). The Sentosa IR too was to be a 'large-scale iconic development and "must-visit" attraction for visitors', but would be a 'world-class tropical resort that offers the whole family a fun and memorable leisure experience. It will broaden Singapore's tourism and entertainment options, complement existing tourist attractions as well as catalyse new tourism investment' (STB, 2006d: 1). The STB also confirmed that key criteria were tourism appeal and contribution, architectural concept and design, development investment, and strength of the consortium and partners.

Eight companies or consortia purchased Marina Bay tender documents and six bought the documents for Sentosa, with international, regional and local businesses all represented. Four Marina Bay proposals were finally submitted by the March 2005 deadline and a five-man Ministerial Committee, headed by the Deputy Prime Minister, was set up to make a final recommendation. It was made public in late May that Las Vegas Sands had been chosen as the bid most closely aligned to government goals, with planned investment of US$3.85 billion which was the largest amount pledged. Las Vegas Sands, best known for the Venetian resort in Las Vegas, is a US-based casino resort operator that will have two properties in Macau by 2007.

Central components of the project were revealed to be a total MICE (meeting, incentive, conference and exhibition) space of $110\,390\,m^2$ and a hotel with about 2500 rooms. Leisure offerings comprise two theatres, a $3700\,m^2$ entertainment zone, an outdoor events plaza, an arts–science museum, $117\,100\,m^2$ of shopping space, celebrity chef restaurants and two floating pavilions to accommodate a micro-brewery and night club. The design was said to form a memorable image for Marina Bay, with three hotel towers and a 'sky park' above, and extensive greenery covering the building facades and roof terraces.

The Sentosa IR bidding process followed the same procedures, although estimated development costs were lower at US$1 billion, but there was a delay in its launch to permit those unsuccessful in the Marina Bay exercise to participate. There were also four final bidders and the winner, announced at the end of 2006, was the partnership between Genting International, operator of the only casino in neighbouring Malaysia, and its sister company Star Cruises, the world's third largest cruise line. News that it had reached agreement with Universal Studios to build a theme park on the site was seen as giving it an edge over competitors.

The IRs are timetabled to open in 2009 and expected to make a major contribution to service-sector earnings and employment, in addition to helping to revitalize tourism in Singapore. They have not been without their critics, however, with strong opposition from some quarters to the presence of a casino on moral and religious grounds. Others have argued that Singapore's image as upright and corruption-free will be tarnished and that economic returns may be disappointing due to competition from other ventures in the region, notably those in Macau. Government has acknowledged these concerns and begun to install regulatory measures such as the establishment of a National Council on Gambling to deal with problem gambling. There will be entrance fees and a credit ban to discourage residents, an exclusion system and some revenue will be diverted to charity. It has also emphasized that casinos will only occupy a very small proportion of the floor space and the IRs will be an exciting leisure facility for residents as well as tourists (STB, 2006b–d).

Conclusion

These are interesting times for tourism in East Asia, and analysis of the attractions in Hong Kong and Singapore reveals some of the problems and opportunities. These will continue to evolve as all destinations strive for recognition and growth in an increasingly competitive tourism industry, exposed to internal and external change. Hong Kong and Singapore are responding to the challenges faced by pursuing comparable tourism strategies in terms of product enhancement, innovation and marketing which are directed at almost identical objectives of pre-eminence as an Asian city destination, with similar types of attraction. Policies are being followed with great energy by tourism agencies, actively supported by governments, and it would be surprising if they did not meet with some success in coming years. Central to such policies are heritage tourism, recognized as a unique selling point of considerable commercial potential, and more modern purpose-built attractions. The latter are very expensive to develop, yet appear of great interest to investors and destination marketers as well as tourists and an increase in their number across the East Asian region appears likely in the future.

References

China Online (2000). Back to the drawing board. 9 September. http://www.chinaonline.com.

Hall, C. M. and Page, S. (eds). (2000). *Tourism in South and Southeast Asia: Issues and Cases*. Butterworth-Heinemann.

HKTB – Hong Kong Tourism Board (2005). *The Year in Review 2004–2005*. Hong Kong Tourism Board, Hong Kong.

HKTB – Hong Kong Tourism Board (2006). Discover Hong Kong: Heritage. http://www.discoverhongkong.com.

HKTC – Hong Kong Tourism Commission (2006). Vision and strategy. http://www.tourism.gov.hk.

HKVAR (undated). Hong Kong Disneyland. Press Release. http://info.gov.hk/Disneyland, accessed 20 November 2000.

Mintel (2005). Singapore. Country report. *Travel & Tourism Analyst*, May.

PWC – Price Waterhouse Coopers (2006). *Global Entertainment and Media Outlook: 2006–2010*. Price Waterhouse Coopers.

STB – Singapore Tourism Board (2004). Uniquely Singapore. Brand presentation. Singapore Tourism Board, Singapore.

STB – Singapore Tourism Board (2005a). *Unique Moments in a Unique Year: STB Annual Report 2004–2005*. Singapore Tourism Board, Singapore.

STB – Singapore Tourism Board (2005b). Singapore Tourism Board Media Release, 4 November.

STB – Singapore Tourism Board (2006a). Uniquely Singapore: what to see. http://www.visitsingapore.com.

STB – Singapore Tourism Board (2006b). Singapore Tourism Board Media Release, 8 February.

STB – Singapore Tourism Board (2006c). Singapore Tourism Board Media Release, 29 March.

STB – Singapore Tourism Board (2006d). Singapore Tourism Board Media Release, 28 April.

Stevens, T. (2000). The future of visitor attractions. *Travel & Tourism Analyst*, **1**, 61–85.

Travel & Tourism Intelligence (1999). Hong Kong. City reports, *Travel & Tourism Analyst*.

UNWTO – United Nations World Tourism Organization (2006). *UNWTO World Tourism Barometer*. United Nations World Tourism Organization.

URA – Urban Redevelopment Authority (1991). *A Future with a Past: Saving our Heritage*. Urban Redevelopment Authority.

The Wall Street Journal (2006). Hong Kong Disney misses target, 5 September.

Leisure day trips have shown a downward trend since 1998 (Natural England, 2006). This is an interesting and perhaps somewhat unexpected finding, as improvements to the road network are acknowledged to have induced traffic growth (DoT, 1994). As tourism trips are clearly discretionary and day visits also often impulsive, one might have expected high levels of induced traffic growth for these journey purposes.

This pattern is mirrored in mainland Europe where Peeters *et al.* (2007) estimate that tourism accounts for between 15 and 20 per cent of passenger kilometres travelled within Europe by surface modes of transport. There has been a fall in domestic tourism trips by car and this is demonstrated in Germany where both the number of trips and the distances travelled (vehicle kilometres) have declined (BMVBW, 2003; Gstalter, 2003).

There is no comprehensive measure of the number of trips or distances travelled to visitor attractions, although they account for 7 per cent of trips in the Leisure Visits Survey (Natural England, 2006).

Modal share of trips to visitor attractions

Dominance of the car in the domestic market

The car dominates UK domestic tourism travel, accounting for around 71 per cent of all trips to and from holiday destinations (UKTS, 2004). The England Leisure Visits Survey of 2005 shows that 68 per cent of all leisure day trips lasting over three hours were taken by car (Table 7.1). There is no comprehensive measure of the car share for journeys to visitor attractions; indeed the survey of visitor attractions published by VisitBritain (2005) is notable for its absence of any transport data. There is no reason to believe that modal shares for visitor attractions are significantly different to travel for all tourism and day visit purposes, although visiting attractions did only account for 7 per

Table 7.1   Main form of transport used for leisure trips of over three hours' duration by destination (%)

	Car	Foot	Bus/coach	Train	Other	Total
Town/city	65	10	8	7	7	100
Seaside town	70	13	6	4	7	100
Seaside coast	80	2	10	2	6	100
Countryside	82	10	2	0	6	100
National parks	91	3	0	0	7	100
Total	68	10	8	7	7	100

Source: Natural England (2006).

cent of trips in the Leisure Visits Survey. However, the modal share for individual attractions will vary considerably depending on a range of factors.

Factors influencing the modal share of visitor attractions

Location of attraction

Perhaps the most significant influence on the modal choice of transport is the location of the attraction. The impact of location on travel behaviour is perhaps initially best demonstrated by an unrelated set of transport statistics. Car ownership in the UK has risen to 26.21 million cars in 2005 (DfT, 2006b), although 25 per cent of UK households consisting of 19 per cent of the population (approximately 12 million) do not have access to a car (DfT, 2006a). Table 7.2 shows the impact of location on car ownership. In rural areas, where public transport is at its poorest, only 11 per cent of households do not have access. However this rises in urban areas, reaching its peak in London which has the most comprehensive public transport network (DfT, 2006a).

The supply of public transport is also a key factor that influences the percentage of tourist and day trip arrivals by public transport. These are also at their lowest in rural areas, most particularly remote areas such as National Parks and highest in large cities (Table 7.2).

Paradoxically, this pattern can cause some concern to attractions with an environmental or 'green' mission statement, which are often located in rural areas. For instance, the National Trust (NT) owns many attractions in rural locations and despite the development of a green transport plan to reduce car dependency, the car share for arrivals at its properties remains stubbornly high and is not falling (Dickinson *et al.*, 2004). Likewise, the Eden Project is unable to meet its own accessibility targets (see case study later in this chapter).

Table 7.2 Household car availability by area type of residence, 2005

	No car	One car	Two + cars	Total	Cars per hour/hold
London boroughs	39	43	18	100	0.83
Metropolitan areas	32	41	27	100	0.99
Large urban	23	45	32	100	1.14
Medium urban	25	43	31	100	1.13
Small/medium urban	23	47	30	100	1.13
Small urban	20	43	37	100	1.24
Rural	11	37	52	100	1.59
All	25	43	32	100	1.15

Source: DfT (2006a).

The impact of location can also be demonstrated in a European context. Research by Gronau and Kagermeier (2007) compared the mode of transport used to travel to four attractions in Germany, all targeting the family-with-children market and all with similar catchment areas of around 90 minutes. The two rural attractions had the lowest public transport shares. One of them, The DinsoaurierPark, had very poor public transport links (fewer than four buses per day) and attracted well over 90 per cent of its visitors by car. Meanwhile the second rural attraction, an open air museum with a frequent bus service to the nearby town (Detmold), attracted 15 per cent of its visitors by bus. In contrast, the leisure facility Mensch and Natur, located in the metropolitan area of Munich, had similar bus frequencies to the open air museum and yet attracted around 33 per cent of visitors travelling by train and then by bus. Gronau and Kagermeier argue that this is because the rail connections to Munich are much more comprehensive than for Detmold, so although the bus frequencies to the attraction itself are similar, it is much easier to make the total journey including interchanges to Mensch and Natur. Their final example, Zoo Hellabrunn, had a similar level of access to Mensch and Natur but constraints on parking, including a charge, increased the share of public transport by further 5 per cent.

The case for travel by public transport becomes overwhelming for visitor attractions sited in the centre of the largest metropolitan areas such as capital cities. Heavy traffic congestion, combined with restricted and expensive parking, adds to the merit of public transport. In the case of London there is the additional disincentive of the central area congestion charge to deter arrival by car.

Profile of visitors

Data from the International Passenger Survey reveals that only 6.7 per cent of overseas visitors to the UK arrived by private car in 2005 (ONS, 2006). Even allowing for car hire by a minority of overseas visitors, the vast majority of trips by overseas visitors to the UK uses some form of public transport, so that attractions with a high percentage of overseas visitors will have lower percentage arrivals by car. This adds to the domination of public transport for attractions in central London. Overseas visitors also impact on the modal split of tourist arrivals in historic towns, contributing to the high bus and coach shares for Oxford and Stratford upon Avon (Table 7.3). Clearly, there are destinations outside major world cities with good public transport infrastructure, where it is customary for overseas visitors to hire cars. Examples include many island destinations, Florida and the Republic of Ireland outside Dublin.

In the UK, day visitors significantly outnumber staying visitors. There are an estimated 872 million day trips of over three hours' duration (Natural England, 2006), compared to 75.5 million domestic holiday trips (UKTS, 2004) and 30.2 million overseas visitors (ONS, 2006). Furthermore, the England Leisure Visits Survey now records day visits made from holiday accommodation as well as

Table 7.3   Mode of travel (%) by visitors to UK historic towns

Destination	Car	Train	Bus/coach	Other	Total
York (1989)	67	20	13	0	100
Chester (1990)	62	13	23	2	100
Bath (1986)	59	17	21	3	100
Cambridge (1994)	55	17	23	5	100
Stratford-upon-Avon (1987)	53	10	34	3	100
Oxford (1991)	48	16	33	3	100

Source: Grant *et al.* (1995).

trips made from home, with the former accounting for a mere 5 per cent of trips. Therefore, visits to attractions are dominated by day visits, even though this can vary significantly between attractions. Interestingly, trips made from holiday accommodation demonstrate a higher car share than trips from home (Natural England, 2006).

Size of attraction

Some very large attractions can be the sole purpose of quite long day trips and even a significant, if not the main, purpose for a staying visit (e.g. Alton Towers in the UK or Disneyland Paris). However, 68 per cent of visitor attractions in England which reported visitor numbers in 2005 are relatively small-scale, attracting under 50 000 visits per annum (VisitBritain, 2005) and these will attract a combination of local residents and opportunistic impulse visits by staying visitors. The transport implications of each scenario are widely different, even when the mode of transport is the same. A long-distance day trip to a major theme park by car will have much greater environmental impacts than a short impulse trip by car (though, as noted in Chapter 4, there is a sharp decline in car use after two hours' journey time) and this has implications for the development of policy to reduce car dependency.

To summarize, public transport's market share is at its highest for those visitor attractions in large cities where overseas visitors form a high percentage of the market and at its lowest for rural tourist destinations with a relatively small resident population, which are dominated by the domestic market and with a higher percentage of visits made by staying visitors.

Reasons for car dominance

The car offers huge advantages over public transport for the visitor. Whilst the cost of acquiring a car can be high, approximately 60 per cent of motoring

Table 7.4 Average cost per passenger mile by mode

	Pence per mile
Rail	17
Bus	22
Motoring fuel costs	6
All motoring costs	24

Source: DfT (2005).

costs are fixed annual charges so the cost of travel 'at the point of use', excluding all the fixed costs of annual road tax, depreciation and insurance, is very low. The Automobile Association (AA) estimates this cost to be around 44 pence per vehicle mile (AA, 2004), or 24 pence per passenger mile (Table 7.4; DfT, 2005). Attendance at visitor attractions is a social activity, usually undertaken in groups with friends or relatives. The car is an ideal unit for groups of four to five people, as there is no incremental increase in the cost of travel for each person until the vehicle is at full capacity. The average car occupancy for day visits and tourism trips is 2.1, which is markedly higher than the occupancy level of 1.2 for the journey to work (DfT, 2006a). The average size of groups for day visits of over three hours is much higher at 4.98, although the average size of family groups is slightly lower at 4.29 (Natural England, 2006). Therefore, those households that have acquired a car primarily for other purposes, such as the journey to work, will find the additional cost of making leisure journeys by car by far the cheapest option.

Furthermore, the price differential between motoring costs and public transport costs continues to widen. Although petrol costs have risen above the rate of inflation, overall motoring costs have risen almost directly in line with inflation, increasing by a mere 4 per cent in real terms since 1990. In contrast, the cost of public transport has continued to rise, by over 20 per cent since 1990 (DfT, 2005). This does not generate optimism for a significant modal switch.

The car also offers greater flexibility than public transport. It does not operate to fixed routes and fixed timetables, and it is widely accepted that the growth of car ownership and car use has brought huge advantages in individual mobility. The increased opportunities are especially important for both holiday trips and leisure day trips. In the case of day trips, car ownership creates opportunities for impulse journeys. This was noted as far back as 1973 when in an essay Colin Buchanan (1973, quoted in AA, 1997; Adams, 1993) eloquently described the impact of car ownership on the quality of life.

I have never managed to make much money, and for the most part, in my half century of motoring, I have made do with second-hand cars. But what an enrichment of life has resulted! Marvellous holidays – camping, caravanning, much of Europe at our disposal in a three week vacation. Short visits in infinite variety – to relatives and friends, to the sea, out into the country, to great houses, gardens, zoos and parks. Spur of the moment trips – it is a fine day so out we go. Why cannot we be less hypocritical and admit that a motor car is just about the most convenient device that we ever invented, and that possession of it and usage in moderation is a perfectly legitimate ambition for all classes of people.

The environmental impacts of tourism transport

The environmental impacts of tourism include energy consumption, noise, pollution, visual intrusion, waste and encroachment. The most important is energy consumption, resulting in carbon dioxide (CO_2) emissions and tourism's contribution to global warming. There is a growing body of literature which confirms that transport is a dominant contributor to visitor attraction environmental impacts. Høyer (2000) calculates that travel to and from the Tyrol region in Austria, together with local transport within the destination area, is responsible for between 40 and 60 per cent of tourism's total environmental impact on the region. A case study of Amsterdam, where international tourist arrivals by air form a significant share of the overall market, estimates the transport contribution at a higher figure of 70 per cent, although local transport around the destination accounts for a mere 1 per cent. In contrast, the share of accommodation is estimated to be 21 per cent, while visiting attractions and other leisure facilities accounts for a relatively small 8 per cent of environmental impacts (Peeters and Schouten, 2005).

Becken and Simmons (2002) study the energy consumption patterns of tourist attractions in New Zealand and conclude that tourist attractions and experience centres generally consume less energy than recreational activities. They go on to note that the total energy use implicated in tourists' recreation amounts to around 1 per cent of New Zealand's total energy consumption. This is minor when compared to the energy requirements of internal and international travel (Becken *et al.*, 2003).

All these case studies demonstrate that to achieve growth within a framework of sustainable development, the transport to and from attractions must be the central policy focus. However, for appropriate policies to be developed, targets must be set and their likely impacts considered.

Government policy

The UK government has acknowledged the need to develop a more sustainable and less car-dependent transport policy (DETR, 1998; DfT, 2004), although progress to date has been slow. The strategy for UK tourism industry is outlined in 'Tomorrow's Tourism', and sets an ambitious target to 'exceed the rate of global growth in the industry by the end of 2010' (DCMS, 1999: 3). The follow-up document 'Tomorrow's Tourism Today' (DCMS, 2004) quantifies this as a £100 billion industry by 2010, which represents a growth rate of around 4 per cent per annum. However, as already outlined in this chapter, elements of the industry are actually beginning to stagnate.

Whilst the policy document advocates a 'wise' growth strategy for tourism, 'one which integrates the economic, social and environmental implications of tourism' (DCMS, 1999: 48), it is less specific on how environmentally sensitive growth can be achieved. However, as the previous section clearly highlights, a more sustainable transport strategy is central. The section on transport issues sets out six specific measures, of which one is in reality dissemination rather than policy. The first two measures are improved quality and delivery of public transport information (Table 7.5). Complex journeys to tourist attractions that require an interchange between modes of transport are difficult to plan and can form a barrier to making these journeys by public transport. In 1999, the English Tourism Council (ETC, since replaced by VisitBritain) produced a video that used a number of scenarios to demonstrate the difficulties of finding out details of local transport services (routes and departure times) in advance of a journey in an unfamiliar location (ETC, 1999). A national integrated transport information service, available online at www.transportdirect since December 2004, has addressed this. However, its effect on modal choice is difficult to determine on current evidence. The third measure, aimed directly at visitor attractions, is the development of green transport plans to achieve a switch away from car use. Examples of such approaches are developed in the following section.

Table 7.5 Tomorrow's tourism proposals for integrating policy

- Improve the quality and accessibility of information available to tourists by developing a national, integrated public transport information service by 2000
- Examine the potential for delivering integrated public transport and tourist information in a user friendly way, including electronic means
- Encourage tourist destination and leisure site managers to produce green transport plans to reduce congestion and pollution from employee and visitor car traffic
- Encourage the upgrading of public transport infrastructure such as facilities for bicycle carriage
- Identify and publicize schemes which utilize transport or visitor management techniques to good effect
- Encourage the creation of new tourism products which integrate walking with cycling or travel by bus and rail as part of the experience

Source: DCMS (1999).

Nevertheless, this rather simplistic approach does beg a number of questions:

(i) Is a significant modal switch away from the car realistic, particularly for longer-distance day visits, given all the advantages of the car in terms of cost and flexibility outline earlier?

(ii) What are the objectives of this modal switch?

'Tomorrows Tourism' sets no targets, it simply presumes that a switch from car to public transport is desirable. Is the aim to reduce Greenhouse Gas (GHG) emissions? If so, then policies need to be directed at the trip from home to the destination area. For day trips, the visitor attraction can develop offers and policies to encourage arrivals by alternatives to the car, but for staying visitors initiatives have to be coordinated at a destination level. There has to be a common approach between attractions and other stakeholders, such as accommodation providers, to discourage staying visitor arrivals by car. This approach has been pioneered by the Swiss association GAST (Gemeinschaft Autofreier Schweitser Touristorte), which encompasses nine virtually car-free tourist resorts (Høyer, 2000).

Policies directed at achieving a modal switch for staying visitors in the destination area, encouraging them to reduce or even forgo the use of their car during their stay, will bring benefits. These will be in the form of reduced congestion, air pollution, noise and visual intrusion, as well as reducing the demand for car parking at the visitor attraction. However, as the case studies have already demonstrated, they will have a minimal impact on GHG emissions.

Furthermore, by targeting a minority of trips, for example the longer-distance day visits, small reductions in the number of visitor arrivals by car will produce disproportionately large reductions in GHG emissions. Savings are not directly related to the volume of the modal switch.

(iii) Can environmental policy objectives be met without a change in modal share by car?

This is dependent on the targets for the transport policy, which it has been established have not been set. Nevertheless, if reduced GHG emissions are the principal aim, then visitor spend, visitor nights and visits to visitor attractions can all see growth without an associated growth in GHG emissions if visitors travel less often but stay longer. A decrease in the share of day visits, combined with an increase in the average length of stay, can reduce the GHG emissions with no reduction in the share of arrivals by car. Needless to say, current tourism trends are moving in the opposite direction, with the increase in short break holidays as well as long-distance day visits, and this will need to change.

Visitor attraction initiatives

The main approaches to divert visitor traffic have been:

- combined transport and admissions tickets offering discounted admission for arrival by public transport (or sometimes by bicycle),

- special bus services to remote attractions from the closest railway station, and
- restrictions on parking at the visitor attraction.

Combined tickets

A number of combined ticket and transport schemes have been tried over the years but results to date have proved disappointing. A combined rail and entrance ticket at Legoland Windsor, with a shuttle bus to and from Windsor station, introduced in the late 1990s, attracted a mere 3 per cent of arrivals (Oswin, 1999) and the Eden Project has also achieved disappointing results. Gronau and Kagermeier (2007) paint a slightly more optimistic picture for combined tickets to 'The Theme Ending' pool facility in Munich, but overall the impact of this approach is at best marginal (Høyer, 2000).

The effectiveness of combined transport and admission tickets can be undermined by the many alternative promotions for reduced entry. Many attractions, but particularly theme parks, offer special deals through loyalty cards such as Nectar and Air Miles, and use vouchers and promotions in newspapers and magazines in their marketing strategies. With such a multiplicity of offers, those arriving by car can often gain admission as cheaply as those arriving by public transport, and the public transport offer seems just another promotion, thereby losing the environmental message.

Special bus services

The National Trust (NT) has developed dedicated coach services from railway stations to certain properties, such as Derbyshire House, and also financially supports bus services to NT properties, often in partnership with local authorities. The concept has been further developed in some areas to link together several visitor attractions or areas of interest, with financial contributions coming from a combination of the attractions themselves and local authorities. Examples include 'The Conservation Express', launched in 2004 in the Purbeck Area of Outstanding Natural Beauty, operating from the station in Wool to connect with Monkey World, Lulworth Castle, Lulworth Cove and Durdle Door. While anecdotal evidence suggests patronage has been very disappointing, it nevertheless operated in 2006 and during the Easter vacation in 2007 and is scheduled to operate over the summer season in 2007. Likewise, the 'New Forest Tour', introduced in 2004, runs a two-hour circular route at hourly frequencies in the New Forest National Park during the peak summer season.

The development of specialist tourist services adds the extra potential to add value to the transport journey and to develop it into part of the leisure experience and create a seamless experience (Schiefelbusch et al., 2007). This can be achieved in a variety of ways, but one approach is through the vehicle itself. The use of vintage vehicles (Robbins, 2003) or open-top buses for scenic views is an example.

Interviews with tourism attraction managers in Purbeck reveal potentially conflicting objectives for public transport initiatives between stakeholders. Their support for the 'Conservation Express' had the principal aim of increasing visitor numbers by making the attraction accessible to non-car-owning households, rather than to switch visitors from car. Although this meets the policy objective of social inclusion, it becomes a promotional tool rather than environmental policy, even though it will achieve growth with only marginal increases in GHG emissions.

Many specialized tourist services have been relatively short-lived. It takes several seasons for a service to become well-used and to achieve its potential. Gronau and Kagermeier (2007) cite the example of tourist transport services in the low mountain regions of Frankenwald and Vogelsberg, where it took three to four years to build up demand. However, subsidized bus services are often

Table 7.6 Travel to National Trust attractions: Prior Park, 1999 (%)

How did you get to Prior Park?

Bus	41
Coach	5
Taxi	2
Bicycle	5
Motorbike	4
Lift	8
Walked	7
Parked/walked	24
Other	4
Total	100

Distance travelled	NT members (%)	Non-members (%)
Under 5 miles	19	23
5–14 miles	41	52
15–24 miles	31	12
25–34 miles	5	7
35–49 miles	3	4
50 miles +	1	2
Total	100	100

set financial or patronage targets, and failure to meet such targets sometimes results in withdrawal of the service before widespread awareness has been allowed to develop (Cullinane, 1997; Dickinson and Dickinson, 2006; Lumsdon and Owen, 2004).

Parking at the visitor attraction

The use of parking policy has already been touched upon in the previous discussion of Zoo Hellabrunn. However, an extreme example of parking constraint is the NT garden at Prior Park in Bath (Table 7.6), which has been opened with no car parking facilities. Visitor numbers have been in line with expectations, with far fewer arriving by car. However, comparison with another NT attraction, Lyford (Table 7.7), indicates that the policy has a significant influence on the distance travelled to the attraction, with visitors from over 25 miles being under-represented, resulting in a smaller catchment area (Table 7.6). Whilst a clear benefit in terms of GHG emissions, the

Table 7.7 Travel to National Trust attractions: Lyford (%)

How did you get to Lyford?

Car	82
Coach	3
Public transport	1
Cycle	3
Motorbike	3
Other	8
Total	100

Distance travelled	1999		2000	
	NT members	Non-members	NT members	Non-members
Under 5 miles	18	25	11	21
5–14 miles	25	26	24	26
15–24 miles	24	27	23	17
25–34 miles	14	9	16	17
35–49 miles	10	11	10	9
50 miles +	9	2	16	10
Total	100	100	100	100

Source: Market Research Group: Bournemouth University.

potential of car restraint policies to hinder tourism growth in the longer term are demonstrated and longer-term monitoring of visitor numbers will be interesting.

Integrated policies for attractions

There is evidence that at least some car users can be persuaded to transfer to public transport services. Analysis of an integrated multi-modal ticket (Wayfarer) used for leisure day trips into the Peak District National Park (Lumsdon *et al.*, 2006) identifies modal switch as being around 42 per cent of users who had a car available for the trip, although the potential does not appear to be uniform across all age groups, appealing disproportionately to older age groups. So how does one begin develop this potential? Dickinson and Dickinson (2006) concluded that the carrot of improved public transport will not achieve a significant modal shift on its own: it must be accompanied by measures of car restraint such as restricted or expensive car parking.

Case Study: The Eden Project

The Eden Project, opened in March 2001, attracted 1.18 million visitors in 2005/6. Although it has a strong commitment to sustainable development, it struggles significantly to influence the travel behaviour of visitors.

Visitor transport

Visitor arrivals are dominated by car (see Table 7.8). This reflects its rural location. Indeed, 82 per cent of tourists arrivals in the South West were by car in 2004 (UKTS, 2004). The attraction encourages visitors to use alternative modes of transport, as demonstrated by a visit to its website (see http://www.edenproject.com/visiting/index.html):

(i) *Cycle*: The attraction is on the National Cycle network and provides both cycle racks and free lockers for cyclists to use. It offers a £3.00 discount on the admission price (over 20 per cent for an adult ticket at £14) for those arriving by cycle. Despite these incentives, the impact on arrivals is disappointing.

   There are difficulties of transferring to cycle. It is an option for some staying visitors and for day visitors from the local area, but for longer distance day visitors the cycle options are:

   • *Travel by train with bicycles*. There are differing policies on carrying bicycles between the UK's Train Operating Companies (TOCs), which is a restraint for those visitors whose journey involves using different TOCs. Bicycles are permitted by First Great Western, the local TOC serving the area. However, our researcher travelled on a Sunday and due to engineering works was unable to take a bicycle because part of the journey was undertaken by a replacement bus service, illustrating the potential constraints.

- *Travel by train and hire a bicycle.* This, however, requires cycle hire facilities seven days per week. The hire shop in St. Austell is not open on Sundays.

Table 7.8 Modal share (%) for travel to the Eden Project

Car	85.8
Coach	12.8
Walk	00.3
Cycle	00.03
Rail	00.3
Bus	00.5
Total	100

Considerable time was taken to research and plan the journey (around four hours) and other rail options using alternative stations were only discovered during the visit. The four-mile cycle ride from St. Austell station over a newly developed trail was spectacular (but quite hilly and difficult).

(ii) *Walk*: This is an option for a small percentage of visitors and is again encouraged by a £3.00 discount on admission.

(iii) *Bus*: There is a discounted combined bus and admission ticket that is now becoming a standard approach. The combined ticket, including travel from St. Austell, is around £2.50 more than admission to the attraction. As with previous schemes, its impact is limited.

(iv) *Car*: The high car share requires a very significant land take and at the busiest periods the attraction has to operate a park-and-ride system from the furthest car parks to the attraction entrance.

This case study shows the constraints attractions face in bringing about a modal shift when acting in isolation. Policies to achieve an increase in cycling require an integrated regional approach from transport operators (rail and bus), retailers and planners.

Other transport

The Eden Project is more effective in achieving an environmentally beneficial influence in other transport elements. All its vehicles are powered by liquid petroleum gas (LPG) and they assist employees who choose to own LPG vehicles by making fuel available (at 5 per cent plus cost).

The Eden Project has developed a Green Transport plan for its employees and encourages car-sharing schemes where commuting by car is necessary.

As a major local employer, the Eden Project has significant leverage over freight transport and deliveries. It sources locally wherever possible, with 87 per cent of catering resources and 55 per cent of all other resources now sourced locally.

Much of the long-distance travel avoided is outside the local area, but there are significant reductions in GHG emissions. However, the Project can also influence the attitudes and behaviour of suppliers through its procurement policy. Influence extends to the vehicles used by local suppliers and the total number of delivery journeys they make. Suppliers are encouraged to combine deliveries, either with other deliveries to the immediate vicinity or with other suppliers to make a single delivery to the Eden Project. Influence even extends to packaging as the Eden Project strives to achieve its ambitious target of becoming waste neutral.

(*Sources*: Eden Project Annual Review 2005/6, see http://www.edenproject.com/about/1449.html).

Conclusions

There is a tremendous paucity of literature on travel to and from visitor attractions and yet, as this chapter has shown, it represents by far the biggest environmental contribution made by the attractions. Its study is essential if both the number of visitor attractions and the visitor numbers to those attractions are to grow in a sustainable manner, and the dominance of domestic day visits in the attraction market requires the initial focus to be on the use of the car. However, simple policies of offering 'carrots' to encourage public transport use (such as reduced admission) and 'sticks' to reduce car use (such as restricted parking), whilst not inherently wrong, will not alone achieve the desired results. Indeed, the target of achieving the largest possible modal switch will not automatically produce the most desirable results. The relationship is a much more complex one and patterns of tourism consumption such as length of stay are equally important. There is a limit to what attractions can achieve acting in isolation by developing their own green plans, and the 'wise strategies' that 'Tomorrow's Tourism' advocates need to be formulated into a coherent integrated strategy combining tourism and transport policies on a regional and national level.

To date, policies to achieve modal switch have not worked. For instance, the NT's green transport plan aims to reduce the car share of arrivals to its properties from the current 90 per cent to 60 per cent by 2020 (Dickinson *et al.*, 2004) but the car share continues to rise, although NT attractions have the added disadvantage that members receive free admission and parking, removing financial levers to influence this group of visitors. There are isolated examples of success and good practice.

Acknowledgement

The authors would like to acknowledge and thank Henrietta Swain from The Centre of Transport Studies at the University of West of England for allowing us to use her perceptive observational data, collected on a visit to the Eden Project in 2007.

References

AA – Automobile Association (1997). *Living with the Car.* Automobile Association Policy.

AA – Automobile Association (2004). *Motoring Cost Tables.* Automobile Association Policy.

Adams, J. (1993). No need for discussion – the policy is now in place. In *Local Transport Today and Tomorrow* (P. Stoneham, ed.), pp. 73–78, Local Transport Today.

Becken, S. and Simmons, D. G. (2002). Understanding energy consumption patterns of tourist attractions and activities in New Zealand. *Tourism Management*, **24**, 343–354.

Becken, S., Simmons, D. and Frampton, C. (2003). Energy use associated with different travel choices. *Tourism Management*, **24**, 267–278.

BMVBW – Bundesministerium für Verkehr, Bau- und Wohnungswesen (2003). *Verkehr in Zahlen 2003/2004.* Bundesministerium für Verkehr, Bau- und Wohnungswesen.

CBS – Centraal Bureau voor de Statistiek (2003). Statline. Statistiek van het personenvervoer. Statistics Netherlands. Centraal Bureau voor de Statistiek http://statline.cbs.nl/StatWeb/table.asp?STB=G1,G2&LA=nl&DM=SLNL&PA=37739&D1=a&HDR=T.

Cullinane, S. (1997). Traffic management in Britain's national parks. *Transport Reviews*, **17**, 267–279.

DCMS – Department for Culture, Media and Sport (1999). *Tomorrow's Tourism: A Growth Industry for the New Millennium.* Department for Culture, Media and Sport, The Stationery Office.

DCMS – Department for Culture, Media and Sport (2004). *Tomorrow's Tourism Today.* Department for Culture, Media and Sport, The Stationery Office.

DETR – Department of the Environment, Transport and the Regions (1998). *A New Deal for Transport: Better for Everyone* (Cm 3950). Department of the Environment, Transport and the Regions, The Stationery Office.

DfT – Department for Transport (2004). *The Future of Transport* (Cm 6234). Department for Transport, The Stationery Office.

DfT – Department for Transport (2005). *Focus on Personal Travel.* Department for Transport, The Stationery Office.

DfT – Department for Transport (2006a). *Transport Statistics Bulletin National Travel Survey: 2005.* Department for Transport, The Stationery Office.

DfT – Department for Transport (2006b). *Transport Statistics Great Britain*, 32nd edn. Department for Transport London, The Stationary Office.

Dickinson, J., Calver, S., Watters, K. and Wilkes, K. (2004). Journeys to heritage attraction in the UK: a case study of National Trust property visitors in the South West. *Journal of Transport Geography*, **12**, 103–113.

Dickinson, J. E. and Dickinson, J. A. (2006). Local transport and social representation: challenge the assumptions for sustainable tourism. *Journal of Sustainable Tourism*, **14**, 192–208.

DoT – Department of Transport (1994). *Trunk Roads and the Generation of Traffic*. Standing Advisory Committee on Trunk Road Assessment. Department of Transport, HMSO.

ETC – English Tourism Council (1999). Video shown at 'Journey to Success' English Tourist Board Conference, London.

Grant, M., Human, B. and Le Pelley B. (1995). Tourism and park and ride. *Insights*, English Tourist Board, London.

Gronau, W. and Kagermeier A. (2007). Key factors for successful leisure and tourism public transport provision. *Journal of Transport Geography*, **15**, 127–135.

Gstalter, H. (2003). Thesen und argumente zu den häufigsten behauptungen zur freizeitmobilität. In *Freizeitmobilitätsforschung – Theoretische und methodische Ansätze* (H. Hautzinger, ed.), pp. 105–118, Studien zur Mobilitäts- und Verkehrsforschung 4.

Høyer, K. G. (2000). Sustainable tourism or sustainable mobility? The tourism case. *Journal of Sustainable Tourism*, **8**, 147–160.

INS – Institut National des Statistique (2006). Services commerce et transport. Institut National des Statistique. http://statbel.fgov.be/figures/d37_fr.asp#7.

Lumsdon, L. and Owen, E. (2004). The Green Key initiative. In *Tourism and Transport: Issues and an Agenda for the New Millennium* (L. Lumsdon and S. J. Page, eds), pp. 157–169, Elsevier.

Lumsdon, L., Downward, P. and Rhoden, S. (2006). Transport for tourism: can public transport encourage a modal shift in the day visit market? *Journal of Sustainable Tourism*, **14**, 139–156.

Natural England (2006). *England Leisure Visits – Report of the 2005 Survey, Leisure Day Visits*. http://www.countryside.gov.uk/Images/England%20-Leisure%20Visits%20Survey%202005_tcm2-31218.pdf.

ONS – Office of National Statistics (2006). *Travel Trends – A Report on the 2005 International Passenger Survey*. Office of National Statistics, The Stationery Office.

Oswin, J. (1999). The role of tourism operators in increasing public transport use. Paper presented to *Journey to Success, English Tourist Board Conference*, London.

Peeters, P. and Schouten, F., (2005). Reducing the ecological footprint of inbound tourism and transport to Amsterdam. *Journal of Sustainable Transport*, **14**, 157–171.

Peeters, P., Szimba, E. and Duijnisveld, M. (2007). European tourism transport and the main environmental impacts. *Journal of Transport Geography*, **15**, 83–93.

Robbins, D. K. (2003). Transport as a tourist attraction. In *Managing Visitor Attractions: New Directions* (A. Fyall, B. Garrod and A. Leask, eds), pp. 86–102. Butterworth-Heinemann.

Schiefelbusch, M., Jain, A., Schafer,T. and Muller, D. (2007). Transport and tourism: roadmap to integrated planning developing and assessing integrated travel chains. *Journal of Transport Geography*, **15**, 94–103.

UKTS (2004). *United Kingdom Tourist Survey 2004*. http://www.staruk.org.uk/.

VisitBritain (2005). *Visitor Attraction Trends – England 2004*. British Tourist Authority.

Part Three

The Management of Visitor Attractions

Part Three of the book focuses on the operational and strategic management of visitor attractions, with a particular emphasis on the fundamental interdependencies involved in managing the various components of the visitor attraction product. Managing visitor attractions successfully requires the effective integration of a wide range of complex and inter-related management considerations, arising both from within and outside the visitor attraction sector. In this respect, the management of the visitor attraction sector can be seen as a microcosm of the wider tourism industry. The challenge for visitor attractions is to achieve this integration with what is frequently a very limited resource base.

A constant challenge for many visitor attractions, particularly those of a heritage or cultural genre, is that of maintaining their authenticity. This theme is examined in Chapter 8, where Philip Feifan Xie and Geoffrey Wall consider the concept of authenticity as it applies to ethnic tourism experiences and ethnic visitor attractions, and discuss the management challenges involved. Tourism has often been accused of having a negative impact on the authenticity of indigenous cultures. Visitor attractions are, however, often perceived as the most appropriate vehicle for protecting and promoting specific cultural identities through 'good' tourism, despite frequent pressures on many attractions to 'commodify' or otherwise 'pollute' the visitor experience. Using a detailed case study of ethnic visitor attractions in Hainan, China, Xie and Wall argue that authenticity can be best thought of as a negotiated process (which they call 'authentication'), the outcomes of which are determined through the complex web of inter-relationships that exist among stakeholders of the visitor attraction.

In Chapter 9, Richard Voase examines how visitor expectations have changed over time and how the expectations of 'old' and 'new' visitors are different. In offering a revised interpretation of what constitutes a 'new' visitor, Voase introduces the concept of the new 'thoughtful' and new 'smart' visitor and explains how 'active' and 'passive' modes of visitor experience require re-definition. In a political context, where 'dumbing-down' continues to be an issue across a range of contexts, Voase discounts the applicability of such a notion in the context of visitor attractions and recommends a strategy that engenders a 'popular' threshold of engagement. This is illustrated through a case study of how one museum, the Royal Armouries Museum in Leeds, UK, is taking account of these new visitor types in its marketing strategies. The chapter also proposes that visitor attractions have much to gain by developing interpretive strategies that enable visitors to build on and extend their own personal narratives. It is through these personal narratives that visitors seek to make sense of themselves, the world around them and the visitor attraction experience. This proposition is illustrated by a further case study, which reports on the author's work on revising the marketing strategy for Lincoln Cathedral, UK.

The issue of authenticity is touched upon again in Chapter 10, which focuses on the management of visitor impacts. In this chapter, Brian Garrod emphasizes the relevance of sustainability issues to visitor attractions and identifies some of the main impacts that the development and operation of visitor attractions can have on the natural and built historic environments. Garrod then goes on to explore what impacts visitors to visitor attractions exert on the fabric of the attraction itself and, more importantly, how these impacts might best be managed. A number of tools for the management of visitor impacts are introduced, and some discussion of their suitability – and indeed their desirability – then follows. A particular problem is that visitor management practices themselves have the potential to compromise the authenticity of the core product of the visitor attraction: resulting in the very outcome that such practices are trying to prevent. The relevant question then becomes not simply *how* to manage visitor impacts but *whether* to manage them at all. The findings of a comparative study of visitor impacts at attractions in Australia, Canada, New Zealand and Scotland are then presented. These go some way to assessing the viability of some of the main tools available to managers of visitor attractions for addressing visitor impacts.

The significance of the schools excursion market to visitor attractions is not widely appreciated in the literature. Chapter 11, by Brent W. Ritchie, Neil Carr and Chris Cooper, begins to address this omission by highlighting the wider management benefits that educational groups can bring to visitor attractions. For example, schools groups can help to fill out the shoulder periods of the tourism season, thereby helping to address problems associated with seasonality. Educational visitors can also provide excellent word-of-mouth advertising and generate repeat visits by their friends and families. Capturing these benefits should not, however, be viewed as an entirely straightforward task. Indeed, catering to the schools excursion market brings its own management problems. Visitor attraction managers need to understand and satisfy the various needs of teachers (including the curricula they are teaching), the children and their parents. Risk and safety issues are becoming ever more prominent in determining whether schools are willing take their students on excursions.

Infrastructure issues, such as suitable accommodation for children and rest facilities for coach drivers, are also important. Through a case study of educational tourism to Canberra, Australia's national capital, the chapter demonstrates how well-targeted research can help managers of visitor attractions to understand the needs, constraints and incentives of schools, and thereby to capture more of the benefits that catering for schools excursions can bring.

As is the case across much of the tourism industry, and particularly in the temperate climatic zones, one of the biggest challenges to operators of visitor attractions is that of temporal variation. This variation can manifest itself over the course of a year (which can be thought of as classic 'seasonality'), over the course of a month or even over the course of a day. When temporal variation is present it brings with it important implications for the management of the visitor attraction, including problems associated with staffing, transportation and accommodation. In Chapter 12, Philip Goulding reviews what is understood by the concept of temporal variation and investigates its operational implications for visitor attractions, both as revenue centres in their own right and more widely as part of the local tourism economy. Within the context of temporal variation being interpreted as a broad and complex phenomenon, Goulding assesses a range of possible management responses and evaluates their likely degree of overall effectiveness. Despite the fact that visitor attractions are often at the mercy of market forces, Goulding argues that through their operational policies, visitor attractions can collectively—and sometimes individually—contribute to, reinforce or combat patterns of temporal variation in a tourism destination. This is particularly the case where major attractions, or groups of attractions, play a catalytic role in promoting and sustaining the destination of which they form part. A case study of the responses of Scottish nature-based visitor attractions to the challenges of seasonality and climate is presented by way of illustration.

The popularity of gardens as visitor attractions continues to increase, yet the associated management issues are complex and pose a number of extraordinary challenges to the visitor attraction manager. Not least, many gardens that operate as visitor attractions were never intended to receive such large number of visitors and this can put immense pressure on the core resources of the garden. Chapter 13, by Dorothy Fox and Jonathan Edwards, begins with an overview of the diverse range of garden attractions and the people who visit them, and then moves on to consider the implications this diversity brings to the challenge of managing them. Such implications range from the constraints imposed on operational decision-making by the vagaries of the weather to the need to cater for 'reluctant visitors', who are merely accompanying those interested in experiencing the gardens. At the same time, operating gardens as visitor attractions actually presents many of the same kinds of management challenge as are faced by other attractions, such as the need to provide appropriate visitor facilities and effective interpretation. These considerations are illustrated though a case study, in which Fox and Edwards present the detailed findings of a recent survey of garden visitors in southwest England.

In Chapter 14, Gianna Moscardo and Roy Ballantyne highlight the significance of interpretation in the management of visitor attractions. Interpretation is arguably the single most important dimension of the visitor attraction product. Indeed, in the 'experience economy' of the new millennium, consumption is becoming less about acquiring commodities and more about collecting experiences. Interpretation, the process which enables visitors to engage mentally and often also physically with what the attraction has to offer, is essential in turning the core resources of the visitor attraction into rewarding experiences that visitors will find it both desirable and easy to consume. Interpretation is also an important ingredient in the pursuit of sustainability goals, not only in terms of enabling the visitor attraction to address its own negative impacts but also in terms of delivering educational messages to visitors for the benefit of society as a whole. What is clear, however, is that interpretation must be effective if it is to achieve these goals. Moscardo and Ballantyne therefore propose a model of interpretation based on making visitors 'mindful'. They also develop the concept of 'hot interpretation' and, through a case study of the District Six Museum in Cape Town, South Africa, demonstrate the benefits to be gained from implementing such an approach.

In many destinations around the world, religion-based attractions serve as the principal draw for tourists. Perhaps more than any other genre of visitor attraction, however, religion-based attractions typically face a range of strategic objectives with considerable potential for conflict among stakeholder groups. In Chapter 15, Myra Shackley illustrates the diversity of religion-based attractions and identifies the management trends and manifold challenges confronting them. For example, how are competitive and operational strategies developed to accommodate divergent organizational goals successfully and how can the operational management of religion-based attractions accommodate the divergent needs of different visitor and user groups? A case study of the Shrine of Our Lady at Knock, Ireland, is then presented. This illustrates the various visitor services required at religion-based visitor attractions. It also highlights the complex interactions between the religious site itself and the public-sector agencies and private-sector firms involved in providing this range of visitor services.

The final chapter in Part Three, by Sandra Watson and Martin McCracken, analyses the role of human resource management in visitor attractions. The human resource is increasingly being recognized as a critical success factor for visitor attractions, particularly in respect of frontline staff. Management challenges revolve around the successful recruitment, training and retention of staff, and the management of human resources is now viewed as a vital ingredient of effective competitive strategy. Against this background, the chapter identifies a strategic human resources management (SHRM) approach, which centres on the devolution of human resource responsibilities to line managers. This approach requires the explicit and proactive support of senior management, as well as the recognition (and reward) of the contributions of line managers to the human resources agenda of the organization. On the other hand, devolving the responsibility for human resources to line managers brings with it a number of challenges, not least in terms of developing strong and productive links between line managers and human resources specialists. There may also be con- flicts in terms of how line managers establish their priorities in dividing their attentions between human resource matters and their various other duties. To illustrate good practice in this area, Watson and McCracken present an in-depth case study of Our Dynamic Earth, a visitor attraction based in Edinburgh, Scotland, which has implemented a human resources strategy based on the SHRM approach.

CHAPTER 8

Authenticating Ethnic Tourism Attractions

Philip Feifan Xie and Geoffrey Wall

Aims

The aims of this chapter are to:

- introduce the concept of 'authenticity' as it applies to ethnic tourism experiences and ethnic visitor attractions, and to suggest that authenticity is a negotiated rather than a fixed attribute,
- suggest that the process of authentication provides a tractable way of examining aspects of authenticity at visitor attractions,
- provide a framework that identifies key stakeholders and five dimensions of authenticity that can be used to guide data collection and its interpretation at visitor attractions, and
- illustrate the utility of the framework through application to ethnic visitor attractions in Hainan, China.

Introduction

Tourism involves the movement of people outside of their normal places of work and residence. As such, it provides participants with novel experiences, often bringing them into contact with unaccustomed places and people. For many tourists, this is a search for the 'other', this being judged in relation to the 'self' and ones usual behaviours and settings. Thus, tourism brings into contact people who are not only strangers to one another, but who may also be members of different ethnic groups. Sometimes, the presence of minority peoples is a visitor attraction in itself. However, even in such places, specific tourism businesses may be created to provide opportunities for tourists to experience aspects of ethnicity. This chapter is concerned with visitor attractions of this type.

In particular, it addresses some of the tensions and trade-offs that should be addressed if such attractions are to meet the goals of the diversity of stakeholders with interests in their operation.

The development of cultural tourism and, in particular, ethnic tourism, which can be viewed as a specific form of cultural tourism, has brought to prominence a number of important questions:

- What is an authentic ethnic visitor attraction and how should such ethnic tourism experiences be provided?
- Can indigenous cultures survive the impacts of tourism?
- Will ethnicity be polluted and ultimately destroyed, or is it possible that tourism can actually nurture a cultural renaissance?
- How can indigenous groups benefit from cultural tourism at acceptable costs?

An understanding of these and related research questions is essential if high-quality tourism experiences based on expressions of ethnicity are to be made available in a sustainable manner.

There is a substantial and growing literature on cultural tourism and ethnic tourism (Cohen, 1988; Jamal and Hill, 2004; Picard and Wood, 1997; Shepherd, 2002; Wall, 1996). Most of these works focus upon the normative issue of whether tourism is beneficial or detrimental to its hosts (Wood, 1998). However, the traditional 'impact' paradigm tends to oversimplify situations, ignoring the facts that tourists and investments in tourism are not always imposed but are often sought, that residents respond and adapt to changing circumstances, and that tourism has such longevity and is so pervasive in some destinations that it is virtually impossible to visualize that place and its people in the absence of tourism (Wall and Mathieson, 2006). Further issues, such as authenticity of experience and commodification of culture, have been hotly debated but little research has paid attention to the concept of authentication, which refers to the identification of those who make claims for authenticity and the interests that such claims serve (Jackson, 1999).

This chapter will elucidate relationships between tourism and culture, particularly in relation to the issue of ethnicity. Terms associated with ethnic tourism will be defined and described, and the state of current knowledge will be assessed. An example of ethnic visitor attractions from Hainan, China, will be presented. It will be concluded that assessment of authentication rather than authenticity may provide a more practical way of addressing quality issues in ethnic visitor attractions.

Cultural tourism and ethnic tourism

Cultural tourism can be viewed from a variety of perspectives. From an ethnographic perspective, cultural tourism can be defined as 'a genre of special interest tourism based on the search for and participation in new and deep cultural experiences, whether aesthetic, intellectual, emotional, or psy-chological' (Reisinger, 1994: 24). From an anthropological perspective, culture is much more than the rituals, ceremonies and dances residents might per-form for tourists at cultural centres or visitor attractions. The richer meaning of culture refers to those activities associated with many private and unknown traditions that are part of the local person's daily life (Fridgen, 1996). Mathieson and Wall (1982) suggested that culture comprises the conditioning elements of behaviour as well as the products of that behaviour. Therefore, ethnic tourism is defined as the absorption by tourists of features resembling the lifestyles of societies observed through such phenomena as house styles, crafts, farming equipment and dress (Smith, 1989). The underlying motiva-tion for ethnic tourism emphasizes understanding contrasting ways of life and the associated interchange of knowledge and ideas (Pigram, 1993). Thus, cultural elements such as handicrafts, gastronomy, traditions, history, music, dance and architecture, whether unmanaged or staged specifically for visitors, can be major visitor attractions.

Ethnic tourism is part of cultural tourism, which is 'a form of recreation combining cultural and natural resources that is marketed to the public in terms of "quaint" customs of indigenous and often exotic peoples' (Smith, 1989: 2). However, the nature of ethnicity is more complex than it might seem to be at first sight. In the field of anthropology, ethnicity does not constitute a new domain of research, but tourism is a challenge to the adequacy of con-ventional cultural theory (Cohen, 1978). There are two basic perspectives regarding the relationship between ethnicity and culture: primordial and sit-uational (Hitchcock, 2001). The former views cultures as static and leads to the assumption that any change imposed by contact with a politically domi-nant state must result in irreversible acculturation. The situational perspec-tive, on the other hand, involves understanding the process by which ethnic identities and boundaries are created, modified and maintained (Barth, 1969). Wood (1980) indicates that culture should not be viewed as being a concrete entity acted upon by forces from outside, but rather as sets of symbols, or as webs of significance and meaning. Culture is not a thing, but a process. Ethnic identity is a feeling 'subject to ebb and flow' (Poole, 1997: 133).

Cultural tourism has long been regarded as a mild oxymoron by some researchers. According to anthropologists, tourists are generally ill-prepared to visit other cultures. Tourists tend to lack information about ethnic cultures and are usually naive about what to expect and how to behave (Fridgen, 1996). The prevailing assumption is that any attempt to use cultural elements to accommodate tourists will cheapen or trivialize the presentation and inter-pretation of ethnic arts and heritage (Kelly, 1994). Tourism research related to ethnicity has concentrated upon describing and understanding the impacts of tourism on host societies (Moscardo and Pearce, 1999). A number of studies have concluded that ethnic tourism is in danger of consuming the phenom-ena on which it is based (see, for example, Altman, 1989; Turner and Ash, 1975; van den Berghe and Keyes, 1984). Ethnic tourism practice may destroy the host's culture or may calcify a culture into a 'frozen' picture of the past.

Cultures are named and stereotyped. The visitors seek to see representations of the culture and the host society provides access to the expected symbols.

On the other hand, research on ethnic tourism also unveils positive impacts. Tourism can promote the restoration of arts, revitalize skills, foster creativity and provide a platform for communities to present themselves positively (Cohen, 1988; Graburn, 1984; Pitchford, 1995). McKean (1973), writing on cultural tourism in Bali, Indonesia, stimulated a reshaping of common perceptions. He concluded that tourism was strengthening the arts in Bali and that, as a result of tourism, there were more dancers, musicians, wood carvers and other crafts persons than there otherwise would have been. Furthermore, he suggested that the Balinese were quite successful in maintaining the boundary between what belonged to their culture and what could be presented to tourists. 'Cultural involution' was proposed as a term to indicate that culture is mutable and that tourism infuses new meanings for local cultures, adding value both economically and psychologically to cultural expressions previously largely taken for granted. Another example is Esman's (1984) study of Louisiana, which suggests that tourism has led to the re-creation of Cajun identity and helped to perpetuate an ethnic boundary that might otherwise have disappeared due to acculturation.

The terms 'touristic culture' and 'touristification' were proposed by Picard (1990) in reference to situations where tourism is so pervasive that it has become an integral part of everyday life. In such situations, the interaction with tourists may be a central component in the definition of ethnic identity. Picard (1995) showed that the Balinese have come to objectify their culture in terms of the arts and to evaluate tourism impact in terms of whether the Arts are flourishing or not. The convergence of tourism and culture in the late twentieth century was presented by Richards (1996: 12) as a pragmatic *fait accompli*, and he suggested that 'in spite of reservations about the potential negative impacts of tourism on culture, it seems that tourism and culture are inseparable'.

Authenticity and commodification

Authenticity can be defined as 'a desired experience or benefit associated with visits to certain types of tourism destinations. It is presumed to be the result of an encounter with true, uncommercialized, everyday life in a culture different than that of the visitor' (Smith, 1989: 31). Concern with authenticity is still prevalent in many areas of endeavour, and is seen by some as an attribute of postmodernity and the growing pursuit of heritage of all kinds (Conran, 2006). The relationship between history and heritage (Lowenthal, 1985, 1996), the portrayal of aboriginal peoples in Canada (Butler and Hinch, 1996; Li and Hinch, 1998; Mason, 2004) and Australia (Altman, 1989; Ryan and Huyton, 2000), and the contested interpretations of the significance of place (Ryan and Aicken, 2005; Tunbridge and Ashworth, 1996) are three examples among many. In tourism research, perspectives have varied from those of Boorstin (1964), who saw tourists as being duped and seduced to visit contrived attractions; to MacCannell (1976), who viewed tourists as modern pilgrims in search of the authentic; to Wang (1999), who argued that there are different types of authenticity; to Cohen (1988), who suggested that authenticity is of differing importance to different market segments. Authenticity is, therefore, a slippery and contested term. Nonetheless, discussion of authenticity has proliferated, since it inherently embodies a myriad of concepts, such as postmodernity, tradition, culture, heritage, legacies, commodification, performance and many others.

The term 'commodification' is used to refer to situations in which a price is placed on artefacts or experiences which were previously not for sale so that cultural expressions become marketable tourism products. The commodification of tourism has been criticized as the 'bastardization' and 'pollution' of previously authentic ethnic cultures for the purpose of touristic display (Wood, 1998). Touristic ethnicity, in other words, is phoney ethnicity, as seen in the so-called airport art and fake ethnic souvenirs. Such tourism is seen as being a 'development which has the power to dilute unique and authentic traditions with standardised stereotypes tailored to the exotic yearnings of the Western traveller' (Oakes, 1992: 3).

There is a growing consensus (Cohen, 1988) that authenticity is a negotiable concept depending upon state regulations, visitors, tourism businesses and host communities and their knowledge of, and belief in, their 'own' past. Each stakeholder can create their own subjective framework of what constitutes the authentic aspects of ethnic tourism. The pursuit of authenticity is what Michel Foucault refers to as 'regimes of truth', involving tensions between authority and autonomy, localization and globalization, evolution and museumification. Shepherd (2002: 196) argues that the current research on authenticity should have 'less focus on identifying what has been commodified and hence no longer counts as "authentic" and more attention on the question of how authenticity is constructed and gets decided'. Ryan (2003) further queries whether 'authenticity' is an adequate framework of analysis and proposes 'authorisation' as a more appropriate term. This is very similar to our perspective in advocating an emphasis on authentication, which is the process through which it is decided whether or not something is authentic. In other words, the authentic is not a fixed property of an object or a situation, but is a negotiated attribute with multiple dimensions whose status is evaluated differently by different assessors. Meanwhile, commodification does not necessarily degrade aboriginal culture; rather, it could be a 'necessary evil' of cultural revival, further suggesting a more complex perspective: that commodification and authenticity are not a dichotomous pair of concepts. Commodification does not necessarily destroy the meaning of cultural products, either for the locals or for the tourists (Cohen, 1988). Commodification of cultural expressions can be interpreted as a means of marking and valuing identity and a step in the finding of the true self through the appropriation of heritage. Furthermore, if hosts are to benefit economically from tourism, it is essential that money is extracted from their visitors.

One of the most notable deficiencies in the existing literature is a lack of attention to the concept of authentication. In other words, there is a dearth of research that seeks to understand who authenticates cultural tourism resources and products: the indigenous peoples, governments at various levels, tourists, or other participants in the tourism system, and how they do this. This chapter suggests, by using a case study of ethnic visitor attractions in Hainan, China, that the concept of authentication not only provides a way of avoiding personal value-laden judgements of authenticity, it is also a practical way of addressing issues of authenticity.

Dimensions of authenticity and authentication

Folk villages are purpose-built visitor attractions that provide visitors with access to expressions of folk culture for a fee. They are essentially small theme parks in which the theme is ethnicity. Folk villages constitute one of the most visible manifestations of ethnic tourism in Hainan, and are probably the most common sites of interaction between members of ethnic minorities and tourists. As such, they provide significant and convenient points of access for the investigation of relationships between tourism and ethnic cultures.

Among the many groups of people with interests in tourism in folk villages, four key stakeholders were identified for investigation: (i) governments at various levels; (ii) tourism businesses, that is, the folk village managers; (iii) visitors and (iv) ethnic communities, in this case represented by dancers performing in the folk villages. Building upon the work of Swain (1989), it is suggested that stakeholders, in their evaluation and attribution of authenticity, may be assessed according to their positions on five continua:

1. *Spontaneity versus commercialism*: this is essentially an indicator of the degree of commodification (Wood, 1997).
2. *Economic development versus cultural preservation*: development implies change and although many changes may be desired, not all changes are desirable. This dimension thus suggests a possible tension and trade-off between economic enhancement and cultural maintenance.
3. *Cultural evolution versus museumification* (the 'freezing' of culture): dynamic cultures are not static but evolve. Thus, although there are signs and symbols with strong associations with particular ethnic groups, this perspective suggests a more 'situational' view of culture (Hitchcock, 2001; Rex, 1986), with ethnicity being continually renegotiated.
4. *Ethnic autonomy versus state regulation*: in the case of ethnic minorities, this dimension contrasts the common desire of minority peoples to control their own destinies in the face of the power that is commonly vested in the majority and the state (Oakes, 1992, 1998).
5. *Mass tourism versus sustainable cultural development*: this dimension contrasts a desire to seek tourism development at almost any cost against a perspective that sees tourism as one possible means of contributing to the well-being of communities, economically, environmentally and socially.

These continua constitute paradoxes and tensions within cultural tourism, and they occur because of the inherent contradictions between stability and change that are found in processes of development. The situation is further complicated by the fact that vibrant cultures are not static but evolve through time. For example, the concepts of spontaneity and commercialism appear to be antithetical. However, it can be countered that commodification may actually be a mechanism that can be used to protect cultural resources and revitalize indigenous cultures. Furthermore, fees may be charged for some cultural experiences and not for others. Destinations that selectively transform cultural resources into tangible products, including visitor attractions, not only facilitate the exchange of cultural experiences for a financial return, they have the potential to create a situation in which sustainable development can be promoted through the careful management of resources. Although ethnic communities may be highly vulnerable to the commercial exploitation of their culture, this does not mean that all commercialism is undesirable. In fact, even though there are risks, ethnic communities stand to benefit significantly from tourism through the associated economic development.

Standardization of ethnic culture through state regulation can lead to the production of staged events such as folk dance performances and costumed photo sessions. However, a focus on the ethnic minority as a tourism resource may also serve as a basis for negotiations between the state and minority communities. Thus, cultural tourism may provide minority groups with a forum for making claims about themselves that may eventually be turned into enhanced local autonomy.

Tourists often expect ethnic minorities to be quaintly traditional: in a state of 'museumification'. While some social and cultural changes are likely to result from tourism and may even be desired, economic development may act as a catalyst for cultural preservation through the enhanced values that are accorded to traditional ways. Thus, at the same time, economic benefits may enhance local standards of living and contribute to the conservation of aspects of ethnic culture.

Mass tourism may cause environmental degradation and a potential clash between cultures. However, selectively choosing or excluding expressions of culture for presentation to tourists may keep sacred or special aspects of culture from being denigrated by mass tourism. Furthermore, staged performances in purpose-built tourist villages or other predetermined locations, may relieve pressures of mass tourism on places that are culturally or environmentally sensitive (Buck, 1978; MacCannell, 1973).

As is implied by the above discussion, the five dimensions in the framework are neither distinct nor easy to quantify. Furthermore, it is not suggested that any one of these dimensions or any particular polar position is inherently superior to another. However, it is suggested that together they provide a more tractable way of approaching authenticity. These components are presented in the form of a conceptual model in Figure 8.1. In this chapter, these dimensions are used to organize the perspectives of the stakeholders in cultural tourism in Hainan folk villages.

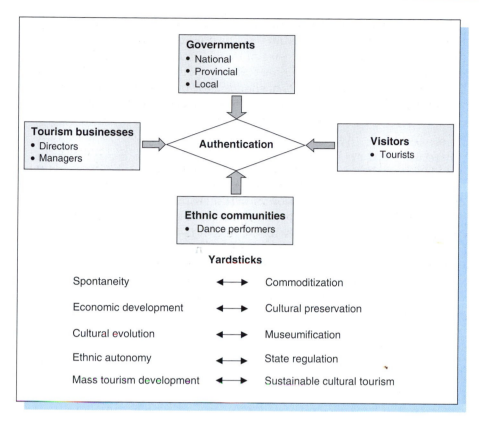

Figure 8.1
A conceptual framework for authentication

The data for the study were collected in Summer 1999 using a variety of research methods. They can be briefly summarized as follows:

1. Locations of folk villages were identified by examining tourism brochures and interviewing tourism authorities.
2. All folk villages were visited, photographed and inventories of their tourism offerings were made (a total of twelve villages, three of them had gone out of business). A map was constructed for the distribution of villages. Managers of the folk villages were interviewed to ascertain information on their perceptions of authenticity.
3. Interviews were conducted with employees of folk villages and, for three sites, with visitors. A total of 139 employees in the folk villages were interviewed (the majority were dance performers). A survey was conducted with visitors to three selected villages and a total of 586 surveys was completed and returned.

Case Study: Ethnic tourism in Hainan

Hainan is a large tropical island located off the southern coast of China. It has a total land area of 33 900 square km² (Figure 8.2). The island was administered by the government of Guangdong Province until 1988 when it became a province. As a special economic zone (SEZ), Hainan is more readily accessible to investors and travellers than most parts of China. While SEZ status has resulted in mixed success with respect to economic development, the ready access to both people and investments that this designation affords is advantageous to tourism. Hainan's tropical climate, splendid beaches, spas, attractive landscapes, cuisine and cultural diversity constitute a solid base on which tourism can be built. Indeed, tourism is already an important economic sector in Hainan. There is a substantial complement of excellent hotels and supporting infrastructure, such as highways and airports. The number of visitors and total visitor expenditures have been expanding annually, the former having grown substantially from just over 750 000 in 1987 to nearly 5 million in 1996 (Chen, 1998), over 7 million in 2001 and, according to provincial tourism statistics, more than 14 million hotel registrations, involving some double counting of visitors, in 2004.

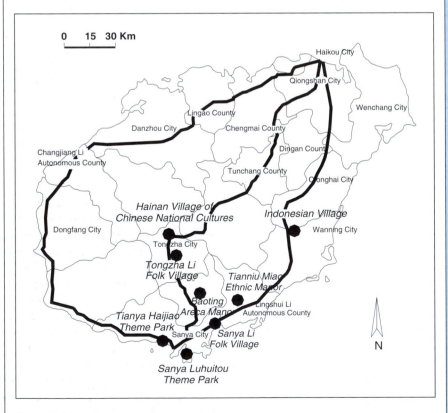

Figure 8.2
A map of Hainan and the folk villages

Nonetheless, the Hainan tourism industry faces many challenges. Most visitors come from mainland China and the number of international visitors continues to be small. While the number of domestic visitors has increased, occupancy rates in hotels declined for many years because of oversupply and many, if not most hotels, operated at a loss. There is a difficulty in finding skilled labour in Hainan and migrants from the mainland take many tourism positions. Members of ethnic minorities, who could make important and distinctive contributions to tourism, are minimally employed in tourism except for some involvement in the informal sector. Thus, while Hainan has great tourism potential, this potential has yet to be realized.

There are 55 ethnic minorities in China that are officially recognized by the Chinese government. They make up 8 per cent of the population, totalling about 96 million people and occupying about 65 per cent of China's total area (Sofield and Li, 1998). While minorities are usually accorded low status in China, tourism has become the most promising industry for Chinese ethnic community development (Swain, 1993).

In Hainan, the Li minority numbers more than 1 million people. Hainan is also home to other ethnic groups including Miao and Hui, each with a population of approximately 60 000 and 10 000, respectively (Hainan Tour Atlas, 1997). Minority populations are concentrated in the south-central part of the island, in the Li and Miao Autonomous Prefecture. The Prefecture covers an area of 1169 square km^2 and has a population of 100 000, 59 per cent of whom are Li (Hainan Tour Atlas, 1997). In addition, there are locations in Hainan with Hui (Moslem) and Indonesian Chinese minorities. Although minority populations are not heavily involved in tourism, their existence is widely publicized in tourism brochures. A number of folk villages have been established where song and dance performances, the enactment of ceremonies, and the availability of ethnic foods and souvenirs provide opportunities for visitors to become acquainted with ethnic cultures (Figure 8.3).

Key issues in the authentication of ethnic tourism in Hainan

Space does not permit the full reporting of all the findings of the research project. Some highlights of the results will be presented for each of the four main stakeholder groups across most of the five continua identified in the framework. In this way, differences in the positions of the stakeholders with respect to ethnic tourism, particularly at folk village attractions, will be revealed.

Governments

National, provincial and local governments all play a part in tourism. At the national level, because national unity is the major guideline when developing ethnic tourism, control is an important issue in the presentation of culture. The national government plays a dual role in authenticating the cultural resources. On the one hand, it supports cultural distinctiveness for economic development, particularly of tourism; on the other hand, it suppresses any 'true' autonomous rights. In terms of commodification, the national government standardizes ethnic markers to fill a symbolic and commercial niche for public gaze. Ethnic attractions, such as tourist folk villages, have been commodified with the support of state policies. In terms of cultural evolution, the policies of the national government seek to 'fossilize' certain

Figure 8.3
The gate of Hainan Folk Village in Baoting County

aspects of cultural tradition, drawing distinct boundaries around local customs, fix-ing them in time and space, and ensuring they remain encased as exhibits for the modern tourists to observe and appreciate. State policies also encourage the Li to be more 'developed' and 'modernized'. The direction of evolution can be seen as a process of 'Hanification', in which the Li minority is subsumed into the Han major-ity (Xie, 2003). The national government places great emphasis on job creation, therefore, cultural tourism is viewed as one of the best ways to minimize the high unemployment rate in ethnic communities. Economic functions have been given precedence and cultural preservation has not received much attention from the national government.

At the provincial level, the focus has also been on economic development and tourism has been identified as Hainan's leading economic sector. The rapid development of tourism holds out the prospect of substantial benefits to the Li communities. Although Li folk villages have been built in response to increased interest from domestic tourists, most administrative positions are occupied by Han people who generally have little knowledge of Li culture. The provincial gov-ernment pays little attention to the negative sides of commodification and muse-umification of ethnic cultures. Instead, mass tourism is highly encouraged by the provincial government. Although sustainable development plans for Hainan have been proposed by the provincial government, it is not clear how these will be implemented.

In the past, agriculture was essentially the only source of income for the Li communities. Tourism is, therefore, a novel idea for the local government and the impacts on the aboriginal communities have yet to be appreciated. Local government plays a passive role in finding a balance between culture and commodification.

Tourism businesses

Village managers pay more attention to attracting and satisfying the tourists rather than presenting authentic aspects of Li culture. The management of the folk villages insists on 'livening things up' so that the visitors will not get bored. They have reduced the length of the 'traditional' dance and incorporate a visitor participation programme at the end. Some employees in the newer villages who wear Li clothing are not of Li origin and, for some, ethnic clothing has become a business uniform and the 'traditional' dance performances have become 'manufactured' routines. Ethnic presentation is in a state of 'museumification', portraying traditional aspects of Li culture as ancient, exotic and fossilized.

Since the business hinges upon the number of tourist arrivals, mass tourism is used to exploit ethnicity for economic purposes. Although tourism businesses could play a key role in balancing cultural preservation and economic development, profit is the major concern. Folk villages have become a combination of ethnic presentations and sales outlets from the numerous vendor stands. The manipulation of ethnic dance programmes and other ethnic cultural events to serve economic interests has resulted in the loss of authenticity and educational value. Spectacle and entertainment are emphasized and authenticity appears to be a flexible notion in folk villages. The concept of sustainable cultural tourism is not widely appreciated or applied.

Visitors

Almost all of the tourists (98 per cent) come from mainland China and visit folk villages as part of organized tours. Direct contact with the ethnic minority is limited and tourism businesses almost always play an intermediary role. Their stop at a folk village is only one of many places visited on a three- or four-day excursion.

Although tourists are interested in ethnic cultures, the majority have little knowledge of ethnicity. They usually lack the time and the depth of experience to understand the more complex and intricate aspects of ethnic culture. They are not well prepared for a tour of a village and their knowledge on ethnicity is generally superficial. As such, it is more appropriate to see them as 'coincidental' cultural tourists rather than as true cultural tourists (Xie and Wall, 2002). Although tourists expect to see non-commercial and non-contrived aspects of ethnic presentation in the villages, the place they visit is, in fact, a highly commercial attraction. Most visitors enjoy their experiences as the villages endeavour to satisfy the touristic gaze and turn ethnicity into 'hyper-reality'.

Ethnic communities

In this research, attention was focused upon dancers as community representatives (Wall and Xie, 2005). In fact the performances are spectacles and the dancers are a young, beautiful and predominantly female subset of Li people. Their performances emphasize romantic aspects of the Li lifestyle and, as such, cannot represent Li culture in its entirety. Nevertheless, dancers are appropriate individuals to consult concerning the authenticity of cultural tourism because they share aspects of their culture with tourists, interact with tourists, are positioned on the interface between tourism and culture on an ongoing basis, and have familiarity with the compromises and trade-offs required to provide an attractive tourism product.

Economic matters are most important for dance performers and skills in ethnic dancing are turned into a good way to make money. They are paid relatively well and the village proprietors strive to make a profit; they are asked to perform as long as tourists visit the village. Mass tourism is seen by dancers as being an optimal strategy since the business prospects for dance performers hinges upon the number of tourist arrivals.

Conclusion

This chapter has provided an overview of the diverse perspectives concerning authenticity of experience as applied to ethnic tourism in general and visitor attractions in particular. It has been suggested that authenticity is not an attribute that is inherent to a place or product, such as a tourist destination or visitor attraction. Rather, it is a status that is ascribed externally. Nevertheless, although authenticity is difficult to define, managers of cultural visitor attractions will be expected to provide authentic experiences as judged by many of their visitors and failure to do so may result in a reduced level of visitor satisfaction. However, the visitors themselves may have divergent views on authenticity and these may differ from those held by other stakeholders, including members of the ethnic group whose culture is being shared with the visitors. As such, the process of authentication merits much more attention than it has hitherto received.

A conceptual framework has been presented, and its utility illustrated through application to ethnic visitor attractions in Hainan, China. It has been shown that different stakeholders exhibit different positions with respect to the various paradoxes associated with authenticity. These positions serve different interests. Thus, for example, in the case of Hainan folk villages, managers have predominantly commercial concerns and strive to make a profit, governments see tourism as a means to stimulate economic development and the employees of the villages welcome economic opportunities in a poor area where job opportunities are few. The tourists do not have high expectations and are largely not in Hainan primarily as cultural tourists. They generally enjoy their visits but would welcome more detailed explanations of the culture that they experience and, in some cases, the availability of more interesting souvenirs. Culture is presented as a series of spectacles and only limited concern appears to exist at present for cultural conservation or for sustainable tourism development more broadly conceived. Although conflicts appear to be few at present, it would be a constructive step to encourage dialogue between representatives of the differing stakeholder groups, perhaps through the organization of 'round tables' so that they can appreciate each other's positions, perhaps leading to an enhancement of their mutual interests.

Is Li culture as portrayed in the folk village attractions of Hainan authentic? This seemingly simple question does not have a simple answer. On the evidence that has been presented, strong cases can be made for both an affirmative and a negative response. Authenticity is not a one-dimensional concept that lends itself to simple interpretation. Nevertheless, it is possible to explore the issues that underpin authentication, as has been done in this chapter. Authenticity is elusive (and often illusive); the investigation of authentication offers a tractable way forward.

References

Altman, J. (1989). Tourism dilemmas for aboriginal Australians. *Annals of Tourism Research*, **16**, 449–456.

Barth, F. (1969). *Ethnic Groups and Boundaries*. Norwegian University Press.

Boorstin, D. (1964). *A Guide to Pseudo-Events in America.* Harper and Row.

Buck, R. (1978). Boundary maintenance revisited: tourist experiences in an old order Amish community. *Rural Sociology*, **43**, 195–207.

Butler, R. and Hinch, T. (1996). *Tourism and Indigenous Peoples*. International Thomson Business Press.

Chen, Y. (1998). South China's legendary island. *China Tourism*, **2**, 6–7.

Cohen, E. (1988). Authenticity and commoditization in tourism. *Annals of Tourism Research*, **15**, 371–386.

Cohen, R. (1978). Ethnicity: problem and focus in Anthropology. *Annual Review of Anthropology*, **7**, 379–403.

Conran, M. (2006). Commentary: beyond authenticity – exploring intimacy in the touristic encounter in Thailand. *Tourism Geographies*, **8**, 274–285.

Esman, M. (1984). Tourism as ethnic preservation: the Cajuns of Louisiana. *Annals of Tourism Research*, **11**, 451–467.

Fridgen, J. (1996). *Dimensions of Tourism.* Educational Institute of American Hotel & Motel Association.

Graburn, N. (1984). The evolution of tourist arts. *Annals of Tourism Research*, **11**, 393–449.

Hainan Tour Atlas (1997). Measurement Publishing Ltd.

Hitchcock, M. (2001). Anthropological reflections on the study of tourism. In *Contemporary Perspectives on Tourism* (G. Wall, ed), pp. 109–128. University of Waterloo.

Jackson, P. (1999). Commodity cultures: the traffic in things. *Transactions of the Institute of British Geographers*, **24**, 95–108.

Jamal, T. and Hill, S. (2004). Developing a framework for indicators of authenticity: the place and space of cultural and heritage tourism. *Asia Pacific Journal of Tourism Research*, **9**, 353–371.

Kelly, R. (1994). The cultural tourist: friend or foe? *Focus on Culture: Statistics Canada*, **6**, 1–3.

Li, Y. and Hinch, T. (1998). Ethnic tourism attractions and their prospects for sustainable development at two sites in China and Canada. *Asia Pacific Journal of Tourism Research*, **2**, 5–17.

Lowenthal, D. (1985). *The Past is a Foreign Country.* Cambridge University Press.

Lowenthal, D. (1996). *The Possessed by the Past: Heritage Crusade and the Spoils of History*. The Free Press.

MacCannell, D. (1973). Staged authenticity: arrangements of social space in tourist settings. *American Journal of Sociology*, **79**, 589–603.

MacCannell, D. (1976). *The Tourist: A New Theory of the Leisure Class*. Schoken Books.

Mason, K. (2004). Sound and meaning in aboriginal tourism. *Annals of Tourism Research*, **31**, 837–854.

Mathieson, A. and Wall, G. (1982). *Tourism: Economic, Physical, and Social Impacts*. Longman.

McKean, P. (1973). Cultural involution: tourists, Balinese, and the process of modernization in anthropological perspective. PhD thesis, Brown University.

Moscardo, G. and Pearce, P. (1999). Understanding ethnic tourists. *Annals of Tourism Research*, **26**, 416–434.

Oakes, T. (1992). Cultural geography and Chinese ethnic tourism. *Journal of Cultural Geography*, **12**, 2–17.

Oakes, T. (1998). *Tourism and Modernity in China*. Routledge.

Picard, M. (1990). Cultural tourism in Bali: cultural performances as visitor attraction. *Indonesia*, **49**, 37–74.

Picard, M. (1995). Cultural heritage and tourist capital: cultural tourism in Bali. In *International Tourism: Identity and Change* (M. Lanfant., J. Allcock and E. Bruner, eds), pp. 44–66. Sage Studies in International Sociology.

Picard, M. and Wood, R. (1997). *Tourism, Ethnicity, and the State in Asian and Pacific Societies*. University of Hawaii Press.

Pigram, J. (1993). Planning for tourism in rural areas: bridging the policy implementation gap. In *Tourism Research: Critiques and Challenges* (D. Pearce and R. Butler, eds), pp. 156–174. Routledge.

Pitchford, S. (1995). Ethnic tourism and nationalism in Wales. *Annals of Tourism Research*, **22**, 35–52.

Poole, M. (1997). In search of ethnicity in Ireland. In *In Search of Ireland: A Cultural Geography* (B. Graham, ed), pp. 151–73. Routledge.

Reisinger, Y. (1994). Tourist–host contact as a part of cultural tourism. *World Leisure and Recreation*, **36**, 24–28.

Rex, J. (1986). *Race and Ethnicity*. Open University Press.

Richards, G. (1996). *Cultural Tourism in Europe*. CABI.

Ryan, C. (2003). *Recreational Tourism: Demand and Impacts*. Multilingual Matters.

Ryan, C. and Aicken, M. (2005). *Indigenous Tourism: The Commodification and Management of Culture*. Elsevier.

Ryan, C. and Huyton, J. (2000). Aboriginal tourism: a linear structural relations analysis of domestic and international tourist demand. *International Journal of Tourism Research*, **2**, 15–29.

Shepherd, R. (2002). Commodification, culture and tourism. *Tourist Studies*, **2**, 183–201.

Smith, V. (1989). *Host and Guests: The Anthropology of Tourism*. University of Pennsylvania Press.

Sofield, T. and Li, F. (1998). Tourism development and cultural policies in China. *Annals of Tourism Research*, **25**, 362–392.

Swain, M. (1989). Developing ethnic tourism in Hunnan, China: Shilin Sani. *Tourism Recreation Research*, **14**, 33–39.

Swain, M. (1993). Women producers of ethnic arts. *Annals of Tourism Research*, **20**, 32–51.

Tunbridge, J. and Ashworth, G. (1996). *Dissonant Heritage: Management of the Past as a Resource in Conflict*. Wiley.

Turner, L. and Ash, J. (1975). *The Golden Hordes: International Tourism and the Pleasure Periphery*. Constable.

van den Berghe, P. and Keyes, C. (1984). Introduction: tourism and re-created ethnicity. *Annals of Tourism Research*, **11**, 343–352.

Wall, G. (1996). Perspectives on tourism in selected Balinese villages. *Annals of Tourism Research*, **23**, 123–137.

Wall, G. and Mathieson, A. (2006). *Tourism: Change, Impacts and Opportunities*. Pearson/Prentice Hall.

Wall, G. and Xie, P. (2005). Authenticating ethnic tourism: Li dancers' perspectives. *Asia Pacific Journal of Tourism Research*, **10**, 1–21.

Wang, N. (1999). Rethinking authenticity in tourism experience. *Annals of Tourism Research*, **26**, 349–370.

Wood, R. (1980). International tourism and cultural change in Southeast Asia. *Economic Development and Cultural Change*, **28**, 561–581.

Wood, R. (1997). Tourism and the state. In *Tourism, Ethnicity, and the State in Asian and Pacific Societies* (M. Picard and R. Wood, eds), pp. 1–34. University of Hawaii Press.

Wood, R. (1998). Book review. Bali: cultural tourism and touristic culture. *Annals of Tourism Research*, **25**, 770–772.

Xie, P. (2003). The bamboo-beating dance in Hainan, China: authenticity and commodification. *Journal of Sustainable Tourism*, **11**, 5–17.

Xie, P. and Wall, G. (2002). Visitors' perceptions of authenticity at cultural attractions in Hainan, China. *International Journal of Tourism Research*, **4**, 353–366.

Rediscovering the Imagination: Meeting the Needs of the 'New' Visitor

Richard Voase

Aims

The aims of this chapter are to:

- explain how 'new' visitors are a product of cultural postmodernization,
- introduce two kinds of new visitor: 'thoughtful' and 'smart',
- show how 'active' and 'passive' modes of experience require re-definition,
- suggest that the alleged 'dumbing down' of culture is a fallacy, and
- recommend the strategy of ensuring a 'popular' threshold of engagement.

Introduction

This chapter aims to offer insights into the character of the 'new' visitor, into the visitor experience and into the act of consumption by which the visitor ingests experiences. Its content applies principally to visitor attractions of a cultural or heritage nature, but there are also wider implications. There are four key features to this chapter. The first is an examination of discourses in common circulation: discourses about the 'thoughtful' consumer, the 'smart' consumer and the 'dumbing down' of culture. The second is the impact of technological change on the way in which human beings use and consume information: this has been termed 'cultural postmodernization'. The third is an examination of the way satisfactions are generated by an encounter with a visitor attraction. An important dynamic is the relationship between the so-called active and passive modes of consumption; and it will be seen that a re-evaluation of our understanding of these terms is desirable. The fourth proposes personal narratives as a paradigm by which the act of consumption, and the meanings that visitors construct in their minds from an encounter with an attraction, can be understood. The chapter concludes by suggesting that a 'popular' approach to the promotion of cultural and heritage attractions is a recommended and rational strategy for engaging the 'new' visitor. A case study of the Royal Armouries Museum, Leeds, UK, documents the *prima facie* effectiveness of such a strategy in a major heritage-based visitor attraction. A second case study, which reports research into the visitor experience undertaken for the Dean and Chapter of one of England's cathedrals, offers evidence of why such a strategy was successful.

'Discourse' and 'ideology'

In order to make this study fully intelligible, it is important to clarify the meanings attached to these two terms. A 'discourse' is a recurring message, or set of messages, which passes back and forth across a range of forms of communication. For example, the alleged dumbing down of culture is a charge which may be advanced by intellectuals who are cultural conservatives; it thus becomes the subject of comment in broadsheet newspapers. It is then discussed around tables in public houses, and also features in academic books such as this one. Thus, the phrase 'dumbing down', and the views attending it, constitute a discourse. 'Ideologies', by contrast, are as invisible as discourses are visible. They are embedded in discourses; they are obscure but powerful meanings which underpin a discourse (Purvis and Hunt, 1993). So, for example, the ideology embedded in the dumbing-down discourse is that to be 'dumb' is a mark of undesirability. The reader might take the point of view that the undesirability of dumbness is so obvious that there is no need for discussion. This point of view would be, in fact, clear evidence of an ideology at work (see Althusser, 1992). When such ideologies are contested, the result can be refreshingly entertaining. The film *Forrest Gump* was an affectionate portrayal of a protagonist whose wisdom and humanity more than compensated for his lack of intellectual prowess. Ideologies are rooted in ideas; they are constructs for shaping meanings rather than templates for realities.

Cultural postmodernization

The most comprehensive study of the theorized cultural shift from a condition of modernity to postmodernity, and its impact upon tourism, is that of Urry (1990). This chapter is not the place to rehearse the full range and complexity of these arguments, but one aspect of the debate is crucial to the present purpose and it is summarized here. The starting point is the miniaturization and spread of informational technology and its consequences (Lyotard, 1984), which unfolds as follows. The increase in television output by means of satellite transmission and augmentation of terrestrial channels, the cheapening and proliferation of desktop computer technology and, most recently, the arrival of the Internet and World Wide Web, have progressively led to a saturating of populations in the advanced world with informational messages. This has led to a democratization of knowledge; everyone can become an 'expert' of sorts. A highly informed, highly educated, well-travelled population is less easily led by appeals to traditional loyalties, such as nation, class, trade union or political affiliation. Hence, individuals are more apt to gather around issues which they themselves have chosen, leading to the proliferation of special-interest groups around environmental issues, conservation, alternative medicine, and so on (Economist, 1994). As individuals gather around chosen interests rather than around traditional loyalties, traditional methods of classifying people and anticipating their behavioural and consumption habits, by socio-economic classification, place of residence, level of education and gender, become increasingly challenged. A structural de-differentiation within society has emerged (Lash, 1990).

The proliferation of the transmission of information, and its democratization, has also led to two other consequences. The first involves the blurring of boundaries between cultural forms such as art, music and travel (Jameson, 1984; Laermans, 1992; Urry, 1990). For example, academic history, when popularized through the medium of television, loses its perceived elite status when it shares a medium with soap operas and quiz shows. Similarly, the deployment of three operatic tenors to accompany a soccer World Cup celebration, in Italy in 1990, was arguably instrumental in removing opera, in the perception of the global public, from the opera house to which it had been hitherto confined. The second consequence is that as cultural knowledge proliferates and spreads via the electronic media, it loses, not unexpectedly, some of its depth. For example, to convey the essence of England under the Tudor monarchs within the space of a 50-minute documentary, and make it engaging television, demands some selection of material. Similarly, a global football crowd may be enchanted by five minutes of the aria *Nessun Dorma*, but may baulk at the prospect of enduring the full duration of the opera from which it was extracted. The demands of the medium become predominant, or as McLuhan memorably observed, 'the medium is the message' (McLuhan and Zingrone, 1997: 151). In the words of Jameson (1984: 60), the consequence is 'the emergence of a new kind of flatness or depthlessness, a new kind of superficiality in the most literal sense'.

The second consequence, crucial to our present understanding, is that this proliferation of knowledge involves not just the dissemination of superficial expertise, but its commercialization and commodification. 'Knowledge is and will be produced in order to be sold, it is and will be consumed in order to be valorised in a new production: in both cases, the goal is exchange' (Lyotard, 1984: 4). So knowledge proliferates and enables the individual to acquire expertise, and increasingly it proliferates on the basis of economic exchange. For example, that which is known as 'heritage' is arguably 'history' in a selected, packaged and consumable form.

The new visitor

At this point the question of the 'new' visitor is addressed. Most practitioners and academics agree that visitors are changing, and that the newness has something to do with increasing levels of sophistication. But like the 'new tourism' (Poon, 1989), the 'new museology' (Vergo, 1989), *The New Sex*[1] and, for that matter, 'New Labour' (Fairclough, 2000), the newness is defined in very general terms. The new visitor is in danger of becoming, if he or she is not one already, a discourse. However, there are already two marked discourses concerning consumer types which have been circulating in recent years, and an appraisal of these reveals that cultural postmodernization has arguably produced, simultaneously, two very different species of sophisticated new consumer.

The first of these will be styled the 'thoughtful consumer'. In the early 1990s, consultants and research organizations began suggesting that future consumers would be variously 'added-value seekers' (Henley Centre for Forecasting, 1992) and 'thoughtful consumers' (Martin and Mason, 1993). These new consumers were discursively linked, in terms of their interest in visitor attractions, with 'a shift in emphasis from passive fun to active learning' (Martin and Mason, 1993: 34) and a general interest in active rather than passive leisure pursuits (Euromonitor, 1992). Ideologically, the discourse was the bearer of assumed values of active = thoughtful = learning. Implicit in these linkages is an assumed binary opposition with passivity, which in turn can be linked with the opposite of whatever 'thoughtful' may be – 'dumb', perhaps? The point to be understood is that these linkages, in ideologically set combinations, are erroneous and misleading. Obviously, it is possible to be an educated person and enjoy passive pursuits. Equally, it is a mistake to conclude that thoughtful people, on a day out, expect to assume an active burden for digesting the experience on offer at a cultural or heritage attraction. These new consumers, sated with messages about the past which are as depthless as they are democratized, embark on a love affair with history in its consumable form, known to us as 'heritage'. This presents challenges to museums professionals; see Davies (1989) for an illustration of the intensity of the debate at the end of the 1980s.

The second species of sophisticated new consumer will be termed the 'smart consumer'. If the thoughtful consumer responds primarily to the postmodernization of knowledge in terms of its proliferation and accessibility, the smart consumer responds primarily to its commodified character. The discourse of smartness appears to have begun, like the discourse of thoughtfulness, in the early 1990s. Allied victory in the first Gulf War was aided by the deployment of 'smart' missiles, which know where they are going. Some automobile manufacturers have produced smart cars, which are unconventionally effective in urban driving and parking situations. Similarly, marketing staff at two major

---

[1] The title of the first book by the fictional anti-hero, Howard Kirk, in Malcolm Bradbury's celebrated novel *The History Man*.

cultural/heritage attractions, in discussions relating to the changing nature of consumers, reported the existence of both the thoughtful consumers, who were ready to engage with the collections, and smart consumers, who were alert to commercial gimmickry and who saw the visit essentially in terms of a transaction, in which economic exchange value was a key feature. These smart visitors were, in essence, consumers who had lost their innocence (Voase, 2002). A hypothetical example may illustrate the difference. A thoughtful and a smart consumer both buy a comparable work of art by a contemporary artist. The thoughtful consumer buys it because he or she likes it, and because the picture resonates with values and memories deep in his or her personal psyche. The smart consumer also quite likes the picture, but the primary product benefit is that the work will increase in pecuniary value. The author would also like to point out that he regards these rationales for ownership to be different from the rationale, so meticulously researched by Bourdieu (1984), whereby original works of art are appropriated as a means of demonstrating social distinction.

'Consuming' the visitor attraction

How do visitors consume the objects and interpretive material which they encounter in a visitor attraction? The vital point is that meaning is not intrinsic to externalities, such as the objects and interpretive material encountered in a museum, but is authored by the visitor in his or her own mind (Campbell, 1990). Meaning resides not in externalities but is defined in the mind of the reader at the point of reading; an insight afforded by the analytic paradigm known as post-structuralism. Outside of an encounter between a reader and a text, there is no meaning. As Derrida (1998: 158) famously observed, 'il n'y a pas de hors-texte' (there is no outside text). In Campbell's (1994: 510) words, 'the individual can be seen as an artist of the imagination, someone who takes images from memory or the immediate environment and rearranges or otherwise improves them so as to render them more pleasing.'

This effect was ably demonstrated by research undertaken at Madame Tussauds, in London, during the 1980s. What was apparent was that the satisfactions which visitors derived from the encounter with a wax figure did not reside in the artistry with which the likeness had been fashioned. Rather, satisfaction resided in the exploration of the memories, feelings and emotions which the visitor associated with the person represented by the wax figure. As a result, Madame Tussauds was re-modelled. Wax figures were removed from their roped-off compounds and placed into settings where visitors could walk around them, touch them and simulate interaction with the person represented by the figure. This relationship could be further simulated by having oneself photographed with the wax figure, photography having been a practice which hitherto, at Madame Tussauds, had been proscribed (Yorkshire TV, 1986).

The implication is that visitors, for example people coming to a museum, will bring with them, in their minds, a set of memories acquired through previous exposure to the subject matter represented by the collections and a set of anticipations based on those memories and constructed through day-dreaming (Campbell, 1994; Kelly, 1997). These daydreams, we can be certain, will not be anticipations based on purely intellectual memories. For example, in the case of a museum displaying and interpreting weapons of war, the anticipations are more likely to relate to personal memories of relatives involved in armed conflict, the fear experienced while watching documentary footage of war situations or simulations in fictional war films, and vicarious concern for victims. Daydreams are not primarily constructs of the intellect; they are constructs of the emotions. As shall be seen, such insights have formed the basis for the promotional strategy of the first case study chosen for this chapter, the Royal Armouries Museum in Leeds.

First, however, further comment is needed with regard to the two discursive features mentioned earlier, and which are arguably crucial to an understanding of the landscape of contemporary consumption. The first will be styled 'the dialectic of the active and the passive', the second 'the discourse of dumbing down'.

The dialectic of the active and passive

It has been shown earlier that agents of the circulation of the discourses surrounding the new consumer are apt to link 'active' modes of consumption with thoughtfulness and learning, and 'passive' modes with fun and whatever may be implied to be in binary opposition to 'learned'. The suggested term was 'dumb'. It has been argued that these ideological linkages are erroneous and misleading. However, there are deeper problems. The first is that it is arguably unsafe to assume that terms such as 'active' and 'passive' are in binary opposition to one another. Rather, they are extremes on a continuum of experience. For example, angling is an essentially passive pastime. It involves sitting by a river or canal for many hours, waiting for a fish to bite. But a retired person who pursues angling as an interest would be discursively regarded as active, and may attract comments such as, 'oh yes, he is very active, he gets himself out once a week to go angling'. Similarly, a group of young friends travelling by train to an arena in a city to hear Robbie Williams issue his injunction to 'Let Me Entertain You' are active in constructing and organizing a day out, even if, as audience members at the concert, they are essentially passive and it is Mr Williams who is doing the entertaining.

The second problem with attempting to label certain pursuits as active and passive is that many pursuits are difficult to categorize in this way. Take, for example, the reading of books. To sit in an armchair for an hour is not most pundits' idea of active consumption, but in a very real sense book reading is active in that it is a mental activity requiring the deployment of intellectual skill. Moreover, the precondition for book reading is the equally active task of informing oneself of what is available, selecting a book and borrowing or buying it. And it does indeed appear that British people are becoming more active as readers and owners of books. In 2004, two-thirds of adults were in the habit of reading books, compared with a little over one half in 1976 (ONS, 1998, 2004). This increased bookishness is not entirely surprising when one considers the major increases in admissions to tertiary education in the UK – an increase from just over 700 000 in 1976 to 2.2 million in 2005 (THES, 2006). And within that period there was an increase of 75 per cent between 1990 and 1995 alone (Marshall, 2001).

It is maybe useful to contrast the intellectually active but physically passive pursuit of book reading with that other armchair pursuit, television viewing. This is widely regarded as the apogee of passive consumption. Televised output has of course expanded greatly during the last twenty years. For example, over the six-year period from 1985/86 to 1991/92, average weekly broadcast hours on terrestrial channels in the UK increased from 477 to 632 hours. This represents an increase of 30 per cent, and does not take into account the proliferation of satellite and cable channels over the same period (PSI, 1993). In that respect, the number of UK households with multi-channel facilities (i.e. satellite, cable and digital TV) rose from 2.3 million in 1992 to 18.6 million in 2007 (BARB, 2007). It may therefore come as a surprise to learn that the weekly hours of television viewing by British adults have remained virtually unchanged – from 27.1 hours per week in 1985, to 25.2 hours in 1994 (PSI, 1996), to 26.1 hours in 2003 (ONS, 2006). Admittedly the overall scale of watching remains considerable, but it is clear that television viewing has not expanded in tandem with the expansion of television output. What can perhaps be safely concluded is that viewers are, by necessity if not by disposition, more selective in their viewing. Furthermore, in common with book reading, television viewing now, in contrast with, say, twenty years ago, involves a range of preconditional planning tasks: deciding which programmes to record for future viewing; deciding which satellite, cable or digital channels are suitable for subscription. While less time is being spent on actual viewing, more time and more mental effort is being expended on the act of choice in viewing. So, consideration of the nature of book reading and television viewing strengthens the notion that the UK population is becoming more active and thoughtful in the broadest sense. Why, then, has a whole discourse emerged surrounding the alleged 'dumbing down' of society?

The discourse of dumbing down

First, the nature of this discourse needs to be specified. The gist is that, for example, school examinations are becoming easier, university standards are being lowered by 'trendy' degree courses (Daily Express, 1996; Smithers and Roff, 2000), democratization of culture has led to erosion of standards (Hartley, 1999) and that a concomitant shortening of attention spans has led an assemblage of 'dumbing' effects, including the tabloidization of the broadsheet press (Engel, 1996; Greenslade, 1997). The pervasiveness of sound bite and spectacle in contemporary cultural expression is taken as indicative of a seldom-articulated but clear inference that a dumbed-down culture, hand in glove with a dumbed-down education system, is producing dumb consumers. However, it does not take many moments' reflection to realize that these claims are not based on observations of cultural *consumption*; they are based on observations of cultural *production*. It is arguably fallacious to infer that, because cultural producers allegedly supply dumb material, the consumers themselves are dumb.

Investigative journalism has yielded some interesting comments on school examinations. Those of the present day were found to be no easier than those of a few decades ago. However, they were qualitatively different. The present-day candidate was required to be more competent in explanation, rather than in description. The emphasis had shifted from 'what' and 'how' to 'why'. Also, the present-day papers were apt to be carefully phrased in a contemporary English in order to be easily understood, or in contemporary jargon, 'accessible' (Elliot-Major, 2000). Set against this, there are concerns in recent years about prescriptive approaches to teaching and examining, leading to assessments which are 'too predictable' (QCA, 2007a), and of a 'focused nature' which limits the scope for the students to express themselves (QCA, 2007b). But broadly speaking, there is a dearth of real evidence to suggest that demands on candidates are lower than several decades ago. According to Elliot-Major (2000), at the interface between production and consumption, which can be usefully termed the 'threshold of engagement',[2] the candidate encounters a paper which is friendlier and easier to understand than its equivalent of several decades earlier. Similarly, in the case of broadsheet press, the popularization of approach should not necessarily imply superficiality. One broadsheet editor argued cogently that the deployment of spectacle ('tabloidization') does not necessarily betoken lack of depth (Rusbridger, 2000).

Linking technological change and consumption practices

So, it does not follow from an apparently dumb threshold of engagement, that content is dumb or that consumers are dumb. There remains, however, the question as to why the dumbing down of the threshold occurs, if as has been shown earlier, the new consumers of both kinds are more knowledgeable and sophisticated. Why must the threshold be visually eye-catching (spectacle) or orally ear-catching (sound bite)? For the explanation, we return to the post-modernization of culture and, in particular, the writings of Lyotard. A consequence of the democratization of knowledge, itself a consequence of the miniaturization of machines and the means of transmitting information, argued Lyotard (1984), is that the big, unifying ideas of modernity – we could mention nationhood, organized religion, monolithic political ideologies – no longer carry the influence they once had. Their component parts are still around, in the form of lesser narratives or to use Lyotard's (1984: 37, 60) term,

---

[2] An excellent term for which the author is indebted to Nick Thompson, formerly of the Royal Armouries Museum.

'*petits récits*'. These are arguably identifiable with the proliferating special-interest groups, mentioned earlier, which have been so successful in recruiting support in the past twenty years. The emergence of flexible ('post-Fordist') production and the substantial replacement of mass markets by segmented markets are arguably other manifestations. In this way, technological change can be seen to be the direct antecedent of the proliferation of information as well as its consequence, namely the sating of consuming populations with informational words and images. Quite apart from the explosion of media output of all kinds, the volume of paid advertising in the UK doubled between 1975 and 1991: expenditure rose from £2700 million to £5400 million at constant 1985 prices (Waterson, 1992). From a later dataset, the volume of paid advertising in the UK increased from £12 000 million in 1989 to £16 500 million in 2003 at constant year 2000 prices (Waterson, 2004). As these proliferating lesser narratives all clamour for attention, it is unsurprising that, in order to get their messages heard, the threshold of engagement is popularized. As a result, sound bite and spectacle are now an integral part of journalistic, commercial and political discourse, but this is not to say that content is dumb, nor should it infer that consumers themselves are dumb.

Personal narratives

How do consumers actually ingest the experience generated from an encounter with a visitor attraction? A useful paradigm for understanding this is that of the personal narrative. The point has been made that meanings do not subsist in the objects and displays which the visitor encounters. Rather, meanings are authored in the mind of the visitor. Reference was made to the remodelling of Madame Tussauds, which was based on the insight that visitors' enjoyment of the wax figure did not subsist in an admiration of the artistry which had produced the model, but in an exploration of the memories and emotions induced by the encounter with the wax figure. The implication is that the visitor arrives at the visitor attraction already equipped with stories in their minds. The encounter with the personality modelled in wax is an opportunity for the visitor to add content to the stories already stored in their minds and memories.

Some recent research has examined the role of narratives in the life of an individual, and the way in which this is salient in visitor attraction encounters. The term 'narrative' is intended to mean something more than a story. A narrative is, arguably, a story plus a discourse. The story is the content of the narrative, and the discourse is its vehicle. Thus, a story such as *Sleeping Beauty* can be told through a variety of discourses, for example cinematic film, ballet or ice show (Chatman, 1978). A narrative in the life of an individual, which can be termed a personal narrative, can therefore be thought of as a story, for which the discourse is the life of the person. A moment's reflection reveals that personal narratives are very common indeed. An everyday example may be the expectation on the part of a human being growing into adulthood that life will involve marriage and children. When a suitable partner presents themselves, the opportunity is embraced as an expected event. There are clichés which embody personal narratives. Some may claim to be a 'survivor'; it may be said of another that they 'fall on their feet'. An accustomed pessimist may greet bad news with the words, 'that's the story of my life'. These are all evidence of stories running through subjects' lives, and these stories have trajectories. As Shankar *et al.* (2001: 429) suggest, 'our lives, too, exhibit the basic features of all narratives; they have a beginning, middle and an end. And so as we grow up we learn about who we are, our history and our culture through stories and by telling stories ... Stories therefore make our lives and ourselves intelligible to us and to others'.

The paradigmatic proposal, therefore, is that the human subjects who constitute the audiences for visitor attractions should be thought of as bearers of personal narratives. At each encounter within the visitor attraction, conscious or unconscious reference to personal narratives is made. The desired outcome is to make sense of the encounter by attempting to incorporate the informational message into the trajectory of one of the personal narratives for which the subject is the bearer. As Escalas (2004: 168) suggests, 'narratives fit the pieces of people's lives together with causal links ... people use stories to understand the world around them, what goes on in their own lives, and who they are as individuals and members of society'.

Evidence of the importance of such visitor predispositions can be found in recent studies. One such study was conducted by Macdonald, Silverstone and Heron amongst visitors to a special exhibition at the Science Museum in London. A conclusion on which the researchers laid particular emphasis was that visitors arrived with a set of preconceptions, which they chose to term 'particular imaginings'. It was seen as the role of the curatorial staff to identify and address these through interpretive processes (Macdonald, 1992). A second example is the research undertaken by McIntosh at three cultural heritage attractions in the UK. Data were collected on the beneficial experiences acquired by visitors. These were then categorized into 'thought processes' relating to affective (emotional) processes, reflection and intellectual synthesizing. The author's conclusion was that the visitors' encounters with the attractions were 'far more sensorily complex and emotion laden' than could be revealed by traditional marketing research techniques (McIntosh, 1999: 55). A third example is the study undertaken by Goulding (2000) into the visitor experience at an open-air museum in the UK. Data were gathered by means of semi-structured interviews, observational research and focus groups. Goulding's conclusion was that the imagining of the visitor was central to the experience.

The theorized thoughtful and smart consumers can clearly be considered as bearers of personal narratives. To be smart is to approach situations in life, whether seeking out the cheapest household-energy supplier or assessing the value of a cultural experience, in terms of economic convertibility. In other words, it is a narrative, which at every opportunity becomes extended. By contrast, to be thoughtful is, perhaps, to shun participation in the search for a cheap household-energy supplier, or to participate grudgingly. To be thoughtful is to seek out and savour those experiences that can extend a personal narrative of reflection, and the pleasures of the mind and heart which can be derived from such reflection.

Case Study 1: The Royal Armouries Museum, Leeds, UK[3]

Armed with these insights, the manager of a visitor attraction can reasonably conclude that content should offer the scope for exploration for the thoughtful consumer, price and value should offer a deal to satisfy the smart consumer, and the initial contact with the visitor, via promotional material, should offer an arresting and popular proposition which appeals not so much to the intellect but to the emotions. Such a policy, implemented at the Royal Armouries Museum, can be linked with significant improvements in visitor numbers. First, some background. The Royal Armouries Museum, which opened in 1996, is an example of a trend whereby collections held by the UK's national museums have been relocated to provincial outstations. Initial annual visitor numbers exceeded 300 000, but thereafter showed a worrying downward trend (see Table 9.1).

Table 9.1 Royal Armouries Museum: annual visitor numbers

Year	1996 (part)	1997	1998	1999	2000
Number	324 110	345 705	292 658	177 334	158 274

Source: Royal Armouries Museum.

The arrival of new marketing staff in the summer of 2000 facilitated a reappraisal of promotional policies. The collections, consisting of weapons and armour from multiple time periods, vividly interpreted, combined with a building which was dramatic in terms of scale and space, were felt to be positive assets. There was felt to be adequate scope for an in-depth exploratory experience in which the emotions, as well as the intellect, could feature. However, implements of war do not have an immediate and obvious appeal to the general public. Indeed, their connotations are, unsurprisingly, somewhat negative. For that reason, a new promotional policy was conceived. The intention was to portray the visitor experience as an encounter with a range of narratives which appealed to all the senses. In the words of the museum's Marketing Operating Plan for 2001/2, this shift involved the replacement of a 'cerebral appreciation' with an 'emotionally driven call to action'.

The principal proposition of the new brochure was to 'discover your sense of adventure'. This was supported with sub-propositions within the brochure to 'see the splendour', 'touch the reality', 'hear the stories', 'smell the fear' and 'taste the victory'.

This approach was adapted for the purpose of business-to-business marketing in the form of attracting sponsorship. A named individual in the targeted business would receive a succession of postcards (Figure 9.1).

---

[3] This case was prepared from interviews with and information provided by Royal Armouries staff. The author acknowledges with gratitude the assistance and information provided by Nick Thompson, formerly Head of Sales and Marketing, and Gillian Harnby, Sponsorship Manager, both of the Royal Armouries Museum, Leeds.

These mailings were followed up by a telephone call from the museum and, subject to level of interest, a personal visit and the handing over of a full brochure. The revised promotional policy was accompanied by an increased emphasis on special events as a provider of a popular 'threshold of engagement' for the visitor. Self-evidently, it is difficult to document an empirical link between changes in promotional policy and changes in visitor numbers; however, month-by-month attendances showed a consistent improvement from October 2000, in comparison with the previous year. Table 9.2 shows the change in visitor numbers during the period in question.

Figure 9.1
(*Continued*)

Figure 9.1

Table 9.2   Royal Armouries Museum: month-by-month visitors

Year	1999	2000	2001
January	9830	7038	9030
February	18 456	14 449	20 656
March	14 434	10 372	15 051
April	17 267	21 157	(aggregate total,
May	12 670	13 038	April–September 2001
June	16 868	11 842	was 154 425[a])
July	19 088	14 792	
August	28 771	22 435	
September	11 165	9538	
October	14 022	18 395	
November	8008	9602	
December	6755	5614	
Total	177 334	158 274	199 162 (to September)

Source: Royal Armouries Museum.
[a] This compares with an aggregate figure of 92 802 visits for the same months in 2001.

Case Study 2: Cathedral visiting

The promotional approach which facilitated the turnaround at the Royal Armouries was not preceded by specific primary research. It was rather the invention of a Head of Marketing and Sales, who was endowed with intuitive knowledge and whose expertise included prior experience in the newspaper industry, where storytelling is the essence of the product. This second case study reports primary research undertaken by the author on behalf of the Dean and Chapter of one of England's cathedrals. Although it is not possible at the time of writing to report action on the recommendations, the research results led to a call for a revised approach to promotion of a kind not dissimilar to that already seen at the Royal Armouries.

The author was invited by the Dean and Chapter of Lincoln Cathedral, England, to conduct research to form the basis of an intended programme of marketing and development activity. The Chapter already had a Marketing and Interpretation Plan, which proposed a conventional segmentation-and-targeting approach and the deployment of database-marketing techniques. The suitability of a generic approach is itself debatable, but in discussions with the client it became clear that fundamental questions needed to be asked. The plan made repeated reference to the 'rich experience' of visiting a cathedral but little was known about what constituted this experience. It was decided that this should be investigated. It was felt that a negotiated or group view of visitor experiences was required to reveal the required insights. Qualitative research, in the form of a focus group, was the chosen methodology. Facilitated by the author, a group of nine individuals, united by being lay visitors and having a memory of having visited a cathedral in England (not Lincoln) within the previous five years for leisure purposes, were led through the experience of visiting a cathedral: before, during, and after the visit. The full report of the research, results and analysis has been published (Voase, 2007). What follows is a selection of key points.

First, the participants were muted in their approval of the interpretive literature which was available. Participants referred to a 'handout', a leaflet typically available free of charge or at minimal cost, to be obtained on entry, and the 'glossy', a polished printed guide which was available to be purchased at the end of the visit. Both these pieces of print were seen as vehicles for architectural and historical facts. Second, subjects became more animated when asked to speak of their behaviour during the visit. The essence of the experience was solitary and reflective. Subjects may separate from their companions in order to enjoy the building at their own pace, and the *modus operandi* involved elements of looking around, and sitting still. The experience appeared to be one of the emotions rather than of the intellect. 'Ambience' was a term used, and seemed to embody that which was being enjoyed. Third, and intriguingly, the subjects appeared to agree on a general sense of dissatisfaction on leaving. One spoke of a 'profound sense of emptiness'. When the group was asked what had been sought but not found, phrases included 'a sense of human connectedness' and a 'sense of human continuity'.

The author concluded from this research that the nature of the visitor experience at the cathedral, as desired by the visitor, had little to do with architecture and history. In contrast, the visitor sought to make sense of the building – an investment of human labour over two to three centuries of construction – in terms of their relationship to the human aspiration, effort and commitment which inspired it. The author's recommendations to the Dean and Chapter thus proposed a rewriting of supporting literature, perhaps through the eyes and mouths of those who built the cathedral, and a promotional approach which addressed the emotions rather than the intellect, or to put it another way, appealed to the heart rather than to the head. The research clearly pointed to an approach consistent with that adopted, with success, at the Royal Armouries.

Conclusion

It is proposed that there is *prima facie* evidence for the following three propositions, of which managers of visitor attractions can usefully take note.

First, cultural postmodernization has led to two kinds of new visitor: the 'thoughtful' and the 'smart'. The former is a product of the proliferation of knowledge under the postmodern condition, while the latter a product of the commodification of that same knowledge. Second, discursive references to 'active' and 'passive' leisure are arguably misleading in the new cultural climate. The terms require redefinition, since to be physically inactive does not betoken mental inactivity. Third, the 'dumbing down' of culture is in fact a lowering of the threshold of initial engagement on the part of cultural producers. Consumers themselves, far from being dumb, are increasingly complex and seek encounters which go far beyond the intellect. The evidence of the Royal Armouries Museum, where promotional policies based on these insights have been implemented, suggest that this approach should be seen as a rational strategy, and can be an ingredient for success. The research into the nature of the visitor experience at cathedrals endorses this too. Fourth, a useful paradigm for conceptualizing the visitor is as a bearer of personal narratives. Evidence suggests that an interpretive approach which enables the visitor to add to and extend the narratives by which they make sense of themselves and the world around them is likely to enhance the experience, and hence make that person more likely to visit the attraction.

References

Althusser, L. (1992). Ideology and the ideological state apparatus. In *A Critical and Cultural Theory Reader* (A. Easthope and K. McGowan, eds), pp. 50–58. Open University Press.

BARB – British Audience Research Bureau (2007). *TV Facts: Multi-Channel Development*. British Audience Research Bureau. http://www.barb.co.uk, accessed 18 March 2007.

Bourdieu, P. (1984). *Distinction: A Social Critique of the Judgement of Taste*. Routledge.

Campbell, C. (1990). Character and consumption: an historical action theory approach to the understanding of consumer behaviour. *Culture and History*, **7**, 37–48.

Campbell, C. (1994). Consuming goods and the good of consuming. *Critical Review*, **8**, 503–520.

Chatman, S. (1978). *Story and Discourse: Narrative Structure in Fiction and Film*. Cornell University Press.

Daily Express (1996). Farce of useless degrees. *Daily Express*, 21 August.

Davies, M. (1989). A loss of vision. *Leisure Management*, **9**, 40–42.

Derrida, J. (1998). *Of Grammatology*. John Hopkins University Press.

Economist (1994). A nation of groupies. *The Economist*, 13–19 August, p. 25.

Elliot-Major, L. (2000). Have exams got easier? Dumb, No. 1: 1066 and all what? Supplement to *The Guardian*, 28 October, pp. 10–14.

Engel, M. (1996). Papering over the cracks. Guardian 2. Supplement to *The Guardian*, 3 October, pp. 2–4.

Escalas, J. (2004). Narrative processing: building consumer connection to brands. *Journal of Consumer Psychology*, **14**, 168–180.

Euromonitor (1992). *The European Travel and Tourism Marketing Directory*. Euromonitor.

Fairclough, N. (2000). *New Labour, New Language?* Routledge.

Goulding, C. (2000). The museum environment and the visitor experience. *European Journal of Marketing*, **34**, 261–278.

Greenslade, R. (1997). The Telegraph, it is a-changin'. Media Guardian. Supplement to *The Guardian*, 3 February, p. 5.

Hartley, J. (1999). Someone's dumb. *The Guardian*, 5 March, p. 20.

Henley Centre for Forecasting (1992). *Inbound Tourism: A Packaged Future?* Henley Centre for Forecasting.

Jameson, F. (1984). Postmodernism, or the cultural logic of late capitalism. *New Left Review*, **146**, 53–92.

Kelly, J. (1997). Leisure as life: outline of a poststructuralist reconstruction. *Loisir et Société/Society and Leisure*, **20**, 401–418.

Laermans, R. (1992). The relative rightness of Pierre Bourdieu: some comments on the legitimacy of postmodern art, literature and culture. *Cultural Studies*, **6**, 248–260.

Lash, S. (1990). *Sociology of Postmodernism*. Routledge.

Lyotard, J.-F. (1984). *The Postmodern Condition: A Report on Knowledge*. Manchester University Press.

Macdonald, S. (1992). Cultural imagining among museum visitors: a case study. *Museum Management*, **11**, 401–409.

Marshall, J. (2001). Vision of lifelong learning put at the heart of OECD target. *Times Higher Education Supplement*, 6 April, p. 11.

Martin, B. and Mason, S. (1993). The future for attractions: meeting the needs of the new consumers. *Tourism Management*, **14**, 34–40.

McIntosh, A. (1999). Into the tourist's mind: understanding the value of the heritage experience. *Journal of Travel and Tourism Marketing*, **8**, 41–64.

McLuhan, E. and Zingrone, F. (1997). *Essential McLuhan*. Routledge.

ONS – Office for National Statistics (1998). *Living in Britain: Results from the 1996 General Household Survey*. Office for National Statistics, The Stationery Office.

ONS – Office for National Statistics (2004). *Social Trends 34*. Palgrave MacMillan.

ONS – Office for National Statistics (2006). *Social Trends 36*. Palgrave MacMillan.

Poon, A. (1989). Competitive strategies for a 'new tourism'. In *Progress in Tourism, Recreation and Hospitality Management: Volume 1* (C. Cooper, ed), pp. 91–102. Belhaven.

PSI – Policy Studies Institute (1993). *Cultural Trends 17*, **5**(1). Policy Studies Institute.

PSI – Policy Studies Institute (1996). *Cultural Trends 25*, **7** (1). Policy Studies Institute.

Purvis, T. and Hunt, A. (1993). Discourse, ideology, discourse, ideology, discourse, ideology. *British Journal of Sociology*, **44**, 473–499.

QCA – Qualifications and Curriculum Authority (2007a). *Review of Standards in GCSE English Literature 2002–5*. Qualifications and Curriculum Authority.

QCA – Qualifications and Curriculum Authority (2007b). *Review of Standards in A-Level English Literature 2000–5*. Qualifications and Curriculum Authority.

Rusbridger, A. (2000). Versions of seriousness, Dumb, No. 2: down the tubes. Supplement to *The Guardian*, 4 November, pp. 14–17.

Shankar, A., Elliott, R. and Goulding, C. (2001). Understanding consumption: contributions from a narrative perspective. *Journal of Marketing Management*, **17**, 429–453.

Smithers, A. and Roff, A. (2000). Are new 'vocational' degrees worthless? Saturday Review, *The Guardian*, 19 August, p. 2.

THES – Times Higher Education Supplement (2006). News: trends and league tables. *Times Higher Education Supplement*, 9 June, p. 20.

Urry, J. (1990). *The Tourist Gaze: Leisure and Travel in Contemporary Societies*. Sage.

Vergo, P. (1989). *The New Museology*. Reaktion.

Voase, R. (2002). Rediscovering the imagination: investigating active and passive visitor experience in the 21st century. *International Journal of Tourism Research*, **4**, 391–399.

Voase, R. (2007). Visiting a cathedral: the consumer psychology of a 'rich experience'. *International Journal of Heritage Studies*, **13**, 41–55.

Waterson, M. (1992). *The Marketing Pocketbook 1993*. Advertising Association and NTC Publications.

Waterson, M. (2004). *The Marketing Pocketbook 2005*. Advertising Association and NTC Publications.

Yorkshire TV. (1986). *The Marketing Mix*. Programme One. Channel 4 Television.

Managing Visitor Impacts

Brian Garrod

Aims

The aims of this chapter are to:

- identify the importance of the notion of sustainability to visitor attractions,
- highlight the relevance of visitor impacts to the issue of sustainability,
- outline the major impacts of visitors on visitor attractions,
- examine a range of tools for managing visitor impacts, and
- discuss the findings of a study of visitor impacts at visitor attractions.

Introduction

It is widely acknowledged that visitor attractions play an important, perhaps even pivotal role in the world tourism industry. Large, often purpose-built visitor attractions are increasingly being employed as instruments of economic regeneration, particularly in run-down urban areas and in locations where traditional forms of tourism have been in decline. Even larger, destination-style, so-called 'mega-attractions' are also now appearing all over the world (Stevens, 2000). These are often linked to the aspirations of governments to establish 'growth poles' in relatively underdeveloped areas (Disneyland Paris being a good example). Then there is the growing number of World Heritage Sites, representing the 'crown jewels' of the world's natural and cultural heritage, and forming the mainstay of the tourism industry of many countries (Leask and Fyall, 2006). At the other end of the scale, meanwhile, there is a multitude of smaller visitor attractions, many of which are independently owned and operate almost on a casual basis. Visitor attractions often represent a major factor in drawing tourists to a particular destination. Visitors to the United Kingdom, for example, typically cite the desire to experience the nation's unique heritage and culture as the most important reason for their trip, and visitor attractions are clearly an important medium of such experiences.

Yet, the visitor attractions sector presently faces the unenviable problem of being pulled between contradictory demands. On the one hand, most visitor attractions are based on specific natural, built, manufactured or cultural assets, the distinctiveness and quality of which forms the core of their 'products'. Opening such sites to visitors carries with it the risk of exposing these self-same assets to a range of potential visitor impacts. Consequently, visitors can compromise the very things that they are coming to see. Even in purpose-built attractions, negative visitor impacts such as overcrowding and traffic congestion around the site can serve to reduce the quality of the visitor experience. As with any other form of business, unless customers receive a product that satisfies their expectations, they will not return to purchase it again and nor will they recommend it to others.

On the other hand, it is axiomatic that visitor attractions need visitors in order to achieve their objectives, whether these are attempting to make profits for their owners, earning revenues to pay for the continuing protection and conservation of the site, educating the public or fulfilling a wider social function. For many visitor attractions, particularly those that are purpose-built, opening to visitors is their fundamental *raison d'être*. For others, being open to the public for at least limited periods of the year is a feature of their ownership, especially when they are owned by membership organizations such as the National Trust in England and Wales. For others again, receiving paying visitors represents an economic lifeline. Without paying visitors, the assets upon which the visitor attraction is based would inevitably have to be sold, converted to alternative uses or fall into disrepair.

The dilemma for visitor attractions is that, generally speaking, the greater the exposure of the site to visitors, the greater is the potential for negative visitor impacts to arise. The incidence of such impacts not only serves to threaten the continued economic viability of the visitor attraction as a commercial concern, but also raises serious questions about the sustainability of the attraction. At the core of the sustainability concept is the requirement that things of value should not be squandered by the present generation, but maintained for the benefit of future generations. If today's visitors damage or even destroy the things they come to see, then those things will simply not be available for future generations to appreciate, enjoy and learn from.

Visitor impacts often pale into insignificance in comparison to the wider environmental threats that are faced by visitor attractions (Shackley, 1998). Historic buildings, for example, are under constant threat from the natural elements, the effects of pollution, the risk of fire and the ravages of time. Visitor impacts can, however, seriously exacerbate such problems. For example, the structural integrity of Craigeivar Castle in Scotland has been compromised literally by the weight of visitor numbers, whose unrelenting passage through the upper floors has left them unsafe for continued public access (Croft, 1994). Meanwhile the growing volume of visitors to the Valley of the Kings near Luxor, Egypt, is thought to have been responsible for a major roof collapse in the tomb of Seti I. The presence of visitors at such fragile sites is clearly a mixed blessing in terms of achieving and maintaining sustainability. While visitors bring the revenues that many sites so badly need to fund their conservation and restoration efforts, they also bring with them impacts that can make the need for such efforts all the more real and urgent.

Sustainability requires that these contradictory demands are effectively tackled, and that a means is found of enabling both access to visitors and the effective protection of the site and its contents from being damaged by those visitors. Typically, the response of visitor attractions has been to introduce some form of visitor management, the aim being to moderate the impacts of visitors while still enabling them to come onto the site, interact with the assets on which the attraction is based and achieve a satisfying experience from their visit.

Types of visitor impact

Visitor attractions are subject to a wide range of negative visitor impacts. A report by the English Tourist Board (ETB, 1991) suggests that visitor impacts tend to fall into the following categories: overcrowding, wear and tear, traffic-related problems, impacts on local community and the impacts of visitor management itself on the authenticity of visitor attractions.

Overcrowding

The problem of overcrowding is highly dependent on the capacity of the site to receive visitors. When a visitor attraction becomes overcrowded, visitors begin to get under each other's feet, the result being that everyone finds it increasingly difficult to move around the site. Once visitors are no longer able to keep moving, queues will begin to form at bottlenecks. Typically such pressure points tend to make themselves evident in the admissions area, near popular exhibits or at particular locations such as shops, refreshment areas and toilets.

Overcrowding might therefore occur either at the level of the site as a whole or in particular parts of it. It can also be a persistent problem or, more usually, be restricted to particular times of the day and days of the year. Shackley (2006) makes the point that this is often the result of the way in which tours are organized. Thus, for example, at the Uluru World Heritage Site in Australia the tightly scheduled itineraries of coach companies tend to coincide, many of them bringing visitors to the same parts of the site at the same times of the day.

The impacts of overcrowding are typically evidenced by visitors feeling that they are unable to appreciate the character or ambience of a site, a reduced opportunity for visitors to see and do everything they want to, and a consequent negative impact on visitor satisfaction. Of course, overcrowding is a highly subjective issue. What feels overcrowded to one person may not seem over-crowded to another, while what is considered to be too long a queue for one person will be perfectly acceptable to another and they will happily wait in it.

Wear and tear

This group of visitor impacts includes trampling, handling, humidity, temperature, pilfering and graffiti. Trampling involves visitors walking on sensitive parts of the site, ranging from carefully manicured lawns, to antique carpets in stately homes, to the very fabric of ancient monuments. A good example of the latter is the erosion caused by visitors walking along the top of Hadrian's Wall, the remains of a Roman defensive structure in Northern England (Gillette, 2000). Trampling may be deliberate or accidental, and is especially likely when the site becomes congested. Handling, on the other hand, is more likely to be a deliberate act on the part of the visitor who cannot resist putting sticky or moist fingers on fragile items, even when they are requested not to do so.

Humidity and temperature, meanwhile, are always unintentional on the part of the visitor; however, they are often unavoidable if the site is to be opened to visitors in significant numbers. The problem is not generally the levels of humidity and temperature themselves, which can quite easily be controlled, but the rapid changes in environmental conditions that tend to occur as visitors move around the site. A good example of the impact of humidity on a visitor attraction is the damage caused to the ancient wall paintings in the tomb of Queen Nefertari in Egypt. The presence of visitors in the tomb raises the level of humidity significantly, causing the paint to flake away from the limestone surface of the inner walls of the tomb. The effect has been so severe that a limit of only 150 visitors per day has been set, with visitors taken into the tomb in small groups, each permitted to stay inside for a maximum of 16 min.

Pilfering and graffiti, meanwhile, are intentional acts on the part of the visitor. Pilfering can range from petty theft in the gift shop or cafeteria, to the theft of valuable exhibits. While the former might be considered a relatively minor problem in terms of the protection of the site, it may nevertheless have important implications for the cash flow and general financing of the attraction. Similarly, graffiti can range from being a minor blemish on the ambience of the site to becoming a very real issue in terms of its protection. For example, Timothy and Boyd (2003) highlight the spray-painting by vandals of several sixteenth and seventeenth century tombstones of St Paul's Church in Melaka, Malaysia. Even though it is possible to clean the paint from the tombstones, the cleaning process is itself likely to result in further damage to their delicately carved surfaces.

Traffic-related problems

Most visitors tend to arrive at a visitor attraction by motor car or by coach. Yet, many sites pre-date the invention of the automobile and were not therefore designed to cope with the traffic generated by visitors. Others are located within city centres, where visitor-generated traffic may exacerbate existing traffic problems. Traffic-related problems include traffic congestion, pollution from vehicle exhausts, the increased risk of accidents, damage to verges and lawns due to poor parking, the restriction of access by thoughtlessly parked cars and coaches and vibration damage to buildings. Traffic problems may be persistent or merely occasional, evidencing themselves only at peak times. They may also be restricted to the site itself or, particularly if the attraction only has a limited amount of parking space, spill over into the locality.

Small historic cities are particularly vulnerable to traffic-related visitor impacts, with relatively small and enclosed city centres being swamped by visitors in the high season. Canterbury in South East England is a good example of a small historic city beleaguered by visitors, many of whom arrive as part of a coach party. Before a series of traffic management measures were introduced during the 1980s and 1990s, traffic in the city centre was increasingly being brought to gridlock by coaches trying to set down and pick up visitors (Curtis, 1998).

Impacts on the local community

Many visitor impacts can spill out into the local community. The potential for poorly parked cars and coaches to restrict access to neighbouring areas has already been mentioned. Another possible impact on the local community may result from the thoughtless and antisocial behaviour of visitors. This may range from visitors unwittingly trespassing on private property, to loutish behaviour by visitors who have consumed too much alcohol in the visitor attraction bar. Visitors may be accused of rudeness towards local people, treating them without due respect or even as curiosities provided as part of the visitor attraction experience. Visitors in large numbers can also cause congestion in local facilities, such as shopping areas or leisure centres. As a result the local community can come to feel besieged by visitors and perceive them to have a negative influence on the local community.

At the same time it is possible to envisage impacts running in the opposite direction, that is, local people having a negative impact on the visitor experience. For example, visitors may feel unwelcome in the vicinity of the visitor attraction because of the way they are treated by the local residents.

Impacts of visitor management on the authenticity of the attraction

Interestingly, the ETB report also identifies the potential of visitor management itself to have damaging impacts on the authenticity of the visitor attraction and the experience it offers. These impacts may take the form of:

- the provision of visitor facilities (for example direction signs or handrails) may have a detrimental effect on the ambience of the attraction,

- adaptations made in order to enhance visitor flow around the site may be considered architecturally inappropriate or felt to compromise the architectural integrity of the site,
- adaptations made to enable access by disabled visitors (for example lifts or ramps) may necessitate the use of inappropriate equipment or materials,
- the need to take measures to ensure visitor health and safety that conflict with the conservation objectives of the site, and
- there may be a tendency towards intrusive interpretation, or interpretation that is not faithful to the history of the site.

These kinds of impact might be considered even more invidious than those outlined above, since they raise the possibility that taking action to remedy visitor impacts might actually result in a worse situation to that which would have arisen in the absence of such efforts. The dilemma for visitor management, then, becomes not simply *how* to manage visitor impacts but *whether* to manage them.

Techniques for managing visitor impacts

The techniques of visitor management can be divided into those that are designed to regulate supply and those that are designed to manage demand for the visitor attraction.

Supply-side techniques

This group of techniques attempts, in a number of different ways, to increase the capacity of the site to receive visitors without being unduly damaged or the visitor experience otherwise being impaired.

Queue management

When the demand for the visitor attraction exceeds the capacity of the site to receive visitors, queues will begin to form. Typically, these take the form of pedestrian queues outside admission points or lines of motor vehicles outside of the main gate. Queues can have a number of adverse impacts on the visitor experience (Barlow, 1999), including:

- Visitors may feel that their enjoyment of the experience offered by the attraction is impaired because they have had to spend a considerable amount of time in queues, either to enter the attraction or to see specific parts of it.
- Some potential visitors may turn away when they see the length of the admission queue; others may join the queue but become bored when it moves forward only slowly, and will go and find something else to do instead.

- Other potential visitors may be put off from visiting the attraction because it has gained a reputation for lengthy queues.
- In order to try to eliminate the queues, staff may be forced to spend less time with each visitor; certain time-consuming features or services may have to be abandoned entirely.
- Staff may become demoralized because they have insufficient time to meet visitors' needs and provide a high-quality experience for every visitor.

Queue management is often the first response to the problem of excess demand, since most other visitor management techniques will take more time to implement. Queue management techniques include:

- snaking the queues, so that they appear to move faster,
- providing literature and displays (perhaps audio-visual) to distract visitors while they queue,
- bringing the queues further into the property, so that visitors can experience its ambience while they wait, and
- entertaining the visitors while they wait in the queue.

None of these measures will of course reduce the size of the queue: they will merely make waiting in the queue more bearable. As such, queue management cannot realistically be viewed as a long-term remedy to the problems of overcrowding and congestion.

Making capacity more flexible

Given a sufficient length of time, visitor attractions can take a number of measures to make their existing capacity more flexible. This can help to reduce or even eliminate queues. Techniques include:

- extending opening hours, or opening for more days of the year,
- opening more admission tills when demand is high, taking them offline when demand subsides,
- increasing staffing levels in periods of high demand, enabling visitor needs to be met more effectively when the site is busy,
- opening additional areas within cafeterias and other facilities during busy times,
- offering or prescribing certain routes, thereby facilitating the free flow of visitors around the site, and
- cross-training staff so that they can work in the busiest areas of the attraction according to demand.

Such measures can be highly effective. However, in the case of many smaller, heritage-based attractions, making capacity more flexible can be extremely problematic. Physical restrictions in the entry hall, for example, may limit the number of admission tills that it is possible to operate.

Increasing capacity

In the longer term, visitor attractions may seek to address the problem of persistent excess demand by investing in additional physical capacity. This can range from building an extension to the gift shop, to constructing an additional building to house particular parts of the collection or visitor activities. The danger, however, is that such efforts may serve to reduce the authenticity of the site, reducing the quality of the visitor experience and potentially compromising efforts to conserve the resource-base of the attraction for future generations.

Site hardening

Other impacts, particularly various forms of wear and tear, are traditionally addressed through the use of 'site hardening' techniques. These include:

- employing security people and room stewards (often volunteers at heritage-based attractions) to provide a physical presence at sensitive locations,
- roping off vulnerable parts of the site,
- the use of glass, Perspex or other materials to encase artifacts or divide off certain areas,
- strengthening of footpaths,
- covering carpets with protective materials, and
- use of prohibitive notices.

At the extreme, site hardening can even take the form of the removal of originals and their replacement with a facsimile. For example, visitors to Hereford Cathedral in England first see a facsimile of the ancient and fragile Mappa Mundi, which they can examine closely before they get to see the original which is safely cocooned behind glass in its purpose-built but less-accessible display area.

Site hardening techniques can be extremely sophisticated, for example a travelator system has been installed at the Tower of London to address a bottleneck at the Jewel House, where long queues would form at busy times. The travelators are switched on at busy times and allow each visitor only a fixed amount of time to see each exhibit before they are whisked onwards (Shackley, 1999).

The problem with almost all site hardening is, however, that it risks compromising the authenticity of the site. This may be a particular problem at heritage-based attractions, where a significant element of the visitor experience may be to gain an insight into how the property may have looked in its heyday. The excessive use of such techniques may also run counter to the conservation objectives of the owners of the site.

Restrictive ticketing and quota systems

Perhaps the most extreme of the supply-side measures available to manage visitor impacts is ticketing that restricts the time of entry (requiring pre-booking), the length of stay, the size of groups, the number of visitors permitted per day or some combination of these. Such measures may be introduced to try to combat overcrowding or address particular forms of wear and tear (such as trampling or visitor-induced humidity). An example is the tomb of Queen Nefertari in Egypt, referred to previously, where a daily quota of visitors has been set along with a maximum dwell time for each party. Visitor attractions are typically reluctant to introduce such measures since they tend to discourage certain types of visitor, particularly the independent visitor and small groups. The casual visitor, meanwhile, can be excluded entirely. Many managers of heritage visitor attractions do, however, prefer such measures to the use of price incentives, which are considered to be even less acceptable.

Demand-management techniques

This group of techniques aims to influence the number or behaviour of visitors in order to moderate their impact on the site and/or its associated artifacts.

Price incentives

One possible pricing technique for managing visitor impacts would be to use elevated admission prices to moderate overall levels of demand. Reducing the pressure of numbers could help to address problems such as overcrowding of the site, traffic congestion or trampling damage to footpaths. The use of elevated admission prices would also accord with the 'user-pays' principle, which states that those responsible for using resources that are vulnerable to damage should be required to pay for the remediation of any user-induced impacts. Increased admission prices can also raise much-needed revenue to fund the attraction's wider strategic goals, such as conservation of the site of or public education.

A potential problem with using price incentives to manage overall levels of demand is that while the demand for visitor attractions tends to be relatively price elastic (responsive) at low prices, as admission prices rise above 'token' levels, demand tends to become increasingly price inelastic (Garrod *et al.*, 2002). In many cases, therefore, elevated admission prices would appear to be a rather blunt instrument in attempting to moderate demand in general.

Charging elevated prices for admission is also highly unpopular among visitor attraction managers (Fyall and Garrod, 1998). Indeed, to many in the heritage establishment, charging for admission at all is considered repugnant. Among the main reasons offered for this standpoint are:

- Charging elevated admission fees may conflict with the wider objectives of the visitor attraction, such as equality access to all social groupings or public education.
- Attractions do not have a legal right to charge for access to public land or public buildings, or a moral right to charge for access to ones own heritage.

- Charging for admission may lead to a bias of concern for those elements of our heritage that can most easily be 'sold' to visitors.
- The cost of collecting admission charges may in some cases outweigh the revenues collected.
- High admission charges may act as a disincentives for impulse, casual and repeat visitors.
- Secondary spend may fall if high admission charges are introduced.
- Charging may also reduce spending elsewhere in the local economy.

Even if raised admission charges are considered objectionable in respect of managing overall levels of demand, they may still be useful tools for managing the nature of demand. For example, price variations might be used to encourage demand at off-peak times and discourage it during the peaks. Special prices can be offered to certain types of visitor. Encouraging school groups, for example, might encourage further visits by their families (Barlow, 1999). It has also been argued that the level of admissions price can help to determine visitors' perceptions of the importance of the site and therefore their behaviour. If visitors pay a relatively high admission price they may be led to understand that they are visiting a particularly unique, pristine or spectacular site, and will need to behave respectfully towards it in the course of their visit (Fyall and Garrod, 1998).

Marketing

Other elements of the marketing mix than price can also be used to manage demand. Visits at off-peak times can be promoted through advertising or joint-ticketing arrangements, heavily used sites can be de-marketed and less intensively used sites marketed as alternatives (Boyd and Timothy, 2006). It might even be desirable to develop new visitor attractions to deflect pressure from more sensitive sites. This has been the strategy adopted by Canterbury in England, for example, where new purpose-built attractions have been developed outside of the city centre in an attempt to reduce the level of pedestrian overcrowding caused by visitors to the cathedral (Curtis, 1998).

Education and interpretation

Education and interpretation also have the potential to serve as tools for managing visitor impacts. Experience has shown that educating visitors about the negative impacts of certain forms of behaviour, informing them how to behave appropriately and encouraging them to act accordingly, can have a critical influence on their behaviour both during and after the visit (Bramwell and Lane, 1993). The following advantages of this approach have been identified:

- People tend to react more positively to requests to refrain from certain forms of behaviour when they know and understand the reasons.

- Visitor impacts can be reduced by offering visitors a more engaging experience, which not only informs them about how to act responsibly but also encourages them to act accordingly.
- Visitor movement both in time and in space can be influenced, for example, by drawing attention to alternative routes around the sites, substitute attractions or different visit times.
- Raising the public's conservation ethic may pay longer-term dividends for the visitor attraction in terms of contributions to charities and other good causes related either directly or indirectly to the work of the visitor attraction.
- Educational and interpretive facilities can bring local economic benefits by employing local people, selling local products (such as local handicrafts), providing services (such as refreshments) and helping to diversify the local economy.
- Local community participation can also be enhanced through the provision of education and interpretation, for example local people can help decide what to educate visitors about and what to interpret.

Education and interpretation would in many ways appear the ideal solution to visitor impacts. The major difficulty with this approach, however, is that the demand for visitor attractions is typically based on recreational rather than educational motivations. While it is true that some visitors will be motivated by the desire to learn about the things they are coming to see, the principal motivation for the typical visitor will be to relax, and to have fun with friends and family. Indeed, going to visitor attractions has been said to be more akin to window shopping than a learning experience. Under such circumstances, it will probably always be difficult to influence visitor's behaviour by means of education and interpretation.

Case Study: Managing visitor impacts at visitor attractions – an international assessment

While the requirement for visitor attractions to develop and implement effective visitor management strategies has long been recognized, empirical studies of the actual visitor impacts concerned remain relatively scarce. Little research has been conducted into the range of potential visitor impacts and their relative importance to different categories of visitor attraction. Without a firm understanding of the nature of the impacts and the susceptibility of different types of visitor attraction to such impacts, strategies aimed at addressing visitor impacts are likely to be ineffective.

A rare exception to the tendency noted above is a study by Garrod *et al.* (2002) into visitor impacts at Scottish visitor attractions. The study sampled 501 managers of paid-entry visitor attractions in Scotland, asking them to share their perception of the importance to their particular visitor attraction of a range of visitor impacts. A response rate of 59 per cent was achieved. The data were then analysed with the assistance of the Statistical Package for the Social Sciences (SPSS).

The study results indicated that traffic-related problems were generally considered to be of relatively little importance by visitor attraction managers, while those considered to be the most serious were firstly the behaviour of local people towards visitors to the attraction and secondly the potential for visitor management itself to compromise the ambience and authenticity of the attraction.

Further data analysis led to three major conclusions. The first was that neither the perceived range nor the perceived severity of visitor impacts was found to vary significantly between different categories of visitor attraction, suggesting that visitor management strategies do not generally need to be tailored to specific visitor attraction categories. Visitor management strategies may thus be readily transferable between visitor attraction categories. The second conclusion was that visitor impacts are only weakly related to visitor numbers, suggesting that such impacts were not the result of visitor numbers exceeding the carrying capacities of the sites concerned. The third conclusion was that visitor impacts are only weakly related to admission prices, suggesting that raised admission pricing is unlikely to result in a significant moderation of visitor impacts. The implication is that rather than attempting to control the overall volume of visitors to a site, visitor management strategies should adopt techniques that aim to influence the behaviour of individual visitors, such as visitor education and interpretation.

While the above conclusions are important in themselves, they are clearly applicable only to the Scottish visitor attraction sector. A further study was therefore undertaken with the aim of identifying the extent to which these conclusions might have a wider international relevance (Garrod et al., 2006). This study sought to replicate the original study in three additional countries: Australia, Canada and New Zealand. A total of 1962 visitor attraction managers were contacted, of whom 721 returned usable questionnaires, giving a response rate of 34 per cent for Australia, 37 per cent for Canada and 41 per cent for New Zealand. These data were then pooled with the Scottish data and analysed as a single data set, again using SPSS. Table 10.1 illustrates the main findings of the analysis.

The findings show a remarkable consistency across all four countries. Overcrowding of the visitor attraction was considered to be a very important or extremely important issue by around a third of all respondents. Only in the case of persistent crowding of the whole site was any significant difference found between countries, with Scottish visitor attraction managers being significantly more likely to be concerned about such impacts. A possible explanation for this finding may relate to differences in the visitor attraction mix across the four countries, with a significantly larger share of those based in Scotland being natural or non-purpose-built attractions such as castles and stately homes. Such properties may be inherently less well-suited to allowing the free movement of people around them. Visitor management measures may also be less feasible where such properties are concerned, particularly if they have the potential to impact adversely on the ambience or authenticity of the site.

The findings for wear and tear impacts also show considerable conformity across all four countries. Only in the case of handling was a significant difference detected, with nearly 60 per cent of Australian visitor attraction managers regarding this impact to be very important or extremely important to their site,

Table 10.1 Visitor impacts at Australian, Canadian, New Zealand and Scottish visitor attractions, percentage of respondents considering these to be very 'important' or 'extremely important'[a]

	Scotland (n = 301) %	Australia (n = 271) %	Canada (n = 321) %	New Zealand (n = 129) %	χ²	d.f.	Significance (%)
Overcrowding							
Occasional overcrowding (whole site)	32.2	32.1	27.8	29.1	1.678	3	–
Occasional overcrowding (parts of site)	42.0	44.6	42.6	44.2	0.339	3	–
Persistent overcrowding (whole site)	35.9	26.9	16.1	30.6	25.963	3	99
Persistent overcrowding (parts of site)	38.5	35.0	26.2	34.2	7.423	3	–
Wear and tear							
Trampling	39.6	43.8	34.3	36.2	4.457	3	–
Handling	43.6	59.7	49.0	55.2	11.939	3	99
Humidity	44.0	50.5	49.2	44.9	2.394	3	–
Temperature	42.5	54.9	48.8	49.5	6.472	3	–
Pilfering	45.0	47.3	63.7	47.9	6.682	3	–
Graffiti	36.3	35.4	28.2	39.6	5.700	3	–
Traffic-related impacts							
Occasional traffic (on-site)	30.7	24.8	33.3	33.7	5.587	3	–
Occasional traffic (local)	25.0	20.7	22.0	24.7	1.264	3	–
Persistent traffic (on-site)	26.4	18.3	18.7	34.4	13.019	3	99
Persistent traffic (local)	27.5	22.8	15.9	28.8	9.603	3	95
Other traffic	36.5	19.3	20.4	24.6	13.447	3	99
Other impacts							
Visitors' behaviour towards locals	42.1	34.9	27.5	37.9	11.927	3	99
Locals' behaviour towards visitors	58.2	57.4	46.1	58.1	9.856	3	95
Visitor management compromising authenticity	57.3	73.7	64.9	68.9	15.237	3	99

[a]Excludes 'don't know' and nil responses.

compared by 55 per cent of managers in New Zealand, 49 per cent of managers in Canada and only 43 per cent of the Scottish sample.

As was the case with the original study of Scottish visitor attractions, traffic-related problems tended to be among those least likely to be viewed as serious. In the case of occasional traffic problems, this perception did not vary significantly across the four countries. Significant differences were found, however, in relation to persistent traffic problems, both on the site and in the vicinity of the visitor attraction, with attraction managers in Scotland and New Zealand being significantly more likely to view these impacts as very or extremely important. This finding might be explained by a tendency for visitor attractions in Scotland and New Zealand to be located on smaller, more cramped sites, which are inherently more difficult to move traffic around.

The findings with respect to social interactions between locals and visitors were also interesting. On the one hand, more than a third of respondents in three out of the four countries considered the behaviour of visitors towards local residents to be a serious issue. Scottish managers were significantly more likely to consider this to be a serious issue for their visitor attraction. On the other hand, more than half of the respondents in all four countries considered the behaviour of local people towards visitors to be a serious problem. Again it was in Scotland where this issue was most widely considered to be important.

The results of the international study also tended to confirm those of the Scottish study in that the majority respondents considered visitor management practices themselves to represent an impact on the ambience and authenticity of the visitor attraction site. This was considered the most serious of all the various impacts considered in the study in the cases of Australia, Canada and New Zealand, with nearly three quarters of respondents in Australia identifying it as being either very important or extremely important. Only in Scotland was this category of impact not the most widely recognized, where it came narrowly second to locals' behaviour towards visitors.

The findings of the international study tend, therefore, generally to confirm those of the Scottish study. Impacts associated with on-site congestion, most forms of wear and tear, and occasional traffic-related problems tended not to vary significantly between the four countries. Contrary to the findings of the original study, however, there are indications that such impacts do vary according to a number of other important variables, such as attraction type and ownership category. Since such relationships are only evident at the international level, it might be concluded that they apply more readily to visitor attractions in Australia, Canada and New Zealand than they do to the Scottish sector. If this is the case, then it may not be sensible to generalize the first of the three conclusions drawn from the original Scottish study, that broadly generic approaches are suitable to managing visitor impacts, irrespective of the particular characteristics of visitor attraction concerned.

The results of the international study also suggest that some caution is required in generalizing the second conclusion of the Scottish study. Indeed, the findings of the international study suggest that while visitor numbers are unrelated to some categories of impact, such as wear and tear, significant relationships are clearly evident in respect of other impacts, such as congestion and traffic-related impacts. Visitor management approaches based on establishing carrying capacities for the site may arguably be more appropriate in such cases.

The results of the international study also tend to support those of the original study in respect of the relationship between admission price and visitor impacts. The original Scottish study suggested at best only a weak relationship between these two variables. The findings of the international study suggest relationships that are undoubtedly stronger in the case of the Australia, Canada and New Zealand; however, they tend to suggest that visitor attractions charging higher admission prices actually tend to suffer more serious visitor impacts. Raising admissions prices does not, therefore, appear to present itself readily as an effective strategy for managing visitor impacts.

Conclusion

Visitor attractions play an important role in the tourism industries of many countries. They also have an important role to play as stewards of the cultural and natural heritage of many countries. These roles often conflict, and one important source of conflict is the potential for visitors to compromise, through a variety of impacts, the very things that they come to see. Visitor attractions are required to walk a fine line between enabling the public to interact with the various elements of their cultural and natural heritage on the one hand, and protecting those elements from the negative impacts of those who come to visit them on the other.

This chapter has identified a range of adverse impacts that people may have on the attractions they visit. These may range from wear and tear impacts on the soft furnishing of a stately home to the physical erosion of footpaths, and from people congestion around a popular exhibit in a museum to traffic congestion around a city-centre visitor attraction. A wide range of visitor management strategies are available to address these impacts and these can be classified either as supply-side strategies, which attempt to increase the capacity of the visitor attraction site to receive visitors without damaging it, or demand-side strategies, which aim to modify visitor behaviour so that they reduce or even eliminate their impact on the site.

A complicating factor is that visitor management may itself be considered to have impacts on the site, particularly if it involves modifying the site so as to compromise its authenticity or if it intrudes overly on the quality of the visitor experience. This opens out a new dimension in the practice of visitor management, in that the task is complicated by the need to identify 'second-best' solutions to the problems faced. Because visitor management can itself have adverse impacts on the visitor attraction, the task of visitor management becomes one of balancing its benefits with its side-effects, rather than simply introducing increasingly strict visitor management measures until visitor impacts are reduced to acceptable levels.

References

Barlow, G. (1999). Managing supply and demand. In *Heritage Visitor Attractions: An Operations Management Perspective* (A. Leask, and I. Yeoman, eds), pp. 157–175. Cassell.

Boyd, S. W. and Timothy, D. J. (2006). Marketing issues and world heritage sites. In *Managing World Heritage Sites* (A. Leask and A. Fyall, eds), pp. 55–68. Elsevier.

Bramwell, B. and Lane, B. (1993). Interpretation and sustainable tourism: the potential and the pitfalls. *Journal of Sustainable Tourism*, **1**, 71–80.

Croft, T. (1994). What price access? Visitor impacts on heritage in trust. In *Cultural Tourism* (J. M. Fladmark, ed), pp. 169–178. Donhead.

Curtis, S. (1998). Visitor management in small historic cities. *Travel and Tourism Analyst*, **3**, 75–89.

ETB – English Tourist Board (1991). *Heritage Sites Working Group: Report to the Tourism and Environment Task Force*, English Tourist Board/Employment Department Group.

Fyall, A. and Garrod, B. (1998). Heritage tourism: at what price? *Managing Leisure*, **3**, 213–228.

Garrod, B., Fyall, A. and Leask, A. (2002). Scottish visitor attractions: managing visitor impacts. *Tourism Management*, **23**, 265–279.

Garrod, B., Fyall, A. and Leask, A. (2006). Managing visitor impacts at visitor attractions: an international assessment. *Current Issues in Tourism*, **9**, 125–151.

Gillette, A. (2000). Managing a museum 120 km long. *Museum International*, **52**, 49–54.

Leask, A. and Fyall, A. (2006). *Managing World Heritage Sites*. Elsevier.

Shackley, M. (1998). Conclusions. In *Visitor Management: Case Studies* (M. Shackley, ed.), pp. 194–205. Butterworth-Heinemann.

Shackley, M. (1999). Visitor management. In *Heritage Visitor Attractions: An Operations Management Perspective* (A. Leask and I. Yeoman, eds), pp. 69–82. Cassell.

Shackley, M. (2006). Visitor management at World Heritage Sites. In *Managing World Heritage Sites* (A. Leask and A. Fyall, eds), pp. 83–93. Elsevier.

Stevens, T. (2000). The future of visitor attractions. *Travel and Tourism Analyst*, **1**, 61–85.

Timothy, D. J. and Boyd, S. W. (2003). *Heritage Tourism*. Prentice-Hall.

CHAPTER **11**
. . . .

School Excursion Tourism and Attraction Management

Brent W. Ritchie, Neil Carr and Chris Cooper

Aims

The aims of this chapter are to:

- highlight the importance of the school excursion market to the attractions sector,
- discuss the management issues surrounding school excursion attraction visits, particularly the need for attraction managers to understand teacher, parent/guardian and school student needs,
- identify some of the major school excursion marketing issues facing attraction managers, including understanding the constraints, segments and possible incentives to encourage school attraction visits, and
- through a case study of Canberra (the national capital of Australia), outline how research can assist attraction and destination managers to understand better the needs, constraints and incentives for school excursion visits.

Introduction

As Ritchie (2003) notes, educational tourism has received little interest from researchers and industry due to a lack of appreciation of the size and potential of this market. Overall, schools tourism is a poorly researched and understood segment of the tourism industry, particularly with regard to its scale, specific nature and needs (Larsen and Jenssen, 2004; Ritchie *et al.*, 2003). Furthermore, as Cooper (1999: 89) suggests, 'the school travel market demands a particular approach in terms of products and promotion, and has its own very different market characteristics and influences'. Attraction managers therefore need to be aware of the demands and nature of the schools market if they intend to develop experiences that meet the needs of teachers and students, and to develop suitable marketing activities that encourage school excursion visitation.

School trips encompass domestic and international trips and student exchanges. Broadly speaking, school trips can be divided into two categories: firstly, there are curriculum-based trips that are directly linked to the lessons taught in the classroom and represent either an integral part or an extension of the formal learning experience. The second type of school trip may be defined as extra-curricular excursions. These are designed outside the constraints of curricular demands and are not linked directly to a particular class or subject of study. Curriculum-based school excursions have the potential to be a significant market for both built and natural attractions. Curriculum-based trips, structured around lessons taught in the classroom, can offer an effective experiential learning opportunity that allows individuals to see how theories and concepts work in reality. Many attraction managers target school excursion groups for educational as well as economic reasons. As Cooper and Latham (1989) suggest, school groups are able to supplement the income of an attraction through spending on merchandise and catering, while many attractions have educational mandates or provide outreach programs with school visits fulfilling an important role within such programs.

This chapter will first outline the size and nature of the school excursion market before examining a number of school excursion management issues that attraction and destination managers need to consider. In particular, this part of the chapter focuses on understanding the need for relevant facilities and educational resources for teachers and students, being aware of safety and risk issues, and infrastructure issues including congestion and relevant facilities for coach drivers. The chapter will then discuss school attraction marketing issues, including the need to understand school constraints, possible incentives and target marketing to increase school attraction visits. Finally, the chapter outlines key findings from an integrated research programme on school excursion tourism in Canberra, the national capital of Australia.

School excursion market

School excursions are not a major income generator for attractions and may never be 'high yield, big business'; however, they do increase the profile of attractions to a group of potential visitors and their parents. Attractions may also garner public acceptance and support through their facilitation of school excursions. Ritchie and Coughlan (2004) contend that marketing to schools is as important as any other market segment for two major reasons. First, young people's attitudes towards a destination and its attractions, both public- and private sector, are likely to be influenced by the experience they have at that time of their lives. As Cooper and Latham (1989) note, school visits are a good investment for the future if there is favourable word of mouth from students. Second, from a tourism visitation perspective, school groups help to bolster off-peak attendances at attractions (Cooper and Latham, 1988). Perhaps an even more compelling reason for better understanding this segment, however, is that cultural attractions such as museums, art galleries and nature parks have become valued as educational and community resources and have a role to play in educating children about scientific and citizenship issues.

A summary of reasons why attractions should target the school excursion market, according to Ritchie *et al.* (2003), includes:

- Schools can be encouraged to visit in the off-peak and quiet times of the day.
- Schools are an excellent source of positive word-of-mouth marketing; children often return with their families.
- Children's exhibits can be newsworthy.
- Schools visits provide an opportunity to promote the non-financial benefits of the visit, including an understanding of such issues as sustainability, environmental concerns, social and cultural issues and issues of race and conflict.
- Children are the adult market of the future.
- The schools market is remarkably loyal and once they have undertaken a successful visit, will return regularly.
- Whilst schoolchildren typically gain entry to commercial attractions at a substantially discounted price, they do spend on retailing and catering.

International curriculum-based trips have been specifically linked with the ability to motivate children to learn foreign languages in an in-depth manner that is not possible in the classroom. The recognition of the value of curriculum-based trips, as an experiential learning tool, is not a modern phenomenon; rather, the field trip has a long history in children's education that can be traced back to at least the 1500s (Tal, 2001). School trips are also utilized to stimulate interest amongst children in specific disciplines and lead to higher-quality learning experiences back in the classroom (Robertson, 2001).

The number of children taking schools trips, especially international ones, is currently expanding. Indeed, Baker (2001) states that in the UK school trips are growing in popularity and although 'local museum visits are still staple fare … even primary schools seem to be opting for residential trips these days'. Although there has been a lack of research into the scale of schools tourism, Cooper and Latham (1989) estimated that in England this market undertook approximately 12 million domestic visits, which is equivalent to 5 per cent of the entire sightseeing market, and generated £8 million annually in the late 1980s. In addition, Revell (2002) stated that, on average, schoolchildren in the UK spend two days on field trips each year. Cooper (1999) notes that, despite official statistics and reports in Europe ignoring school trips, the market is a significant one with an estimated 70 million pupils and students in Europe alone making an estimated 100 million day trip visits and 15–20 million overnight trips during 1998. However, a decline in the number of primary school children in European and other developed nations indicates that the overall school population is likely to continue to decline in these countries for the foreseeable future (Ritchie *et al.*, 2003). This situation is confirmed by declining birth rates in most of the developed countries of the world. Despite the potential size of the school market, a major assumption of marketers, education officers and planners is that the market is generic or homogeneous, when clearly the only commonality is that it all originates in schools. The schools market is diverse in origin, age, purpose of visit, pattern of visit, length of stay, needs and requirements for a satisfying visit. Indeed, this market is becoming more sophisticated with demands for high standards in access, accommodation, educational services, interpretive materials and interactive educational experiences.

Catering for various ages and attitudes, providing high-quality educational material and interactive learning experiences, having well-qualified staff and keeping visitors entertained is a challenge for all sectors of the tourism industry engaged in school visits, but especially for attractions. As Cooper (1999) rightly notes, there is a need to understand the school excursion market including their motivations, needs and constraints. Future development of the experience means identifying the product more closely with the needs of this market and their suppliers. This provides a challenge for attraction managers who must consider the needs of a range of school excursion stakeholders including teachers, parents/caregivers, coach drivers and other attraction providers as well as the students themselves.

School attraction management issues

Estimates suggest that around 50 per cent of the volume of school visits are day trips with the remainder comprising overnight stays (Cooper, 1999). For day trips, the focus of the visit is usually an attraction such as a theme park, museum, art gallery, science centre, garden, zoo or wildlife park. Here, the tourist sector is involved in providing transportation as well as the focus of the visit itself. However, for overnight stays, the accommodation sector also becomes involved. Typically, these trips last up to a week, utilize budget accommodation such as youth hostels or guesthouses, and use coach or minibus transport at the domestic level.

School excursion management issues from the perspective of both teachers, parents/caregivers and destinations (including attraction managers), for the purposes of this chapter, can be summarized into three main themes: (i) attraction facilities and educational resources, (ii) safety-and-risk issues and (iii) infrastructure issues including congestion and facilities for school excursion support services such as coach companies.

Attraction facilities and educational resources

A range of specialist facilities and resources are often required to cater adequately for a school excursion group. As Cooper (1999: 100) suggests, 'from the point of view of schools and teachers, they need to be convinced of the curriculum value of the visit. They will look for this to be demonstrated by the provision of educational materials and resources – this is a central element in the development of the schools product and maximization of its curricular value'. Therefore, attraction managers must ensure that they can adequately supply a range of facilities and resources relevant to the school excursion market including:

- free classroom facilities,
- free indoor packed lunch room/outdoor eating area,
- free familiarization visits for teachers,
- free coach/car parking,
- free adult or accompanying passes depending on the size of the group,
- access to a specialist education team,
- access for special needs, and
- secure storage for belongings.

Justification of school excursions by teachers is mostly made on the basis of educational or curriculum reasons. Therefore, it is vital that attraction managers provide educational resources including pre-visit packs, on-site facilities including rooms, storage and places for eating, as well as post-visit information materials that make direct links to relevant curriculum. A national study of teachers in 1985 in England, determined that services such as teacher resources and student packs, as well as lunch rooms and specialist education staff were very important components of the school excursion experience (Cooper and Latham, 1989). For instance, 72.9 per cent of teachers surveyed in England suggested that teacher educational packs were important, while 55.3 per cent stated that pupil education packs were important to the success of school trips (Cooper and Latham, 1989). In Australia, national research found that 89 per cent of teachers indicated that teacher pre-visit education packs were important while 40 per cent noted that teacher packs at the attraction were also important, indicating the importance of understanding more clearly not only the information needs of teachers but also the timing of information provision (Coughlan et al., 1999).

Many attractions also provide educational officers or a specialist education team to cater towards this market. Indeed, research from Cooper and Latham (1989) and Coughlan et al. (1999) found that 44.7 per cent and 63 per cent of teachers, respectively, felt that specialist educational staff were important for school excursion visits to attractions. School excursion groups consisting of different age groups may require different materials and support. For instance, Ritchie et al. (2003) suggest that younger children have different energy levels and may respond better to tactile and physical displays and more inputs from an education officer than older children who may be more self-sufficient.

Furthermore, Howard (2000) suggests that primary and secondary school teachers, and teachers from country and city areas, showed differences in their venue choice for school excursions based on these characteristics. Understanding the size, scope and nature of the visit group is vital in providing school excursion groups with a quality experience. It is therefore vital to provide lively, exciting and memorable material for teachers and pupils, as well as to plan these into the development of an attraction or destination from the start. These materials should be both age- and subject-specific. Educational materials and displays should:

- encourage pupils to interact with others,
- allow pupils to relate to the material,
- reward pupils wherever possible,
- not preach or over teach,
- make the teacher's job easier and less stressful,
- provide especially for the 9–13-year-old age group, and
- keep it simple.

Furthermore, pre-visit information should also be provided and may include:

- map and details of location,
- details on what there is to see,
- logistics of visit,
- teachers, and possibly student pre-visit packs, with ideas for pre-visit, post-visit and on-site activities, and
- safety-and-risk assessment information.

Such information does not need to be provided in hard-copy format, but could be provided on attraction websites or destination websites developed specifically for school attraction visits.

Safety and risk issues

Despite the variety of sources of pressure being exerted on the educational systems of a variety of countries to stop field trips, probably the largest issue is related to the deaths, accidents and other incidents that occur on school trips, and how they are portrayed in the media. For example, in the UK it has been estimated that seven children died while on school trips in 2001 and 47 between 1985 and 2001 (Revell, 2002). Considering that these deaths were examined in detail by the media, it is not surprising that Robertson (2001: 78) has claimed that 'parents are increasingly nervous about allowing their children to participate in out-of-school activities'.

With teachers and other organizers of school trips increasingly facing criminal charges and the process of public inquiries when a child is injured or killed while on a field trip, it is only parents who are having second thoughts about educational trips. In addition to death or injury, the revelation that over one-third of British school children aged 16 or under have had sexual experiences whilst on holiday, 60 per cent of which involved penetrative sex, shows how schools and teachers may face litigation linked to field trips (Lacey, 2001). Speaking after the publication of the sexual behaviour of children on school trips, Nigel de Gruchy, General Secretary of the National Association of Schoolmasters Union of Women Teachers (NASUWT), which is the UK's second largest teacher's union, suggested that teachers are increasingly being held liable by parents for the behaviour of students while they are on school excursions (Lightfoot, 2001).

Faced with the threat of legal action as a result of incidences that occur during field trips, the NASUWT now advises its members not to organize or go on school trips (BBC News, 2002). While not participating in field trips removes the risk of litigation and/or criminal charges from teachers and schools, it also robs students of the opportunity to take part in school trips and experience the educational benefits associated with them. In effect, the blame culture and litigation mentality increasingly being cultivated around the world could lead to the end of school trips (Robertson, 2001). The British government has attempted to reduce the risk associated with school trips by providing teachers with highly detailed field-trip preparation guidelines. While these are, in theory, a sensible approach to risk management, as Baker (2001) states, 'just reading them [the guidelines] could frighten you off organising a trip'.

Perceptions of safety, particularly in an era of global security and terrorism, may also affect school excursion trips. Some evidence is provided in the context of Canberra, Australia, where a major bushfire in January 2003 destroyed a range of camping grounds and lodge-style accommodation, which catered for school groups. Although the fire did not affect the central city area, where most of the national institutions and attractions are based, perceptions of widespread damage and destruction seriously affected attraction visitation levels, with school visit numbers in the months during and after the bushfire dropping by approximately 50 per cent. Furthermore, anecdotal evidence suggested school visit numbers dropped by as much as 30 per cent at attractions which placed temporary security structures directly in front of their buildings in response to the 9/11 terrorist attacks. Risk-assessment and safety materials should be provided by attraction managers to teachers and school coach operators to reduce the concerns that teachers and parents/guardians may have.

Infrastructure issues

Although school groups are primarily influenced by teachers, and to a lesser extent by parents/guardians, children can influence destination choice based on their physical needs, age and their ability to undertake long trips away from school and home. According to Thornton et al. (1997) accommodation, facilities and distance required to travel will determine whether a location is feasible for a school group to visit. If a destination has high-quality attractions with educational merit but poor support infrastructure such as school-friendly accommodation, poor accessibility from a destination or attraction perspective and lacks suitable medical facilities, this could influence teachers' choice of destination.

Primary schools with younger children are more likely to travel shorter distances than those with older children. The behaviour and needs of children can also significantly influence a school attraction visit. According to Cooper and Latham (1988), most educational visits last less than four hours due to students' inability to cope with travel. Summer months are the most popular time for school excursions in England, while Cooper and Latham (1988) noted in their study that attractions in England did not appear to use school groups to increase their shoulder or off season. Large numbers of school visits in the peak summer season can cause congestion issues and contribute to general visitors' perceptions of school visits as 'noisy and unruly', resulting in a negative perception of both the attraction and the youth population. In Canberra, nearly 40 per cent of all interstate school visits occur in August and September, primarily due to the school year and the sitting dates of parliament, a major attractor for school visits.

Despite attempts through pricing and promotion to increase the number of school visits to the first half of the year, this has proven to be difficult. For instance, as the case study notes, in 2006 an increase of interstate school student numbers by 18.4 per cent from the previous year was recorded. However, the first half of the year only received an increase of 12 per cent compared to 2005, while August recorded a 11 per cent and September a 24 per cent increase. One strategy to deal with overcrowding and the potential disturbance of general visitors is for attractions to hold longer opening hours during the peak season or offer school groups after-hours entry possibly including attraction 'sleep overs' providing a unique experience (although this may only be viable for overnight trips).

Although suitable accommodation may not be as important as attractions with educational merit, it may be important to those teachers who are experienced with overnight school excursions. Accommodation that provides school-friendly dorms and catering services in a cost-effective way are increasingly attractive to school teachers and to parents/guardians who are increasingly required to at least partially fund school excursions. For instance, 8.6 per cent of teachers surveyed in Canberra in 2005 indicated that they were overall very dissatisfied or dissatisfied with their accommodation, while over 11 per cent were very dissatisfied or dissatisfied with the accommodation meals and approximately 7 per cent with the rooms (Ritchie and Uzabeaga, 2006). The standard of product and operators' lack of understanding school group needs were the most common negative experiences teachers noted in the 2005 survey.

It was suggested earlier in this chapter that teachers require additional support facilities and educational resources. However, the needs of support services such as coach drivers and coach companies are often ignored by attraction managers. They too require certain infrastructure or support services in order to help facilitate school attraction visits, including:

- easy-to-navigate maps and clear coach signage,
- adequate (perhaps free) coach parking facilities,
- toilets and facilities for drivers, and
- refreshments (perhaps free) for drivers.

The biggest concern for the majority (39.2 per cent) of coach drivers surveyed in Canberra was the lack of sheltered areas for lunches and the lack of parking at attractions (28.4 per cent), while 9.1 per cent of those who made positive comments noted good coach parking and ease of navigation, while 6.8 per cent said Canberra had good signage (Ritchie and Uzabeaga, 2006).

School attraction marketing issues

Marketing to schools requires a distinctive approach. The education market is loyal and once attracted and satisfied with the services of a destination tend to become regular, repeat visitors. According to Cooper (1999), destinations should have a pro-active and professional approach to promoting themselves to the educational travel market. From a marketing point of view, it is important to recognize the differences in type of school and age of children and consider the elements of the marketing mix which may attract certain schools (see Table 11.1). This is for three key reasons.

Table 11.1 Possible incentives linked with the marketing mix for school excursion tourism

Product	Price	Promotion	Place
Better-quality accommodation	Discounted accommodation	Access to online information	Access to online information
More school-friendly attractions	A rebate per student	A destination planner to assist organizing	A destination planner to assist organizing
Special offers and packages	Special offers and packages	Information seminars held in your region	Access to risk-and-safety information
A special event related to your curriculum		Familiarization tours	
State-based curriculum programmes			
Special exhibitions Special programmes at attractions			

Source: Dale (2007).

Firstly, when mapping the catchment areas of a destination or attraction for potential school visits, research shows that schools are reluctant to take younger children on longer distances and will confine journey time to around an hour (Cooper and Latham, 1988). This severely limits the potential catchment for destinations and attractions. For older children, distances travelled can be greater, but schools still like to complete the visit within the school day.

Secondly, the timing of marketing to schools is crucial and will depend upon the age of the children involved. Dependent upon climate, many countries concentrate their visits into the spring and early summer months. Decisions on such visits are generally taken early in the school year: September/October in the northern hemisphere, and February/March in the southern hemisphere. For younger children, decisions on visits are made approximately one semester ahead of the trip, whereas senior schools tend to operate on an annual cycle. This variation in visit decision-making is important from a marketing point of view, as schools will be more receptive to promotion at certain key times of the year.

Finally, the person in the school who makes the visit decision also varies by the age of the children. For younger groups, the head teacher, or deputy head, makes the decision. For older children, the subject teacher makes the decision. This is also the case for tertiary education groups where the lecturer makes the decision.

Because of the very personal nature of contact with schools and individual teachers, marketing to schools tends to use relationship-marketing approaches such as direct mail. However, other approaches and incentives such as free familiarization visits and price discounts are essential if the promotion is to convert to a visit. Other techniques include (Cooper and Latham, 1989):

- contact with educational authorities,
- direct mailing to schools with newsletters and excursion planning information,
- poster campaigns,
- marketing special events which may be relevant for school groups,
- editorial coverage,
- advertising in the educational press,
- attendance at school visits fairs, and
- attendance at teacher conferences and seminars.

In order to understand better the decisions made by schools concerning destination choice, and how schools come to these decisions, marketers need firstly to be aware that the school market is not a homogeneous one, and that segmentation of the schools market by characteristics may help to target and help overcome the constraints schools may face. Leisure and tourism researchers have been increasingly interested in the role of travel constraints and how these are likely to affect leisure patterns. Yet few studies have thus far been undertaken relating to the constraints faced by school excursion tourism decision makers and what this may mean for school attraction marketing.

According to Crawford and Godbey (1987), such constraints can be placed into three major inter-related categories that move sequentially from the most proximal (intrapersonal) to most distal (structural).

- *Intrapersonal*: These exist when individuals fail to develop leisure or tourism preferences. Examples for school excursion tourism include relevance to curriculum, student behaviour or travel logistics.
- *Interpersonal*: These exist because of a lack of social interaction. Examples include staff shortages or a lack of willingness on the part of teachers to take excursions.
- *Structural*: These are factors that intervene between preferences and participation. Examples include lack of information, cost, timetabling, funding or distance to the attraction.

Dale (2007) identified that as school size grew, so did the importance and influence of interpersonal constraints, while school-related structural constraints became less of an issue. The research also discovered that as the experience level of the teacher increased, intrapersonal constraints was less of an issue but destination-related structural constraints (such as appropriate accommodation, facilities, etc.) became more important constraint for teachers.

The role of the marketer in converting latent into effective demand is to overcome those constraints that research may uncover. Some of these constraints may be inter-related. Due to a staff shortage at a school, teachers may not have a strong willingness to commit to planning school trips. Similarly, student behaviour may have an influence on staff willingness to organize a school excursion. Ultimately, the challenge remains to align the marketing mix more closely with the possible constraints faced by the latent market. In most cases, this will have implications for the further development of the school attraction product, its pricing, promotion and distribution (see Table 11.1).

Furthermore, it should be noted that schools face differing constraints depending on their size, staffing, type, the socio-economic profile of the parents/guardians and their location. The following case study examines how an integrated and strategic research programme can help both attraction and destination managers to understand the constraints and possible incentives to encourage school excursion visits, as well as to understand the needs of teachers, students and support-service providers such as coach drivers.

Case Study: Canberra, national capital of Australia

Canberra is located approximately a 3-hour drive south of Sydney and a 7.5-hour drive from Melbourne, and sits in the Australian Capital Territory (ACT). Canberra is a high-profile destination for the schools market both within the ACT in particular and in Australia in general. The national capital enjoys several major strengths in providing educational tourism experiences and supporting infrastructure. A significant feature is the concentration of major national attractions in a relatively small area. Many national attractions have allocated significant resources to educational programmes, including educational officers, which are curriculum-related and devised to cater for different groups. In contrast, the major weakness of Canberra as a schools destination lies less with its image as with the capacity of its attractions and supporting infrastructure to deal with school visits.

In 1998, attraction managers, accommodation operators and the ACT and Federal government formed the National Capital Educational Tourism Project (NCETP) consortium, the role of which was to develop and market Canberra as a schools excursion destination. Their activities include marketing Canberra as a schools destination, securing funding to offer programmes and rebates to encourage school excursions, as well as developing a research programme to examine the size, nature and value of schools excursion tourism. This research programme included ongoing research to:

- estimate and track the size of the market by gathering data on interstate school excursion numbers at attractions each month and providing yearly estimates,
- understand visiting teachers' perceptions of Canberra as a schools destination, their satisfaction with their current trip, the nature of their trip and their school socio-demographics,
- understand coach-driver school excursion itineraries, and their needs and requirements, and
- examine the nature of the national latent market and school excursion demand, constraints, possible incentives and perceptions of Canberra as a schools excursion destination.

Key findings from the visiting teacher and coach driver research include:

- Interstate school visit numbers have grown from an estimate of 108 000 in 1998 to 144 326 in 2006.
- The most popular months for school excursions to the national capital are the second half of the calendar and academic year. A range of marketing initiatives have been used to encourage visitation to the first half of the year and thereby reduce congestion, including discounted accommodation and attraction-entry fees, behind-the-scenes tours and special programmes.
- The length of stay of school visits is approximately 2.8 nights and over half of schools visiting the national capital in 2005 were from country or regional areas.
- Average expenditure per student is up to AUS$457.65 compared with AUS$328.20 in 2003. This results in an estimated AUS$40 million in gross state product for the ACT compared with AUS$34 million in 2003.
- Just over 98 per cent of teachers in 2005 felt that a visit to the national capital impacted their teaching, with 24 per cent noting it helped their government and democracy units and that it assisted, reinforced and enhanced their students' learning (18.9 per cent).
- Nearly half (46.7 per cent) of respondents were aware of the NCETP prior to a visit to the national capital. Furthermore, 13.8 per cent noted that the NCETP had influenced their decision to visit the national capital, while 58.7 per cent noted that they used the NCETP directly in planning their visit in 2005.

- Almost one-third (31 per cent) of teachers were able to identify that they had a negative experience in the ACT, with the most common negative experiences relating to accommodation utilized by the visiting groups. Generally, these issues related to poor service, especially in relation to problems with the meal packages and the accommodation facilities in general. One-sixth (16.7 per cent) mentioned rude or impatient staff, while 5 per cent mentioned overcrowding at attractions as a negative experience.
- Teachers wanted more evening activities and more physical experiences for students to complement the intellectual/educational experiences.
- Just over half (51.3 per cent) used the educational travel rebate along with contributions from pupils (63.4 per cent) and parent funds (51.3 per cent) to finance their school excursion.
- The biggest concern for the majority (39.2 per cent) of coach drivers was the lack of sheltered areas for lunches and the lack of parking at attractions (28.4 per cent).

The results provide information for attraction managers to develop marketing, product-development and improvement strategies, as well as to lobby government for rebate schemes to assist school excursion travel. Regular research is also used to help attraction managers assess satisfaction levels with the educational tourism product and potential issues that may need addressing.

Key results from the latest national study of 1134 teachers were:

- Perceived safety (70.9 per cent) and ability to cater for school groups (69 per cent) were rated very important factors when deciding on an overnight school excursion destination. Additional important attributes were cost, followed by safety and security of children.
- Attractiveness of incentives in their capacity to encourage respondents to visit the national capital were a rebate per student (66.5 per cent), special offers and packages (60.3 per cent) and discounted accommodation (59.1 per cent).
- Important factors for school attraction visits were discounted admission (77.9 per cent), teacher education packs (76.4 per cent) and guided tours (72.7 per cent), followed by student education packs (62.1 per cent).
- The majority of respondents were not able to take as many excursions as they had liked (72.5 per cent). The cost of travel (83.0 per cent) and lack of funding (76.4 per cent) imposed constraints to schools taking overnight school excursions.
- A high proportion (90.2 per cent) of respondents were involved in or planned to take an overnight excursion in the 2006 calendar year. The majority of these stay away for one night (29.9 per cent), followed by two nights (22.7 per cent).
- Of the overnight excursions undertaken or planned during 2006, the average length of stay was 2.9 nights, the average number of students was 47 and the distance travelled was on average 431 kilometres.
- The most common mode of transport was hired coach or bus (80.1 per cent) and own coach or bus (12.3 per cent). The average maximum distance respondents would travel by road was 560 kilometres, while the maximum distance by air was 3013 km.

- The type of accommodation most commonly used by schools were purpose-built dormitories (21.6 per cent) and motels (11.9 per cent).
- When planning overnight school excursions the methods used by schools are directly booking with attractions/accommodation (59 per cent), coach/bus companies (44.9 per cent) or using previous experience (44.2 per cent).

This information has provided detail on the size and scope of overnight school excursion constraints to participation and possible methods of overcoming such constraints. In particular, safety and risk issues are now paramount and teachers are looking for cost-effective attractions. Also important are educational resources such as education packs, guided tours and student education packs, suggesting that attraction managers need to provide suitable resources (human and material) for school excursion groups. The large number (90 per cent) of schools currently planning an overnight school excursion indicate the potential size of the market. Although the majority of those unable to take more trips mentioned a lack of funding, just over one-half were aware of the educational travel rebate scheme. Promotion of the rebate scheme, special offers and packages, and discounted accommodation were noted as possible tools to overcome the constraints for overnight school excursions.

Finally, incentives for encouraging school excursion travel were also shown to differ (Dale, 2007). Access to online information was less important to schools in regional centres than other schools, whereas the help of a destination planner was more important for rural schools compared to regional centres. Better-quality accommodation was more important for primary schools compared to secondary schools, while those with a dedicated excursion planner placed more importance on better-quality accommodation, discounted accommodation, rebates and special attraction programmes than those without an excursion planner.

Conclusion

This chapter has highlighted the importance of the school excursion market to attractions as well as tourism destinations. There is generally a lack of research into school excursion attraction visits. However, this chapter has identified that attraction managers need to understand teacher, parents/guardians, school students and even the needs of support-service providers such as coach drivers and coach companies in order to provide an educational and rewarding experience and build repeat visitation. Safety-and-risk issues are putting pressure on the educational system to stop field trips, despite their educational benefits. Injuries, deaths and sexual activity cause concern for both teachers and parents/guardians. As Robertson (2001: 78) suggests, 'accepting that accidents do happen, we should learn from them and try to help teachers, parents and children better understand the nature of risk. We need to set standards which achieve the required level of safety while avoiding a culture of over-regulation and bureaucracy'.

Infrastructure problems may result as school attraction visits often take place in the peak summer season, creating potential negative impacts on other visitors. This chapter has provided some suggestions as to how overnight school excursions could deal with this issue through providing after hours entry or 'sleep overs'. Furthermore, school excursion support services may not be perceived as directly relevant to attraction managers, but increasingly schoolteachers are placing greater importance on school-friendly accommodation. Subsequently, this chapter has argued that the school excursion market should be treated like any other market with appropriate and targeted marketing activities developed by attraction and destination managers. Elements of the marketing mix can be used by managers to try and convert latent demand into effective demand through the development of innovative products, pricing incentives, clear promotional strategies and distribution channels that meet the needs of school groups.

Supplying the schools market is a very specialized activity, demanding careful product development and a sound knowledge of the needs of schools, which is often lacking due to a limited research into this market. This chapter has provided a case study of a research programme undertaken in Canberra, the national capital of Australia, to illustrate how research can assist school attraction product development and marketing activities. More research is required to understand more fully this neglected market, especially concerning the role that parents/guardians and children themselves play in school excursion visits, helping to move the research focus away from teachers and tourism providers. As part of this focus, the influence that a school visit has on future destination and attraction loyalty and on educational outcomes should be examined in more detail.

References

Baker, M. (2001). Second thoughts about school outings. *BBC News*. http:// news.bbc.co.uk/hi/english/education/features/mike_baker/newsid_142 6000/1426203.stm.

BBC News (2002). Fresh school safety review pledged. http://news.bbc. co.uk/hi/english/education/newsid_1862000/1862840.stm.

Cooper, C. (1999). The European school travel market. *Travel and Tourism Analyst*, **5**, 89–106.

Cooper, C. and Latham, J. (1988). English educational tourism. *Leisure Studies*, **9**, 331–334.

Cooper, C. and Latham, J. (1989). School trips: an uncertain future? *Leisure Management*, **9**, 73–75.

Coughlan, D., Ritchie, B. W., Wells, J. and Tsang, A. (1999). *Schools Educational Tourism Project Research Report*. Centre for Tourism and Leisure Policy Research, University of Canberra.

Crawford, D. and Godbey, A. (1987). Reconceptualising barriers to family leisure. *Leisure Sciences*, **9**, 119–127.

Dale, N. (2007). Identifying strategies to overcome constraints to school excursions: an Australian case study. Unpublished Honors Dissertation. Centre for Tourism Research, University of Canberra.

Howard, J. (2000). Parks as schools: what do teachers want from an excursion? *Parks and Leisure Australia*, **2**, np.

Lacey, H. (2001). Foreign tongues. *The Guardian*, 29 May.

Larsen, S. and Jenssen, D. (2004). The school trip: travelling with, not to or from. *Scandinavian Journal of Hospitality and Tourism*, **4**, 43–57.

Lightfoot, L. (2001). Alarm as pupils claim to have sex on school trips. *The Telegraph*, 24 May.

Revell, P. (2002). Trips that end in tragedy. *The Guardian*, 11 March.

Ritchie, B. W. (2003). *Managing Educational Tourism*. Channel View Publications, Clevedon.

Ritchie, B. W., Carr, N. and Cooper, C. (2003). School's educational tourism. In *Managing Educational Tourism* (B. W. Ritchie, ed), pp. 130–180. Channel View Publications, Clevedon.

Ritchie, B. W. and Coughlan, D. (2004). Understanding school excursion planning and constraints: an Australian case study. *Tourism Review International*, **8**, 113–126.

Ritchie, B. W. and Uzabeaga, S. (2006). *Discover what it means to be Australian in your National Capital: Size and effect of school excursions to the National Capital, 2005*. Centre for Tourism Research, University of Canberra.

Robertson, E. (2001). Risk needs to be managed, not feared. *Geographical*, **73**, 78.

Tal, R. (2001). Incorporating field trips as science learning environment enrichment: an interpretative study. *Learning Environments Research*, **4**, 25–49.

Thornton, P. R., Shaw, G. and Williams, A. M. (1997). Tourist group holiday decision-making and behaviour: the influence of children. *Tourism Management*, **18**, 287–297.

CHAPTER **12**
. . . .

Managing Temporal Variation in Visitor Attractions

Philip Goulding

Aims

The aims of this chapter are threefold:

- to examine and review what is understood by the concept and components of temporal variation in tourism,
- to examine the operational implications of temporal variation to visitor attractions, both as revenue centres in their own right and as part of the wider local tourism economy, and
- to examine potential attraction management responses to temporally variable markets and the expectations of visitors.

Scotland's tourism industry and its visitor attractions are the context of many of the findings and analysis in this chapter, including a case study highlighting the challenges of temporal visitor management in Scotland's nature-based and wilderness attractions operators. A broad view of what constitutes an 'attraction' is adopted in this chapter.

Introduction

The importance of visitor attractions to many local, regional and even national tourism economies has been well documented. In many parts of urban and rural Scotland, they are critical (Garrod, 2003) and represent a cornerstone of destination pull. Indeed, their ability to stimulate market development and overall visitor spend, to interpret and present aspects of cultural heritage and create local honeypots has been recognized by public agencies such as Highlands and Islands Enterprise (2002) and most recently the Scottish Executive (2006). Many attractions include all-weather facilities, and as such have the potential to generate market demand throughout the year. Despite this, temporal variation through imbalances in demand and supply remains endemic in the visitor attraction sector. This is particularly the case in the cool temperate climatic zones, within which a significant part of the world's tourism activity takes place (Baum and Hagen, 1999).

Visitor attractions display complex relationships with the temporal nature of tourism in their destination areas. On the one hand, they are typically at the mercy of the seasonal and periodic nature of market forces, which can manifest in either predictable or sometimes chaotic demand patterns during the course of an operating day, week, month or year. Yet through their operational policies, attractions can collectively, and sometimes individually, contribute to, reinforce or combat patterns of demand disparity in a tourism destination, especially where major attractions, or groups of attractions, play a key role in promoting and sustaining the destination of which they are part. There is a growing range of options available to attractions as to how they respond to temporal challenges. However, before exploring such relationships and options, it is pertinent to consider what is meant by 'temporal variation'.

Towards an understanding of temporal variation in tourism

Historically, the term 'seasonality' has been used as shorthand to convey the peaks and troughs of temporal imbalances in tourism, particularly from a visitor demand perspective. Yet the operational challenges faced by visitor attractions point to a much more complex temporal canvas than dealing with simply 'seasonal' variation. In contrast to most forms of commercial overnight guest accommodation, the inventory and space of commercially operated permanent attractions is temporally perishable throughout the operating day, as well as from day to day and across the time spectrum of weeks, months and 'seasons' (Pender and Sharpley, 2005). Moreover, for many attractions operators, demand disparity between quiet and peak visitation periods can generate external (community/destination) costs as well as internal costs arising from variable service operation. Temporally concentrated demand patterns and trading periods, irrespective of the timescale, do not provide economic advantages for a fixed facility attraction with high fixed costs.

For the purposes of this study, temporal variation is deconstructed into 'seasonality' and short-term periodic variation.

'Seasonality' in a tourism context is usually understood to refer to market-derived temporal imbalances. Grant *et al.* (1997) refer to the peaks and troughs of visitor numbers during a calendar year, while Butler's (2001: 5) definition of 'seasonality' provides a broad approach: '[a] temporal imbalance ... which may be expressed in terms of dimensions of such elements as numbers of visitors, expenditure of visitors, traffic on highways and other forms of transportation, employment and admissions to attractions'.

There is an inherent vagueness in the terminologies applied to seasonality. The term 'shoulder' period is used extensively in tourism to denote a period of time linking 'peak' demand and periods of least demand, although there is often little evidence of criteria used to denote the characteristics of the 'shoulder period'. Similar vagueness applies to the terms 'off peak', 'high season', 'mid-season' and 'low season'. This is especially pertinent, given the market peculiarities of individual attractions, when public-agency intervention or destination-wide collaborative initiatives are used to promote seasonal extension policies, 'low season' market growth, seasonal employment, and so on. The 'twin peaks', 'multi-peaking' or 'non-peak' characteristics of demand (Butler and Mao, 1997) may even render concepts of a defined 'shoulder' or 'low season' obsolete in some locations.

Seasonality is thus generally accepted to be a demand-driven phenomenon (Butler, 2001; Lundtorp, 2001), in which the vagaries of the market dictate opening and closing patterns of businesses and facilities and the levels of service provided at certain times of the year. However, a reliance on knowledge or understanding of demand patterns and characteristics to explain seasonality is an oversimplification. In addition to demand-led market forces, factors that collectively influence the seasonal nature of tourism to a location and its attractions include:

- the role of underlying causal factors (such as institutional holidays, climate, social conventions and evolving patterns of work-life balance),
- supply-side factors (such as local labour availability, planning constraints, transport access and corporate decisions on opening and closure), and
- wider community and resource implications, such as the role of local stakeholders in determining facility use across the year; and of environmental constraints and policy, for example seasonal closure (conservation/preservation/community recovery) or spreading demand and facility use across the year (for example, local economic sustainability).

Figure 12.1 illustrates the inter-connectedness of determinants and influences on seasonal patterns. There is growing acceptance that a multi-dimensional approach is necessary to understand patterns of seasonality (Butler, 2001).

Temporal imbalance needs to be recognized as being more than a 'seasonal' effect. Apart from 'seasonality', it is also important to consider the implications of short-term periodic temporal variation (Frechtling, 2001; Lundtorp, 2001; Pender and Sharpley, 2005), the significance of which has been generally much under-represented in the tourism literatures.

The phenomenon of *monthly fluctuation* in tourism is inherently predictable (Frechtling, 2001). However, unusual or *ad hoc* events not occurring annually,

Demand-oriented factors

Market analysis: temporal trip/spend characteristics of existing market sectors – historic trends

Consumer research: travel-timing characteristics, trip decisions, motivational research, work-life balance changes, destination image analysis, additional holiday/break analysis

Development of market segment profiles by temporal flexibility

Niche marketing

Development of season-extending new products – consumer responsiveness

Causal factor analysis

Natural influences:
- *climatic* variables at point of trip generation and destination
- *spatial* attributes (remoteness, access, distance)

Institutional influences:
- public holidays, religious festivals, calendar effects, holiday entitlement, tax year, business customs, etc.

Socio-cultural factors:
- inertia/habit/mind-set
- fashionability
- social necessity

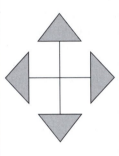

Resource Implications

Environmental factors:
- overuse/degradation of natural resource in peak season
- degradation of physical resource in peak season

Resource competition:
- demands of other seasonal economic activities on labour force, land, capital

Socio-cultural factors:
- community recovery
- tourism versus socio-cultural conflicts – e.g. religious observance in peak seasons

Supply-driven perspectives

Capacity limitations: destination carrying capacity, fixed on-site capacity, transport access and capacity

Operating decisions: e.g. corporate opening/closure policies (heritage attraction agencies, local authorities); marginal cost/revenue relationships; threshold cost/revenue targets; utilization thresholds

Labour force: availability, training needs, flexibility

'Lifestyle' or 'hobby' businesses – not necessarily profit/target driven

Figure 12.1
Perspectives of seasonality
Source: Adapted from Goulding (2006).

such as the Oberammergau Passion Play, localized one-off events such as the Tall Ships Race visit, or special temporary 'flagship' exhibitions such as the Gold of the Pharaohs, will distort the temporal balance of tourism in the locations where they are held. Furthermore, *calendar effects* such as the number of weekends in a month and movable festivals such as Easter will add to the distortion of short-term periodic trends (Frechtling, 2001), such as weekly and monthly visitor arrivals or visitor throughput performance in attractions. Other short-term irregularities such as a one-off conference or a demand-surge following the opening of a new facility also impact on visitor numbers and revenue. However, the inclusion of periodic variation relating to shorter-term fluctuations in demand, such as within the course of a day, from day to day, weekday to weekend and week-by-week variations, is still far from widespread under the umbrella of temporal performance imbalances in tourism analysis. Lundtorp (2001) provides some rationale for its consideration as part of the broader operational canvas, noting that variations in the number of visitors during the course of a week can be of great importance for the attraction and the destination of which it is a part.

Many small tourism amenities in seasonal operating environments experience periods of intense daily work patterns during peak seasons. For independent proprietors, in particular, this may impact on their trading behaviours and operating decisions at other times, especially the desire for periodic rest and relaxation (Goulding, 2006). Figure 12.2 provides an illustrative summary of temporal variation.

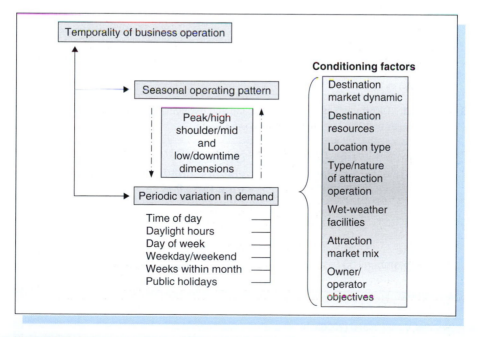

Figure 12.2
Conceptual framework of temporality for visitor attractions

Periodic variation therefore contributes to an understanding of temporal cycles in tourism that may be seen as distinct from longer-term patterns of *seasonality*. Temporal 'downtime' may represent a more meaningful descriptor in operational and economic terms.

Operational implications of seasonality for visitor attractions

The dynamic of an attraction's composite visitor market and the temporal characteristics of each market segment clearly influence the overall spread of revenues and visitor numbers. While this seems to state the obvious, many attractions continue to be over-dependent on highly seasonal or temporally fixed market sectors, such as families with school-age children. In Scotland, there is a marked temporal difference between overseas and domestic holiday visits, as illustrated in Table 12.1. Around 70 per cent of visits to attractions occur during the second and third quarters of the year, which are influenced significantly by the summer-oriented overseas-visitor holiday market. Indeed, there is some evidence of a trend towards greater concentration in the summer months by overseas visitors in recent years (STB, 2001; VisitScotland, 2006a), mainly at the expense of the spring months. In less accessible peripheral areas of Scotland, the degree of seasonal concentration of overseas visitors is more acute.

Operating to seasonally defined periods has long been a characteristic of Scottish attractions. The visitor attractions monitor (VAM) represents the closest measure to a national census of visitor attractions within Scotland.

Table 12.1 Distribution of visitors to Scotland and to Scottish visitor attractions, by quarter

Quarter	UK visitors' holiday trips (%) 2005	Overseas visitors' holiday trips (%) 2005	Visits to attractions all visitor markets (%) 2005
January–March	18	8	16
April–June	26	20	29
July–September	33	61	38
October–December	23	12	17

Source: VisitScotland (2006a, b).

The 2004 VAM identifies 251 Scottish attractions as operating for less than nine months of the year from a survey total of 642, almost 40 per cent of the total (VisitScotland, 2005a). Nine months is the cut-off point used in the survey to define 'seasonality' in operations. An extension of the definition to include attractions operating for longer trading seasons while still having periods of closure would almost certainly increase this proportion. Seasonally closing attractions include such primary and iconic regional attractions as the Balmoral Estates (Grampian), Cawdor Castle (Highland), Dunrobin Castle (Sutherland), Floors Castle (Borders), Glenfinnan Monument (Highland), Mount Stuart House and Gardens (Isle of Bute) and the Museum of Flight (East Lothian).

The most prevalent – and over-represented in terms of seasonal attractions – are those operated as charities or trusts and privately owned and managed attractions. It should be stressed that 'charities' and 'trusts' as listed within the VAM cover a spectrum of organizational types and legal arrangements (Leask, 2003), ranging from local community-run heritage centres, especially on island communities, to large estates such as some of the Borders and Perthshire historic houses. As with privately run businesses, seasonal operation may reflect specific motivational or influencing forces within the contexts of community, social and environmental objectives, as well as revenue generating considerations. Scotland's two largest attractions estates, Historic Scotland and the National Trust for Scotland, have relatively few managed attractions in their respective portfolios that operate seasonally or on restricted opening hours, reflecting their partnership in Scotland's national tourism seasonal extension campaigns.

Irrespective of the forms, causes or manifestations of temporal variation, there are some fundamentally universal implications for attraction operators. Two of the main ones are labour-related and capacity utilization issues.

Labour force issues

A seasonally defined tourism destination can create instabilities in the local labour market, especially in tourism-dependent rural or peripheral locations. In their analysis of tourism in peripheral regions of northern Europe and maritime Canada, Baum and Hagen (1999) noted the negative impact on the quality of service delivery caused by the short-tourism season, which in turn reduced the competitive edge of amenities and visitor attractions in those places. A number of contributory issues were identified, discussed below.

Recruitment of staff

The disproportionate cost to the organization of hiring staff for relatively short periods (as little as ten weeks in some cases) inhibits the development of progressive remuneration packages for those employees. Moreover, short seasonal working contracts may limit the pool of local labour willing and able to undertake such work. Citing the case of the Swedish island of Gotland, Baum and Hagen noted the dependence of operators on school and university students to fill vacancies. The end of the island's tourism season is determined as much by the flight of labour at the start of the academic year (15 August) as by consumer demand.

An additional recruitment issue for some heritage attractions is that highlighted by Deery and Jago (2001). They note the specialist craft skills required by some attraction operators to authenticate the visitor experience. Such skills, for example wheelwrighting, operating coal or textile machinery, may be unique to a particular attraction and in short supply in the local workforce, who are in turn more inclined to take up permanent posts than seasonal or temporary ones.

Cost of training and development

Given that this is spread over a shorter time-span, attractions may be less willing to invest in training and development for their seasonal staff, particularly where the work pattern is predominantly part time. The Association of Scottish Visitor Attractions (ASVA) encourages its members to demonstrate commitment to raising service quality through extending training opportunities to all staff, both seasonal and permanent.

Commitment of seasonal workers to the operation

Although it is accepted that an element of the labour force will prefer short-term contracts of either full- or part-time nature, for other job starters there remains an issue of commitment to the organization. Faced with competition from other service sectors offering the prospect of more permanent employment (for example retail, hospitality and call centres), seasonal attractions may have to carry the costs associated with relatively high-staff turnover rates. In the 2004 VAM survey, 'poor seasonality' is cited as the second highest staff retention problem for among Scottish attractions operators. However, little in the way of structured, comparative research has been done into the retention and turnover of seasonal staff in the attractions sector.

Heritage attractions and those operated by trusts often rely to a significant degree on volunteer staff. Table 12.2 shows the degree of prevalence of seasonal and volunteer staff in Scotland's visitor attractions, 20 per cent and 40 per cent respectively in 2004, from a sample of 549 operations. Jago and Deery (2001) note the increasing complexity of volunteers' motivations in heritage attractions and the ascendancy of personal development as a desired unremunerated reward. Accordingly, seasonal attractions relying on such staff may increasingly find themselves having to address issues around volunteer management and development to ensure their commitment to return the following season.

Table 12.2 Permanent versus seasonal employment in Scottish visitor attractions, 2004

Employment type	Percentage	Total employees
Full-time permanent	27	3167
Part-time permanent	13	1456
Full-time seasonal	8	950
Part-time seasonal	12	1331
(Unpaid volunteers)	40	4661
Total	100	11 565

Source: VisitScotland (2005a).

Loss of skills and experience at the end of the season

Inter-linked with commitment is the problem of consistency, where valued skilled staff are unavailable for the following season. Given that the essence of visitor attractions service delivery is often the interactions between the staff and the customers, consistency in service quality from year to year may depend on continuity of the skills, experience and personal qualities of front-line staff.

Capacity utilization

Although 'problems' associated with temporal imbalances are most often considered in terms of underutilization, demand-peaking can be just as problematic for visitor attractions. Symptoms of peak overutilization include:

- Congestion, including overflowing car and coach parks, on-site traffic congestion, exceeding natural or built carrying capacity and visitor bottle-necking.
- Diminished visitor satisfaction from the experience: excess queuing, limited dwell time in popular areas, limited access to guides or other on-site staff, diminished service in retail or catering units, limited access to toilets, child-care facilities and so on, all contribute to lower satisfaction levels.
- A heightened level of wear and tear on the core resource and its ancillary infrastructures, including degradation of the physical fabric of buildings, exhibits, furnishings, gardens and parkland attributable to the volume of visitor throughput. This may be compounded if there is a deficiency in the level of visitor management and control at peak times.

- Externalities (community costs) including off-site parking, grass verge degrad-ation, traffic congestion and resultant costs of extra traffic management to the local community, increased levels of litter, noise and carbon pollution.

Visitor attractions can employ a range of supply-rationing methods to over-come capacity constraints during periods of peak demand (Garrod, 2003). Most typically these include queue management, cordoning car parking, limiting access once carrying capacity is reached. Increasingly, popular large attractions are following the example of Madame Tussauds in introducing timed ticketing as a way to smooth demand peaks. Recent additions include the London Eye and the Queen's Gallery at Buckingham Palace.
Characteristics of temporal underutilization include:

1. Perishability of the unit of production:
   - The element of permanency in the physical structure of attractions means that most attractions are relatively inflexible in adapting to lower scales of operation during quiet periods. Closure of rooms within his-toric houses or parts of museums, for example, may have little impact on lowering variable costs but risks lowering visitor satisfaction.
   - Underachievement of revenue-earning potential during much of the operating season.
   - Temporal demand or closure patterns in core attractions render ancillary revenue-generating components perishable (for example on-site cater-ing, garden centres, retail sales outlets). There is a clearly defined inven-tory in cost and revenue-generating terms in many attractions (e.g. preserved railways, theme park rides, special exhibitions) the contribu-tions of which can be temporally measured.
2. Cash flow, revenue and profit contribution are concentrated into a short operating period and subsidize fixed and variable costs over the full oper-ating period. Findings from previous large-scale studies undertaken by Leask et al. (2000) into Scotland's visitor attractions indicated that these financial considerations are the key reasons for attractions operating sea-sonal closures or restricted opening patterns during parts of the year. A more recent survey of independently operated seasonal businesses in Scotland has reiterated this finding (Goulding, 2006).
3. Opportunity costs of idle space, equipment and staff for much of the oper-ating period, where the attraction is operating below its fixed capacity to produce.
4. Capital investment: the income-concentrating effect of temporal variation can deter capital investment in tourism infrastructures and at destinations generally. For private-sector attraction operators, the shorter the season, the greater are the risks in recouping investment costs and the longer the payback time required.

In the increasingly competitive and uncertain national and international market place for leisure and tourism, overcoming the issues outlined above requires ever more resourceful and imaginative measures. Some of the main management responses to temporal variation are discussed in the next section.

Management responses to temporal variation

In the first instance, it must be acknowledged that the need or case for 'solving' or 'overcoming' temporal imbalances is not universally accepted, especially where natural resources form the base of a managed attraction. Mathieson and Wall (1982) were among the first to advocate the cause for dormant periods being necessary for the recovery of social and ecologically fragile environments, many of which may be heritage-based resources. Clearly, temporal operation may be necessitated where a nature-based attraction is built around a natural cycle such as birdlife migration. This is the basis of seasonal closure in the Loch Garten Osprey Centre in Speyside and the Royal Society for the Protection of Birds (RSPB) Forsinard Reserve in Sutherland.

The sustainability debate has swung strongly in recent years towards 'managing' temporality through adaptation to seasons and periodic variations. In their study of operators on the Danish island of Bornholm, Getz and Nilsson (2004) observe three types of operator response to 'dealing with' extended periods of low demand. These include 'capitulating' to the condition, which sooner or later leads to business failure; adopting 'coping' strategies, which embodies the idea of accepting prevailing temporal conditions but adapting to them; or more positively, adopting 'combating' behaviours, tactics and strategies to actively reduce disparities in demand and operating levels.

Coping with or accepting temporal variations

Attraction operators may either maintain the operational *status quo* or concentrate their response efforts on redeploying resources more efficiently. This could involve:

1. Devoting more effort to visitor management in peak periods.
2. Attempting to shift demand within existing peak periods (for example through extending daily opening and/or closing times, negotiating with tour groups and coach parties to vary arrival and dwell times as appropriate and incentivizing such arrival shifts through pricing, promotional packaging and/or parking tariffs).
3. Tackling some of the implications of seasonal employment as discussed above.
4. Optimizing the use of the 'low season', quiet days, early mornings or late afternoons or non-trading periods as appropriate, for maintenance and repair tasks, attending trade fairs or other forms of business networking, training, business planning, marketing, inventorizing or recuperation.

Employ tactical responses to seasonal extension

These usually focus on marketing mix elements, including:

1. *Product extension and development.* Typical among these elements in the context of historic houses are the staging of *ad hoc* events where space permits, such as seasonally themed horticultural shows, classic vehicle rallies, food and drink demonstrations, craft fairs, antiques fairs and farmers' markets. Such events have the advantage of utilizing otherwise unemployed ground space that can be sub-let for events. Several of the historic houses in the Scottish Borders, for example, use the winter and early spring 'down time' for non-touristic revenue-generating activities, such as promoting themselves as film locations, hosting seminars and extended corporate hospitality events. Museums, galleries and themed commercial attractions can develop educational and community events to coincide with otherwise quiet periods, around the school curriculum or with local businesses, media and charities, for example hosting fundraising activities.

    Product-extension initiatives in quiet periods may focus on the non-core features of the attraction, including retailing and food/beverage provision, where these are seen as viable revenue centres in their own right.

2. *Pricing.* Temporally based pricing techniques remain an underutilized tool among attraction operators. This is particularly so in the case of seasonal pricing differentiation. Many attraction operators keep seasonal price differentiation narrow, concentrating instead of offering additional product benefits in non-peak periods. For example, entry to temporary exhibitions, craft demonstrations or ancillary on-site attractions can be included in the gate price in shoulder or low season periods or during quiet periods during the week.

    'Periodic' pricing is increasingly employed as a reward for early morning or late afternoon arrival during quieter periods of the year, to encourage greater spread in visitor flows. However, where time-differentiated pricing is used, the main objective is often to shift existing demand away from peaks rather than to create additional off-peak demand.

    To survive the challenges arising in recent years from UK government policy of free entry to prominent museums in public ownership, commercial operators will have to employ ever-more creative temporal pricing policies designed not simply to meet fixed cost contributions or other financial targets, but as importantly to encourage repeat visitation and customer loyalty in the longer term.

Take a strategic view of maximizing revenue opportunities, which might include:

1. *Market diversification.* As an example, the Scotch Whisky Experience (SWE) in Edinburgh has successfully developed lucrative corporate hospitality, meetings and small functions markets. Initially on the back of its core

attraction, these have become self-sustaining and separate markets in their own right.

2. *Investment in facilities, interpretation and services.* To achieve the above market diversification, the SWE invested in converting office space into prestigious meeting rooms.

3. *Adopting yield-management philosophies* as creatively as in other sectors, such as hotels, budget airlines and car hire. Though the cost structures of most attractions reflect high fixed to variable cost relationships, there is plenty of scope for attractions operators to be more responsive to temporal revenue contributions.

Collective responses

On a broader front, it is increasingly recognized that attractions need to be proactive in destination area market development and adopt a more commercial outlook, where once a curatorial outlook pervaded (especially in public-sector attractions).

Numerous forms of collective response channels are available to visitor attractions to mitigate the effects of temporal variation. Local 'explorer pass' attraction initiatives have operated successfully in London, Edinburgh, North Wales and Orkney, among other places. However, there is always the danger that participation in joint promotional initiatives can result in exacerbating an existing demand pattern, if it succeeds in generating more business at peak times. Accordingly attractions operators need to be mindful of their principal priorities between generalized or temporally targeted demand generation.

More formalized consortia enhance collective marketing (such as the Sussex Top Attractions Consortium), while trade associations, such as the Historic Houses Association and the Independent Museums Association, are able to lobby government in policy areas that impinge on the overall viability of their sectors. A more common route of participation for operators is active involvement in destinational seasonal extension marketing campaigns and, particularly in the case of multiple attractions operators, involvement in national-level season-extension strategies.

While the shoulder or low seasons may offer a natural 'space' for collaboration compared with the peak season, commercial sensitivities can limit their effectiveness. For example, collective seasonal extension pricing promotions by locally competing attraction operators can be a double-edged sword. Fyall *et al.* (2001) noted the reluctance of larger (that is, higher profile) attractions to engage in off-season joint ticketing initiatives, when the risk of reduced dwell time and secondary expenditure by visitors has a greater impact than in peak season periods. On the other hand, similar initiatives in Scandinavian countries have been seen to garner success through collaboration (Natural Capital, 2004).

Finally, the role of governments and their public-sector agencies must be considered as part of the overall management response to temporal variation in tourism, which has been seen as a symptom of market failure in tourism, and as such forms the rationale for government intervention. The issue has been addressed in a wide range of public-policy issues beyond direct tourism initiatives, including proposals to stagger academic holidays (notably by the European Commission), rural development and transport policy. Table 12.3 identifies a range of public sector as well as attraction specific (supply-side) responses to seasonality, as surveyed by Goulding (2006) and Natural Capital (2004, on behalf of Scottish Enterprise) in Scotland.

Table 12.3 Supply-side strategies for coping with or combating temporal variation

Attraction responses	Public-Sector policy responses
'Combat' responses: adoption of temporal extension strategies and practices	*'Combat' responses: adoption of temporal extension policies and practices*
• Year-round opening • Extended hours/days of opening • Temporal pricing • Market diversification: eg educational trips, local communities • Product extension/diversification • Events strategy • Promotional activities (quiet period awareness raising) • Participate in collective promotions and business networks (e.g. destination marketing initiatives, travel trade incentive visits)	• Fiscal incentives • Labour force incentives – e.g. training initiatives • Staggering of school holidays • Business support services geared to seasonal extension, e.g. marketing, financial advice • Creation, support or participation in seasonal extension programmes (e.g. events strategies) • Weather-friendly planning policies (e.g. towards wet-weather facilities)
Acceptance of/coping with temporal disparities	*Acceptance of/coping with temporal disparities*
• Offer reduced capacity in line with resource limitation (e.g. reduced staffing level) • Lower service level, e.g. part closure of non-essential amenities • Full seasonal closure of all facilities • Temporary closure (e.g. during lowest revenue periods) • Restrict opening/closing times • Use downtime for maintenance, repair and upgrading work • Manage customer expectations	• Environmental regeneration initiatives • Infrastructural repairs, road repairs, etc. during low seasons and non-event periods • Focus business support on high season initiatives • Support off-season community initiatives (e.g. local arts festivals)

Sources: Adapted from Goulding (2006) and Natural Capital (2004).

Case Study: Managing customer expectations in bad weather and low-season periods: the experience of nature- and wildlife-based attractions

Scotland's natural environment and the range of things to see and do have long been recorded in visitor attitude surveys as the principal reasons why leisure visitors holiday or take breaks in Scotland (VisitScotland, 2005b). Natural landscapes and managed wildlife resources are key attractions in the country's armoury of tourism assets. Indeed nature- and wildlife-based attractions represent a growth sector among Scotland's diverse tourism attractions sector. Examples of the diversity and range are shown in Table 12.4.

In addition to the above-managed attractions, Scotland's tourism economy has witnessed rapid growth in recent years of wildlife tour and excursion operators.

Table 12.4 Principal nature-based attractions in Scotland

Name and location	Visitors 2005	Free or paid entry
Scottish Seabird Centre, North Berwick	143 000 (estimated)	Free
Vane Farm RSBP Reserve, Kinross	76 000[a] (estimated)	Entrance fee
Lochwinnoch RSPB Nature Centre	40 000	Free
Loch Garten Osprey Centre, Nethybridge	33 000	Entrance fee
Scottish Wildlife Trust, Dunkeld	22 000	Free
Cairngorm Reindeer Centre, Aviemore	8500 (estimated)	Entrance fee
Caerlaverock Wildlife & Wetlands Trust, Dumfries	18 000	Free
Jedforest Deer & Farm Park, Jedburgh	17 000	Entrance fee
Falls of Clyde Wildlife Reserve, New Lanark	15 600[a]	Free
St Cyrus Nature Reserve, Montrose	15 400	Free
Insh Marshes Nature Reserve, RSPB, Kingussie	12 000 (estimated)	Free
Loch Gruinart Nature Reserve, Argyll	10 500	Free
Bright Water Visitor Centre, Isle of Skye	4500[a]	Free

Source: VisitScotland (2006b).
[a]2004 data.

While visitor attitudes remain positive towards Scotland's natural amenities, expectations of good weather and the seasonal differences of Scotland at different times of the year tend not to feature as major deterrents for visitors (Natural Capital, 2004) even though 'the weather' is typically cited as a source of disappointment in visitor attitude surveys. For operators, the twin issues of 'seasonality' and managing visitors' expectations during peak and non-peak periods and in inclement weather are frequently expressed concerns (Natural Capital, 2004; Scottish Executive, 2006). The first of these manifests as a 'catch 22' situation insofar as seasonal closure of attractions might itself be a deterrent to visiting a locality while on the other hand lack of visitors in quiet periods is uneconomic and is known to be a primary cause for site closure (Butler, 2001). At stake is the issue of managing visitor expectations during both peak and non-peak periods.

Clearly, wet-weather facilities at essentially open-air attractions can be considered a 'front-line' approach to providing enhancements during inclement weather. However, for many nature-based attractions, there are limits to the degree to which enclosed visitor centres can substitute for the experience of 'closeness' to the natural attraction. Yet many of Scotland's nature-based attractions manage to operate a long operational season for visitors. For the nature-based attractions sector as a whole, patterns of visitation reflect the overall distribution of Scottish attractions (VisitScotland, 2006b). Yet for such operators, the specific temporal issues relating to the habitat and breeding cycles of their core natural and wildlife attractions pose added operational challenges.

Capitalizing on the weather and time of year

Around the world, nature reserve and wildlife-spotting operators take advantage of what otherwise might be termed adverse or sub-optimal conditions. Promoting the advantages of wet weather, cloud cover and reduced daylight hours can be used to effect in viewing wildlife. For example, spotting whales, dolphins and basking sharks in the Irish Sea is often easier in wet weather than in bright sunlight, while geese and other large bird species in flock formations can be seen to more striking effect during daybreak and when the sun is low in the sky.

Using a calendar approach to chart the arrival, breeding cycle, behaviours and departure of different species throughout the year can be a tool to engage visitors – especially locals and those with a particular interest in the natural resource – and encourage repeat visitation. This is demonstrated by the Scottish Seabird Centre in North Berwick which capitalizes on opportunities to tempt visitors to return to the Centre to see subsequent arrivals of migratory and breeding seabird species. Remote cameras and webcams record 'live' activity in seabird colonies while interpretation boards and videos of the species' lifecycles, habitats and behaviours provide a contextual educational base to the live viewings.

The RSPB has promoted educational activities related to biodiversity studies around its managed sites in various parts of Scotland (e.g. Mersehead Reserve on the Solway Firth and Lochwinnoch Nature Centre in Ayrshire). Bird watching is inherently seasonal and is promoted accordingly, with late-autumn and early-winter migration watching promoted as 'seasonal highlights' (RSPB, 2007). Expectation management includes detail to the information on seasonal dress codes and equipment to heighten the experience. This supplements information on seasonal, diurnal and nocturnal conditions and what can be seen within the protected habitats at different times. Interpretation of the sites for visitors is therefore based on the ethos of realistic rather than raised expectations.

Table 12.5 Incentivizing visits to natural attractions during quiet or low-season periods

Temporal demand management system	Management issue	Visitor acceptability
• Advance reservation required in peak periods • No reservation required in quiet periods Eligibility requirements: • Preferential access for attraction/reserve supporters/wildlife enthusiasts or local community members at all times • Temporally restricted access to 'general' visitor markets	Limit peak period disturbance and site degradation	High if communicated widely; low if not (accepted practice in some natural areas)
	Market segmentation favouring engaged visitors to ration access	Perceived low acceptability among passing/generic visitors and potentially among local businesses
• Regulated entry to certain areas during peak periods; closure of fragile/sensitive areas • Open less frequented areas in quiet periods (within determined carrying capacities)	Temporal zoning to reduce habitat disturbance	High: accepted environmental management principle
• Temporal pricing dis/incentives (peak time and high season add-ons or quiet period /low season reductions)	Partitioning demand	Moderate: accepted principle. Value for money perceptions
• Enhanced encounters during quiet periods (e.g. availability of site guides, demonstrations, educational talks, close-up viewing, extended dwell times)	Service level differentiation	High among off-peak/quiet period visitors

Sources: Adapted from Newsome *et al.* (2002) and Natural Capital (2004).

Visitor management approaches

In nature reserves and managed wilderness sites in cool temperate areas where the core attraction is available throughout the year (e.g. deer parks, protected marine areas or enclosed wetland reserves), there is often an ecologically driven pressure to spread visitor demand away from traditional peak patterns. This is particularly the case for popular attractions close to major visitor honeypots. Numerous management strategies and actions have been tried and tested around the world, with varying degrees of success. Table 12.5 illustrates the range of potential demand management approaches pertinent to temporal spreading in nature-based attractions. The emphasis here is on incentivization.

Ultimately, the success of any visitor expectation management technique will be through the combined effectiveness of its communication channels and the message, i.e. the ability to articulate the reasons for implementing temporal supply access or market differentiation. The challenges of temporal management are different and arguably greater for nature- and wildlife-based attraction operators than for most other attraction types, given the potentially harmful impacts of concentrated 'over-visitation'. However, the case study has illustrated that the options available for capitalizing on the seasons and climate are many and varied.

Conclusion

This chapter has demonstrated that for visitor attractions operators, temporal variation in demand and supply can be deconstructed into components of 'seasonality' and short-term periodic variation. Temporal variation should be treated as a broad and complex phenomenon, rather than seen purely in terms of fluctuations in visitor numbers or spend. As has been demonstrated, it encompasses a variety of perspectives beyond the immediacy of the market place. For attractions operators, these perspectives raise many issues in managing visitor demand, identifying and possibly influencing the wider causes of temporal imbalances and acknowledging the wider destinational impacts of seasonality. However, 'coping' or 'acceptance' strategies may be more appropriate than the need to 'combat' temporal variation.

The case study of nature- and wildlife-based operations illustrates the dichotomy of managing temporal market imbalances around an inherently perishable resource. Some causal factors, such as climatic conditions and seasonal daylight hours, are clearly beyond the control of tourism attractions and destination management organizations. However, attractions can capitalize on short days or inclement weather. Moreover, they are not powerless to extend the temporal basis of the operations, even if a twelve-month operating season or a seven-day operating week remain unrealistic targets. Attractions in or close to urban areas may be best placed to take advantage of wider markets and the 'honeypot' effect of visitor attraction clusters. Nevertheless, all attractions can benefit from considering their responses tactically or strategically, or indeed by accepting or adapting to temporal 'down time' in a proactive way in which the mission to promote realistic visitor expectations is paramount.

References

Baum, T. and Hagen, L. (1999). Responses to seasonality: the experiences of peripheral destinations. *International Journal of Tourism Research*, **1**, 299–312.

Butler, R. W. (2001). Seasonality in tourism: issues and implications. In *Seasonality in Tourism* (T. Baum and S. Lundtorp, eds), pp. 5–21. Pergamon[v3].

Butler, R. W. and Mao, B. (1997). Seasonality in tourism: problems and measurement. In *Quality Management in Urban Tourism* (P. Murphy, ed), pp. 23–90. John Wiley & Sons.

Deery, M. and Jago, L. (2001). Managing human resources. In *Quality Issues in Heritage Visitor Attractions* (S. Drummond and I. Yeoman, eds), pp. 175–193. Butterworth-Heinemann.

Frechtling, D.C. (2001). *Forecasting Tourism Demand: Methods and Strategies*. Butterworth-Heinemann.

Fyall, A., Leask, A. and Garrod, B. (2001). Scottish visitor attractions: a collaborative future? *International Journal of Tourism Research*, **3**, 211–228.

Garrod, B. (2003). Managing visitor impacts. In *Managing Visitor Attractions: New Directions* (A. Fyall, B. Garrod and A. Leask, eds), pp. 124–139. Butterworth-Heinemann.

Getz, D. and Nilsson, P.A. (2004). Responses of family businesses to extreme seasonality in demand: the case of Bornholm, Denmark. *Tourism Management*, **25**, 17–30.

Goulding, P. (2006). Conceptualising supply-side seasonality in tourism: a study of the temporal trading behaviours of small tourism businesses in Scotland. Unpublished PhD, University of Strathclyde.

Grant, M., Human, B. and Le Pelley, B. (1997). Seasonality. *Insights*, July, A5–A9.

Highlands and Islands Enterprise (2002). *Submission from Highlands and Islands Enterprise to the Scottish Parliament Enterprise and Lifelong Learning Committee's Inquiry into Tourism*. HIE, Inverness.

Jago, L. and Deery, M. (2001). Managing volunteers. In *Quality Issues in Heritage Visitor Attractions* (S. Drummond and I. Yeoman, eds), pp. 194–217. Butterworth-Heinemann.

Leask, A. (2003). The nature and purpose of visitor attractions. In *Managing Visitor Attractions: New Directions* (A. Fyall, B. Garrod and A. Leask, eds), pp. 5–15. Butterworth-Heinemann.

Leask, A., Fyall, A. and Goulding, P. (2000). Scottish visitor attractions: revenue, capacity and sustainability. In *Yield Management Strategies for the Service Industries* (A. Ingold, U. McMahon-Beattie and I. Yeoman, eds), 2nd edn, pp. 211–232. Continuum.

Lundtorp, S. (2001). Measuring tourism seasonality. In *Seasonality in Tourism* (T. G. Baum and S. Lundtorp, eds), pp. 23–50. Pergamon.

Mathieson, A. and Wall, G. (1982). *Tourism: Economic, Physical and Social Impacts*. Longman.

Natural Capital (2004). *Green Tourism Approaches to Weather and Seasonality: Final Report*. Scottish Enterprise.

Newsome, D., Moore, S. and Dowling, R. (2002). *Natural Area Tourism: Ecology, Impacts and Management*. Channel View.

Pender, L. and Sharpley, R. (2005). *The Management of Tourism*. Sage.

RSPB (2007). Mersehead: Seasonal Highlights. www.rspb.org.uk/reserves/guide/m/mersehead/seasonal_highlights.asp.

Scottish Executive (2006). *Scottish Tourism: The Next Decade. A Tourism Framework for Change*. The Scottish Executive.

STB (2001). *The Scottish Visitor Attraction Monitor 2000*. Scottish Tourist Board.

VisitScotland (2005a). *Visitor Attraction Monitor 2004*. VisitScotland/Moffat Centre for Travel and Tourism.

VisitScotland (2005b). *Tourism Attitudes Survey 2005*. VisitScotland.

VisitScotland (2006a). *Tourism in Scotland 2005*. www.scotexchange.net/tis_summary2005updated.pdf.

VisitScotland (2006b). *Visitor Attraction Monitor 2005*. VisitScotland/Moffat Centre for Travel and Tourism.

CHAPTER **13**
· · · ·

Managing Gardens

Dorothy Fox and Jonathan Edwards

Aims

This chapter introduces the range of gardens that are presented to the public as visitor attractions, the popularity of which continues to increase. The complexity of managing such outdoor sites, which in the majority of cases were not initially developed or designed to receive large numbers of visitors, is discussed. Also discussed are some of the factors that influence an individual's decision to visit a garden.

The specific aims of this chapter are to:

- provide an overview of garden-based visitor attractions,
- identify and characterize the visitors to gardens, and
- examine the issues involved in managing sites which are both natural and social spaces and which were not initially developed as visitor attractions.

Introduction

While data regarding the popularity of gardens as visitor attractions globally are not currently available, official figures for the UK (VisitBritain, 2006) suggest that in the early years of the twenty-first century gardens represent 7 per cent of the attractions section and account for 5 per cent of all visits. These figures are almost certainly an underestimate, as they do not recognize the attraction of gardens associated with historic properties, a category of attraction that accounts for 12 per cent of all visits, and nor do they recognize the visits to the many hundreds of private gardens that open to the public on an occasional basis. One estimate is that between 300 and 400 million visits are made to historic parks and gardens in the UK each year (English Heritage, 2002). In France, there were 784 gardens open to visitors in 2002, an increase of more than 10 per cent over the five-year period. The number of visitors is also expanding; a survey of 405 French gardens revealed that in 2000, they had 25 million visitors compared to 18.5 million in 1999 and 11.5 million in 1998 (Comité Départemental du Tourisme de l'Yonne, 2003). Gardens are not purely attractions in Europe, they feature prominently in the promotion of countries in all parts of the world and a number of them are designated as World Heritage Sites (WHS). The award of WHS status to Suzhou Gardens in China and the Garden Kingdom of Dessau-Wörlitz in Germany serves to demonstrate the universal value attributed to gardens as representative of different cultures.

In practice, the designation of 'a garden attraction' spans a diverse group of attractions, with no single attribute to define them or to distinguish, for example, between a garden and a park. Definition is complicated further, as few gardens constitute attractions in their own right. Many are just one part of an attraction which has another draw, for example, the historic house which the garden complements. The garden may be the principal part of the attraction or it may be subsidiary, and many gardens may have additional services that attract visitors, such as tearooms and plants for sale. VisitBritain includes botanical gardens as well as arboreta within its garden category, whereas Connell (2005) excludes urban parks from her study of British gardens. However, garden-based attractions are usually permanent spaces where one of the purposes of cultivating plants is to give pleasure to the public. This definition includes the permanency of the space because 'show gardens' are also constructed. Some of these last just a few days at horticultural shows, for example, at the Chelsea Flower Show, while others may be open to the public for several months at garden festivals, which are often popular as catalysts for regenerating areas, for example, in Germany and other countries.

Whilst a garden-based attraction aims to provide a pleasurable experience during a visit, it may also be maintained for other purposes. Many gardens are conserved for their historical aspects because, for example, their layout is attributed to a leading garden designer, such as the Lutyens/Jekyll garden at Hestercombe in England or Beatrix Farrand's designs at Dumbarton Oaks in the USA, or the garden may have a direct association with a nationally important person, for example, Monet's Garden at Giverny in France. Three gardens in England are WHSs: Blenheim Palace, Fountains Abbey and Studley Royal Water Garden, and the Royal Botanic Gardens at Kew. Additionally, in England there were 1531 historic parks and gardens recorded in the Register of Parks and Gardens of Special Historic Interest, which is maintained by English Heritage (English Heritage, 2002). Approximately 10 per cent of properties are of international importance and are classified as Grade I. Around 30 per cent are considered of exceptional historic interest and are awarded Grade II* status. The remainder have been identified as of sufficient interest to merit national designation Grade II. More recently, gardens have adopted environmental aims, for example Wakehurst Place in Sussex, England, contains the Millennium Seed Bank Project. Meanwhile, the Eden Project in

Cornwall in South West England has unambiguous environmental objectives and is designed to deliver a programme of educational events for both the public and for schools. Other gardens have a commemorative function: the gardens in London adjacent to the United States Embassy and the British Memorial Garden in Hanover Square, Lower Manhattan, have both been implemented to remember those who lost their lives in New York in September 2001.

Development of gardens as attractions

Gardens and parks that are now open to the public as attractions developed in five main ways: first, as outputs of different cultures, often created when a given culture was at its most powerful. The Alhambra and Generalife gardens in Southern Spain created in the thirteenth and fourteenth centuries maintain, despite many alterations, their Islamic character while the gardens of the Mughal emperors of the sixteenth and seventeenth century India were, it is claimed (Adams, 1991), some of the most magnificent gardens seen on earth.

Second are those gardens that initially complemented a domestic property. Whilst many gardens were developed for the pleasure of their owners or to provide flowers, fruits and vegetables for their households, some were deliberately created at least in part, to impress visitors by displaying the owner's wealth or their overseas travels. The restored sixteenth-century gardens of the Chateau de Villandry in the Indre et Loire in France was originally constructed in the 1530s for Jean le Breton, the then French Finance Minister. Chatsworth in Derbyshire, England is the stately home of the Duke and Duchess of Devonshire and its garden is famous for the 300-year-old Cascade, which falls 200 m down a hillside. In contrast to these large internationally renowned gardens, there are in England more than 3000 much smaller domestic gardens that are opened to the public for a few days each year to raise money for charity. The largest organization to support owners in this way is the National Gardens Scheme, but the British Red Cross and the Royal National Lifeboat Institute have similar schemes.

Third, gardens were and are developed as scientific collections. Following the foundation of a botanic garden in Pisa, Italy, in 1543, the University of Oxford Botanic Garden was established in the UK in 1621. Planted to provide plant specimens for teaching students, it is now open to the public. Botanical gardens (as they are often known) are rarely planted purely for aesthetic reasons: usually the plants are grouped by country of origin, by taxonomy or by their economic value. However, many botanic gardens are frequently located in or near major cities and consequently receive many visitors. The Royal Botanic Gardens Sydney has around three million visitors annually; the Kew botanic gardens in London receive in excess of one million and the Chicago Botanic Garden receives 750 000.

Fourth, many gardens and parks that created during the late nineteenth or early twentieth centuries as a deliberate result of municipal action to provide recreational facilities for residents. Duthie Park, which was donated to the city of Aberdeen in 1880, is a typical example. It covers about 18 hectares (44 acres) and contains a bandstand, fountains, ponds and statues, as well as over 120 000 roses.

The fifth way in which gardens have developed as visitor attractions is through being adjacent to other institutions. For example, many plant nurseries and garden centres develop display gardens for visitors, for example, The Flower Fields in Carlsbad, Southern California, were developed as an additional source of revenue for a nursery specializing in the production of the highly ornamental Giant *Tecolote ranunculus.* Other gardens form part of zoos or museums; for example, in the garden of the American Museum, near Bath, is a replica of George Washington's garden in Virginia, USA.

Connell (2005) created a database of 1223 gardens in 2000 that open to the public on a regular and/or commercial basis and estimated that a total of 5000 gardens are open to the public in Great Britain. Most gardens have private owners or are held in trust for not-for-profit organizations, such as charitable trusts, educational establishments or local authorities. The principal owner of gardens in the UK is the National Trust, which looks after 200 gardens and 67 landscape parks in England, Wales and Northern Ireland. English Heritage has 21 properties that have gardens as a part of the attraction and the Royal Horticultural Society owns four gardens, including Wisley in Surrey. It is the UK's leading gardening charity and all of the gardens are open to the public as well as the organization's members.

Garden visitors

Knowledge of the characteristics of visitors and what they seek from their trip is essential for any attraction. Data from France show that more women (59 per cent) make visits than men and that the average age is 48, with 46 per cent of visitors coming from the higher occupational groups. More than 30 per cent of garden visitors come from the same department or region and, on average, 16 per cent are international visitors (Comité Départemental du Tourisme de l'Yonne, 2003). Similar findings are reported in North America: for example Steinhauer's (2004) study in Alabama indicates that here again women represent the majority of the visitors. In Canada (Lang Research Inc., 2001), women are more likely than men to visit or express an interest in visiting gardens, together with mature singles and couples.

Survey data published by Berry and Shepherd (2001) show that at two National Trust properties in the South of England, Scotney Castle, a garden in Kent, and Bateman's, the country home of Rudyard Kipling in East Sussex, 60 per cent of visitors were females. The data from a British survey by Connell (2004a) suggest that middle-aged or older people have a greater propensity to visit than young people and that there is also a significant bias in favour of the higher occupational groups, repeating the French findings. In 2005, 56 per cent of visitors were on a day out, 36 per cent were domestic tourists and 8 per cent were from overseas (VisitBritain, 2006). This profile is however by no means universal, Ballantyne *et al.* (2006) report and support the findings of the Australian Bureau of Statistics which suggests that the highest visitation to Botanic Gardens in Australia is by 25–34-year-olds, followed by 35–44-year-olds, and that the majority in the 30–39 age category visited with children, a 'younger' age distribution, in contrast to Western European experience.

In Britain, Connell (2004a) found that when she asked visitors to describe themselves in one of three ways, 70 per cent stated that they had a general gardening interest, 10 per cent had a special horticultural interest and 20 per cent wanted a pleasant day out. She also established that those with a special horticultural interest were likely to visit more frequently (at least once a month) and that whilst those visitors with a general interest also were frequent visitors, it was to a lesser degree, but almost half visited gardens at least once a month. Those with no interest at all visited a few times a year or less than once a year.

Studies from across the world show that visitors have similar reasons for visiting gardens. In Australia, research carried out at the Royal Botanic Gardens, Sydney and Brisbane, (Hatherly, 2002) identified the percentages of visitors giving the following reasons for visiting (Table 13.1).

Studies carried at out Hodges Gardens, Louisiana, USA (Legg and Kim, 1990) and Brisbane Botanic Gardens in Australia (Ballantyne *et al.*, 2006) employing factor analysis techniques demonstrated the importance of key benefit dimensions (Table 13.2; average scores are given in brackets).

In Britain, Connell (2004a) notes that 53 per cent of visitors scored visiting 'a nice environment' highly and 51 per cent 'the tranquility'. Next in importance were the horticultural aspects and getting ideas for ones own garden. Interview data describing visitor experiences in two of the gardens of the

Table 13.1 Reasons for visiting the Royal Botanic Gardens, Sydney

Reason for visiting	% of respondents
Relaxation	21
Aesthetics	19
Peace/tranquillity/refuge	18
Sightseeing/general interest	17
Walking/jogging	9
Botanic	5
Educational	5
Horticultural	3
Thoroughfare	3

Source: Hatherly (2002).

Table 13.2 Benefit dimensions of those visiting Hodge Gardens, Louisiana and Brisbane Botanic Gardens

Benefits sought Louisiana	Average score based on a 7-point scale	Benefits sought Brisbane	Average score based on a 7-point scale
Natural beauty awareness	4.00	Enjoying gardens	4.74
Aesthetic enhancement	3.64	Passive enjoyment	4.42
Social bonding	3.61	Restoration	3.94
Commodity-related	3.36	Learning and discovery	3.23
Outdoor learning	3.20	Social contact	2.47
Stimulation seeking	1.91	Learning about gardens	2.51
		Personal self-fulfillment	2.04

Sources: Legg and Kim (1990) and Ballantyne *et al.* (2006).

Smithsonian Institute in Washington, USA, provide further details (Smithsonian Institution, 2005). One interviewee said:

I find it very relaxing. I like to see what is growing, where it's growing, the colour combinations. I hate weeding, I hate gardening, but I just enjoy this garden so much.

Another said:

I love the fountains too. Just sitting and listening to the running water in a place like this. ... It really is part of the beauty of it. Not just the flowers, but the water and the plants together.

Together, these studies identify the main reasons for visiting gardens. First, the setting draws the visitor; that is, the peace and tranquility, the naturalness and the freedom they offer. Second, horticultural aspects attract visitors, particularly the aesthetic value of the garden and the associations visitors an form with their own domestic gardens. Additionally, the studies identified reasons that could be generic to any attraction, for example, social bonding (the opportunity to go out for a day) and opportunities for learning and self-fulfillment.

Gardens as natural–social spaces

Gardens are different to most attractions in that they cannot offer a standard-ized product. The imagescape is in a state of constant transformation because nature interacting with anthropogenic actions creates and shapes a garden. A tree may have grown naturally in a location or may have been transplanted there by a gardener. Conversely, a self-seeded plant may have been over-looked by a gardener or may have been deliberately left *in situ* as part of the design. A species that may be indigenous to an area, may have become nat-uralized or reintroduced. For example, the genus *Magnolia*, was once naturally abundant in Britain, but has had to be reintroduced by gardeners. The wind and animals, as well as people, have carried out hybridization of plants and the actions of gardeners, as well as climate, influence the shape and size of the flora. For these reasons, gardens must be considered as social–natural spaces.

It is suggested that gardens occupy a greater proportion of the land area in Britain than in any other country (Thompson, 2003). Natural environmental explanations for this phenomenon include first the temperate climate experi-enced as a result of Britain's position on the westerly edge of Eurasia and the warming effects of the Gulf Stream. It provides a good growing environment: Southern England, for example, has a growing season of nine or more months. Second, the distribution of glacial drift has created frequent changes in the underlying solid rock and consequent variation in soil types, enabling a wider variety of plants to grow. Finally, Thompson suggests that repeated glaciations led to the depletion of the range of natural flora, which encour-aged the enrichment of gardens by plants brought back by Britain's long his-tory of colonial expansion and exploration. This final example further illustrates the problems of distinguishing the 'natural' from the 'social' dimension of gardens.

Whilst on the one hand, a garden can be influenced by the surrounding physical context, its topography, the soil type, macroclimate and microcli-mate (e.g., a frost pocket at the bottom of a slope), on the other its social loca-tion influences the number of residents and tourists within reasonable travelling distance and its ability to attract staff. Its position will also deter-mine the level of competition from other gardens or attractions, and whether collaboration in marketing or other aspects of management is possible.

The cultivation and presentation of a garden varies continuously on a sea-sonal and long-term basis. The pleasure for many visitors is to see plants in flower, but the length of flowering is determined not only by the species or variety but also by the meteorological conditions, therefore the timing of when a flower is in bloom can be unpredictable. An owner who seeks to pro-mote their garden on the basis of a particular species being in flower can have difficulties in knowing exactly when that might be. The National Trust, in England, for example, have large collections of snowdrops at several gardens including Kingston Lacy in Dorset and Lacock Abbey in Wiltshire, but poten-tial visitors have to telephone the organization to find out exactly which weeks the properties will be open to see these displays.

Maintenance is essential in any attraction, but planning a maintenance regime in gardens where there is a constant process of growth and decay, and where nature and people interact, is more challenging. Grass mowing, for example, will need to be carried out frequently if the weather has been mild and wet, but needs to be done on dry days and this is the time, when more people are likely to visit. Furthermore, routine tasks such as mowing and hedge cutting require machinery that can detract from the ambience of a garden. Other manual tasks such as planting and pruning have less impact and many visitors see this as an opportunity to speak to the gardeners and obtain advice or information.

Gardens are subject to fashion and the changing needs of visitors, but changes initiated by management can require longer time spans than when using man-made materials. Whilst smaller plants can be quite quickly incorporated into a design, a mature hedgerow cannot be and takes time to develop. Over the long term, the appearance of the garden can change naturally, for example, as trees grow their impact aesthetically in a landscape can be beneficial or detrimental. They may also force out other planting through their uptake of water from the soil or create shade in which sun-loving plants cannot develop. Nature can also have an impact over much shorter timescales. Dutch Elm disease is a fungus spread by a beetle that can reach epidemic proportions. In Southern England, 20 million trees were lost to the disease between 1971 and 1980. Then in October 1987, a storm swept England, having a devastating effect on gardens; a further 20 000 trees were destroyed overnight at Wakehurst Place in Sussex.

Although seasonality in visitor numbers provides a challenge for many attractions, in gardens the seasonality of the planting can be used as a marketing opportunity. A positive example of climate change, which has led to a variation in normal temperatures and hydration impacting on flowering times, is at Trelissick in South West England, where 30 plants were recorded in flower in January 1991. In January 2004, this figure had risen to 220 (Watson, 2006) and therefore a longer growing season may well encourage more visitors to gardens rather than less. However in northern Japan, the earlier flowering of the cherry trees has had the opposite effect. Normally, their flowering in the city of Hirosaki coincided with the 'Golden Week' holiday in May, but in 2004 the trees flowered 10 days earlier and the number of Golden Week visitors fell from 2 million to 600 000.

If the climate continues to change, there will be other alterations to growing seasons and the management of gardens may need to adjust their planting to reflect this. The UK Climate Impacts Programme (Bisgrove and Hadley, 2002) suggests a 10–20 per cent reduction in autumn rainfall, higher autumn temperatures and cooler nights developing from clear skies. Whilst this could lead to an earlier leaf fall in Britain; it could also encourage the enhanced development of autumn leaf colour as a result. Gardens such as the Ness Botanic Garden in Cheshire in North West England, which holds the largest collection of *Sorbus*, a species of trees renowned for its autumn colours, already has lower annual rainfall than average for the West Coast of England and is therefore in a strong position to attract visitors in the 'shoulder' period.

Heritage gardens may find it harder to grow the plants associated with the initial design or the period of the property, which may make their conservation objectives difficult to achieve. Less predictable weather may also result in greater fluctuations of income for owners, making investment in the garden more problematic. More immediate impacts may come from the visitors' behaviour. Grass paths are seen as particularly vulnerable and the soil after exceptionally wet or dry weather may become severely compacted. To ease movement around a garden may therefore require either the replacement of grass with hard surfaces or the use of intensive management techniques developed originally in the sports turf industry. Visitors may become unsatisfied with their visit if, for example, there are empty flowerbeds due to unsuitable planting conditions. Similar feelings may be aroused by brown rather than green grass, tender plants destroyed by early frosts, and plants damaged by the geographical spread of pathogens or pests.

Gardens as social–natural spaces

Gardens are social spaces not only because of the work of the gardeners that create and maintain them but also in the way that visitors experience them. The non-natural infrastructure of gardens, including car parks, tearooms, toilets as well as the interpretation, plant labelling, etc. are all aspects of the socially mediated environment. So too, are intangible aspects such as the helpfulness of staff and the welcome that visitors perceive. Gardens have diverse meanings to different people. Hatherly (2002) showed how hard and soft landscaping and appropriate interpretation in the Cadi Jam Ora garden in the Royal Botanic Gardens, Sydney was able to demonstrate the indigenous community's connections with the site. Prior to 1788, the land where the botanic gardens now stand was home to the Cadigal people, but this had never been acknowledged in the gardens. The interpretation included a 50-m long storyline describing the city's history from the perspective of its indigenous population. Hatherly's research showed that whilst many visitors did not go specifically to see the Cadi Jam Ora, they were interested in learning about the indigenous heritage of the garden and could recall most of the objectives of the project.

In the south west of England, the Lost Gardens of Heligan have been restored. Whilst the work was being carried out, the nature of the lives of the people who had lived and worked on the estate over the previous 400 years emerged. The association between the discovered artefacts and the past produces a sense of place for visitors in the present. Connell (2004b: 190) suggests that this 'creates a social, historical and cultural context and gives meaning to the garden beyond its essential charm as an environment or visitor attraction'.

Some gardens and parks were designed as public places and they would look strange if they were empty; the other visitors are an integral part of the space and therefore subject to the 'collective' tourist gaze (Urry, 2002). Other places, however, are subject to the 'romantic' gaze. Walter (1982: 298) gives the example of Stourhead in England to illustrate:

... the romantic notion that the self is found not in society but in solitudinous contemplation of nature. Stourhead's garden is the perfect romantic landscape ... designed to be walked around in wonderment at Nature and the presence of other people immediately begins to impair this.

Nonetheless, garden visiting usually occurs with the companionship of family or friends. Connell's survey (2004a) in Britain confirmed 85 per cent of visitors were not alone and that about half of these were with a partner, 11 per cent of respondents were in organized groups and 13 per cent of visits were part of a family with children. In Britain, gardens have the lowest number of child visitors of all attraction types (VisitBritain, 2006), although as noted above this is not necessarily the case in other cultures.

The management of gardens

Managing gardens as visitor attractions poses the same demands as managing visitors at other attractions and, equally, a diversity of responses is found. The location of a garden clearly influences issues of access in terms of relationship to public transport and for the many gardens where the majority arrive by car or coach at parking facilities and drop-off points. Toilet provision might reasonably be expected and the provision of catering and retailing clearly represent opportunities for revenue, particularly if they are available to not only to visitors to the garden but also to those just passing by. Many gardens have the potential to offer very attractive settings for dining and entertainment, and this opportunity has been exploited by the numerous gardens that compete as venues for weddings and/or other social events such as plays, concerts, firework displays and events specifically targeting the family market such as Easter egg hunts.

In larger gardens, orientation may well be required, and this may accompany policies to offer information and interpretation recognizing the need to balance the aesthetic and social experiences visitors require with interests that may range from naming the plants to broader environmental and social issues.

Most gardens were not designed as visitor attractions but today, either by accident or design, find themselves as part of an expanding attractions sector. The Napier Botanical Gardens in North Island, New Zealand, provides an appropriate illustration. These gardens were overdue for restoration and revitalization to make the gardens fit for visitors in the twenty-first century. A report prepared for the city council (Environmental Management Services Limited, 2000) highlights some of the issues that arise for gardens as a consequence of their initial creation. For example, the public entrance to the gardens was underdeveloped and therefore needed to be redefined to reflect the special character of the gardens and to attract visitors in. The car parking too required extending and upgrading to enable this to happen. Security of the gardens was reevaluated and it was proposed that a 1.8-m fence be erected, secondary gates be closed, surveillance cameras be installed and limited hours of access to the garden be introduced. This would ensure public safety after dark and reduce the incidence of plant theft and vandalism, which were then a major issue.

Paths required resurfacing and widening to 1800 mm which would make it possible to carry greater numbers of visitors than ever originally envisaged, and steeply sloping paths needed to incorporate ramped sections and handrails to permit safer and more extensive access. Advice was also given that those plants with thorns or prickles or with low hanging branches together with poisonous plants needed to be removed or else not be planted at the edge of paths.

Recommendations were made about the signage and interpretation in the gardens. Unlike gardens developed to complement a dwelling, plant labels have always been an integral part of botanic gardens. However, contemporary needs extend beyond botanical information to include visitor orientation, traffic flow and entrances to 'disabled access' areas, for example. Demand for interpretation, too has expanded and at Napier, they sought to explain the plants' historical significance to the gardens. Attracting increasing numbers of visitors, however, has ongoing consequences as the next example demonstrates.

Sissinghurst Castle, in South East England, is a National Trust property, which was once the home of Vita Sackville-West. It had first opened to the public in 1938 under the auspice of the National Gardens Scheme (Benfield, 2001). In 1967, when the garden was donated to the National Trust, the number of visitors rose from a maximum of 28000, whilst in private ownership to 67000 in the first year of Trust ownership. The approach by management during the 1970s and 1980s was to facilitate greater number of visitors, for example, by adding paths, catering facilities, a gift shop, etc. By the end of that period, however, more than 100000 additional visits were being made each year and the realization came that '... the large numbers of visitors was clearly acting to diminish the psychological, particularly the aesthetic, nature of the garden tourism experience' (Benfield, 2001: 210). During the early 1990s, various restrictive systems were trialed, culminating with the introduction of a timed-entry system in 1992 and a total cessation of paid advertising of the garden in 1997. Visitor numbers have since remained stable.

Case Study: Garden visitors in England

Understanding the behaviour of visitors to gardens is essential for the long-term viability of the attractions. A study in Southern England sought to explore what influenced garden visiting and the findings relating to some of the effects of the natural and social environment are reported here. The area of the study is renowned for its natural beauty. In the South it has award-winning sandy beaches and to the West is Poole Harbour, one of the world's largest natural harbours, leading to the West Dorset Heritage Coast, a WHS. The Cranborne Chase and West Wiltshire Downs Area of Outstanding Natural Beauty is to the north and to the east is the New Forest National Park. There are 191 gardens in the County of Dorset open to visitors, of which 41 open on a regular basis. Two, the Abbotsbury Sub-tropical Gardens and Athelhampton House and Gardens, are listed Grade 1 by English Heritage. Bournemouth, the main resort in the area, is a leading tourism destination with 5.5 million visitors and a tourism industry worth £350 million each year.

In the first phase of the research, a cluster survey of residents, based on post-codes in the BH postcode area in East Dorset and West Hampshire, was carried out in November/December 2002. The sample size was 932 households, from which the adult who would next celebrate their birthday was asked to complete the questionnaire. A total of 345 were completed or partially completed, giving a response rate of 37 per cent. Subsequently, interviews with a sample of visitors selected purposively (based on convenience) were undertaken with visitors to gardens. There were three pay-to-visit gardens (Compton Acres, a commercially operated Grade 11* listed garden in Dorset; Wakehurst Place and a garden opening for the National Garden Scheme), and the public Pleasure Gardens in the town of Bournemouth. In order to gain a better understanding of the dynamics of decision making within a pair or group of visitors, the interviews were carried out within the decision-making group. All the interviews used the grand tour question approach (Spradley, 1979). In this method, only one broadest possible question is asked. In this case it was, 'What made you come here today?' Further questions were then asked, in an informal way, to encourage respondents to expand on their initial response.

The influence of the weather

It has been shown how the prevailing climate and the weather associated with it impacts on a garden, but the weather also influences whether a visit to a garden takes place and the quality of the experience of the visitor. Meteorological data for England show that as the number of hours of sunshine increases, and to a certain extent as the amount of rainfall decreases, the number of garden visits increases. In 2003, England had a long hot summer with the second lowest rainfall since 1766 and had the highest level of garden visiting ever recorded. In contrast, the country experienced its wettest summer since 1912 in 2004 and there was a 6 per cent decrease in visitor numbers.

The qualitative data from the study show why this occurs. First the 'right' weather can be particularly important in creating satisfaction with a garden visit. For example, a man at Compton Acres said:

I think it's just nice to come at this time of the year when the weather is good really. You can just wander round without getting soaked.

Another man there said:

... well we were coming here once before and we got to the gates and it poured with thunderstorm so we went off ... we'll definitely go today, as it's a nice day.

This type of reaction to inclement weather is supported by the results of the residents' survey. Over three-quarters of respondents said that if they were told it was going to rain all day, just as they were leaving home, they would not continue with the visit to a garden. Over half would cancel the visit, if the same circumstances occurred, as they arrived at the entrance to the garden.

But the weather can also prompt a trip out, as this elderly woman said:

> … we're a bit off the cuff. We look at the weather and suddenly think we'll do something.

It is not always the weather itself that has the effect; it can be through the social agency of a weather *forecast*. These can help people anticipate whether a visit will be enjoyable and the best time to go.

> Interviewer (I): '… what made you think of coming today?'
> Man in the Pleasure Gardens: 'Cause the weather. I don't think the forecast's very good, so we've come today'.

Participants also showed that because they can anticipate what an attraction will be like in different weather conditions, the weather could also determine which type of attraction to visit:

> I: 'What made you choose the garden rather than the beach today?'
> Man at Compton Acres: '… Just, uh, the weather not being so nice, so you know, we thought we'd do a detour on the gardens. We thought we'd have a look'.

One visitor to Compton Acres expressed her disappointment in the way the garden looked, confirming how the weather can also have a secondary influence on people through its effect on the planting in a garden. Clearly, her expectations of what a garden should look like had not been met, although she attributed responsibility for the state of the planting on the gardeners rather than the weather, demonstrating her assessment of the garden as a cultural rather than a natural artefact.

> So far here I really am disappointed. You know, so, everything seems so dead, it seems so dried up. I mean where you've got bare patches, even there, dry patches and all there, just dry and dying because they haven't been watered.

The influence of family and friends

A visitor's companions can be instrumental in providing information about a garden, making a visit happen and influencing the quality of the visit experienced. Transmission of information by word of mouth within families or friends is a key source of knowledge about visiting a garden. A 58 per cent share of respondents in the resident survey who had visited a garden had been inspired to visit by a friend, and 46 per cent had been inspired by a family member. A person may simply be reliving their own experiences or they may be advocating visiting, as this man interviewed at Compton Acres showed.

> I think I'd recommend it to some friends really… if they want a day out …

Less often recognized is that companions can be influential in encouraging a visit, as this woman interviewed at Wakehurst Place revealed.

> I'm a great one for thinking I'll do a thing, um and then I just think, oh shall I be bothered, but if somebody else'll come along ... I don't always need people to go along with, but happy to do it on my own, but, but, you know ... I just need that little bit of shove, now and again, to make me do things ...

The respondents in the resident survey were asked who most wants to visit a garden. In about two-thirds of cases, the respondent and their companion both wanted to visit gardens, but in about a third of cases ($n = 84$), either the respondent (21.6 per cent) or their companion (10.2 per cent) wanted to visit more.

The qualitative data provide examples of individuals who are like this. Here is an extract from an interview with a sixth-form student, in the public Pleasure Gardens in Bournemouth. When asked if he ever visited gardens he replied:

> Sixth-former: With my parents really
> I: 'It wouldn't be your choice though?'
> Sixth-former: 'Not really'.
> I: 'But if they go, you'll go with them?'
> Sixth-former: 'Yeah'.

Prime movers and secondary participants

From examples such as this, it was observed that some individuals, specifically those who most wanted to visit, were instrumental in making a visit take place and so these were labelled the prime movers. The others visited, but were less influential in promoting a visit, so these were labelled the secondary participants.

With the quantitative data, the researchers were restricted in establishing the identity of all secondary participants, because only data from the study respondents were available; there were no data from their companions. But of the male respondents, 12.1 per cent said that their companion wanted to visit more, compared to 9.1 per cent of women. For female respondents, 26.1 per cent said that they wanted to visit more, compared to 14.1 per cent for men. So taken together, these figures suggested that the 'reluctant' visitors were more likely to be male than female. About a quarter of all secondary participants did not visit a garden in 2002, but 42.6 per cent made one or two visits, 21.0 per cent made three to four visits and 12.5 per cent made five or more visits. Male secondary participants made more repeat visits than female ones. If these visitors are 'reluctant' to visit, it makes one question why in fact they go.

In an open question asking 'why do you visit a garden with your family or friends?', responses of some of those who stated that their companion likes to visit more than they do, could be identified as truly reluctant, for example:

> For something to do (young woman)
> To occupy my mother (middle-aged woman)

The second group of secondary participants, however, seemed to gain *some* pleasure from the visit, either vicariously, for example:

A treat for an older member of my family (middle-aged man)

or by also enjoying the visit, just not as much perhaps as the prime mover. An example of this was:

To enjoy the pleasure of it with loved ones (young woman)

The survey instrument included closed questions on what motivated the respondents to visit gardens. First they were asked how enjoyable they thought a visit to a garden would be. Only 2.6 per cent of the entire sample did not think or did not know that a visit to a garden would be enjoyable. Amongst the prime movers, about half thought it would be very enjoyable and the other half thought that it would be quite enjoyable. With the exception of one secondary participant who said they did not know, all the so-called 'reluctant' visitors thought a visit to a garden would be enjoyable, and a quarter of them that it would be very enjoyable. Their enjoyment may result from different sources however. The first quote is from a woman interviewed at Compton Acres, clearly, she is a prime mover and it is the garden that is providing the pleasure.

We just love going round gardens really. We just enjoy it, it's very pleasing and this is really wonderful.

Contrast this to a further extract from the teenager quoted above who was asked whether he enjoyed visiting with his parents:

Teenager: 'Sometimes. Lots of time I just want to go to the café, in the gardens ....'
I: 'So the gardens themselves aren't the appeal?'
Teenager: 'Not really'.

The respondents in the resident survey were also asked how important a variety of possible reasons were to them when visiting a garden. These were cross-tabulated with their responses to the question as to who most likes to visit a garden. It was thought that the respondents who themselves were most enthusiastic about visiting would give similar responses to those who thought that they and their companion both liked to visit and this was the case.

Reasons for visiting gardens

Two of the reasons given for visiting gardens (Table 13.3) that may well be common to other visitor attractions, relaxation and the companionship of family or friends, were equally as important to both the prime movers and the secondary participants. Other generic reasons, however, such as enjoyment, peace or solitude, exercise, freedom and for lunch or tea, showed a reduction in importance to the secondary participants. The reasons that are based on the horticultural aspects of garden visiting, the pleasure of viewing the garden, inspiration, learning or being informed, buying plants and comparing ones own plants showed variable reductions in importance to the secondary participants. For some variables, the reduction was only slight: for example, over 90 per cent of the secondary participants

Table 13:3 Reasons for visiting gardens given by prime movers and secondary participants

	Respondent is the prime mover (%)	Respondent is the secondary participant (%)	Respondent and companion are both prime movers (%)
To relax	90.0	88.9	91.9
To be with family or friends	64.0	65.4	69.2
To enjoy myself	93.9	76.0	90.0
The peace/solitude	82.2	68.0	80.5
The exercise	60.8	47.8	54.6
The freedom	57.2	48.0	62.2
For lunch or tea	36.0	16.7	42.4
The pleasure of viewing the garden	98.2	92.6	98.9
Inspiration	80.0	57.6	72.4
To learn or be informed	72.5	62.5	72.8
To buy plants	45.2	23.1	42.2
To compare my plants	43.4	23.1	44.2
To see unfamiliar plants	73.6	73.0	74.6
Gardens are safe places to walk	67.3	65.3	66.3
Curiosity	61.5	73.1	62.9

stated that they experienced pleasure from viewing the garden, whilst in regard to comparing plants in the visitors garden the difference was much greater. On the other hand, when asked the importance of seeing plants that they were unfamiliar with, each group responded almost identically. Also unexpected was the finding that one reason, namely 'curiosity', reversed the trend of greater importance of reasons to prime movers by showing a 10 per cent increase in importance to the secondary participants. These findings indicate that both the prime mover and the secondary participant responded in not dissimilar ways to the aesthetic dimension of the garden visit experience, but that the secondary participant was less enthused by the more practical details of gardens and gardening.

The qualitative data provide a more in-depth view of the reasons prime movers and secondary participants give for visiting. This interview with a middle-aged couple in a privately owned garden open under the National Gardens Scheme shows the woman's enthusiasm for visiting gardens, her husband's interest in the architecture of the owner's cottage and their shared pleasure in having a cream tea:

Woman: 'I love gardens so that's, it's my main hobby, my main interest'.
Man: '... I'm interested in the architecture of the old buildings. So it's the setting of the garden and the architecture, so my interests are somewhat different ...'.

Woman: '… and it's again a sort of an excuse to get out and um …'
Man: '… have a cream tea'. (laughter).
Woman: '… well we don't, we don't always do that … today we have. If I wasn't interested in gardening, would you come?'
Man: 'No I don't suppose so'.
Woman: '… It's more sort of the National Trust places I suppose where you find the house interesting and I look at the garden …'

The next interview was with a young woman and her husband who were visiting Compton Acres. It shows how people will do something that they wouldn't choose to do, as company for each other.

Woman: 'It was my decision really, yes'.
Man: '… I don't mind gardens, but it's not my thing but … I don't mind having a look'.
I: 'And sometimes do you … go to places that he'd like to go to?'
Woman: 'Yes. I don't play golf, but I normally walk round the golf course and things like that, so yea'.

Social agency can also shape a visit. Some participants' comments referred to how going with someone else enhanced the benefits of visiting alone, for example:

More enjoyable than going on my own (middle-aged woman).

And:

More interesting with company (middle-aged man).

This woman stressed the importance to her of being with her family when she visited Kingston Lacy:

We'll go, but then again we'll meet family. We've got three daughters and we all went over there for the snowdrop day. We took a flask and sandwiches. See that, that's what I like. … Having all the family there, I didn't even look at the snowdrops, because we were too busy nattering.

So does it matter to participants whom they visit with? This resident considered members of her family as possible companions:

I: 'When you visit a garden, does the person you go with change the way you feel about the garden? Or do you always go with your Mum?'
Resident: 'Usually my Mum'.

I: 'Would you take your children?'
Resident: 'No … because they haven't got the slightest interest, they'd be bored senseless. I took my daughter once … she would have been about 12, we were at … a tiny garden at Corfe, she was "when are we going home", "when are we going to the cafe", "what are all those flowers for"…'.

I: 'And what about your boyfriend, would you take him to a garden? ... Have you?'

Resident: 'No I haven't. Would I take him, I'd take him and he'd tolerate it'.

These data demonstrate the influence of the weather and a person's companions on a garden visit and yet neither can be controlled by management. Instead, therefore, ways must be sought to mitigate their influence and enable a positive visitor experience to take place. Garden owners, for example, could consider the provision of all-weather facilities. Large greenhouses or conservatories not only can provide an adapted environment for growing a more diverse range of plants, but also can offer an alternative environment for visitors if the weather is inclement.

Diverse facilities for family members that do not have the same interest in horticulture can be provided, but these must be compatible with the ambience of a garden that the majority of visitors seek. At Exbury Gardens, for example, in Southern England, a 12¼-gauge steam railway follows a one-and-a-quarter mile circular route designed to pass through a series of individual themed gardens. Part way through the 20-min journey passengers can alight and explore more distant parts of the 200-acre woodland garden. Several of the participants spoke during the interviews about this garden and always referred to the steam train as part of the appeal of a visit, for the fun it provides for children and the accessibility to the gardens it gives to the less able.

Conclusion

This chapter has given an overview of the range and diversity of gardens that may be described as visitor attractions, although in many instances this is a secondary function. An analysis of the profile of visitors and of the experiences they seek demonstrates that whilst interests in plants, garden history and design will attract some visitors, it is the creation of a social space within the nature that attracts significant numbers of visitors. This in many ways intangible combination is to some extent what distinguishes gardens from many other types of visitor attraction, as the interviews with visitors demonstrate. For example, gardens provide what is perceived as a sympathetic and secure environment for families with young children, as a mid-week visit to many gardens with a café or restaurant will clearly demonstrate. A review of the range of factors that contribute towards a garden visit, most commonly a family or group visit, has clearly shown that those responsible for their management need to consider how visitors may have conflicting priorities and are seeking different experiences from visiting. Meanwhile, some of the factors that are beyond their control can be ameliorated with careful planning and investment. Developments in recent years in garden attractions around the world demonstrate an awareness of these visitor demands, be they in the provision of quality catering and retailing or in the increasing recognition of the value of non-intrusive and sympathetic interpretation. As with those historic properties that receive visitors, many gardens were not developed initially as visitor attractions and imaginative management may be required to facilitate access and provide facilities, while at the same time preserving the experience of enjoyment, relaxation and pleasure that characterize the experience sought by the majority of garden visitors, be they the 'prime mover' or the secondary participant.

References

Adams, W. H. (1991). *Gardens Through History: Nature Perfected*. Abbeville Press Publishers.

Ballantyne, R., Packer, J. and Hughes, K. (2006). Exploring visitors' motives, expectations and experiences in Brisbane Botanic Gardens. The 6th International Congress on Education in Botanic Gardens, 10–14 September 2006. Botanic Gardens Conservation International. http://www.bgci.org/educationalcongress/pages/preface.htm.

Benfield, R. W. (2001). Good things come to those who wait: sustainable tourism and timed entry at Sissinghurst Castle Garden, Kent. *Tourism Geographies*, **3**, 207–217.

Berry, S. and Shepherd, G. (2001). Cultural heritage sites. In *Cultural Attractions and European Tourism* (G. Richards, ed), pp. 159–171, CABI.

Bisgrove, R. and Hadley, P. (2002). Gardening in the global greenhouse: the impacts of climate change on gardens in the UK. *Technical Report*. UK Climate Impacts Programme. http://data.ukcip.org.uk/resources/publications/documents/Gardens_master.pdf.

Comité Départemental du Tourisme de l'Yonne. (2003). *Le tourisme de jardins*. http:www.tourisme-yonne.com/pro/statistiques/tourisme_jardin 2003.pdf.

Connell, J. (2004a). The purest of human pleasures: the characteristics and motivations of visitors in Great Britain. *Tourism Management*, **25**, 229–247.

Connell, J. (2004b). Modelling the visitor experience in the gardens of Great Britain. *Current Issues in Tourism*, **7**, 183–216.

Connell, J. (2005). Managing gardens for visitors in Great Britain: a story of continuity and change. *Tourism Management*, **26**, 185–201.

English Heritage (2002). State of the Historic Environment Report 2002, *English Heritage*.

Environmental Management Services Limited (2000). *Napier Botanical Gardens Restoration Project*. http://www.napier.govt.nz/council/docs/reports/botanic.rest.pdf.

Hatherly, J. (2002). *Myths About Visitors to Botanic Gardens*. http://amol.au/evrsig/pdf/MA2002hatherley.pdf.

Lang Research Inc. (2001). *Travel Activities and Motivation Survey: Horticultural Tourism Report*. Lang Research Inc. http://www.tourism.gov.on.ca/english/tourdiv/research/tams.html.

Legg, M. H. and Kim, J. M. (1990). Visitor market structure analysis: a benefit-oriented approach. In *Leisure Challenges*: *Proceedings from the 6th Canadian Conference on Leisure Research*, 9–12 May 1990. University of Waterloo (B. Smale, ed), pp. 124–128, University of Waterloo Press.

Smithsonian Institution (2005). *Visitor Experiences in the Enid A. Haupt and the Mary Livingston Ripley Garden.* Office of Policy and Analysis, Smithsonian Institution. http://www.si.edu/opanda/Reports/Reports/HSD%20Gardens.pdf.

Spradley, J. P. (1979). *The Ethnographic Interview.* Holt, Rhinehart and Winston.

Steinhauer, M. M. (2004). An examination of public garden visitors adult learning style preference. *Journal of Integrative Psychology*, **5**, 42–49.

Thompson, K. (2003). *An Ear to the Ground.* Transworld Publishers.

Urry, J. (2002). *The Tourist Gaze: Leisure and Travel in Contemporary Societies*, 2nd ed. Sage.

VisitBritain (2006). *Visitor Attraction Trends England 2005.* http://www.tourism-trade.org.uk/Images/Attractions%20Survey%20-%20Final%20 Report%20-v2_tcm12-28144.pdf.

Walter, J. (1982). Social limits to tourism. *Leisure Studies*, **1**, 295–304.

Watson, A. (2006). Climate change – feeling the effect yet? *The National Trust*, **108**, 66–69.

CHAPTER **14**
• • • •

Interpretation and Attractions

Gianna Moscardo and Roy Ballantyne

Aims

The aims of this chapter are to:

- define interpretation and outline the roles it can play in the management of visitor attractions,
- describe a model and principles for the design of effective interpretation services in visitor attractions, and
- describe some of the challenges and future issues associated with using interpretation in visitor attractions.

Introduction

Interpretation is an essential component of visitor experiences at visitor attractions. Many of the activities and services provided at visitor attractions, such as guided tours, information signs, self-guided walks and guide books, are forms of interpretation. Interpretation plays two critical roles in visitor attractions: it helps in the creation of visitor experiences and it is a valuable tool in supporting the sustainability of the attraction. This chapter will define interpretation and discuss these two roles in more detail. A model for designing effective interpretation will then be presented. The chapter will also examine a number of challenges for interpretation in visitor attractions, including the need to find ways to present places and topics related to the darker side of human history and nature.

What is interpretation?

There are two ways to define or describe interpretation. The first is to list the forms of interpretation and the second is to focus on its goals and key characteristics. In thinking about forms of interpretation it is typical to include such activities as:

- guided walks and tours,
- lectures and audio-visual presentations,
- signs, panels or exhibits that provide information about the attraction and its heritage or significance,
- guidebooks, pamphlets or brochures, and
- information centres.

Using this list it could be suggested that interpretation incorporates all the various ways in which attraction managers seek to communicate with their visitors.

Traditionally, interpretation has been a formally recognized and central element of museums, historic houses, archaeological sites, art galleries, zoos, aquaria, national parks and gardens. It is worth noting that interpretation is also sometimes referred to as visitor education or animation. More recently, interpretation has become a recognized element of other types of attraction such as theme parks, wineries and urban entertainment precincts. This growth in the use of interpretive activities reflects growing competition between attractions and increasing expectations from visitors (Harris, 2005).

Given the wide range of places where interpretation is used, it is not surprising to find that there are many formal definitions available. Table 14.1 provides a selection of these definitions which take the second approach of describing the

Table 14.1   Selection of formal definitions of interpretation

Visitors as a central focus	Management as a central focus
A means of communicating ideas and feelings which help people understand more about themselves and their environment (IAA, cited in Kohl, 2005)	An educational activity that aims to reveal meanings about our cultural and natural resources. Interpretation enhances our understanding, appreciation, and, therefore, protection of historic sites and natural wonders (Beck and Cable, 1998)
[A] communication process which aims at helping people to discover the significance of things, places, people and events … Helping people change the way they perceive themselves and their world through a greater understanding (McFarlane, 1994)	The goal of interpretation is a change in behaviour of those for whom we interpret (Risk, cited in USNPS, 2005)

goals and key characteristics of interpretation. These definitions have been organized into two categories reflecting an important difference in approaches to thinking about interpretation. In the first column there are definitions which are centred on the visitor or audience, and these definitions feature words such as communication, understanding, significance and changes in perception. In the second column there are definitions with a stronger management focus, and these feature words such as education, appreciation, protection and changes in behaviour. The visitor-centred definitions also have a broader focus with an emphasis on people understanding the world or environment as a whole, while the management-centred definitions tend to concentrate on specific sites. While these two approaches are not incompatible, the management-centred definitions do tend to place the visitors as more passive receivers of interpretation and this can lead to interpretation becoming more like propaganda than persuasive communication (Harris, 2005). Thus, for the purposes of this chapter a more visitor-focused definition will be used. Interpretation will be defined here as a set of information-focused communication activities, designed to facilitate a rewarding visitor experience, that encourages visitors to be receptive to a management or sustainability message.

The roles of interpretation in visitor attractions

The two approaches to defining interpretation mirror two key themes in the broader business literature: the creation of consumer experiences and the importance of sustainability. While Pine and Gilmore's (1999) book *The Experience Economy* brought the concept of experience as a key element of consumption into the broader business literature, experience has always been at the centre of understanding why visitors go to attractions and what they get out of engaging in various tourist and leisure activities (Cohen, 1996). A number of authors have noted the increasing desire of consumers in general, and travellers in particular, for multi-dimensional and personalized entertainment and leisure experiences (Matathia and Salzman, 1998). In addition to the growing importance of the experience, sustainability issues have also emerged to dominate first the business and academic literature and, more recently, the popular media. These two themes can be seen as directly related to the key roles that interpretation can play in attractions: building rewarding visitor experiences and supporting sustainability.

Building rewarding visitor experiences

According to Pine and Gilmore (1999), an experience is a memorable event that evokes a range of positive emotional or affective responses in the participant. The key to successful visitor attractions is the creation of opportunities for visitors to have a rewarding experience. Interpretation can play an important role in experience-building by providing a range of activities for visitors to participate in, offering visitors mental and physical access to a site or topic of importance, and by providing visitors with a story about the significance of the place they are visiting.

The Cradle of Humankind World Heritage Area provides an example of the use of interpretation to build rewarding visitor experiences. This World Heritage Site is located in South Africa, north-west of Johannesburg and covers an area of approximately 47 000 ha, incorporating a number of different archaeological excavations. The area was given World Heritage status in recognition of its large number of fossil sites, including several caves that have yielded important early hominid fossils and information on the evolution of humankind. The challenge for creating a rewarding tourist experience in such a place is that much of the physical evidence is not easily seen or recognized and the large number of sites makes it difficult to build a coherent picture of the significance of the area. One of the solutions to this challenge was the development of an interpretive visitor attraction called Maropeng. This takes the form of a museum and visitor centre built in a central location within the World Heritage area. The building is distinctive as it is designed to resemble an ancient burial mound or tumulus. This building houses a number of displays explaining the history of the site, the fossil discoveries and their significance and the evolution of various hominid species (see Maropeng Aafrika, 2007; Cradle of Humankind, 2007, for more information on these areas and sites).

Another example of interpretation building rewarding visitor experiences can be found on the Otago Peninsula near Dunedin on New Zealand's south island. This area is home to a number of rare and significant wildlife populations including the only albatross breeding colony on the mainland in the southern hemisphere. The royal albatross breeding area on the Taiaroa peninsula has been a popular site for visitors since the 1960s (Parry and Robertson, 1998). This wildlife site has become the focus of a visitor attraction, the Royal Albatross Centre. This attraction uses interpretive displays, audio-visual presentations and guided tours to build an experience for visitors that includes more than simply watching the birds. The interpretive centre provides visitors with an insight into the significance of the site and the colony, details about the birds and a range of different ways to observe the colony in action. Without the interpretation provided, only visitors with pre-existing knowledge of the colony would be able to access the site and appreciate its significance. In addition, the Centre provides a mechanism for managing visitor impacts on the wildlife. Surveys of visitors to the Royal Albatross Centre confirm that the interpretive aspects of the Centre make an important contribution to their satisfaction with their experience. Even those surveyed on days with almost no albatross activity reported high levels of satisfaction (average of 8 on a scale where 0 referred to not at all satisfied and 10 very satisfied) (Saltzer, 2003).

These results are consistent with studies conducted with visitors in a number of different types of attraction and other tourist settings that demonstrate the importance of interpretation as both an expected feature of the experience and as a critical factor in visitor evaluations of the quality of their experience. For example, in a study conducted with visitors to an Australian indigenous attraction, the most important motivation for visitors was learning new things and increasing knowledge (Moscardo and Pearce, 1999). In a study conducted at historic houses in the United Kingdom, Frochot (2004) reported that the largest visitor group was amateur historians interested in learning about how people lived in other times. Even when learning or increasing knowledge and understanding are not major motives for a visit, there is evidence that effective or quality interpretation can make a significant contribution to visit satisfaction. Moscardo (2006), for example, reporting on a survey of nearly 4500 visitors conducted at 15 wildlife-based visitor attractions in New Zealand and Australia, concluded that quality interpretation and the amount visitors felt they had learnt about a species or setting were two of the most significant factors contributing to overall satisfaction.

Supporting sustainability

The second part of the definition of interpretation is about building on the rewarding experiences to encourage visitors to be receptive to a management or sustainability message. There are three main types of these management and sustainability messages. First, such messages play the traditional role of encouraging visitors to behave in ways that minimize their negative impacts on the specific setting being presented. Second, there are messages related to broader or global conservation or sustainability messages. A number of attractions seek to encourage people to take home a conservation message and to change their behaviour in their homes and workplaces to more sustainable practices. Third, there are messages related to supporting the sustainability practices of the attraction itself. There is increasing pressure on all businesses to improve their sustainability practices and visitor attractions are beginning to develop and publicize sustainability policies and practices aimed at limiting the negative impacts of their business operations on the environment and local communities. For visitor attractions, a key element in the successful implementation of such policies and practices will be encouraging visitors to comply with sustainability practices such as water and waste reduction.

There are numerous examples of the use of interpretation in the first role of managing visitor impacts on heritage sites. It is common to find signs and other forms of interpretation devoted to explaining why visitors should not touch certain objects, should stay on paths or should limit flash photography. In Philadelphia, for example, the Liberty Bell is an important historical artifact on public display. A number of signs are used to explain to visitors why they should not touch the actual bell and there is an exhibit allowing people to touch a replica of the words printed on the bell.

There are also many examples of the second role for interpretation – the take home conservation or sustainability message. Returning to our Maropeng example in South Africa, the final section of the displays on hominid evolution features a series of panels looking at the ways in which some of our uniquely human features have resulted in major environmental and social problems and visitors are asked to write a message about how they will challenge what they do when they return home to tackle these problems. The British Museum of Natural History in London also has a large exhibition on ways visitors can improve environmental impacts and reduce resource use and waste production when they leave the museum.

The third role is still emerging as various visitor attractions recognize the importance of improving their operational or business sustainability. A number of attractions have extensive sustainability programmes. For example, Greenwood Forest Park in Wales has won a number of environmental awards and acclaim for its programmes to reduce resource use and waste production, enhance the local environment, balance carbon usage and support local community projects (see Greenwood Forest Park, 2007, for further details). If visitor attractions follow the same sustainability path as other forms of tourism business such as hotels and resorts, then it will become increasingly important for them to enlist the support of their customers in meeting sustainability targets. Kingfisher Bay Resort on Fraser Island of the eastern Australian coast is an example of a tourism business with extensive interpretation both about the environment the resort is located in and about the sustainability practices of the resort itself. This second form of interpretation seeks to explain to visitors what they can do to minimize their environmental impacts while staying at the resort and why that is important to the resort. Studies of visitors and their experiences at this resort show that exposure to this interpretation does play a significant role in encouraging visitors to support management sustainability practices (Lee and Moscardo, 2005).

Principles of effective interpretation

The discussion thus far has been based on the assumption that the interpretation offered to visitors to attractions is of a high quality. Like all other aspects of visitor attraction design and management the effectiveness of interpretation depends upon the quality of its design and implementation. Table 14.2 provides a summary of the results of two critical incident studies conducted with tourists seeking to understand memorable experiences at visitor attractions. The first asked about wildlife-based attractions (Woods and Moscardo, 2003), while the second examined visitor attractions in general (Benckendorff *et al.*, 2006). The critical incident technique is a qualitative research method designed to generate descriptions of critical or memorable social or service episodes (see Chell, 1998, for more details). In the two studies presented in Table 14.2, the content analysis of the key themes that recurred in the most memorable visitor attraction experiences revealed a set of features most likely to be associated with a rewarding tourist experience. The visitor attraction features reported in Table 14.2 are not surprising as they are consistent with an extensive body of literature reporting on the results of evaluations of a number of different types of interpretation across a wide range of attractions and tourist settings. These results can be organized into a set of principles

Table 14.2 Key features of memorable visitor attraction experiences

Wildlife-based attractions	Visitor attractions in general
Critical incidents collected from 790 tourists, with incidents reported from attractions on every continent except Antarctica	Critical incidents collected from 356 tourists, with incidents reported from attractions on every continent except Antarctica. The main types of attractions included were theme parks, leisure attractions in shopping precincts, museums, science centres, and historic sites
• New experiences/animals	• Variety and change in the activities available
• Variety or diversity in the activities and animals	• Multi-sensory experiences
• Opportunities to interact and take control	• Opportunities for visitors to interact with exhibits or displays and make choices
• Multi-sensory experiences	• Finding information of personal relevance or interest
• Clear and easy to follow physical orientation	• Exhibits that allowed you to take a new or different perspective on something
	• Realistic displays/entertainment
	• Interesting information
	• Comfortable
Source: Woods and Moscardo (2003).	*Source*: Benckendorff *et al.* (2006).

that are consistent with a psychological approach to human experience referred to as mindfulness theory (Langer and Moldoneau, 2000).

Mindfulness theory comes from social psychology, where it is used to explain a large variety of everyday behaviours (Langer, 1989). According to mindfulness theory, in any given situation a person can be mindful or mindless. Mindfulness is a state of active cognitive or mental processing. Mindful people pay attention to the information available in the environment around them, react to new information and learn. Mindless people, on the other hand, follow established routines or scripts for behaviour and pay minimal attention to the environment and/or new information. Mindfulness has been shown to result in more positive perceptions of an experience, better responses to management requests and conservation messages, excitement, learning and satisfaction in leisure and tourism settings (Moscardo, 1999).

So what then are the conditions that contribute to mindfulness? Moscardo (1999) suggested a mindfulness model for communicating with visitors in interpretive settings based on studies conducted into interpretation. This model is depicted in Figure 14.1. This model can be used as the basis for the following principles for effective interpretive design in visitor attractions.

Good orientation and attention to visitor comfort

Visitors need to be able to find their way around easily, understand how to plan and organize their visit and be comfortable so that they can focus on the interpretive experience. Visitor attractions need to have good way-finding systems and information at the entrance or foyer about the facilities available, the schedules for the day and advice on how to plan a visit. In addition, visitor

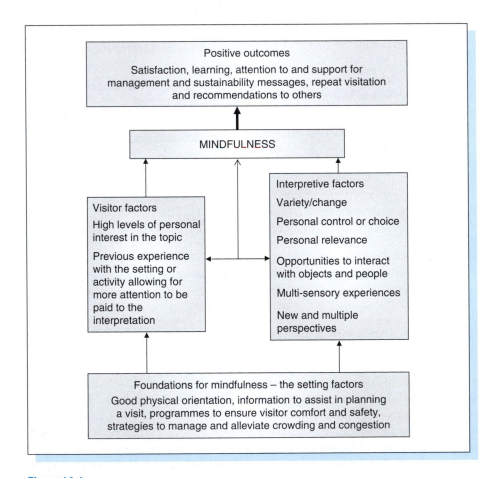

Figure 14.1

A mindfulness model of effective interpretation for visitor attractions attraction managers need to plan for rest areas, temperature control and access to food and drink. Crowding and queues also need attention and careful management (Pearce, 2005).

Personal relevance and/or importance

One of the most powerful ways to encourage mindfulness (Moscardo, 1999) is to build a link between the interpretation topic and something of personal relevance or importance to the visitor. There are a number of ways to connect interpretive material to visitor interests and knowledge. At the simplest level, analogies and metaphors can be used to connect new information to things that visitors are likely to already know or be familiar with. Interpreters can also use stories that provide a human dimension to the interpretive topic. In addition, the interpretation could be organized around universal themes such as altruism, family life, food acquisition, danger and discovery (Davis and McLeod, 2003). The reader is directed to Pierssene (1999) for more information and example on the use of themes in interpretation.

Variety or change in an experience

There are a number of ways that change can be incorporated into an interpretive experience. These include the use of range of different media, the development of activities that vary in terms of the level of physical and mental input required by the visitor with a balance between more active and more contemplative opportunities, seasonal events programmes and the development of different facets of the interpretation topic. Even text on signs and panels can be varied in a number of ways (see University of Queensland, 2007, for more details on applying this and other interpretive best-practice principles to text on signs, displays and in exhibits). The NASA space centre outside Houston is a visitor attraction offering a wide range of different interpretive activities including a guided bus and walking tour of the space centre, interactive computer displays on various aspects of space travel and static displays of spacecraft and theme park, like rides simulating aspects of space travel.

Personal control or choice

One way to include variety in interpretation is to give visitors choices and options. This allows the visitors to create their own unique and personal experience. Examples of such options could include having different themes that visitors could follow on a self-guided tour or walk in the attraction, the embedding of different levels or layers of detail in interpretive signs so that visitors can elect to investigate some topics in more detail and the opportunity to pursue special interests in more detail on websites, in libraries or through the use of computer technology.

Opportunities to interact with objects and people

An exhibition space in the National Museum of Australia offers an example of the use of computer technology to allow for visitors to interact with both the interpretive content and other visitors. In the kSpace Futureworld exhibition, visitors can create their own futuristic vehicles or living spaces. Once these are finished, the computer combines the designs of all the participants and creates a futuristic city for the visitors to explore in a 3D presentation. Interaction does not, however, require complex technology. The key is to allow visitors some measure of participation and social interaction. A number of activities offered to visitors at the Polynesian Cultural Centre in Hawaii are low-tech examples of participation. At this visitor attraction visitors can get a temporary Maori tattoo, learn to dance or try their hand at traditional food preparation methods.

Multi-sensory experiences

While traditionally interpretation is based around reading and looking, it is easily possible to incorporate touch and kinaesthetics as additional sensory experiences by offering a variety of objects for visitors to handle and feel. In addition, new technologies allow for the incorporation of sound, smell and climate effects into the interpretive experience. The Antarctic Centre, a visitor attraction in Christchurch, New Zealand, provides a special room where visitors can experience the cold and windy conditions of Antarctica.

New and multiple perspectives

Finally, effective interpretation challenges visitors to reassess their perceptions by offering new and different perspectives on a topic or content area. At one level, such new and/or multiple perspectives can be generated by offering differing viewpoints from different people. At the Independence Historical National Park visitor centre in Philadelphia, for example, an introductory video presents the events of the American War of Independence from the perspective of four different individuals each with a different political view. Special effects and technology can also be used to provide different physical perspectives.

Challenges for interpretation in visitor attractions

Despite the evidence presented earlier about the important role that quality interpretation can play in contributing to visitor experiences and satisfaction, not all people are advocates of its use (Howard, 2003). Major criticisms of the use of interpretation cluster around the major themes of threats to authenticity, excessive interpretation and conflict over what topics or interpretive content to include (Harris, 2005; Howard, 2003; Pearce, 2005). All of these themes can be seen as reflecting the reality that decisions on what to include in interpretive presentations, and how much to restrict the visitor experience, reflect political values and power differentials (Moscardo, 2001). Nowhere are these issues more clearly present than in the interpretation of hot topics such as war and dark tourism places, such as sites of massacres and prisons.

Interpreting 'hot' events and places

Interpreters today are expected to provide more than just information in their stories relating to places that have experienced 'hot' or emotional events. Uzzell introduced the term 'hot interpretation' into the field of heritage interpretation in 1988 (Uzzell, 1989). According to Uzzell and Ballantyne (1998), the concept of hot interpretation 'arose as a response to the failure of many interpretive designers and providers to acknowledge that visitors to heritage sites do not experience heritage simply as a cognitive experience. The principle behind hot interpretation is that although a detached, cool and objective approach to the presentation and assessment of information and subsequent decision-making is seen as highly desirable in our society, there are many decisions that we make in both our private and public lives where a purely rational Vulcan-like approach to the world is difficult, impossible or even undesirable. Whenever we are presented with choices we rarely stand by as disinterested observers. Of course, we hope our judgements will be thought through carefully, having drawn on as much information as possible and weighing up all the pros and cons of alternative options. However, our feelings, emotional instincts and reactions play an important role in our decision-making'.

Emotions colour our memories and experiences and thus our selective attention to information. ... There are some areas in heritage interpretation which have a strong affective and emotional impact on people. This might be because the interpretation touches on personal memories for instance such as at battlefield sites where loved ones were killed. Interpretation could equally have resonance at a collective level such as at a site where a nation achieved its independence from a colonial power or where a pressure group won a famous battle to protect a threatened landscape. Likewise, emotional responses could be fired through interpretation related to issues which evoke strong ideological beliefs and convictions such as the protection of a rare bird or plant species or the opposition to non-renewable energy sources such as nuclear power.

'Interpretation that appreciates the need for and injects an affective component into its subject matter, *where appropriate*, is "hot interpretation". Hot interpretation accepts that we are subject to a full repertoire of emotional responses – the palette is very varied, more varied than is typically acknowledged, anticipated or encouraged through interpretation ... Hot interpretive experiences are today fairly common, particularly where they are used for "touristic" purposes – to emotionally engage visitors in order to better convey the meaning and significance of the heritage of the people, places, events and artifacts' (Uzzell and Ballantyne, 1998: 165). Internationally, there has been an explosion of hot interpretive tourist experiences in museums around the world with the most well known being the 'holocaust' experiences in Washington, DC (Holocaust Museum), Berlin (Jewish Museum) and Los Angeles (Museum of Tolerance). Many war museums today have also changed their interpretive experiences to provide greater hot experiences: it is no longer as common to find museums that interpret only the 'machines of war' without any interpretation of the impact of such machines upon people.

Notwithstanding the desirability of providing hot interpretation for touristic purposes, it is as a 'platform' for delivering behavioural change – interpretation motivating visitors to address social and environmental challenges facing society – that hot interpretation holds such potential. It is the 'community development function' (Uzzell and Ballantyne, 1998) of hot interpretation that is expected to increasingly play an important role in motivating community to undertake actions to remediate and address important social and environmental problems.

A good example illustrating the way in which the community development function of hot interpretation has been used to facilitate community healing in post-Apartheid South Africa is seen in the development of the District Six Museum in Cape Town, which is described in the following case study. Permission has been obtained from *Curator* to reproduce in the case study below a section of an article 'Interpreting Apartheid: visitors' perceptions of the District Six Museum' (Ballantyne, 2003: 280–281) that briefly describes the District Six Museum (see also Ballantyne and Uzzell, 1993).

Case Study: District Six Museum, Cape Town, South Africa

District Six was so named in 1867 as the sixth municipal district of the port of Cape Town, South Africa, and housed a vibrant, mixed-race community, once known as 'the soul of Cape Town'. With the advent of Apartheid laws after 1948, those people living in the racially mixed area of District Six experienced increased racial discrimination that characterized the implementation of the system. As one ex-resident commented:

> At work we had to use separate toilet facilities; there was hardly any eating place in town where we could now sit down and have a meal. At the railway station we suddenly had to use a separate entrance. The same applied to subways ... the railway ticket boxes, the buses and trains, the post office, the hospitals – everything was segregated.
>
> (Fortune, 1996: 118)

On 11 February 1966, District Six was declared a 'White' area under the Apartheid Group Areas Act (1953) and over the following 15 years, 60 000 people were forcibly removed, their houses razed to the ground by bulldozers and resettled in government provided 'apartments' on the bleak, sandy, windblown wastes of the Cape Flats. As ex-residents commented on the experience of being 'resettled' in one of the new townships:

> Oooo, don't talk about that, please don't talk about it to me. I will cry. I will cry all over again. … There was a change. Not just in me, in all the people. What they took away they can never give it back to us! … It won't ever be the same again (weeping). It cannot be the same … I cannot explain how it was when I moved out of Cape Town and I came to Manenberg … Oooo my God, was my whole life tumbling down! … They destroyed us, they made our children ruffians.

(Jeppie and Crain, 1990: 31–32)

> It was not necessary to lock the front door. The house was going to be demolished … I didn't even bother to pull the door closed. Number 14 would exist no more … I started to cry. I sobbed as if someone had just died. I didn't care … The place was our home, after all.

(Fortune, 1996: 129)

More than 30 years later there are now plans to resettle District Six, but at present the scar on the slopes of Table Mountain still remains. The weed-choked rubble, framed by the still evident street pattern, is a stark visual reminder of the brutal impact of Apartheid laws upon people of colour. It is a space imbued with memories and charged with feelings and emotions – the visual blemish in the townscape mirroring the emotional scars borne by past inhabitants and their families. As Blake (1999: 9) comments, 'the barren landscape of District Six is at once an open wound in Cape Town and a well healed if unsightly scar. It is a hole (needing) to be filled to mend the fabric of the city, to integrate a systematically and forcibly fragmented community and nation'.

The District Six Museum is located in the deconsecrated Methodist Church that is one of the few remaining buildings at the edge of what was once District Six. Readers are directed to District Six (2007) for a visual overview of the museum and its exhibits. Many artifacts such as the street signs kept by a bulldozer driver when the area was demolished, a street map on the floor, 'recreated' rooms and photographs of the site, are displayed in the museum. Ex-residents act as guides, telling visitors about the area as well as their own personal stories. Visiting the District Six Museum is clearly a hot interpretive experience where displays elicit deep personal memories and emotions, especially on the part of ex-residents, as they recall the history and community spirit of the area. An important focal point in this regard is the 'memory cloth', a calico sheet (now well over 100 m long) upon which past residents and visitors write personal comments. Writing and reading such memories is a very moving part of visiting the museum both for past residents and other visitors – it is not uncommon for individuals to be moved to tears as they confront words that hint at the real impact and hurt of the removals upon community members. For instance,

> Here we lived. Here we loved. Here we laughed. Here we served, worshiped … We all loved District Six. We all have fond memories. We all long to come back. (BU)

> In respect of and in memory of my mother and father who lived out their lives in that marvellous community of District Six. … We shall not morn their

> passing on but keep a memory of their struggles for future generations to strengthen their beliefs against the Capitalist bastards! (GM and SM)
>
> I am sorry for what was done through the Apartheid era. Keep up South Africa! Keep up! We will survive. (W)
>
> SP from Arundal St came to reclaim her land on the 1st Oct. 1998 – FOR SURE!!!
>
> My childhood dreams were shattered by the forced removals of 1966. (LL)

Interpretation at the museum is especially 'hot' for ex-residents and those with direct experience of the destruction of District Six because the artifacts and stories connect with their memories and personal experiences.

Conclusion

Interpretation is a central element of the visitor experience in many attractions. For some it is the primary reason for their existence, while in others it is the one thing that all visitors expect to find. Interpretation can also be an important tool for managing visitors. But to achieve these goals interpretation must be effective. A substantial body of research and practice evidence tells us that effective interpretation

- is organized around themes,
- allows visitors to find and build personal connections,
- offers a variety of experiential dimensions,
- is interactive and multi-sensory,
- gives visitors choices and control over their experiences,
- offers new and/or multiple perspectives on the topics being presented, and
- is part of a comfortable setting where it is easy for visitors to find their way.

It is important to remember these principles as one looks to the future of visitor attractions. Being able to design interpretation which incorporates multiple perspectives gives visitors choices and control and which encourage visitors to participate and interact is likely to become increasingly important in responding to greater range of visitor expectations, backgrounds and needs. Finally, it is also likely that in the future visitor attractions will have to provide much more evidence of their commitment to sustainability practices and it is here that effective interpretation may again play an important role.

References

Ballantyne, R. (2003). Interpreting Apartheid: visitors' perceptions of the District Six Museum. *Curator: The Museum Journal*, **46**, 279–292.

Ballantyne, R. and Uzzell, D. L. (1993). Environmental mediation and hot interpretation: a case study of District Six, Cape Town. *Journal of Environmental Education*, **24**, 4–7.

Beck, L. and Cable, T. (1998). *Interpretation for the 21st century*. Sagamore.

Benckendorff, P., Moscardo, G. and Murphy, L. (2006). Visitor perceptions of technology use in tourist attraction experiences. In *Cutting Edge Research in Tourism* (G. Papageorgiou, ed). Available as pdf file on CD.

Blake, A. (1999). Keep it real. In *District Six Museum Newsletter*, 4 October.

Chell, E. (1998). Critical incident technique. In *Qualitative Research Methods and Analysis in Organizational Research* (G. Symon and C. Cassell, eds), pp. 51–72. Sage.

Cohen, E. (1996). A phenomenology of tourist experiences. In *The Sociology of Tourism* (Y. Apostolopoutos, S. Leivadi and A. Yiannakis, eds), pp. 90–111. Routledge.

Cradle of Humankind (2007). Cradle of Humankind World Heritage site. http://www.cradleofhumankind.co.za/.

Davis, H. and McLeod, S. L. (2003). Why humans value sensational news: an evolutionary perspective. *Evolution and Human Behaviour*, **24**, 208–216.

District Six (2007). District Six Museum. http://www.districtsix.co.za.

Fortune, L. (1996). *The House in Tyne Street: Childhood Memories of District Six*. Kwela Books.

Frochot, I. (2004). An investigation into the influence of the benefits sought by visitors on their quality evaluation of historic houses' service provision. *Journal of Vacation Marketing*, **10**, 223–237.

Greenwood Forest Park. (2007). Family adventure. http://www.greenwood-forestpark.co.uk/.

Harris, D. (2005). *Key Concepts in Leisure Studies*. Sage.

Howard, P. (2003). *Heritage Management, Interpretation and Identity*. Continuum.

Jeppie, S. and Crain, S. (1990). *The Struggle for District Six: Past and Present*. Buchu Books.

Kohl, J. (2005). Putting environmental interpretation to work for conservation in a park setting. *Applied Environmental Education and Communication*, **4**, 31–42.

Langer, E. J. (1989). *Mindfulness*. Addison-Wesley.

Langer, E. J. and Moldoneau, M. (2000). The construct of mindfulness. *Journal of Social Issues*, **56**, 1–9.

Lee, W. and Moscardo, G. (2005). Understanding the impact of ecotourism resort experiences on tourists' environmental attitudes and behavioural intentions. *Journal of Sustainable Tourism*, **13**, 546–565.

Maropeng Aafrika (2007). Maropeng Aafrika. http://www.maropeng.co.za.

Matathia, I. and Salzman, M. (1998). *Next: Trends for the Future*. MacMillan.

McFarlane, J. (1994). Some definitions of interpretation. *Heritage Interpretation International News*, July.

Moscardo, G. (1999). *Making Visitors Mindful: Principles for Creating Quality Sustainable Visitor Experiences through Effective Communication*. Sagamore.

Moscardo, G. (2001). Cultural and heritage tourism: the great debates. In *Tourism into the Twenty First Century: Reflections on Experience* (B. Faulkner, G. Moscardo and E. Laws, eds), pp. 3–17. Cassell.

Moscardo, G. (2006). Is near enough good enough? Understanding and managing customer satisfaction with wildlife based tourism experiences.

In *Tourism and Hospitality Services Management* (E. Laws, B. Prideaux and G. Moscardo, eds). CABI.

Moscardo, G. and Pearce, P. L. (1999). Understanding ethnic tourists. *Annals of Tourism Research*, **26**, 416–434.

Parry, G. and Robertson, C. J. R. (eds). (1998). *The Royals of Taiaroa*. Otago Peninsula Trust.

Pearce, P. L. (2005). *Tourist Behaviour: Themes and Conceptual Schemes*. Channel View.

Pierssene, A. (1999). *Explaining our World: An Approach to the Art of Environmental Interpretation*. E & FN Spon.

Pine II, B. J. and Gilmore, J. H. (1999). *The Experience Economy*. Harvard Business School Press.

Saltzer, R. (2003). Understanding visitor–wildlife interactions: a case study of the Royal Albatross Centre, Otago Peninsula, New Zealand. Report prepared for the CRC for Sustainable Tourism.

University of Queensland (2007). Interpretative signage: principles and practice. http://www.talm.uq.edu.au/signage/.

USNPS – US National Park Service (2005). What is interpretation? US National Park Service. http://www.cr.nps.gov/nr/publications/bulletins/interp/int4.htm.

Uzzell, D. L. (ed.) (1989). The hot interpretation of war and conflict. In *Heritage Interpretation: Volume 1 – The Natural and Built Environment*, pp. 33–47. Belhaven.

Uzzell, D. L. and Ballantyne, R. (eds) (1998). Heritage that hurts: interpretation in a post-modern world. In *Contemporary Issues in Heritage and Environmental Interpretation: Problems and Prospects*, pp. 152–171. The Stationery Office.

Woods, B. and Moscardo, G. (2003). Enhancing wildlife education through mindfulness. *Australian Journal of Environmental Education*, **19**, 97–108.

Management Challenges for Religion-Based Attractions

Myra Shackley

Aims

The aims of this chapter are to:

- illustrate the diversity of religion-based attractions,
- identify major management trends and challenges,
- distinguish religious from secular visitor attractions, and
- consider visitor motivations.

Introduction

Religion-based visitor attractions form an immensely diverse assemblage, varied in scale, location, visitor motivation and management style. Most are sites that are sacred to one or more religious traditions, including many places of worship or pilgrimage that have been receiving visitors for hundreds or thousands of years (McGettigan, 2003). But the category also includes crassly commercial theme parks with some religious motifs, as well as many sites which fall somewhere on the continuum between these two extremes. The writer has attempted elsewhere to classify sacred sites (Shackley, 2001) and to provide an overview of some site-specific management issues (Shackley, 2002, 2004). Conceptual frameworks for the study of religious tourism are often based around the work of Cohen (1979) and Smith (1992). This chapter, however, focuses especially on several operations management issues especially significant at religious sites which have become visitor attractions, and introduces the recent phenomena of commercially managed visitor attractions based on a religious theme. The subject is currently attracting a great deal of academic interest, including edited books by Fernandes *et al.* (2003) and Timothy and Olsen (2006), both of which focus on pilgrimage and spiritual journeys but include a consideration of the site management issues experienced at the end of such journeys (Olsen, 2006). This has also been applied to religious sites associated with relatively little known traditions, such as the case of Haifa's Baha'I Gardens in Israel (Collins-Kreiner and Gatrell, 2006), which attracts both Baha'I pilgrims and secular visitors with different socio-spatial practices, concluding that differing motives define the activity space of visitors and contribute to a separation of tourist and pilgrim experiences which has been utilized by the municipality in the creation of a specific visitor attraction.

Classifying religion-based attractions

The range of religion-based attractions in the world is enormous, and the problem of classifying them could be tackled in any number of ways (Vuconic, 1996). They could be divided, for example, by religious tradition, by the level of site utilization, by the balance between the worshipping community and by the number of tourist visitors. They could be categorized by management type (sacred or secular, public or private sector) or by size (which can vary from a small isolated shrine to an entire city such as Jerusalem, a small state such as the Vatican or tens of square miles of cultural landscape). Recently, there has been some international attention given to the social, physical and economic impact of religious sites which are significant visitor attractions (Raghunathan and Sinha, 2006; Raj, 2003). Religious sites could be divided roughly on the basis of the number of visitors each receives on the premise, as the difficulty of managing a religious site is in direct proportion to the number of people who visit it, or by the length of time the visitors stay. A typology of visitors could also be constructed, perhaps on the basis of the distance they have travelled, which could be a pilgrimage of several hundred miles or a journey just round the corner from their homes. The context of the site could be a means of classification whether, for example, it was urban, rural, linear or nodal, and how it was linked to other attractions (van der Borg *et al.*, 1996). It might form part of a pilgrimage or cultural route or have been included in a marketing promotion that encourages visitors to sample a number of linked attractions in the course of one tour or visit. An even simpler division of religious sites would split off those sites actively used for worship from those which, while still visited by tourists, are, in religious terms, only of historical or archaeological interest.

Broadly speaking, religion-based visitor attractions can be either:

- components of the natural environment (e.g. sacred mountains, lakes, groves, islands),

- human-made buildings, structures and sites originally designed for religious purposes which may now also be attracting tourists, and
- human-made buildings with a religious theme designed to attract tourists.

Inevitably, some sites combine elements of all three categories. A further category, of special events with religious significance which take place at non-religious sites, could also be added. This typology is unpacked further in Shackley (2001). Although for many people the idea of a religion-based attraction is synonymous with built heritage, this is not globally true. Many cultural landscapes (including those of Uluru in Australia, Sagarmartha in the Himalayas or the Tien Shan mountains in China) include sacred sites, elements of built heritage and the component parts of a local religious tourism industry. A nodal site such as St Katherine's Monastery in Mount Sinai (Egypt) may be the focus of an entire sacred landscape, venerated by adherents of different worshipping traditions and also visited by casual tourists (Shackley, 1998). In addition to the single nodal building (e.g. a cathedral, shrine, temple or mosque), built religious heritage may also consist of entire towns like Jerusalem, Amritsar, Varanasi or Assisi. This category of religion-based attractions could also be extended to include 'New Age' sites such as Glastonbury (although Glastonbury also has an older, Christian religious heritage). There is also a difficult and controversial category of secular sites associated with socially traumatic or politically significant events which have become sacralized, including some battlefield and Holocaust sites, and localities associated with the slave trade in West Africa.

Trends in today's consumer services marketplace have also created a new category of purpose-built religious tourism attraction that to some extent makes a commodity of the religion which it purports to promote. Instead of being based around a traditional sacred site, these new attractions have been devised to create a visitor environment with a religious theme, but without any authentically sacred elements. In some cases, the motives for such projects are blatantly commercial, but most claim educational motivation. Many substitute a sanitized experience for one which is either historically unavailable or geographically or socially undesirable. 'Nazareth Village', a new project in the town of Nazareth in northern Israel, is an example of the latter, where a first-century village is being re-created near the supposed location of Jesus' childhood home. The objective is to enable visitors to experience what life would have been like at that time, but the project moves from museum to theme park with items such as the 'Parable Walk' where visitors can speak with costumed volunteers acting in character. Published justification for the scheme has included the observation that contemporary urban Nazareth not only resembles a building site but is also overshadowed by a huge cathedral and has a high Arab population, leading to disappointment from overseas visitors who had anticipated simple rural life. A more extreme example of this genre has now been constructed near Orlando in Florida. The US$16 million 'Holy Land Experience' developed by Zion's Hope, a non-profit making and non-denominational Christian ministry, has opened this Park on 15 acres near Universal Studios and attempted to re-create Jerusalem, down to the camel prints in the cement, Goliath burgers and strolling Middle Eastern minstrels (see Holy Land Experience, 2007). The park has encountered much opposition from local Jewish leaders and has also fallen foul of tax inspectors who deemed it to be a theme park (and thus liable for property tax) rather than a religious and educational entity as its developers claim. There are other American examples, starting with Heritage Village (O'Guinn and Belk, 1989; Shackley, 2001) and projects still in the planning stage include 'The Holy Lands' religious theme park in Mesquite, Nevada and Marianland, a Catholic theme park containing replicas of major Marian sites including Lourdes, proposed for south Texas. Such projects are likely to flourish in the future if American tourists become increasingly reluctant to visit Christian religious sites in the Middle East and Europe because of anxieties about security. Major Buddhist projects in construction include the huge Maitreya project near Buddha's birthplace in north India, as well as the largest Buddhist temple outside Asia which opened on the outskirts of Denver in 2003 as a result of 14 years of work and US$2.7 million of voluntary donations.

Many such artificially created religious sites make such travel substitution their major selling point. This is not a new idea. Shoval (2000) pointed out that the St Louis World Fair in 1904 included a 13-acre 1:1 model of Jerusalem. But this kind of substitution is in direct opposition to the pilgrimage ethic that stresses the need to leave normal life (including its constraints and conveniences) behind. There is a marked contrast between the product offered by a religious theme park and the experience of the sacred that might be gained by a visitor to a sacred site. The religious tourism market (Bywater, 1994) is thus divided between religiously motivated tourists seeking an authentic religious experience, and tourists who utilize religious sites as a background for other activities. Religious sites have always been commercial; the selling of souvenirs is an integral part of all major religious traditions. It is only a small step from building entrepreneurial opportunities to take advantage of visitors to religious sites to building entire environments to attract new categories of visitor. But this is a recent trend; by far the majority of the world's religious tourism attractions are the sacred sites.

Managing religion-based attractions

What is the core product of a religious site? The main benefit to the consumer/visitor is intangible and subjective, including atmosphere and spiritual experience (Brown and Loades, 1995). Within the world of secular heritage, visitor attraction managers are generally trying to optimize visitor numbers and revenue while minimizing adverse impact. Many religious sites generate no revenue from visitors at all, none generate sufficient to cover operating costs. Religious sites (unless purposely built for commercial reasons) have limited capacity to generate revenue from visitors, although their existence generates a lot of money for associated private-sector operators.

Moreover, religious sites are usually encumbered by tiers of public- and private-sector interests, which can vary from the volunteers directly involved in their day-to-day management, through to UNESCO's World Heritage Committee if the site has been placed on the World Heritage list. There will be national, regional and local governmental organizations, non-governmental organizations (NGOs), charities, pressure groups and other organizations concerned with the site. These represent the interests of local people, the religious establishment, planners at regional and national levels, tourism, resource management and a host of others. Considering sacred heritage as a product encounters problems, since by comparison with other elements of the service sector, such sites lack integrated management. There is seldom any linear agreement between resource use through production to 'sale' and subsequent 'consumption' by visitors or worshippers.

The effectiveness of the management and marketing of a religious site is related to the type and size of the religious tradition represented. Many religious sites have rigidly hierarchical, clerically-dominated management structures, which may have functioned in the same way for thousands of years. Such structures are largely unaffected by modern management trends, with the exception of their peripheral activities (often financial). Some religious sites seem not to be managed at all, and merely exist in a management vacuum where things happen by custom and nobody is too bothered with achieving specific targets. Others (but very few) are competent professional organizations, with proper accounting systems and business plans. Unless the site is one of the above-mentioned commercially run religious attractions (and many might consider this concept a contradiction in terms), its managers might not recognize themselves as such but might prefer to identify themselves primarily as facilitators of worship and custodians of a site or building. Only built heritage (rather than landscapes) is usually managed, and the site manager of a religious site is almost always starved of resources. His (operating religious-based attractions is an almost exclusively male prerogative) operations are usually grossly undercapitalized. Moreover, he will probably see dealing with planning or financial issues or other aspects of operational management as something that he neither wishes to get deeply involved with, nor has the ability to cope with at the required level. The managers of religious sites are usually religious leaders, to whom concepts such as product development and strategic planning may be quite foreign. And perhaps, in spiritual terms, this is a good thing. Yet when sites become visitor attractions, which may necessitate coping with thousands, and sometimes millions, of visitors each year, operations management is no longer a luxury: but it becomes essential.

Management methods vary and site managers have to perform a delicate balancing act. However they need to preserve the site, which may be ancient, fragile and weighed down by traditions, which means that the installation of visitor facilities becomes unfeasibly expensive, if not downright impossible. Yet to conserve the site requires money (and sufficient cash will never be forthcoming from worshippers) and money comes, directly or indirectly, from visitors. Visiting a religious site is, or should be, an emotive experience and site managers are also charged with the task of preserving that elusive spiritual quality referred to as 'spirit of place'. At the same time they must facilitate the religious use of the site (if, indeed, the site is active) and catering for the frequently conflicting demands of worshippers and visitors. Sacred sites often rely heavily on volunteers to assist with day-to-day operations, with all the problems that provides. They are not (primarily) commercial operations, yet are functioning in a commercial world where customers have become more discerning and more critical, can choose between competing destinations and have easier access to information.

Seasonality and visitor flows

Very few religious sites take active steps to restrict overall visitor numbers, but many popular sites have problems in controlling visitor arrivals. There are exceptions to this generalization: at the Church of the Holy Sepulchre in Jerusalem, the tiny Chapel of the Angel, which contains the stone on which the angel sat to tell of Christ's resurrection (Matthew 28:1), is so small that only four visitors can enter at any one time, placing an obvious limit on numbers. At religious sites where there are very high levels of visitation or marked seasonal variations, it is often necessary to manage visitor flows to, around and within sites in order to optimize multiple use. Sometimes, visitor access to a religious site is controlled by the type of transport required to reach it. The easiest access systems to control are, inevitably, to islands and the most difficult are at complex urban sites. For example, visitor access to Holy Island (Lindisfarne) off the Northumbrian coast can be gained only when the causeway road is exposed at low tide. Access to the pilgrimage destination island of Iona in Scotland is by ferry, and markedly seasonal. Fifty times more visitors use the ferry in August than in January, yet the ferry size and operating costs remain roughly the same. During July and August, large numbers of visitors cause congestion around Iona Abbey and the ferry landing, with the rest of the island largely deserted. One management strategy under consideration is a combination of better signage and better information which might disseminate visitors more widely throughout the island if the footpath network could be rationalized and stabilized. Most access issues are closely connected with ever-present financial considerations. For example, since 1999 visitors to the ancient site of Jericho in Jordan Valley of Israel can now reach the neighbouring Monastery of the Temptation, high on a mountainside above the village, by a new cable railway. Many claim that the railway is a visual pollutant and destroys the 'spirit of place' of the area. However, the reason for its construction was not to assist with visitor flow but to generate revenue in a West Bank area with little access to tourism development funding.

Many sites, especially in India, are suffering under the weight of increased visitor numbers, within an infrastructure which is unable to cope, giving cause for concern about the heavy level of environmental impact (Guo, 2006; Jutla, 2006). In particular, India's spiritual heritage and major pilgrimage destinations have attracted academic interest, notably the sites of Braj in Uttar Pradesh, a centre of Vaishnava pilgrimage (Cloesen, 2005) and the Rockfort Temple at Tiruchirapalli in Tamil Nadu. The latter site, which constitutes an entire sacred landscape, attracts more than 40 000 visitors per year into a crowded and chaotic environment where the calm and quietness which originally attracted pilgrims has been replaced by commercial chaos and heavy traffic (Raghunathan and Sinha, 2006). The Archaeological Survey of India takes a monument-based approach to conservation, which limits understanding of the relationship between monument and context. Raghunathan and Sinha (2006) proposed a series of measures including delineation of a pedestrian zone to regulate the pilgrim path through the site and limit commercial access, thus improving the quality of the visitor experience.

Visitor flows within sites can be controlled in various ways. In the case of a religious attraction where an entrance fee is charged, access to the entire site may be restricted by the utilization of some kind of 'pay perimeter'. This refers to that portion of the site that can only be accessed after payment of a fee. Some sacred sites designate a pay perimeter spatially located beyond an area where normal worship or prayer takes place, allowing both paying tourists and non-paying visitors access to the facility. But such arrangements are frequently resented. Some sacred sites make the payment voluntary. Lincoln Cathedral has recently adjusted its pay perimeter so that visitors entering the building are able to get an excellent overview and panorama of the nave for free. They are also able to enter a small chapel reserved for prayer and gain access to the cathedral bookshop without charge, but cathedral catering is within the charging zone. Like all sacred sites, some areas are no-go areas either reserved for staff, administrative or storage use, or for sacramental purposes, where unlimited visitation is not encouraged. Other visitor flow management methods include queue control, which is often used for special exhibitions such as the Turin Shroud or art exhibitions in religious buildings.

Access to and around religious sites can therefore be physically limited and controlled, but it can also be socially limited by policies that include the implementation of booking and queuing systems, which may or may not be associated with various types of charges. Charging for access to sacred sites is a highly emotive issue and one that frequently causes disagreement on the grounds that access should be universal, a human right. However, only those sites which charge have accurate visitor records. The following case study is intended to illustrate the way large-scale religious tourism can be an integral part of destination development, and what commercial opportunities it presents.

Case Study: The Shrine of Our Lady at Knock, Ireland

The Shrine of Our Lady at Knock is one of the many Christian pilgrimage sites in Europe which has developed over the last 150 years (including all the major Marian shrines such as Fatima and Lourdes) and receives 1.5 million visitors each year (Shackley, 2006). It is of immense economic significance to a relatively undeveloped area of western Ireland, and a major element in the Catholic pilgrimage network of Europe. Knock was a small, obscure bog-side village in County Mayo where, on 21 August 1879, a vision of Our Lady accompanied by St Joseph and St John appeared, surrounded by a soft brilliant light. The apparition lasted for about two hours and had 20 witnesses, with the light visible for miles around. Validated by a commission of enquiry, it generated a great wave of religious enthusiasm in Ireland and steady growth in visitor numbers. Today, Knock remains a great centre of prayer and pilgrimage. It is primarily a location for organized group tours, many requiring facilities for the disabled, rather than for individual pilgrimage. A huge new circular church catering for 10 000 people was completed in 1976, accompanied by landscaping of the extensive shrine grounds, the building of the Knock Folk Museum and assorted oratories, churches, confessional halls, assembly and processional areas. This large area is necessary: in 1993 more than 40 000 people attended a single mass on the visit of Mother Teresa of Calcutta. Mayo County Council has reconstructed the small village of Knock by widening streets and roads, building a new shopping centre and constructing a huge car park. The shrine is served by its own airport, Knock International Airport, some 11 miles to the north. This was opened in 1985 and developed by the Connaught Regional Airport Company with the mission to provide a gateway to open up this disadvantaged region of Ireland and help the shrine to achieve its full pilgrimage potential. Currently, Knock is linked to different Irish and English airports by scheduled and charter flights, including budget airlines such as Ryanair. Tourism to Knock is seasonal with little (including the tourist office) open outside the main tourism season, May–October. Knock is not just a pilgrimage destination but also a major visitor attraction. Its religious visitors come mainly as day trippers, motivated by a desire to see where the apparition happened (and with the faint hope that it might happen again), and the wish to share in the sanctity of a holy place. Some wish to pray for healing, others use a visit as a focus for family or community life and some are simply curious. The shrine itself generates very low levels of income (as donations) from its visitors, with most money being made by private-sector service businesses. No precise visitor data is available as the shrine is open access, but it is thought that the percentage of non-Irish and international visitors is increasing, partly as a result of easier air access and partly as a result of the decline in Catholic religious observance in Ireland. The shrine at Knock has no 'official' catering outlets except those within hospices and care centres within the shrine enclosure, although this is relatively unusual. Despite the small size of Knock village (only 400 people) and a limited population base within the surrounding catchment area, more than 70 local businesses have developed in the village, which cater primarily to visitors and pilgrims.

The above short case study illustrates that the visitor services required at Knock are much the same as those at any other religious tourism attraction, being dominated by transport, parking, information, catering, accommodation and merchandising. Most of the 'religious' infrastructure that is included within the shrine grounds (churches, basilica, confessionals, shrine office, some convents and monasteries) is provided and managed directly by the religious authorities which manage the shrine (although these may include partnership or franchising arrangements with bookshops or catering outlets). However, the facilities inside the shrine grounds are limited in number and always greatly exceeded by the number of private-sector firms operating outside and around the shrine to cater to the needs of visitors. Retailing and catering facilities are provided primarily by the private sector, but the commercial significance of the site may be illustrated by the fact that it is of sufficient economic importance to warrant the construction of an international airport. Tourism to Knock is changing from being primarily domestic to being more mixed. Irish tourism (both domestic and international) is flourishing: visitor numbers and revenue grew by approximately 4 per cent in 2003, with Ireland gaining market share in its main markets (Shackley, 2006). Although primarily a religious visitor attraction, tourism to Knock is driving the development of infrastructure in western Ireland but the impetus is coming not from the Catholic church but from private-sector investment in nearby secular urban destinations including Galway and Westport.

Conclusions

One of the most interesting features of tourism to religion-based attractions is that visitor numbers continue to increase at the same time that the number of people in regular worshipping congregations decline. This is clearly the case at Knock: a thriving tourism destination in a country whose traditional Catholic faith is in decline. However, this observation applies more to Western, Christian sites in the developed world than to, for example, major Hindu, Buddhist or Muslim pilgrimage sites in the developing world that continue to attract huge numbers of seasonal visitors. With the West becoming an increasingly secular society, it will be interesting to see whether this trend continues, and equally interesting to speculate on the reasons for it. Are visitors to religious sites looking at a quick-fix substitute for the commitment required to become a regular worshipper? Has spending a short time in a religious building become a substitute for prayer and worship? Since most (but not all) religious sites are major historical sites of great significance to the cultural tourism sector, it seems likely that continued growth in cultural tourism also plays a part in the phenomenon. It is, of course, very difficult to generalize as the motivations of visitors to a major sites (such as St Peter's in Rome) will include a whole spectrum from eagerly anticipated pilgrimage to idle curiosity. The phenomenon of travel substitution is also likely to become more important, at least in the short term, and it would be surprising if there were no considerable growth in purpose-built managed religion-based attractions offering the experience of pilgrimage with none of the dangers and inconveniences. Religious sites in Europe and the Middle East will certainly receive fewer visitors from America in the conceivable future, and any escalation in international terrorism could also result in a reduction in visitation to prominent buildings such as cathedrals, mosques and temples if they are perceived as terrorist targets. However, international insecurity may also be partially responsible for an increase in popularity of religion-based attractions as people turn to religion as a source of comfort, strength and explanation at times of unrest. But the priorities of site managers will always include the need to generate visitor revenue, balancing tourists with worshippers and juggling conservation priorities. But it seems likely that religion-based attractions will continue to flourish and diversify during the next decade, providing their visitors with at least a fleeting encounter with the numinous in an increasingly secular world.

References

Brown, D. and Loades, A. (eds) (1995). *The Sense of the Sacramental*, SPCK.

Bywater, M. (1994). Religious travel in Europe. *Travel and Tourism Analyst*, **2**, 39–52.

Cohen, E. (1979). A phenomenology of tourism experiences. *Sociology*, **13**, 179–201.

Cloesen, U. (2005). Braj, center of Vaishnava pilgrimage. *Acta Turistica*, **17**, 1–26.

Collins-Kreiner, N. and Gatrel, J. D. (2006). Tourism, heritage and pilgrimage: the case of Haifa's Baha'I Gardens. *Journal of Heritage Tourism*, **1**, 32–51.

Fernandes, C., McGettigan, F. and Edwards, J. (eds). (2003). *Religious Tourism and Pilgrimage*. ATLAS-special interest group 1st Expert Meeting. Tourist Board of Leiria/Fatima (Portugal) and ATLAS.

Guo, C. (2006). Tourism and the spiritual philosophies of the 'Orient'. In *Tourism, Religion and Spiritual Journeys* (D. Timothy and D. Olsen, eds), pp. 119–121. Routledge.

Holy Land Experience (2007). Holy Land Experience. Expect to be inspired! http://www.theholylandexperience.com/.

Jutla, R. S. (2006). Pilgrimage in Hinduism: historical context and modern perspectives. In *Tourism, Religion and Spiritual Journeys* (D. Timothy and D. Olsen, eds), pp. 220–237. Routledge.

McGettigan, F. (2003). An analysis of cultural tourism and its relationship with religious sites. In *Religious Tourism and Pilgrimage* (C. Fernandes, F. McGettigan and J. Edwards, eds), pp. 13–37. ATLAS-special interest group 1st Expert Meeting. Tourist Board of Leiria/Fatima (Portugal) and ATLAS.

O'Guinn, T. C. and Belk, R. W. (1989). Heaven and earth: consumption at Heritage Village USA. *Journal of Consumer Research*, **16**, 227–238.

Olsen, D. H. (2006). Management issues for religious heritage attractions. In *Tourism, Religion and Spiritual Journeys* (D. Timothy and D. Olsen, eds), pp. 104–119. Routledge.

Raj, R. (2003). The Hajj: pilgrimage to Makka, journey of a lifetime or a tourist phenomenon? In *Religious Tourism and Pilgrimage* (C. Fernandes, F. McGettigan and J. Edwards, eds), pp. 141–151. ATLAS-special interest group 1st Expert Meeting. Tourist Board of Leiria/Fatima (Portugal) and ATLAS.

Raghunathan, A. and Sinha, A. (2006). Rockfort temple at Tiruchirapalli, India: conservation of a sacred landscape. *International Journal of Heritage Studies*, **12**, 489–505.

Shackley, M. (1998). A golden calf in sacred space? The future of St Katherine's Monastery, Mount Sinai (Egypt). *International Journal of Heritage Studies*, **4**, 123–134.

Shackley, M. (2001). *Managing Sacred Sites: Service Provision and Visitor Experience*. Continuum.

Shackley, M. (2002). Space sanctity and service; the English cathedral as heterotopia. *International Journal of Tourism Research*, **14**, 1–8.

Shackley, M. (2004). Managing the cedars of Lebanon: botanical gardens or living forests? In *The Politics of World Heritage* (D. Harrison and M. Hitchcock, eds), pp. 137–146. Channel View.

Shackley, M. (2006). Empty bottles at sacred sites: religious retailing at Ireland's National Shrine. In *Tourism, Religion and Spiritual Journeys* (D. Timothy and D. Olsen, eds), pp. 94–104. Routledge.

Shoval, N. (2000). Commodification and theming of the sacred: changing patterns of tourist consumption in the 'Holy Land'. In *New Forms of Consumption: Consumers, Culture and Commodification* (M. Gottdibner, ed), pp. 251–265. Rowman and Littlefield.

Smith, V. L. (1992). Introduction: the quest in guest. *Annals of Tourism Research*, **19**, 1–17.

Timothy, D. and Olsen, D. (eds) (2006). *Tourism, Religion and Spiritual Journeys*. Routledge.

van der Borg, J., Costa, P. and Gotti, G. (1996). Tourism in European heritage cities. *Annals of Tourism Research*, **23**, 306–321.

Vuconic, B. (1996). *Tourism and Religion*. Pergamon Press.

CHAPTER 16

Managing Human Resources in Visitor Attractions

Sandra Watson and Martin McCracken

Aim

The aim of this chapter is to analyse how visitor attractions can take a strategic human resource management (SHRM) approach to enhance their people management. In particular, the role that line managers play in implementing human resource strategies is explored. In order to illustrate some of the key issues, real life examples taken from a Scottish visitor attraction are discussed in a case study at the end of the chapter. This chapter seeks to:

- highlight influences on visitor attractions in relation to managing people,
- identify the philosophy and underlying values pertinent to a SHRM approach, and
- examine the role that line managers play in implementing a SHRM approach by studying a visitor attraction case study of good practice.

Introduction

Delivering tourism products and services to increasingly discerning customers in highly competitive and dynamic market conditions, presents a range of organizational challenges. To remain competitive, tourism providers in Scotland must continue to meet and ultimately exceed customer expectations.

This is in the context of a less buoyant market in terms of both UK (traditionally Scotland has been over-reliant on the UK tourist) and overseas visitor numbers (Atkinson, 2000). This downturn in numbers may be attributed to a number of factors, including a heightened perception of threat from international terrorism, increased marketing activity by other international destinations and ultimately the strength of the British pound sterling.

Despite these issues, it has been argued that the visitor attraction sector does offer visitors an enhanced experience whilst staying in Scotland and is an important revenue and employment provider. However, the philosophy of continuous improvement is required amongst attractions if they are to continue playing this vital role. This message is conveyed most starkly by authors such as Leask *et al.* (2000: 215) who suggest '... that if the visitor attraction sector in Scotland is to have a viable long-term future, then it will have to find new ways of doing things, and develop a more strategic approach to managing its activities'. It is the view of the authors that one of the major activities that is vital for attractions to enhance is the strategic management of employees.

This view was formed after carrying out empirical research with key industry experts (Scottish Tourist Board, National Trust for Scotland, Scottish Enterprise and Historic Scotland) who promote and manage visitor attractions in Scotland. Many of these experts noted that the impact of key environmental factors, related to legislative changes (requirements on health, safety and employment issues), developments in technology and rapidly evolving socio-economic trends, would have a major impact on how visitor attractions manage their staff. The industry experts also underlined that increasing globalization, greater competition and demographic changes would raise the need for visitor attractions to be more creative. In essence the impact of such environmental factors further emphasizes the need to attract, retain, develop and effectively manage staff so that they can effectively offer a valued product and experience to visitors (Watson and McCracken, 2002).

The wisdom of ensuring that employees are treated well is encapsulated in the service–profit chain developed by Heskett *et al.* (1994). They identify important relationships between employee satisfaction, loyalty and productivity, organizational profitability and consumer loyalty. The evidence and logic of the service–profit chain indicates that there is a close relationship between customer satisfaction, service quality and employee satisfaction. Oakland and Oakland (2001: 773) support this assertion in their observation that in world-class organizations, it is now widely acknowledged that 'effective people management and development is one of the primary keys to achieving improvements in organizational performance'. It is interesting to note that in terms of competitive strategy, service organizations have recognized the importance of service as a basis for differentiation. Heskett *et al.* (1994) argue that the correlation between employee and customer satisfaction emphasizes the need for a quality internal working environment that makes an effective contribution to employee satisfaction, particularly in terms of systems and mechanisms that enable service workers to create satisfaction for customers. Given this increasing dependence on high service quality in the tourism industry, ensuring that there is a systematically selected, properly trained and highly committed workforce in place is now essential for all visitor attractions.

Even though the tourism industry in the UK is a major employer, and is expected to grow over the next 10 years, there are clearly many challenges ahead for the sector. The workforce is characterized by a reliance on a young (34 per cent are under 25 years of age) and mobile part-time workforce (54 per cent work part-time, with a further 10 per cent on a casual or temporary basis). Over 17 per cent of employees are from overseas with 11 per cent of employees from ethnic minorities based within the UK. Additionally, it is estimated that female employees constitute 67 per cent of the workforce, with two-thirds of them working on a part-time basis (People1st, 2006). The management of employees in the tourism industry is often described as informal, being shaped by both its product and labour markets, with evidence of many visitor attractions failing to adopt good-practice models of human resource management (Keep and Mayhew, 1999).

Research examining human resource (HR) practices in the tourism industry has reported these as largely lacking in sophistication. Indeed, when the nature of tourism labour markets were explored recently by Watson (2006), it was found that there were still clear weaknesses in many organization's procedures in relation to unspecified hiring standards, multiple entry points, little training, unsophisticated promotion procedures and low skills requirements. Such assertions reflect earlier findings from research commissioned by the Skills Task Force investigating the nature, pattern and extent of skill requirements and shortages in the UK leisure sector and found that a significant skills gap existed amongst the workforce. The authors of this report noted that the apparent lack of entrepreneurial and management skills was particularly worrying, as were the deficiencies in information technology and customer-care skills in addition to the absence of good-quality training for volunteers (Keep and Mayhew, 1999). This last point reinforces the assertions of several other authors in the field (Graham, 2000; Jago and Deery, 2001) who have found that the tourism sector is particularly poor at managing (normally unpaid) volunteers effectively.

It is the underlying belief of the authors that the increasing competitiveness in the environment, allied to the labour market characteristics discussed above, may prove to be catalysts for the visitor attraction sector to adopt a more systematic human resource management (HRM) approach. Fundamentally, this requires an understanding of the importance of effective people-management strategies for sustaining business performance through addressing such areas as:

- selecting and retaining quality staff,
- training and development to meet new and changing demands, and
- managing the employee–employer relationship to meet organizational objectives.

With this in mind, the next section explains the rationale of a strategic approach to HRM and discusses the vitally important role that line managers need to play in the delivery of SHRM.

Strategic human resource management

Whilst the term human resource management (HRM) is now universally used in organizations, there has been widespread debate into its meaning and significance. In the 1980s, HRM began to be acknowledged as a more distinct and valuable management function, and it was frequently cited as a factor explaining why certain organizations were successful. Storey (1995: 6) defines HRM as 'a distinctive approach to employment management which seeks to achieve competitive advantage through the strategic deployment of a highly committed and capable workforce, using an integrated array of cultural, structural and personnel techniques'. An essential difference between those organizations that fully embrace HRM and those who do not is their acknowledgement of the vital importance of managing employees in a strategically coordinated way.

In seeking to explore the link between HRM and the strategy of the organization, authors in the 1980s developed models asserting a strategic approach to HRM, resulting in the evolution of the concept of SHRM. Writers in the arena of SHRM emphasize the importance of aligning HRM to organizational strategy. The alignment of HRM activities to organizational strategy, and the harmonization of HRM activities are considered fundamental. With this in mind, Storey's (1995) seminal HRM model is based upon four key tenets:

- *Beliefs and assumptions* (of HRM): underlying belief that people are critical to business success.
- *Strategic qualities* (of HRM): people issues are considered at the organization's highest level.
- *Critical role of managers* (in ensuring the successful delivery of HRM strategies): line managers are the key players in managing people.
- *Key levers* (which also ensure that HRM strategies can be implemented): culture of the organization and integration of people-management procedures enhance people management.

Storey (1995) asserts that if an HRM perspective is central to an organization's activity there will be underlying beliefs that stress the importance of staff. Based on these assumptions, the professional management of staff should enhance competitive advantage and, in the final analysis, enhanced human capability and commitment should be a distinguishing feature of successful companies. Therefore, SHRM can be viewed as a process that is concerned with ensuring that long-term human resource issues are effectively aligned to the structures, values, culture, commitment, performance and development of staff to meet the goals of an organization (Armstrong, 2000).

In addition, there has also been academic attention given to the notion of a best-practice model of HRM that emphasizes the importance of high-commitment or high-performance work practices in any organization. In seeking to explore the impact of HR practice on performance, Boxall and Purcell (2003) put forward a model, which argues that the fundamental rationale of HRM is centred on three basic notions, namely ability, motivation and opportunity (AMO). Within this approach they assert that for staff to perform above the basic minimum they must have the *ability*, i.e. the skills and knowledge, be *motivated* to work well and be given the *opportunity* to deploy their skills and contribute to the organization. In essence, HR polices and practices should encourage or induce staff to demonstrate positive discretionary behaviour by linking into employee commitment, motivation and job satisfaction. Purcell *et al.* (2003: 8) highlight 11 interrelated HRM areas of importance, which are:

- careful/sophisticated recruitment and selection,
- training and learning and development,
- providing career opportunities,
- information sharing and extensive two-way communication,
- involvement in decision making,
- team working,
- appraising each individual's performance and development,
- pay satisfaction,
- job security,
- job challenge/job autonomy, and
- work-life balance.

In addition, they highlight the need for these policies to be mutually enforcing and 'concerned with creating an able workforce, motivating valued behaviours and providing opportunities to participate' (Purcell *et al.*, 2003: 8). The manner in which these policies are implemented by front-line managers, their values espoused by top-level management and the cultivation of organizational culture are seen as important influencers on employee discretionary behaviour. What is evident from research work into SHRM and performance is that there is a perceived link between policies and practices, the manner in which these are implemented and their impact on employee discretionary behaviour. The authors believe that ultimately there is need to examine the nature of HRM strategies, policies and practices, their perceived importance in the organization, the role of managers in their implementation and the values and culture in which they are set in the visitor attraction sector. The case study, which is discussed in the latter part of this chapter, aims to illustrate that in at least this visitor attraction there is great scope to adhere to the principles of SHRM in this sector.

Inherent in this SHRM concept is the 'centre-stage' role for line managers (Renwick, 2003). Since the advent of HRM, there has been some debate about devolving aspects of HRM to line managers. Indeed, the devolving of human resource activities to line managers has received much attention by both academics and practitioners in Europe over the last decade. Various reasons for this devolution have been cited, including restructuring, downsizing and an increased need to focus on encouraging employee inputs for improving their competitive edge (Renwick, 2003). Several researchers assert that by assuming some HRM responsibility line managers can positively influence employee commitment and, ultimately, business performance. For example, Cunningham and Hyman (1999: 9) highlight the role of line managers in promoting an 'integrative culture of employee management through line management'. Thornhill and Saunders (1998) also signal the role of line managers in securing employee commitment to quality, while it has been argued that in order to increase productivity, devolution of HRM to the line is required (IRS Employment Review, 1995). To illustrate such assertions further, research findings contained in a Chartered Institute of Personnel and Development (CIPD) report indicated that when line managers participate in coaching and guidance, communication and involvement, there has been positive influence on overall organizational performance (Hutchinson and Purcell, 2003). A key finding from this report is that to gain line managers' commitment to people management, strong organizational values that emphasize the fundamentals of people management and leadership are required (Hutchinson and Purcell, 2003). As organizations, particularly those in the visitor attraction sector, need employees' input to help achieve competitive advantage, involving line managers in HRM surely cannot be disputed.

Research on the progress of devolution of operational HRM activities and its consequences illustrates that many organizations are now coming round to understanding the importance of vesting HRM responsibility with line managers and are reaping the rewards of such deliberate and sustained strategies. Renwick (2003), in investigating line managers' views on HRM roles across three organizations, found evidence that line managers were often willing, flexible and took a professional and considerate attitude to HR and employees. Similarly, Whittaker and Marchington (2003), in their case study focusing on senior line managers' views on devolving HRM to line managers, found that the key ingredients for an effective strategy of devolution was proactive explicit support from senior management, and their recognition (through effective reward strategies) of the contribution that line managers make in the HR arena of their organizations.

However, giving line managers responsibility for HRM has also been noted as being 'problematic' (McGovern et al., 1997). Challenges lie not least in the relationship between line managers and HRM specialists (Cunningham and Hyman, 1999); 'the ability and willingness of line managers to carry out HR tasks properly' (Renwick and MacNeil, 2002: 407), and line managers' knowledge of company policies (Bond and McCracken, 2005). Other researchers have also found tensions between line managers' general functional versus HR responsibilities. For example, Whittaker and Marchington (2003) noted that HR took second place in relation to other business needs of sales and marketing and finance, and Renwick (2003) found that often there was lack of time and/or ability, distraction from general managerial focus, as well as tensions concerning HR specialists' expectations in relation to the completion of scheduled HR tasks by line managers.

With the above in mind, the authors feel that the literature, whilst asserting that there is a clear responsibility for line managers to undertake HRM roles and tasks, also recognizes that to secure involvement the issues of task delineation, support, training and trust are crucial for effective devolvement of HRM to line managers in tourism. In addition, the key inhibitors of and barriers to involvement centring on lack of time, work priorities, capability, comfort and trust, still need to be addressed in many tourism organizations.

In order to explore the nature of HRM in the visitor attraction sector in more detail, an example of good practice is explored in the following case study. The organization and leadership of SHRM, the culture and values underpinning HRM strategies, the mutually reinforcing nature of HRM practices and the role of line managers in implementing these are all discussed. Within this framework the 11 interrelated HRM areas of importance presented by Purcell *et al.* (2003) are revisited.

Introduction and background to case organization

The Dynamic Earth Charitable Trust (DECT) was established in 1995 when Scottish and Newcastle Plc gifted the City of Edinburgh 10 acres of land to locate a building of architectural note which could serve to educate the people of, and visitors to, Edinburgh. The resulting interpretation and visitor centre, Our Dynamic Earth (ODE), is situated at the base of a volcano that last erupted 350 million years ago, and displays and informs the public about issues relating to geology and the natural environment. In order to collect data for this case study, the authors carried out a semi-structured interview in December 2006 with the Commercial Director of the attraction (please note: reference is also made to material from an earlier interview carried out in 2000 with the then CEO). Several areas were investigated to inform and further our understanding of how HRM strategy and practices can help visitor attractions achieve their overall business strategy.

In terms of general background information, the business is owned by the DECT and is operated by a not-for-profit organization, Dynamic Earth Enterprises Ltd (DEEL). Hence, any profit generated through the operation of ODE is allocated to the DECT to further its aims and objectives. As noted above, the broad remit of ODE is to provide continuing education in earth sciences and to promote awareness and understanding of the properties, behaviour and characteristics of ODE. Ultimately, it seeks to achieve this aim by providing a high-quality, well-researched and accessible exhibition to a wide base of visitors, ranging from the general public and schoolchildren to special-interest geological groups.

The top management team consists of the CEO, a Commercial Director, Operations Director, Marketing Director and a Science Director, who are responsible for 12 managers, 8 supervisors and 66 employees. Of these staff,

49 per cent work in shift patterns, with 23 per cent on part-time contracts. Only 5 per cent of staff are employed on a seasonal basis and there is an even split between male and female employees, with over a third of staff having been employed for less than one year. The diverse nature of employees was raised a number of times in the interview with the Commercial Director. He felt that the changes in the types of employees who were applying to the organization reflected structural changes in the leisure sector labour market, where in the early years applications from Australians, Americans and Swedish nationals were high, but currently ODE was felt to be relying heavily on Polish employees. It was noted that there was a big diversity of staff and skills requirements, ranging from food and beverage operations, to sales and education.

As alluded to above, there are three operational dimensions within the ODE visitor attraction: visitor service, retail and merchandizing; corporate entertainment (encompassing banqueting and conferences); and education of earth sciences. The Commercial Director felt that the third of these is considered to be the cornerstone of the business: 'education is what the organization is really about'. These three components of the business are reflected in how core teams of employees are assigned within the attraction. Firstly, there is a core team of food and beverage workers who deliver banquet and conference services. Secondly, a team of scientists and educators is responsible for delivering the educational product. Finally, ticketing, retail and attraction services, as well as maintenance workers, have a key role in ensuring the efficient and effective delivery of service and facilities for the whole of the attraction. This results in the need to manage potentially different perspectives within the attraction and, vitally, to communicate to all staff that they are part of an organization which has to serve the needs of three very diverse sets of customers. As the Commercial Director indicated 'staff need to have an appreciation of what is going on in the other departments'.

The importance to ODE of looking outwardly was discussed by the Commercial Director. It was noted that ODE is a member of a number of forums which are designed to help improve quality of provision across the tourism and educational attraction sectors, including the Scottish Science Centres Network (SSCN) and the Unique Venues of Edinburgh (UVE) group of attractions. Funded by the Scottish Executive, the SSCN is designed to promote science throughout Scotland by drawing upon the knowledge of all the visitor attractions in the network to share best practice, drive up commercial performance and provide a complementary and cohesive approach to formal science education provision in schools and further higher education colleges. With this in mind, it was not surprising to note that in 2007 over 45 000 schoolchildren visited educational exhibitions in ODE and that the science education division of the attraction has recently participated in a successful inspection by Her Majesty's Inspectorate of Education (HMIE). The UVE initiative was initiated by a small number of highly specialized attractions (23 leading venues in Edinburgh and the Lothians) to encourage partnership working and knowledge sharing in relation to customers and best practice.

ODE has also been graded as a 5-Star Visitor Attraction by the Scottish Tourist Board (now known as Visit Scotland), illustrating the continued commitment to excellence in customer care. The Star Awards Programme focuses on the most important operational aspects in any tourist organization, such as standard of the welcome, hospitality and service and how the attraction is presented (e.g., the standard of the toilets, shop and café). To further illustrate this commitment to quality in service provision, ODE also carries out its own mystery shopping exercise. The Commercial Director observed that such a system is particularly useful in that it provides good-quality specific feedback to employees about service levels. As a result of the comments and suggestions which are received through this mechanism, training interventions can be focussed on any perceived weaknesses in service. In the same vein, the attraction also organizes for key employees the opportunity to visit other organizations to gauge working practices or, as the Commercial Director described them 'the little gems that we could adapt to our attraction here'.

Examples such as the mystery shopping experience illustrate that, since its inception, ODE has considered its employees to be critical to its business success. This feature was something that the first Chief Executive, who was interviewed by the authors in 2000 as part of earlier research into the attraction, noted when she said … given in an interview to the authors in April 2000 'we're in a business where the people are actually making the business happen, therefore, it is imperative that we understand this and manage the attraction with staff being seen as central to its success'. Such consideration for staff permeates throughout the organization, from a strategic perspective to the day-to-day operations. Further evidence of the strategy of linking people issues to strategic goals is shown in the fact that the attraction received an Investors in People (IiP) award in February 2000, and have since been successfully reviewed in 2003 and 2006.

In seeking to understand how the HRM approach is organized at ODE, we provide an overview of its strategic approach prior to analysing their specific practices using 11 key components proposed by Purcell *et al.* (2003) as a framework.

SHRM in our dynamic earth

Overall responsibility for HRM falls within the remit of the Commercial Director, who devises the HR strategy in conjunction with the other directors at Board of Trustee meetings. Such high-level alignment of HR to the businesses goals means that the organization constantly reviews HR implications of any proposed operational issues. For example, when the business expanded its corporate business, HR issues were considered as an integral component of that strategy.

The critical role played by line managers in the implementation of HRM in the organization should also be seen as fundamental to its strategy. The fact that there is now no dedicated HR specialist employed in the organization (the HR manager left in 2005) underlines the need for the Commercial Director to work in tandem with line managers to ensure that HR issues are managed effectively. Although the attraction does employ the services of an employment law specialist on certain issues, in the main it is the line manager's job to undertake staff planning and appraisals, recruitment, learning and development needs identification and manage disciplinary and grievance procedures. The Commercial Director felt that the major reason why this devolving of HRM strategy to line managers seemed to work well could be attributed to the 'open positive culture' which mean the ODE has been described as 'a fantastically gelled organization' by HMIE.

Careful/sophisticated recruitment and selection

The careful cultivation of an inclusive and stimulating organizational culture was raised as a fundamental reason why ODE has been successful. With this in mind, it is not surprising that the selection of staff centres on attracting individuals who will 'fit into' this organizational culture. In the interview with the Commercial Director, the essential cornerstone of the ODE culture could be summed up in the phrase 'making science fun'. Hence, a fundamental quality of staff at all levels is excellent communication and customer-service skills, and a key part of the selection process is profiling individuals on the basis of how well they could work together in teams. Hence group interviews were used, as well as situational exercises to determine individuals' styles of communication.

It was interesting to note that the attraction had recently changed its policy for recruiting the guiding (tour guides and special display staff) employees and that the softer skills of personality, communication and excellent customer service were felt to be much more important than technical science knowledge. Such an innovation clearly underlines the seriousness with which ODE takes the issue of employees fitting into the 'generally inclusive culture ... it is genuine and not lip service and we have found that people who have ownership in anything are much more likely to make it work'.

Training and development

Clearly, the issue of training and development is an integral aspect in Purcell's model of SHRM. In ODE, there were several examples where up-skilling of current employees and effective initial training and development of new employees was evident. For example, a new innovation in the attraction was the introduction of new 'theme characters' into the exhibition in 2006. The Commercial Director noted that after prior trials the previous year, using existing guiding staff, ODE had given many more staff the opportunity to participate in the programme.

We have mascots – they wear dinosaur outfits which goes down a storm with all the families and that gives a really warm reception .... We have also an explorer character who wanders through the galleries dressed as a traditional jungle explorer performing what we call 'crowd busting'. If they see a big crowd in a gallery, they will go and entertain with a number of relevant props for where they are in the attraction. That is an extra member of staff but it has worked very well. It is very good for staff and customer interaction. So we are planning to do more of that next year and what that department manager has to look at is – how many are we going to do and what days of the week are we going to do it.

Clearly if members of staff want to take on such roles, there is a need to ensure that they have the necessary skill requirements. For example, as a mascot or jungle explorer there may be a need for more scientific skills training than for one of the other guides. This issue of further up-skilling can also be linked to the role of line managers, who need to think clearly about how best to utilize staff time and consider who may be best suited for such roles, in terms of qualifications, and so on, as well as when is the best time to provide relevant skills and knowledge training. The commercial director noted that such issues also provided 'knock-on' effects for the attraction where departmental and line managers will also need to be properly trained to ensure they can mange such situations properly.

Providing career opportunities

The above examples illustrate the general ethos in ODE surrounding training and development, and how skills development is linked to further career development. It was noted that in certain departments, especially banqueting and catering, many employees were interested in gaining vital experience that could allow them to pursue longer-term careers. With this in mind, a policy for the attraction was offering key employees the opportunity to participate in job rotation so that they get varied experiences and skills. As the Commercial Director elaborated:

I am always looking at things with an eye on HR as well when we are thinking about moving into different areas. … We have to think about up-skilling – are there people who are supervisors at the moment – could they take over in new roles for example like into a management role to cope with the business expansion?

(ODE Commercial Director)

Although support for continued progression was a feature of the attraction, the Commercial Director noted that senior management in ODE implicitly understood that the majority did not have long-term career aspirations within the attraction, so the focus was on ensuring that they do a good job whilst they are employed, with training, development and facilities to encourage commitment. Many examples were given, illustrating the techniques that were used to instil commitment to the attraction amongst such staff, for example free coffee and drinks and subsidized meals were available, as well as regular staff social events and parties.

Information sharing and extensive two-way communication

The inclusive nature of the culture at ODE was something that was discussed at length above. Throughout the discussion with the Commercial Director in December 2006 and, indeed, with the CEO in the first round of research in 2000 the emphasis that the attraction placed on sharing information and communicating with staff was made clear. Hence communication is a central ethos of the attraction, where a range of vehicles, including consultative committees and staff suggestion schemes, are used to emphasize a strong focus on open and informal communications.

It was noted that efforts were made to ensure that staff clearly understood both the commercial and educational aspects of the business. For example, at the regular morning meetings, line managers communicate clearly any important current issues. In addition, any particular issues relating to the employees roles are discussed at the weekly training sessions. For example, guide employees receive current updates on scientific issues of interest to the attraction at the weekly science training and information sessions. More formally, ODE held regular Staff Consultative Committee meetings and management meetings where important issues surrounding staff development and information exchange were discussed to diffuse best practice amongst the departments. As well as these formal avenues, the Commercial Director also felt that real efforts are made to 'make sure that it [effective communication] happens more informally too, where staff will stop you in the corridor with new ideas and that is very useful too'.

Involvement in decision making

The Commercial Director put forward a number of useful examples, which clearly illustrate the level of involvement of staff. Presentations are given to staff on the results of visitor surveys in order that staff can be made aware of the commercial implications of decisions made at the highest levels. Such information is discussed at the regular Staff Consultative Committee meetings, where the implications for different aspects of the business are indicated and staff members are encouraged to suggest ways of improving the business. Most interestingly, it was indicated that when the induction programme had been redesigned the previous year, employees were canvassed for views on what the programme should actually include. He noted that the resulting programme received commendations from the IiP assessor:

For the IiP report we reviewed and refreshed our induction training and asked people what they thought we should do with it. We asked questions like if you were to have induction training right from the start what would you like to see in it? So we got fantastic feed back but the IiP assessor commented that 'how would they not like the systems when they helped to make it.

(ODE Commercial Director)

In addition, it was noted that the progress made though eliciting views and promoting involvement through the new induction programme, which was described as a 'shining beacon' for involvement, is to be rolled out in the future in relation to the appraisal process.

We are going to be reviewing the appraisal system in the New Year and we are going to have a look at our processes and include refresher training on appraisals for everybody. So we are going to take people from all different levels in the organization and I will be the director involved there, there will be a couple of managers and supervisors and a couple of staff and that will be the working group and we will meet every couple of weeks. They will go back and talk to their peers and we will hopefully get some feedback from staff to decide on how we improve the system.

(ODE Commercial Director)

Team working

In order for ODE to have an inclusive and progressive culture in place, the importance of team working is clearly important. It was noted that as a result of having the three core businesses under the one roof there was a need for much cross-departmental collaboration to ensure that the overall objectives of the attraction could be met. It was noted that in the staff development sessions, much effort was put into ensuring that information was exchanged between different departments. For example, with the ticket desk and the sales team, as the attraction now qualifies for 'gift aid' there is a need to for effective collaboration to ensure that money is claimed back properly from the Inland Revenue.

Another indication of the open culture was the fact that there was also no segregation of staff levels and although everyone was required to wear a name badge, supervisors were not seen to be any different from other staff by visitors. This is seen as appropriate to the kind of product being offered and the culture at ODE.

Appraising each individual's performance and development

The issue of appraisals was discussed briefly when involvement and decision making was covered. It is, however, interesting to note that a higher degree of sophistication than anything that has been used before in relation to staff appraisal is proposed for the future. Hence, instead of only systematic appraisal for the managerial level, who are assessed on their 'leadership and development of others', there are moves to look at all levels of staff through a formal performance-review system: The Commercial Director noted that this will affect all employees in the attraction, including staff who might only be employed for a summer season. Indeed it was noted that ODE has an assessment review after the initial six weeks of employment because it is conceivable that within 10 weeks staff may return to university or move elsewhere.

In addition, employees are provided with opportunities to develop to their fullest potential. Training is provided on a regular basis and there is a combination of on- and off-the-job training opportunities. As indicated by the Commercial Director

There are dozens of examples of people who have moved through the organization and we love to do that and do it when we can. I am a good example, I joined the company just before we opened in May 1999 and came onboard as Retail Manager. But a couple of months after we opened I became the Operations and Retail Manager and then a couple of years ago I became Commercial Director.

(ODE Commercial Director)

Pay satisfaction

Remuneration is discussed at the highest levels of the organization, with departmental directors liaising through the Remuneration Committee which is made up of the Board of Trustees and the CEO. The process is designed to be inclusive and to allow for a degree of flexibility; hence managers can influence payment levels of the higher achievers. Another important element in the remuneration strategy is to undertake benchmarking with respect to pay levels and conditions of service to ensure that employees' payment is in line with local competitors. The fact that the organization has a relatively low labour turnover is evidence that the payment strategy outlined above works well.

Job security

As noted above, the remuneration strategy is comprehensively researched and planned to ensure fair and equitable payment that is allocated to all employees and this may contribute to the low labour turnover rates in ODE. In addition, the fact that the organization has a warm and inclusive culture has been a recurring theme described and again it is felt that offering employees an appropriate level of job security contributes to this culture. Overall the organization has a workforce of 93 including salaried staff – directors, full-time hourly paid and part-time hourly paid – who may only work at the weekend or even only one day a week. However, to ensure that this number stays stable, the attraction uses more flexible labour in the form of agency staff when there is a need. For example, the Commercial Director commented that

For corporate events we use agency staff. Last week at the Christmas party nights we had 540 guests so we had about 60 agency staff for those events. We cannot afford to keep those agency staff all the time, but we have the core team managing those agency staff.

(ODE Commercial Director)

277

Job challenge/autonomy

It has been illustrated that the culture of the organization is very much aligned to ensure that employees at all levels are well looked after and suitably challenged in their roles. The examples of the innovations in guiding such as the jungle explorers and the use of mascots clearly illustrate how the attraction seeks to stimulate and use the creative ideas of their employees. When data were first collected in 2000, one of the main objectives of the then CEO was to take the lead in encouraging a culture where staff and their contributions are valued. At that time, she discussed how 'managing the culture is everything we do, even the staff uniforms are a reflection of what this culture is all about: open, friendly, young, contemporary'. It is clear that this culture has been perpetuated since the organizations initiation, where the attractions personality is felt to be essential in guiding everything that is done.

The organisation has a personality that governed what we can do and our personality is Indiana Jones: an explorer who is adventurous and yet has some credibility in that he is a university professor – so brave, exciting – and the uniform was designed to reflect that and the staff were asked to keep that in mind.

(ODE Commercial Director)

This commitment to allowing staff to use their own initiative and autonomy is perhaps best reflected in a final example, where a member of staff was allowed to pursue his own initial idea of designing a Braille version of the guiding material for blind customers. It was noted that this particular employee came forward and asked if it would be possible to develop such an innovation, and ODE dually obliged and attempted to help as much as possible.

Work-life balance

Whilst there is no specific work-life balance policy in operation, staff workloads are monitored through a clocking in and out procedure with weekly hours being monitored, to ensure that staff are not working excessively long hours. This information is then used as part of HR planning for the coming year. In addition there is no time off in lieu without prior permission, policy in place to discourage staff from working overtime. In essence, staff work-life balance issues are considered at a strategic level.

Conclusion

The authors contend that adopting a SHRM approach as illustrated in the paragraphs above is vital to ensure the future success of visitor attractions in a competitive environment. In addition to highlighting the fundamentals of SHRM, discussion has also centred around the notion of best-practice models of HRM, one that emphasize the importance of high-commitment or high-performance work practices in any organization (Huselid, 1995). In line with these principles, Boxall and Purcell (2003) put forward a model of the fundamental purpose of HRM being centred on three basic notions of AMO. In essence, this involves encouraging staff to demonstrate positive discretionary behaviour by linking into employee commitment, motivation and job satisfaction. All of these approaches reflect an underlying belief that people are the key to competitive advantage, and that HR decisions are made and supported by top management, engaging line management commitment to HR policies and developing a culture which encourages communication and involvement in decision making. A fundamental component of a SHRM approach is the involvement of line managers in HRM roles and tasks. This involvement requires support, training and trust for effective implementation of HRM strategies.

As an illustration of how a SHRM approach can help enhance the performance of a visitor attraction, the above case illustrates good practice. ODE's strategies and policies are built upon the AMO principles as presented by Boxall and Purcell (2003), that enhance employee desire to become involved, demonstrate discretionary behaviour and feel valued, whilst linking this to their strategic imperatives.

References

Armstrong, M. (2000). *A Handbook of Personnel Management Practice*, 7th edn. Kogan Page.

Atkinson, P. (2000). The strategic imperative: creating a customer focused organisation. *Change Management*, October, 8–11.

Bond, S. and McCracken, M. (2005). The importance of training in operationalising HR policy. *Journal of European Industrial Training*, **29**, 246–260.

Boxall, P. and Purcell, J. (2003). *Strategy and Human Resource Management*. Palgrave.

Cunningham, I. and Hyman, J. (1999). Devolving human resource responsibilities to the line: beginning of the end or new beginning for personnel? *Personnel Review*, **28**, 9–27.

Graham, M. (2000). The impact of social change on the roles and management of volunteers in Glasgow museums. PhD thesis, Glasgow Caledonian University.

Heskett, J. L., Jones, T. O., Loveman, G. W., Sasser, W. E. and Schlesinger, L. A. (1994). Putting the service–profit chain to work. *Harvard Business Review*, March–April, 64–174.

Huselid, M. A. (1995). The impact of human resource management practices on turnover, productivity, and corporate financial performance. *Academy of Management Journal*, **38**, 635–672.

Hutchinson, S. and Purcell, J. (2003). *Bringing Policies to Life: The Vital Role of Front Line Managers in People Management*. CIPD Research report.

IRS Employment Review (1995). Changes in personnel. *Industrial Relations Survey*, December, 4–9.

Jago, L. K. and Deery, M. (2001). Managing volunteers. In *Quality Issues in Heritage Visitor Attractions* (S. Drummond and I. Yeoman, eds), pp. 194–217. Butterworth-Heinemann.

Keep, E. and Mayhew, K. (1999). *The Leisure Sector*. Skills Task Force Research Paper, No. 6.

Leask, A., Fyall, A. and Goulding, P. (2000). Scottish visitor attractions: revenue, capacity and sustainability. In *Yield Management Strategies for the Service Industries* (A. Ingold, U. McMahon-Beattie and I. Yeoman, eds), 2nd edn, pp. 211–232. Continuum.

McGovern, P., Gratton, L. and Hope-Hailey, V. (1997). Human resource management on the line? *Human Resource Management Journal*, **7**, 12–29.

Oakland, S. and Oakland, J. S. (2001). Current people management activities in world-class organizations. *Total Quality Management*, **12**, 773–788.

People1st. (2006). Skills needs assessment for hospitality, leisure, travel and tourism sector. http://www.people1st.co.uk.

Purcell, J., Kinnie, N. Hutchinson, S., Rayton, B. and Swart, J. (2003). *Understanding the People and Performance Link: Unlocking the Black Box*. CIPD.

Renwick, D. (2003). Line manager involvement in HRM: an inside view. *Employee Relations*, **25**, 262–280.

Renwick, D. and MacNeil, C. M. (2002). Line manager involvement in careers. *Career Development International*, **7**, 407–414.

Storey, J. (1995). *Human Resource Management: A Critical Text*. Thomson Learning.

Thornhill, A. and Saunders, M. N. K. (1998). What if line managers don't realize they're responsible for HR? Lessons from an organisation experiencing rapid change. *Personnel Review*, **27**, 460–476.

Watson, S. (2006). Contextual understandings of hospitality management development: a realist approach. PhD thesis, Napier University.

Watson, S. and McCracken, M. (2002). No attraction in strategic thinking. *International Journal of Tourism Research*, **4**, 367–378.

Whittaker, S. and Marchington, M. (2003). Devolving HR responsibility to the line. Threat, opportunity or partnership? *Employee Relations*, **25**, 245–261.

Part Four

Marketing Visitor Attractions

Part Four of this book focuses on a theme of considerable importance to all visitor attractions: that of marketing. While there has been considerable growth in the literature on the marketing of visitor attractions in recent years, arguably much of what is said about visitor attraction marketing remains premature. Firstly, there is presently little known about the fundamental nature of the visitor attraction product by those marketing them, particularly those sites of a heritage nature. Secondly, there is frequently a lack of suitable marketing information available upon which to make sound judgements about marketing strategy. The marketing research-base of many attractions remains extremely limited, and where research has been undertaken it is arguably still relatively unsophisticated. This has implications for the management and marketing of visitor attractions, severely limiting the scope for effective marketing. Thirdly, whereas branding is a major marketing issue in most other parts of the tourism industry, to date it has played a relatively limited role in the visitor attraction sector. As with marketing research, where branding does exist it has tended to deliver limited benefits. Finally, there is also a tendency in the literature to talk about the marketing of individual visitor attractions in isolation from one another. Pressures in the funding and visitor marketplaces are serving as catalysts for a more collaborative response from many visitor attractions, especially the smaller, resource-poor attractions that often constitute the majority in visitor attraction sectors around the world.

In Chapter 17, Stephen Boyd begins to address some of the above issues with particular reference to heritage visitor attractions. In view of the complex nature of the heritage product, Boyd provides some new insights by taking the discussion beyond the conventional marketing mix and examining new areas where opportunities exist to market heritage tourism. Boyd highlights the importance of the need to move towards a position of sustainability of the heritage product, and examines a variety of new areas where opportunities exist to market heritage tourism such as dark tourism, heritage trails and routes, and personal heritage and pilgrimage, to name but a few. Boyd's chapter concludes with a case study on the marketing of the Titanic and the maritime heritage of Belfast, Northern Ireland.

Whereas the focus of Chapter 17 is on the marketing of a new attraction, Chapter 18 by C. Michael Hall explores the marketing and management of an attraction over time: Hagley Park in Christchurch, New Zealand. Hall begins the chapter by introducing the important role of urban parks as visitor attractions before demonstrating how a visitor attraction can in fact become part of the sense of place of the local users of an attraction. Thereafter, the chapter illustrates how marketing and management policies of an attraction can change over time before indicating how institutional arrangements influence management policies and the very nature of the visitor resource.

Chapter 19 analyses another important aspect of marketing: that of pricing. With an updated detailed case-study investigation of the competitive marketing and pricing practices of theme parks in Central Florida, Bradley Braun and Mark Soskin spell out a number of lessons for managers of large-scale, predominantly themed, visitor attractions. After an initial discussion of the evolution of the Central Florida theme park industry, the chapter discusses how the industry has developed strategies to cope with the maturing of their markets and how it has confronted both demand shocks and growing competition from elsewhere. The large-scale and highly commercial nature of such attractions offers challenges and opportunities quite different to many of the examples outlined in the preceding two chapters. With considerable financial sums required for the investment and re-investment in ride technology, detailed research, as a foundation for sound management decision-making, is a necessity rather than a luxury. This is particularly the case in mature market conditions, where industry structures are still emerging and where there are evident changes in global tourism markets. Braun and Soskin use a demand estimation model to illustrate the nature of the pricing relationships and strategic interdependencies in the sector; a demand model being made possible by the richness of data available in this part of the wider visitor attraction sector.

Given the increasingly difficult competitive environment in which many visitor attractions now find themselves, Part Four concludes with an exploration of the extent to which collaborative marketing strategies offer a potential solution to problems and challenges too large or complex for individual attractions to address in isolation. In Chapter 20, Alan Fyall outlines the conditions in the visitor attraction sector that encourage a collaborative approach to marketing and identifies some of the benefits and drawbacks of collaboration. More specifically, he explores the situations where collaborative strategies are most appropriate and desirable, and introduces a set of guiding principles for effective collaboration. With reference to a case study on the recent Rembrandt 400 initiative undertaken in the Netherlands, the feasibility of collaboration is examined, with the author concluding that competing attractions are no longer the competitive threat they once were: they should now be viewed as the source of future strength and collaborative survival.

CHAPTER 17

Marketing Challenges and Opportunities for Heritage Tourism

Stephen W. Boyd

Aims

The aims of this chapter are to:

- illustrate the complexity of 'heritage' and heritage tourism,
- outline the unique challenges of marketing heritage tourism: understanding the client, an evolving marketing mix, how should heritage be paid for, branding and authenticity,
- examine new areas where opportunities exist to market heritage tourism: dark tourism, ordinary landscapes and people, heritage trails and routes, personal heritage and pilgrimage, and
- highlight, through a case study, the challenges of marketing a heritage attraction prior to its completion and ahead of when it can be appreciated: the Titanic, the centenary of her sinking in 2012 and her association with Belfast, Northern Ireland.

Introduction

Heritage tourism, which typically falls under the purview of cultural tourism (and vice versa), is one of the most notable and widespread types of tourism and is among the very oldest forms of travel. Towner (1996) commented that the ancient Egyptians and Romans, as well as the nobility of medieval times, travelled to experience historic places of cultural importance. In its modern form, heritage tourism has come under the radar of interest of many international travellers. The World Tourism Organization is often quoted as stating that over 40 per cent of all international travel has an element of heritage and culture associated with it. A major challenge for heritage managers is how to match that demand with visitors that cover the spectrum from passive to serious heritage visitors, offering them existing products as well as developing a range of new products and experiences, which are often versions of the former.

To most scholars, heritage is about the present-day use of the past (Ashworth, 2003; Graham *et al.*, 2000). Heritage is, however, selective, being formed by those elements of the past that society wants to keep, this selection being based on its cultural value (what society values) and its economic value (what the tourist industry values), to create the heritage tourism experience. Timothy and Boyd (2003: 7–8) refer to this as the 'experiential heritage environment', which is 'influenced and shaped by a mix of elements that include supply, demand, the nature of the heritage landscape that has been conserved and protected, the impacts that heritage creates and leaves within destination regions, how heritage attractions and resources are managed, how it is interpreted, presented and at times commoditized, as well as the role politics plays in forming the heritage experience'. Marketing this 'experience' is further compounded by the need to embrace the holistic nature of the term to involve its natural, cultural, historical, built, industrial and personal components, and to present each as they exist within destinations. Furthermore, heritage tourism should be viewed as a type of tourism that traverses a mix of landscapes and settings (pristine natural to urban artificial), where overlaps occur with other types of tourism (ecotourism, cultural tourism, urban tourism) (Boyd, 2003; Timothy and Boyd, 2003). Failure to adopt such a holistic and inclusive understanding of heritage will perpetuate a myopic perspective that limits what elements of heritage within a setting are presented to visitors.

Discussion in this chapter is centred on a number of themes that include market reach, marketing mix, economics of heritage tourism, branding and authenticity. Future marketing opportunities that are presented include thanatourism, ordinary landscapes and people, heritage trails and routes, personal heritage and pilgrimage. In the first edition chapter by the author, considerable attention was given to the challenge of creating sustainable heritage tourism development. This reworked chapter does not explore the topic of sustainability other than to make these few passing points. Sustainability has been part of the lexicon of tourism scholars for some time now, and while 'sustainable' criteria have been well espoused – in the case of heritage tourism authentic products, learning opportunities, societal involvement – and these must remain as central pillars to build heritage tourism opportunities and environments that have long-term viability. At the same time it is important to recognize what Hall (1998: 24) observed almost a decade ago: 'it is unlikely that *heritage* tourism will ever become truly sustainable beyond anything more than the most local of cases' (italics added by author). This chapter concludes with a case study that highlights the challenges of marketing a future heritage tourism attraction, and one that is constrained both in a spatial and temporal sense. In this case the time is 2012 and the centenary of the sinking of the Titanic, while the place is Belfast, arguably the birthplace of Titanic.

Challenges

Market reach

Heritage is not homogeneous; it exists at different levels and scales, namely world, national, local and personal (Timothy, 1997). Many heritage tourism sites have been ascribed as having world status and universal appeal, and we know them as World Heritage Sites. Research, however, shows that many of these sites are only visited for a very short time and that while they draw large masses of tourists, the visit itself is likely to be only a small part of a more extensive itinerary (Boyd and Timothy, 2006; Leask and Fyall, 2006). Timothy (1997) commented that the vast majority of heritage tourism opportunities lie outside of the World Heritage Site category and that at a national, regional and local scale, a plethora of opportunities exist to tell local stories and to sell local heritage landscapes. Despite the scale at which heritage tourism opportunity exists, the challenge will be to appeal to both the passive heritage visitor (akin to the mass tourist) and the serious heritage visitor (akin to the special-interest traveller), and to market to different ends of the visitor spectrum.

Psychographics provide one mechanism to assist with marketing. Plog (1973, 1991) proposed that tourism places develop differently as a result of the types of visitors they attract. For those visitors displaying psychocentric tendencies of preference for nearness, home comforts and familiar surroundings, local heritage products are often sought out, and if long distance travel is involved, then the familiar sites associated with. Thus, for example, the Grand Tour circuit of Europe may become a possibility, particularly for those travelling from within Europe or North America. In contrast, visitors keen to explore cultural heritage sites (e.g. temples of Asia, the ruins of the Mayan and Aztec civilization), experience the culture of First Peoples and their traditions (e.g. sites in the interior of Australia, the peripheral regions of Canada and the Pacific Ocean) are, in essence, creating new Grand Tours and displaying allocentric tendencies of a preference for distant, unusual and challenging experiences. Timothy and Boyd (2006: 2) noted that as the range of resources that function as attractions in heritage tourism increase, there is a need to 'understand better the supply side of heritage tourism, including how resources are marked as heritage sites in different cultures and the unique management challenges and solutions in different heritage settings'. McKercher and du Cros (2002), albeit working in the context of cultural tourism, established a typology of cultural tourists according to the experience sought and the importance of cultural tourism in the decision to visit a destination. They identified five types of cultural tourists: purposeful, sightseeing, serendipitous, casual and incidental. This categorization can equally apply to the heritage tourist, and such thinking may be more beneficial than viewing the heritage tourist spectrum as 'passive visitor' through to 'serious visitor'. Marketers of heritage tourism should take note of this.

Marketing mix

Considerable attention has been paid to the topic of the marketing mix within the tourism marketing literature (see for example Holloway, 2004). The conventional view has been to market on the basis of product, place, promotion and price. Others state there is merit in adding to this list the 'P's with people, programming and partnerships (Boyd, 2003; Mill and Morrison, 1998). The first is argued on the basis that ultimately the heritage tourism product must be focused on the people involved and the experiences they desire; this requires marketers to address the intangible aspects of place and opportunity. Programming is better understood to involve the provision of events and festivals. The heritage tourist, and in particular the cultural heritage tourist, is particularly drawn to events and festivals as they offer a suitable way of presenting the intangible qualities of destinations and their people. With respect to partnerships, Bramwell and Lane (2000) attach this to the wider ideas of collaboration and network development. While considerable attention has been paid by scholars to collaboration and partnership, discussion of network development has been less prevalent within the field of heritage tourism, and confined to research on food and wine tourism (see Hall *et al.*, 2000). In the context of heritage tourism, Boyd (2000) examines heritage tourism opportunities for Northern Ireland and refers to networks as part of the formation of attraction clusters. New 'P's are constantly being added to the original mix, recent ones being passion, purpose, performance, potential, pass-along, position, practice and profit, which in turn provide greater scope and flexibility in how heritage tourism may be marketed in the future.

Heritage economics

Where the economic impact of heritage tourism is concerned, marketers need to take into account two related subjects, namely that of price elasticity and willingness to pay. Little is known about the former with regard to heritage tourism, other than through some early works that indicated the higher the price for admission, the lower the attendance will be (Herbert *et al.*, 1989). Related to this, among site managers there are several concerns and problems associated with people paying for the use of 'their own heritage'. These include the over-commercialization or commoditization of heritage and the exclusion of people who cannot afford to pay entry fees. There is also a danger of the commercial side of site management occupying too much time and effort, thereby taking time and resources away from the more important goals of conservation and interpretation (Fyall and Garrod, 1998; Garrod, 2003).

Ensuring authenticity

The idea of authenticity has been of concern to tourism scholars for many years. The debate within heritage tourism circles around those that argue that people travel in a constant search for authentic experiences and genuine places (e.g. MacCannell, 1979), as opposed to those that suggest that tourists do not seek truly authentic experiences (e.g. Herbert, 1995; Moscardo, 2000) and are able to discern artificial from authentic heritages (Urry, 1995). The reality may be that the desire of most tourists is to experience a holiday that is entertaining, enjoyable and memorable (Halewood and Hannam, 2001; Moscardo, 2000). Much of what exists in the form of heritage centres and 'living museums' today offer visitors an inauthentic experience, where the past has been distorted through inventing places (e.g. Land of Oz, Kansas), by sanitizing (e.g. pioneer villages free of disease, death, poverty and starvation; see Bartel, 1990) or idealizing the past (e.g. Monterey, Cannery Row; see Hall, 2003), and by celebrating only the 'winners' of society, to the exclusion of the 'ordinary people' of history (Timothy and Boyd, 2003). Further to this is the need for marketers to accept that authenticity is a relative term and that it cannot be generalized but rather shaped by the visitor's own social conditioning, and that meaning may be attributed in part to their background and how they interpret what they are gazing upon (Timothy and Prideaux, 2004; Wall and Xie, 2005). The dangers are nevertheless evident in that in striving to ensure an accurate picture of the past is presented to visitors, there is the danger that heritage tourism spaces become fossilized spaces that fail to always show the 'present' within the 'past'.

Branding

Branding is another term that has become common in marketing today, developing its own lexicon of terms, two of which are positioning and image. Both terms have particular resonance when it comes to World Heritage Sites (Boyd and Timothy, 2006) as Destination Marketing Organizations (DMOs) are often too quick to brand destinations with certain labels and to promote areas around well-known symbols, such as UNESCO's World Heritage Site (WHS) logo. Among the dangers of using the WHS logo is the possible exclusion of recognition of many other opportunities and hence experiences that WHS regions that do not have WHS status have to offer visitors. Research in New Zealand has revealed that while many tourism businesses promote themselves as part of the wider WHS region, beyond that of the site itself, this does not always translate in the mind of visitors who fail to recognize the brand as many are even unaware they are within a WHS region (Hall and Piggin, 2003).

New opportunities

New heritage tourism opportunities are constantly emerging. These include thanatourism, ordinary landscapes and people, heritage trails and routes, personal heritage and pilgrimage (Timothy and Boyd, 2006). This process serves to broaden the scope of heritage attractions as conceived by scholars like Prentice (1994).

Thanatourism, or dark tourism, is not a new tourism product, but the interest in places associated with death, atrocity, disaster and suffering have increasingly come under the radar of the heritage tourist. Some of the most popular tourist attractions for the heritage-minded tourist include concentration camps, prisons, slave centres and sites where famous people have died (Ashworth and Hartmann, 2005). Ground Zero in New York, where the twin World Trade Center towers once stood, has become a space of meaning; a space that is almost sacred and is representative of national identity. As the sixth anniversary approaches, the site has become a major visitor attraction that appeals across the entire heritage tourist spectrum.

The interest in ordinary landscapes and ordinary people is a reaction to their absence in most heritage spaces. Society has always celebrated the winners of society and commemorated them by erecting statues, memorials or gardens. Their societal position and achievement is often reflected in the buildings they left to future generations. Heritage tourism has promoted the lifestyles of the elite within society over the 'heritage of the ordinary'. There is, however, limited understanding as to how favourably today's heritage visitor will gaze upon mundane remnants of the past such as farms, houses, schools, factories, cemeteries, jails and villages. The lives of the peasantry and working class in general are as important as the lives of the powerful within past societies, and the opportunity exists within the heritage tourism industry to offer these alternative narratives of a region's past.

Heritage trails and routes have been around for ages and exist at various scales, from mega-trails such as the Silk Route, to national trails like the Mormon trail across America, to small-scale urban trails like the Boston Freedom Trail (Timothy and Boyd, 2003). Trails offer the opportunity to market a mix of attractions and individual sites together for tourists, as opposed to selling the importance of the route in an historical context. While trails should be marketed as an entity, it is often the individual attractions they connect that appeal to visitors; hence the reason why few visitors would value experiencing the entire route, an exception being those engaged in pilgrimages. Some scholars (see Hall, 2005) have questioned if pilgrimage is part of tourism given the obligatory dimension associated with it. It may, however, be argued that pilgrimage or religious tourism is part of heritage tourism firstly because the locations and structures that are visited (e.g. Mecca) have become important heritage attractions and destinations, and secondly because the route itself has become an historical phenomenon and gained recognition as an important element of religious tourism (Timothy and Boyd, 2006).

Lastly, personal heritage, better known as roots tourism, and visits to ancestral homelands and regions are emerging as a new heritage tourism opportunity. Considerable attention has been paid as of late by tourism scholars to diasporas, the desire of tourists to connect with past ancestry and trace their family genealogy (Coles and Timothy, 2004), and the importance that tourists place between heritage places and their own individual identity. It offers new scope to broaden the market appeal of many destinations.

The following case study examines the challenges of promoting a new heritage attraction/opportunity which has strong temporal and spatial constraints.

Case Study: Marketing of the Titanic and the Maritime heritage of Belfast, Northern Ireland

The tourism industry of Northern Ireland has matured over the past decade against a political climate of establishing a more peaceful and safe environment for residents and visitors alike. With the end to the 'troubles', Northern Ireland today welcomes around 2 million out-of-state visitors and records 10 million bed nights each year, with the industry sector contributing around £500 million to the Northern Ireland economy. The lead destination marketing organization, the Northern Ireland Tourist Board (NITB), has since 2004 embarked on a 'Strategic Framework for Action' programme which comprised three elements: attracting visitors, business enhancement and communicating effectively. One aspect of business enhancement involves the development of a number of 'signature projects' in order to deliver international 'stand out' for Northern Ireland. One of these is Titanic (Maritime) Belfast. Northern Ireland, and in particular the shipbuilding yards of Harland and Wolff, Belfast, is home to the Titanic as well as her sister ship the Olympic. Commissioned by White Star Line, these ships were conceived to restore the pre-eminence of the company within the golden age of travel at the start of the twentieth century.

Conceived, designed, built and launched in Belfast, Titanic was the subject of pride for the city: over 10 000 onlookers cheered on 31 May 1911 when the ship was launched and towed to the then new Thompson Outfitting Wharf and Graving Dock to be transformed into the floating palace of legend. Despite the tragic events of 15 April 1912, when Titanic sank five days out of Southampton on its maiden voyage, it has remained the subject of enduring pride over the years for the city of Belfast. Five years ahead of commemorating the centenary of the tragic sinking of the Titanic, Belfast has embarked on a project to transform the former docks and surrounding region, aptly named the Titanic Quarter, into what will emerge as the largest urban waterfront renewal space in Europe, comprising tourism, commercial, educational, residential and recreational and leisure elements. At the centre of this space a visitor centre is planned, shaped in the design of the White Star logo, that will tell the story of the Titanic to visitors and residents alike. The marketing of an attraction that is designed to commemorate a specific event, and one which is still in the future, is beset with challenges that are somewhat unique but do have some similarity to hosting of hallmark events. These include developing an attraction that has a future beyond the event, the substantial upfront building costs involved with no assurance that when opened will have sufficient appeal to recover these costs, the extent to which a single attraction can be developed into a wider brand and related to the surrounding region, and its varied functions and activities. At present, the Thompson Dry Dock lies dormant and the Harland and Wolff drawing offices are abandoned and the only permanent Titanic exhibition which includes items such as original Titanic artefacts, vintage photographs, newsreels, recordings and music related to the ship, is housed at the Ulster Folk and Transport Museum, Cultra, outside of Belfast.

The theme of the Titanic holds significant economic, cultural and regeneration opportunities for all of Northern Ireland and not just the city of Belfast; a finding from the detailed concept and economic feasibility study that was commissioned by the NITB and Belfast City Council in 2004. On its release on 1 September 2005, Alan Clarke, Chief Executive of the NITB commented that 'the completion of this report means that Belfast is closer to establishing a world class attraction that will compete against the best in the world' (Belfast City Council, 2007a). Original design plans included

- a centrepiece visitor centre building, shaped in the form of the White Star logo,
- the creation of a 'ghost ship' on the Thompson Dry Docks (a unique light-sculpture of the ship that would be visible across the Belfast harbour skyline), and
- a large-scale industrial sculpture park, alongside a hotel, conference and convention centre.

The Titanic/Maritime Belfast signature project is part of a larger Titanic Quarter initiative. The Titanic Quarter encompasses 185 acres of Queen's Island, on the eastern banks of the River Lagan, and covers most of the former Harland and Wolff shipyard site. It extends from Abercorn Basin to Belfast Lough. It is adjacent to the region known as Laganside, a region of Belfast's waterfront that underwent renewal between 1987 and 2001 (see Timothy and Boyd, 2003), and combined with the Titanic Quarter will transform a now derelict site into a sustainable and smart city region of the future which will be more than just about tourism but rather it will be about citizens living and working in a core multi-functional space. The wider waterfront development is projected to cost over £3 billion, with £70 million being the estimated cost to establish a Titanic-themed visitor attraction within the historic area of the shipyard where the liner was built. It is expected that it will take 15 years to transform Belfast's Titanic Quarter, becoming the largest waterfront development project in Europe and creates over 20 000 new jobs over the next 15 years (Titanic Quarter, 2007).

Success of the developing the Titanic tourism attraction, one element of the larger Titanic Quarter vision, requires public- and private-sector involvement. Partnership is currently in place that include Belfast City Council, the NITB, Titanic Quarter Limited and Titanic Forum, the latter representing all local Titanic interest groups. In August 2006, the signature project was short-listed for the Big Lottery Fund's Living Landmarks Programme, receiving a development grant to help prepare its application to the programme. If successful, the Titanic Signature Project will be eligible for support funds of between £10 million and £25 million: a substantial contribution towards overall building costs. This announcement will be made towards the end of summer 2007.

A number of destinations are expected to host events on the centenary in 2012, including Southampton (from where the ship sailed on 10 April), Cherbourg, France (where she dropped anchor on the evening of 10 April to pick up a further 247 passengers), Queenstown (Cobh) on the south coast of Ireland (from where she sailed at 1.30 pm on 11 April) and St Johns, Newfoundland (where many of the survivors were taken). While it is a centenary of a tragedy, it is important that Belfast positions itself over other destinations associated with the ship's maiden voyage. In the years running up to the centenary event, Belfast has embarked on a number of programmes where the Titanic brand is becoming associated with the city. These involve hosting an annual Titanic Made in Belfast Festival (which runs for a week in April to coincide with the anniversary of the ship's maiden voyage), the design of an interactive Titanic trail, and tours of the Harland and Wolff shipyards from the River Lagan (as part of the events that are run across the Festival period).

The Titanic Made in Belfast Festival is a celebration of the ship, her city and the artisan skills of the people who built the ship. The week-long festival involves exhibitions, living history and storytelling, viewing the Titanic Memorial Plague in Belfast City Hall (a replica of the plague left in 2005 on the bridge of the Titanic to remember those who died in the tragic sinking), viewing of SS Nomadic, the last floating link to the Titanic now returned to Belfast to be restored for the centenary (built to carry first and second-class passengers out to the Titanic when she called in to Cherbourg, France), and boat tours to the actual place on Belfast Lough where Titanic was launched on 31 May 1911. Belfast City Council state that for the 2006 festival, an estimated 18 700 visitors were in attendance, resulting in a total gross economic impact of £608 500. A survey of visitors by Millward Brown Ulster Consultants revealed a very high proportion of respondents (91 per cent of 111 surveyed) stated they would visit a visitor attraction about Titanic in the Titanic Quarter. Those aged 55 and over and from a C2DE background were most keen to visit a visitor attraction about the Titanic.

A Titanic Trail, with a duration time of 2.5 hours, takes in the buildings and monuments associated with RMS Titanic, including the shipyard where she was designed, built and launched. While walking trails have become familiar in most cities and developed along specific themes and topics of interest, this trail development is unique as visitors are offered an interactive trail experience. The Node™ Explorer (portable device, developed by Awakin Limited) uses Global Positioning Systems (GPS) technology to take visitors back to the future, leading them on a tour of the city sites associated with the Titanic story, from the grounds of the City Hall to Queen's Island (site of the slipways, related docks) as well as offering them a vision of what the Titanic Quarter will look like on completion. A range of still images, video footage, dramatic reconstructions, text and audio clips are employed to enable visitors to experience a fully interactive trip through time, telling the Titanic story and the key figures associated with its history. The interactive trail was launched in August 2006, and the Explorer technology offers an opportunity to revolutionize the visitor experience by being able to offer them a level of engagement with destinations not previously possible (current figures of 600 users since August 2006, personal correspondence, John Bustard, 26 March 2007). While the interactive Titanic Trail has yet to be trailed over the peak visitor period, Belfast City Council have further plans to broaden the experience beyond Titanic to include trails to the city's Cultural and Queen's Quarter using this technology.

There is no certainty that Big Lottery monies will become available to assist with the build of the Titanic visitor attraction. In this case, Belfast will continue to build the Titanic brand by adding new elements of the Titanic story. For instance, Belfast celebrated the 95th anniversary of the maiden voyage with the launch of a new initiative, the Titanic Nomadic Convention. With the return of the Nomadic to Belfast in 2006, there is expectation that this may act as a catalyst to develop a world-class Titanic Museum. The 2007 Convention saw delegates from Titanic Associations from France, Britain, USA, Germany and Switzerland. Dave Custy of the Belfast Titanic Convention stated that 'it is important that we promote Belfast as the birthplace of the Titanic' and he went on to state that the convention 'highlights the rich heritage in the shipbuilding and also opens up Northern Ireland as an economically viable tourist attraction creating an annual foundation for the Titanic Signature Project in 2012' (Belfast City Council, 2007b).

Kerrie Sweeney, NITB and Manager of the Titanic Signature Project stresses that in the event that Big Lottery's Living Landmarks funding is unsuccessful, the NITB is still committed to the completion of a Titanic visitor attraction, and that public–private funding arrangements will have to be sought. Alongside completing funding applications, she stresses the importance of building on the range of bottom-up Titanic products that currently exist (i.e. the trail, festival and convention). A new initiative to be rolled out over 2007 is Titanic signage across the city that allows visitors to walk from the City Hall down to the Titanic Quarter. In addition to this is a press campaign as the international media at present do not see Titanic as associated with Belfast. According to Sweeney there is a lot of work to be accomplished in order to build the brand, an observation she pointed out was stressed in the 2005 Concept Plans to Belfast City Council (personal correspondence, 15 March 2007).

The marking of the centenary of the sinking of the Titanic will be a sombre occasion. Over the years, numerous museums have been set up that are dedicated to the Titanic. Belfast must establish the Titanic brand on the competitive advantage that it is the only place where visitors will be able to tour the shipyards where the legendary ship was built. The long-term viability of the Titanic Signature Project is its location, adjacent to Laganside, with its café; culture, entertainment (Waterfront Hall) and sporting arenas (Odyssey Complex; Northern Ireland's biggest visitor attraction). In time the Titanic Quarter will be transformed and offer a unique cultural experience (bars, restaurants, cafes, water-based leisure facilities, hotel and cruise ship facilities, and conference venues, as well as the Titanic attractions) and this mix of opportunity the region will offer visitors will create a visited space that is sustainable. The most import-ant elements of this vision, namely the Titanic attractions, are only starting to be developed, but in the interim years leading up to 2012, Belfast must ensure that its connections to Titanic are internationally recognized.

Conclusion

This chapter has presented several strands of thinking about marketing heritage tourism. Today's student of heritage needs to be aware that the scope of the subject is constantly changing, expanding to include new topics and linking with many other forms of tourism. As a concept, heritage should be marketed to include its various elements and a holistic approach to the topic is beneficial. This chapter illustrates that considerable scope remains as to how heritage tourism is marketed, that the marketing mix is constantly evolving beyond the traditional approach of product formulation, price, place and promotion. Research is further needed to understand the position of heritage tourists when it comes to how we pay for that heritage and the type of products they want to view, where they are authentic or inauthentic. New opportunities exist to broaden the appeal of heritage to a wider market to include dark tourism sites, the appreciation of the 'heritage' in ordinary places that tell the stories of ordinary people, trails and routes of varying scale and themes, and the attachment to personal heritages, pilgrimages and roots.

As heritage tourism continues to gain in recognition and importance, these new opportunities need to be explored against the more conventional heritage spaces and products, and the approach to marketing requires a better understanding of visitors interested in things heritage.

References

Ashworth, G. J. (2003). Heritage, identity and places: for tourists and host communities. In *Tourism in Destination Communities* (S. Singh, D. J. Timothy and R. Dowling, eds), pp. 79–97. CABI.

Ashworth, G. J. and Hartmann, R. (eds). (2005). *Horror and Human Tragedy Revisited: The Management of Sites of Atrocities for Tourism*. Cognizant.

Bartel, D. (1990). Nostalgia for America's village past: staged symbolic communities. *International Journal of Politics, Culture and Society*, **4**, 79–93.

Belfast City Council (2007a). Lord Mayor hails a new dawn in Titanic Quarter. http://beslfastcity.gov.uk.

Belfast City Council. (2007b). Press Release, 5 February.

Boyd, S. W. (2000). Heritage tourism in Northern Ireland: opportunity under peace. *Current Issues in Tourism*, **3**, 150–174.

Boyd, S. W. (2003). Marketing challenges and opportunities for heritage tourism. In *Managing Visitor Attractions: New Directions* (A. Fyall, B. Garrod and A. Leask, eds), pp. 189–202. Butterworth-Heinemann.

Boyd, S. W. and Timothy, D. J. (2006). Marketing issues and world heritage sites. In *Managing World Heritage Sites* (A. Leask and A. Fyall, eds), pp. 55–68. Butterworth-Heinemann.

Bramwell, B. and Lane, B. (eds). (2000). *Tourism Collaboration and Partnerships: Politics, Practice and Sustainability*. Channel View.

Coles, T. E. and Timothy, D. J. (eds) (2004). *Tourism, Diasporas and Space*. Routledge.

Fyall, A. and Garrod, B. (1998). Heritage tourism: At what price? *Managing Leisure*, **3**, 213–228.

Garrod, B. (2003). Managing visitor impacts. In *Managing Visitor Attractions: New Directions* (A. Fyall, B. Garrod and A. Leask, eds), pp. 124–139. Butterworth-Heinemann.

Graham, B., Ashworth, G. J. and Tunbridge, J. E. (2000). *A Geography of Heritage: Power, Culture and Economy*. Arnold.

Halewood, C. and Hannam, K. (2001). Viking heritage tourism: Authenticity and Commodification. *Annals of Tourism Research*, **28**, 565–580.

Hall, C. M. (1998). Historical antecedents of sustainable development and ecotourism: new labels on old bottles? In *Sustainable Tourism: A Geographical Perspective* (C. M. Hall and A. A Lew, eds), pp. 13–24. Longman.

Hall, C. M. (2003). Politics and Place: an Analysis of Power in Tourism Communities. In *Tourism in Destination Communities* (S. Singh, D. J. Timothy and R. Dowling, eds), pp. 99–113. CABI.

Hall, C. M. (2005). *Tourism: Rethinking the Social Science of Mobility*. Pearson Education.

Hall, C. M., Johnson, G. and Mitchell, R. (2000). Wine tourism and regional development. In *Wine Tourism Around the World: Development, Management and Markets* (C. M. Hall, E. Sharples, B. Cambourne and N. Macionis, eds), pp. 196–226. Butterworth-Heinemann.

Hall, C. M. and Piggin, R. (2003). World heritage sites: managing the brand. In *Managing Visitor Attractions: New Directions* (A. Fyall, B. Garrod and A. Leask, eds), pp. 203–219. Butterworth-Heinemann.

Herbert, D. T. (ed.) (1995). *Heritage, Tourism and Society*. Mansell.

Herbert, D. T., Prentice, R. C. and Thomas, C. J. (eds). (1989). *Heritage Sites: Strategies for Marketing and Development*. Avebury.

Holloway, J. C. (2004). *Marketing for Tourism*, 4th edn. Prentice Hall.

Leask, A. and Fyall, A. (eds) (2006). *Managing World Heritage Sites*. Butterworth-Heinemann.

MacCannell, D. (1979). *The Tourist*. Schocken Books.

McKercher, B. and du Cros, H. (2002). *Cultural Tourism: The Partnership between Tourism and Cultural Heritage Management*. Haworth.

Mill, R. C. and Morrison, A. M. (1998). *The Tourism System: An Introductory Text*. Kendall/Hunt.

Moscardo, G. (2000). Cultural and heritage tourism: the great debates. In *Tourism in the 21st Century: Lessons for Experience* (B. Faulkner, G. Moscardo and E. Laws, eds), pp. 3–17. Continuum.

Plog, S. C. (1973). Why destination areas rise and fall in popularity. *Cornell Hotel and Restaurant Administration Quarterly*, **14**, 13–16.

Plog, S. C. (1991). *Leisure Travel: Making It a Growth Market … Again!* Wiley.

Prentice, R. C. (1994). *Tourism and Heritage Attractions*. Routledge.

Timothy, D. J. (1997). Tourism and the personal heritage experience. *Annals of Tourism Research*, **34**, 751–754.

Timothy, D. J. and Boyd, S. W. (2003). *Heritage Tourism*. Prentice Hall.

Timothy, D. J. and Boyd, S. W. (2006). Heritage tourism in the 21st century: valued traditions and new perspectives. *Journal of Heritage Tourism*, **1**, 1–16.

Timothy, D. J. and Prideaux, B. (2004). Issues in heritage and culture in the Asia Pacific region. *Asia Pacific Journal of Tourism Research*, **9**, 213–233.

Titanic Quarter (2007). Phase Two of Titanic Quarter Plans. Submitted 9 January.

Towner, J. (1996). *An Historical Geography of Recreation and Tourism in the Western World: 1540–1940*. Wiley.

Urry, J. (1995). *Consuming Places*. Routledge.

Wall, G. and Xie, P. F. (2005). Authenticating ethnic tourism: Li dancers' perspectives. *Asia Pacific Journal of Tourism Research*, **10**, 1–21.

CHAPTER 18

Marketing and Managing an Attraction Over Time: The Case of Hagley Park, Christchurch

C. Michael Hall

Aims

The aims of this chapter are to:

- indicate the important role of urban parks as visitor attractions,
- demonstrate how a visitor attraction can become part of the sense of place of the local users of an attraction,
- illustrate how marketing and management policies of an attraction can change over time, and
- indicate how institutional arrangements influence management policies and the nature of the visitor resource.

Introduction

Parks and gardens are an integral part of the landscape of modern cities. Yet despite their recreational significance there is surprisingly little literature on their role as visitor attractions in their wider sense, particularly in terms of how this role has evolved and changed over time (see Hall and Page, 2006, for a review). This chapter will first discuss the nature of parks and their changing visitor function before going on to examine the case of Hagley Park in Christchurch, New Zealand.

Evolution and development of the concept of urban parks

Parks are designated public or shared open spaces provided for leisure and outdoor recreation (Hall, 2004). Parks range in scale from small, highly environmentally modified urban parks, including public gardens, to large national parks with wilderness characteristics. The creation of public parks is primarily a function of Western attitudes towards nature and a reaction to industrialization and urbanization, although examples of public urban open space can now be found throughout the world (Hall and Page, 2006).

Although parks are presently seen as public space, their origin lies in private leisure space. Wealth and power were prerequisites to garden creation in Western society until the mid-nineteenth century as the establishment of gardens and parks reflected the financial or political ability to turn land from productive uses for farming or housing to 'non-productive' uses related to leisure. Importantly, such changes in land use also required the development of attitudes to nature that regarded the availability of land for leisure as being socially and aesthetically desirable.

Together with the gradual closure and privatization of common land used for grazing and hunting in Europe, known as the enclosure of the commons, the park idea has its origins in the ordered pleasure gardens of Europe in the Middle Ages and the Renaissance (Mitchell, 2001). Such private gardens continue to the present day, including private parks such as Bedford Square in London. Together with royal gardens and estates, initially accessible only by the aristocracy (for example, Regents Park in London), such gardens gradually became shared recreational spaces for the elite, then available to the general public over time.

The enclosure of common land between 1760 and 1820 led not only to a revolution in commercial agricultural production but also the nature and aesthetics of the English landscape. The agricultural landscape was transformed into a commercial space of regular, hedgerowed fields, and by changes in the aesthetics of garden design. The latter was a result of the influences of landscape designers such as Capability Brown and Humphry Repton, who moved away from tight, enclosed spaces to expansive landscapes of trees, lakes and lawns, which are now represented as the ideal English or temperate countryside (Hadfield, 1985). These landscapes have influenced parks internationally in terms of both aesthetic conceptions and design, being referred to as parkland scenery to the present day, even if they remain in private hands.

In Britain, the first official government recognition of the need for urban public parks came in 1839 with a report to Parliament by the Select Committee on Public Walks (Hall and Page, 2006). The case for urban public parks for recreation was taken up by the public health movement and by intellectuals who believed the new industrial areas to be evil as well as unhealthy places, and who actively campaigned for the creation of parks as a source of healthy recreation and moral regeneration (Conway, 1991). In 1840, the first public park in Britain was given to the city of Derby by philanthropist Joseph Strutt. The first municipal park in Britain was established in Birkenhead in 1843. In some British cities, such as Leicester and London, the few commons that had survived the enclosures were gradually converted from grazing areas to parks for public recreation (Hall and Page, 2006). Significantly, the history of grazing had actually contributed to the commons' parkland nature and provided an aesthetic for their retention as public open space. As Hadfield (1985: 315) comments, '… many Victorian gardens, and … public parks, were within a permanent setting of a Brown or Repton landscape. The artistic merit of these were [sic] never questioned, and they were allowed to mature unharmed'.

In the latter half of the nineteenth century, public open space was an important source of civic pride, with the Victorian public parks containing refreshment and tearooms, fountains, lakes and ornamental trees and gardens that reflected the private parkscapes of the rural elite in an urban setting (Conway, 1991). The Victorian emphasis on public parks and gardens as a means of healthy recreation and sport as well as aesthetic education was exported throughout the British Empire and was incorporated into urban planning practice in Australia, Canada, India, New Zealand and South Africa as well as in the United States (Taylor, 1999). Table 18.1 provides some examples of major urban parks around the world. Botanical and zoological gardens were also

Table 18.1 Examples of urban public parks and public open space

Name	Location	Size (ha)
The Mall	Washington DC, USA	2670
Fairmont Park	Philadelphia, USA	1692
Chapultepac Park	Mexico City, Mexico	850
Phoenix Park	Dublin, Eire	712
City Park	New Orleans, USA	610
Golden Gate Park	San Francisco, USA	406
Kings Park and Botanic Gardens	Perth, Western Australia	406
Stanley Park	Vancouver, Canada	400
Englischer Garten	Munich, Germany	370
Central Park	New York, USA	341
Hyde Park	London, England	255
Centennial Park	Sydney, Australia	222
Hagley Park and Botanic Gardens	Christchurch, New Zealand	192
Royal Park	Melbourne, Australia	188
The Regent's Park	London, England	166
Mount Royal Park/Parc du Mont-Royal	Montreal, Canada	101

often integrated with park developments. Such gardens were usually associated with the formation of societies with scientific and economic interests, although they often received a degree of government support in recognition of their educational role. Throughout the British Empire such gardens also served an important social function because they not only included plant and animal species that reminded the British settler of 'home', but also served as a base for the spread of such species in the new country through the activities of acclimatization societies (Tritenbach, 1987).

The moral and social control dimensions of park creation and use has continued through the twentieth century to today. Members of the garden city movement believed that their new cities with their parks and open spaces would provide a basis for the development of stronger community values (Wilson, 1989). Despite a lack of empirical evidence, the belief that participation in sport helps to reduce juvenile delinquency has also been a major impetus in the provision of parks and recreational facilities in post-World War II urban developments. Since the 1960s and the growth of environmental concerns, urban parks have also become recognized as significant environmental resources, while the extended period of time over which urban parks have existed has also meant that many of them now hold significant heritage values. In addition, increased mobility means that many parks have become significant international tourist attractions in their own, particularly in larger urban centres. However, the conservation of environmental values and their promotion as tourist attractions arguably represents yet another layer of demands on the multipurpose, multiple values nature of public parks.

Hagley Park, Christchurch, New Zealand

Christchurch is by far the largest urban centre in the South Island of New Zealand. With a population of 360 500 people as on June 2006 the city is the major service, education and administrative centre of the South Island as well as being a transport hub and the international gateway. In terms of domestic tourism, there were almost 6 million day visits and 2.39 million overnight visits (6.12 million visitor nights) to the region in 2005, resulting in a total spend of NZ$918 million. In terms of international tourism, there were 549 000 day visits and 2.1 million overnight visits (6.5 million visitor nights) resulting in a total spend of NZ$1077 million (Canterbury Development Corporation, Christchurch Canterbury Tourism and Christchurch City Council, 2006).

Hagley Park was named after the country seat of Lord Lyttelton, the Chairman of the Canterbury Association, a Church of England colonist group that established Christchurch. The Park is Christchurch's premier metropolitan park and was the original source of the city's tag line as 'the garden city', which dates from 1906. Established in 1855 shortly after the arrival of British settlers to the region, the Park is integral to the city's sport, leisure and recreation, as well as to its sense of place. Hagley Park and the Christchurch Botanic Gardens, which it encloses, comprise an area of 192 ha. Centrally located, the Park has also long been an important element of the city's domestic and international tourism marketing; a role that has only been reinforced by its situation adjacent to the cultural precinct of Christchurch which features art galleries, museums, arts and crafts stores, heritage buildings, restaurants and cafes.

The Park is made up of three parcels of land (Little Hagley Park, North Hagley Park and South Hagley Park) that are classified Recreation Reserve under the New Zealand Reserves Act 1977. The Botanic Gardens are classified as a Local Purpose (Botanic Gardens) Reserve under the Reserves Act. Although the Act is administered by the Department of Conservation, the same national body responsible for National Parks, the Christchurch City Council (CCC) is the administering body with respect to both the Park and the Botanic Gardens.

The openness of the Park make exact visitor numbers extremely difficult to ascertain. According to the CCC (2006a, b) the Botanic Gardens receive an esti-mated 1.2 million visits each year, which probably represents about 600 000 individuals who pass through the gates. 'This makes the Gardens one of the most popular visitor destinations in Christchurch and certainly the most popu-lar passive recreation area' (CCC, 2006a: 41). Council surveys suggest that about 75 per cent of all Christchurch residents will have visited the Gardens in a 12-month period. As well as being used for casual recreation, Hagley Park is also a major sport and event facility, with a number of playing fields and a pub-lic golf course, which means that the amount of annual visits is possibly of the order of 5 million visits a year. Table 18.2 reports some of the results of seasonal surveys of visitors to the Botanic Gardens undertaken in 2004 for the CCC (2006a, b). Unfortunately, the statistical validity of the surveys cannot be ascer-tained. Nevertheless, the growth of the city and region's population and the likelihood of increased tourism means that there is increased visitor pressure on the Park and Botanic Gardens. The Park is regarded by the CCC as 'Christchurch's equivalent of Central Park for New York City' (2006c: 12). Yet, like Central Park, Hagley is coming under increased pressure from local and non-local visitors alike, and is being called upon to meet a wide range of envir-onmental, recreational and tourism values. According to the CCC:

Within ten years there could be about two million visits to the Botanic Gardens annually. Although there has not yet been rigorous determination of the value of this use, the Gardens visits represent at least 30 million dollars if equated to income equivalence for the time spent in the Gardens. The public health values of this large green space have yet to be calculated but will be significant and may well be in the tens of millions of dol-lars. Hagley Park and the Botanic Gardens are first and foremost open space areas for the enjoyment of the public, both Christchurch residents and visitors. Combined, they are a significant open space area by world standards. (CCC, 2006b: 12)

As a result of visitor pressures in terms of both the numbers and the range of activities being undertaken in the Park and Gardens, the CCC undertook a master planning process in 2006–2007. The process had three core elements: the development of a master plan for both Hagley Park and the Botanic Gardens, and the development of separate management plans for Hagley

Table 18.2 Profile of visitors to the Christchurch Botanic Gardens

Item	Profile
Visitor origin	50% of visitors are from Christchurch 20% are from the United Kingdom and 20% from Australia
Repeat visitation	65% of visitors
Gender	Female visitors outnumber males by more than 10%
Age	22% of visitors are 20–29 in age 20% are in the 60+ age group
Travel to gardens	58% private car 24% walk 12% taxi
Social dimensions	Almost 75% of visitors come with family and friends 2% visit a tour or tour group 13–20% visit with children (differs seasonally)
Reasons to visit	88% walk 52% relax 43% to look at trees and plants 37% pass through
Sources of information	Almost 90% of Christchurch based visitors say that they have 'always known about it' Of visitors from outside Christchurch, 36% stated they got information from a guide book

Source: Derived from Christchurch City Council (2006a, b).

Park and the Botanic Gardens. The plans were to be developed in light of the previous plans that had been developed for the Park and Gardens, as well as the various planning processes and policies of the CCC. The elements of this process are outlined in Figure 18.1.

An obvious question is why this planning structure? Although the Park and Gardens are coterminous, they are classified differently under national law (the Reserves Act 1977) as noted above. The Botanic Gardens and the Park also serve different purposes and, although there is only limited empirical research to support this, almost certainly have different audiences. For example, dogs are prohibited from the Botanic Gardens, yet they are allowed in Hagley Park. Observational research by the author suggests that something in the order of

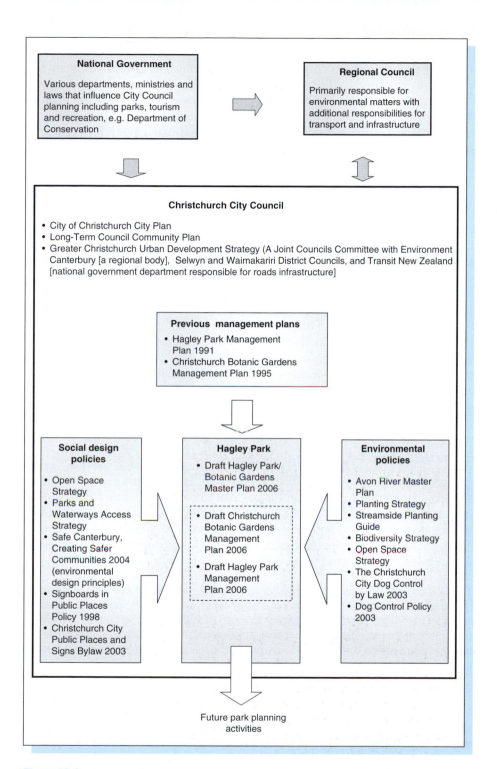

National Government

Various departments, ministries and laws that influence City Council planning including parks, tourism and recreation, e.g. Department of Conservation

Regional Council

Primarily responsible for environmental matters with additional responsibilities for transport and infrastructure

Christchurch City Council

- City of Christchurch City Plan
- Long-Term Council Community Plan
- Greater Christchurch Urban Development Strategy (A Joint Councils Committee with Environment Canterbury [a regional body], Selwyn and Waimakariri District Councils, and Transit New Zealand [national government department responsible for roads infrastructure]

Previous management plans

- Hagley Park Management Plan 1991
- Christchurch Botanic Gardens Management Plan 1995

Social design policies

- Open Space Strategy
- Parks and Waterways Access Strategy
- Safe Canterbury, Creating Safer Communities 2004 (environmental design principles)
- Signboards in Public Places Policy 1998
- Christchurch City Public Places and Signs Bylaw 2003

Hagley Park

- Draft Hagley Park/ Botanic Gardens Master Plan 2006

- Draft Christchurch Botanic Gardens Management Plan 2006
- Draft Hagley Park Management Plan 2006

Environmental policies

- Avon River Master Plan
- Planting Strategy
- Streamside Planting Guide
- Biodiversity Strategy
- Open Space Strategy
- The Christchurch City Dog Control by Law 2003
- Dog Control Policy 2003

Future park planning activities

Figure 18.1

Hagley Park institutional planning context 2006–2007

400 dogs and their owners use the Park on weekdays, with approximately 600 using it on weekends. Although there are likely to be seasonal differences, a conservative estimate would suggest that this means that there are around 150 000 visits by dog owners to the Park each year, who usually then do not go to the Botanic Gardens. Similarly, the Park is used extensively for organized sports (cricket, golf, netball, rugby, soccer, touch); the majority of participants again do not use the Botanic Gardens.

The Master Plan, which is a statutory document reviewed under strict procedures laid out in the Reserves Act 1977, is designed to provide strategic direction and vision for the Park and the Gardens, while the Management Plans provide policies to guide the ongoing management of each of the areas. However, the values associated with the Park and Gardens and their interpretation in management, planning and marketing is not static. Such planning documents therefore illustrate a number of themes associated with their status as visitor attractions and the weight of public memory that is often associated with them making change difficult. The visions and goals that have been determined for the Park and Gardens under the most recent formal planning process (Table 18.3) are therefore the current mark of a legacy of contestation and debate between stakeholders over the attraction's use and management. Therefore, from the perspective of understanding how the attraction is managed presently and in the future, further analysis of the attraction may shed light on management practices and strategies.

Purpose

Under the plans of the Canterbury Association, Hagley Park was set aside as a reserve forming the western boundary of Christchurch before the town was even inhabited. In 1855, Hagley Park was formally reserved by the Canterbury Provincial Council (Canterbury Association Reserves Ordinance, Session V, No. 2, 1855) 'for ever as a public park' (para. 4) 'though lands may be let' (para. 5) (Archives New Zealand (a)). Under paragraph 4 of the Ordinance:

The land commonly known as Hagley Park ... shall be reserved for ever as a public park, and shall be open for the recreation and enjoyment of the public: Provided that it shall be lawful for the Superintendent to set apart so much of the said land as he shall think fit for plantations, gardens, and places for public amusement, and to made Regulations for the use and preservation thereof, and to lay out public roads through the said Park, and to make Regulations from time to time for the depasturing of cattle therein.

The wording of the Ordinance is fascinating as it sets out some of the immediate difficulties of managing park areas in terms of balancing 'use and preservation' – a legacy that exists in both urban parks and national parks to the present day (Hall and Page, 2006). Although the park was not established for some of the same aesthetic reasons as the first National Parks, it is noticeable that the park was clearly designed to take advantage of the river that ran through it (now called the Avon River). In fact the original map of the proposed city of

Table 18.3   Vision and goals for Hagley Park and the Christchurch Botanic Gardens

Vision	Goals
Hagley Park For Hagley Park to remain an iconic inner-city open space for the City of Christchurch – a place for present and future residents and visitors for recreation and enjoyment	To protect and enhance Hagley Park's existing and historical environmental values, its landscape qualities and its botanical features
	To provide areas for recreational and sporting activities for the benefit of the public that are compatible with Hagley Park's environmental and open space qualities
Christchurch Botanic Gardens The Christchurch Botanic Gardens is foremost in celebrating and presenting plant diversity through collections and programmes, including promoting the relationships that people have with plants	To protect and enhance the Botanic Gardens existing and historical environmental, values its landscape qualities and its botanical features
	To provide areas for visitor experience/activities and programmes expected of a botanic gardens of international standard that are compatible with the Botanic Gardens inherent environmental and open space qualities

Source: Christchurch City Council (2006b).

Christchurch from 1850 also had a botanic gardens located to the East of the city (Archives New Zealand (b)). While not making a claim that Hagley Park is the world's first National Park, its origins appear to be derived from more than just the English commons and public park tradition that existed at the time (see above), and perhaps was also a wider reflection of emerging aesthetic and environmental sensibilities, albeit a substantially modified environment in the English landscape tradition. Indeed, such was the clear recreational use intended for the area that a squatter was ordered to remove himself from the land four years prior to its formal reservation (Archives New Zealand (c)).

As with many parks that are substantial visitor attractions, contestation over purpose has existed over much of the life of the attraction. For example, even though the grazing of animals was allowed on Hagley Park for much of the nineteenth century, similar to other colonial parks such as Kings Park in Perth or even the Royal National Park in Sydney, recreational needs came first. A lease agreement for depasturing on Hagley Park and the Christchurch Domain dated 1852 stated that: 'The license shall not be construed as conveying any right ... to use it for any other purpose than pasturage ... [and] as giving a right to prevent the use of the land included in it by the Public for the purposes of recreation and amusement such as cricket, racing and other sports and games' (Archives New Zealand (d)). Indeed, it is quite possible that grazing was seen as a way of encouraging English country-park-like qualities. An applicant for a lease to pasture animals on Hagley Park in 1867 noted that he would 'lay down English grass' (Archives New Zealand (e)). However, when a proposal was put forward to develop a cattle market on Hagley Park in 1868, it was met with a strong response from the local community:

We the undersigned inhabitants and ratepayers of Christchurch and the adjoining districts beg respectfully to protest against the occupation of any part of Hagley Park as a cattle market.

   We conceive that any alienation of the Park reserve from its original purpose would be a public wrong and that the cattle market proposed would be one of the most injurious encroachments that could be made on a place set apart for public recreation. (Archives New Zealand (f))

The level of opposition clearly indicates the high recreational value that was attached to the Park soon after the establishment of the city. This is all the more remarkable given that Christchurch was then economically dependent on agriculture. Nevertheless, this pattern has been preserved consistently over the past 150 years. For example, there was opposition to the construction of hospital buildings at the south-eastern edge of the park in the 1850s and 1860s and again in the 1920s. However, the greatest opposition has been to the development of more roads in the park.

   The idea of having roads for carriages and horses, as in London's Hyde Park, was mooted over the years but specific proposals were rejected, as was a proposal to set out a cycle track around the Park in 1897. Automobiles first attempted to enter the Park in 1904, when it was proposed to construct a scenic drive. However this was defeated; such developments were not regarded as an appropriate recreational activity. From the 1950s through to the 1970s, successive city council bodies sought to extend a motorway through the northern section of the park despite massive opposition (Archives New Zealand (g)). For example, the April 1970 report of the CCC's Works and Services Committee argued that 'other recreational areas were a substitute' for those that would be lost by road construction and recommended 'that the council continue with the project, despite the 7,827 objections against it' (Archives of New Zealand (h)). In fact, such was the significance of the motorway proposal that it was a factor in the 1971 local council elections and opposition to road-building proposals led to a change in the council. As a result, the Christchurch

City (Reserves) Empowering Act came into force in 1971, containing clauses stating that the City Council 'shall not, without the consent of the Minister, appropriate any part of Hagley Park for parking places for vehicles unless that part is already appropriated for that purpose at the commencement of this Act' (Sec. 5 Sub. 2) and that 'no part of Hagley Park may be taken or set apart under the Public Works Act 1928 for any public work whatsoever' (Sec. 5 Sub. 4, in CCC, 2006c: 39). More recently, proposals in the 1990s to extend the city's tourist tram service into the park also received significant opposition.

Managing stakeholders

Although the recreational values of the park have clearly been dominant over its history, there is substantial contestation and change over how those values can be expressed. For example, until the period immediately following World War II there was substantial regulation over leisure activities in the Park that reflected some of the mores of the local elite with respect to appropriate activities and behaviour. In the 1930s, discussions over the bylaws for the park indicated that there had been a proposal to prohibit sport and games on a Sunday. Although Sabbath restrictions did not proceed, other restrictions were put in place, with bylaws that meant no fishing, aeroplanes, firearms, dogs (unless led) or people carrying large packages. In addition, permission for assemblages and picnics were required:

No person shall be permitted to picnic within the limits of the Park or Gardens without the permission of the Board, and then only at such places as may be assigned by the Curator, and the person representing the persons for which the privilege of holding a picnic is applied for will be held responsible for the proper conduct of the party using the place, and for any damage that may be done. (Christchurch Domains Board by laws circa 1931 in Archives New Zealand (i))

Such restrictions, which no longer hold, nevertheless reflect broader issues with respect to the type of recreation visitors can engage in. One of the dominant issues is potential conflict between organized sports on the one hand and passive and informal recreation on the other. The Park has been used as a sporting venue since shortly after the commencement of European settlement. Cricket clubs first played on South Hagley Park in 1867. Polo occupied the largest area of the park in the late nineteenth century, with football well established by the end of the century as well. In 1902, a 12-hole golf course was established in North Hagley Park. The course is utilized by both club members and paying visitors, although its viability is regarded as limited because of its capacity to compete with 18-hole courses. An approach by the Golf Club to the Council in 1990 to extend the golf course in the Park to gain a further six holes resulted in strong public opposition. The CCC's 1991 Hagley Park Management Plan noted that during its public consultation phase, submitters emphasized the value of the area proposed for conversion to a golf course 'as an informal recreation ground, valued for kite flying and by the surrounding residents as a venue for exercising dogs' (CCC, 2006c: 51). Nevertheless, while the efforts of an organized sporting group failed on this occasion, the management plan notes that as of 2006 there were 22 associations and clubs that regularly use sports and sites, with only one, the Canterbury Horticultural Society, not being a sporting club. In addition, five schools have been allocated specific sporting areas. Given this situation it is therefore not surprising that the draft management plan states that:

There is a need to retain a balance between the provision of facilities for organised sporting codes and catering for the more passive and informal recreational users of Hagley Park. The sports grounds must not be allowed to encroach into any of the traditionally passive recreation areas, such as the woodlands. The open spaces where the organised recreation is concentrated should be retained as open space. (CCC, 2006c: 46)

The relationship between stakeholders and park management is therefore clearly one that is greater than just programming activities in the attraction area over time and space. The type of visitor and the activities they engage in actually affects the way the Park as an attraction is managed over time with respect to facility provision and landscaping as passive recreation is associated with woodland and open space with organized sport. Indeed, 'the facilities used by the passive recreational user vary from those required by organised sport. Rather than focusing activities on sports grounds, passive recreational users prefer the woodland and/or waterside areas for their activities' (CCC, 2006c: 77). However, observations by the author would suggest that such a demarcation actually only exists when the open space sports grounds are actually being used for sporting competitions as, outside of that time, they still get substantial use from joggers, dog walkers, people out walking, and groups of family and friends.

Although the Draft Management Plan notes the importance of 'balance' between sports and informal recreation, the management plan process actually favours organized interests such as sporting clubs. The CCC's own outline of the process indicates that as soon as the need for a new plan is identified it should then be discussed with affected and interested parties including residents/resident groups, community boards, sports clubs/schools, other organizations, council units (CCC, 2006c: 9). Such a process reveals an institutional bias in the way that users of the Park are incorporated into the process, with those users with an organization framework for their interests, such as sporting associations, clubs and schools, clearly better able to influence management policy processes than informal users. Indeed, given the extent of passive recreational use, it is perhaps somewhat surprising that, as far as can be ascertained, as opposed to the Botanic Gardens (see Table 18.2), there was no attempt to survey passive recreationists and visitors to the Park during the period in which the Draft Management Plan was being developed and then reviewed, although public comments on the draft plan were invited. At the time of writing, the final Management Plan had not been decided upon but the influence of organized interests in the draft could clearly be seen. For example, several statements in the 1991 Management Plan with respect to 'management problems … becoming increasing apparent' as a result of sporting events, 'damaged sports grounds' and 'a gradual change in emphasis from intensive organised forms of recreational to more passive/informal recreation needs to occur' were deleted from the 2006 draft (CCC, 2006c: 73, 74). Similarly, a statement in the 1991 Management Plan that 'sporting codes which currently occupy areas required for other forms of recreation, or which have an undesirable impact on the park, shall be progressively relocated to suburban sports grounds' was substantially modified in the 2006 draft to become:

All occupations of Hagley Park for organised sport shall be assessed as to how each contributes generally to the benefit the public is able to gain from use of the Park and shall be compatible with the prime purpose of the Park to provide areas for (a) outdoor recreation and sporting activities, and the physical welfare and enjoyment, of the public and (b) the protection of the Park's open space character and natural environment, prior to the issue or renewal of any formal occupation agreement. (CCC, 2006c: 74)

Unfortunately, the Draft Management Plan provides no assessment as to how such an assessment would occur. Such issues are not exercises in semantics. Management policies differentially affect user groups and serve to allocate the way in which visitor attraction space can be used both in the short-term, through booking and exclusion policies, and in the long-term, through the nature of landscaping. Indeed, there are differences in the perceptions of different users groups with respect not only to how much of the grounds should be open space but also to the type of landscape that should be represented.

Marketing, representation and image

Although Hagley Park has been significant as a local recreation resource since its reservation, its role as an attraction for visitors to the city was well established by the end of the nineteenth century. For example, from April to July 1882 it was host to a privately run New Zealand International Exhibition that attracted over 250 000 people. The Gardens were also an important scenic feature of postcards, photographs and promotional material on the city. Nevertheless, the role of the Gardens as central to the city's landscape iconography was confirmed in 1906 when Christchurch hosted a government-sponsored New Zealand International Exhibition to promote trade and tourism that ran from 1 November 1906 to 15 April 1907. The exhibition attracted nearly two million visitors at a time when the country's population was less than one million. This figure was partly helped by special rail fares being available to encourage New Zealanders to visit, although there was also significant visitation from overseas. Significantly, in terms of the appropriateness of recreation at the Park the Domain Board refused to allow the amusement area from the Exhibition known as Wonderland to remain in Hagley Park. The Press newspaper commented that leaving it on the site would be a 'hideous blot … on a delightful piece of sylvan scenery', especially as the entertainment was 'not especially healthy or refined' (*The Press*, 1907: 8). Yet, perhaps more significantly from a marketing perspective, the British Commissioner to the Exhibition, Sir John Gorst, referred to Christchurch as a 'garden city', superseding the previous 'city of the plains' or 'city of trees' (CCC, 2005; Deverson, 2001).

The 'garden city' moniker was clearly welcomed in a city that sought to promote its English landscape heritage. The Christchurch Beautifying Association, formed in 1897, sought to encourage the Garden City image and identity, while the official report on the International Exhibition also praised the 'sylvan' landscape, 'a very Eden of shade and flowers' (Cowan, 1910: 16, 17). Hagley Park and the Botanic Gardens have therefore been integral to the 'garden city' image and promotion (CCC, 2006a, c) for over a century although, like many environmental attractions, its managers have historically had little influence over the representation of the park in the marketing activities of destination marketing organizations or private operators.

Nevertheless, the marketing of the Park appears about to change substantially, with a shift from passive or no conscious marketing to one in which active marketing is utilized. Figure 18.2 indicates the changing marketing context with a new Marketing Strategy proposed in the 2006–2007 planning process. Several changes can be evidenced. First, the Hagley Park/Botanic Gardens Draft Master Plan emphasizes the need for a Marketing Strategy (CCC, 2006b). Second, a section on marketing has been added to the Draft Management Plan for the Botanic Gardens (CCC, 2006a), although one has not been added to the Hagley Park Management Plan (CCC, 2006c). Third, the Botanic Gardens Management Plan clearly suggests that a marketing orientation needs to be developed, so that 'the gardens brand is widely disseminated and made known and marketed effectively to known and potential users and among related institutions' (CCC, 2006a: 205). Tourism is a clear focus in the 'market position' of the Gardens, along with the development of partnerships:

There needs to be a firm commitment to an objective to increase the number of visitors using the Gardens – such a commitment might make it easier to secure more resources in the future ... It needs to be decided how vigorously the Gardens should pursue new customers and profile itself as being 'the' premier attraction in Christchurch, and to what extent joint marketing is sought, for example, with the Cultural Precinct. (CCC, 2006a: 209)

By themselves, such statements would appear to be standard practice for visitor attractions. However, in the context of the history of the Park and Gardens, such changes are arguably revolutionary as they demonstrate a position in which the Gardens will shift more towards a consumer and relationship focus, rather than there being primarily an internal focus on the environmental resource. Moreover, the attention to marketing for the Gardens and not the remainder of the Park also suggests that the shift in focus means that the Park will not be developed as a product in the same way as the Botanic Gardens will. However, arguably the shift in orientation reflects problems facing many

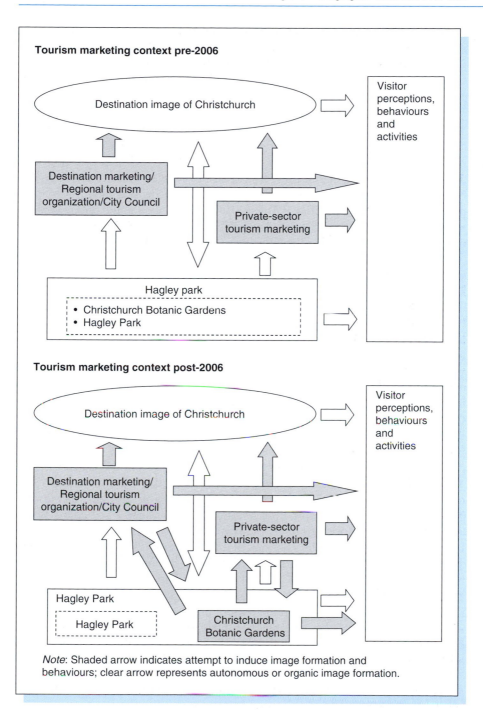

Figure 18.2
Changing tourism marketing context for Hagley Park

publicly owned visitor attractions that serve a wide variety of stakeholders and which increasingly need to become externally focussed in order to assist their own long-term survival as an institution.

Conclusions

This chapter has presented an examination of some of the changing dimensions of the management and marketing of a visitor attraction over time. Urban parks have been significant visitor resources for over 150 years, yet their role and use has changed in that time. In the case of Hagley Park in Christchurch, New Zealand, recreation has been a key focus over its history and has served to protect the park from significant physical change. However, the nature of what recreation is appropriate and what is not has changed, with consequent implications for management practice, for users and for the Park landscape itself.

The Park planning process since the early 1990s has also indicated further shifts in management strategies. First, organized interest groups, particularly sporting clubs and associations, have appeared to have had a greater influence in Park management practices. This has led to open space being primarily managed for formal users and woodlands for informal users. Second, a greater strategic marketing orientation is being adopted with respect to meeting the perceived demands of the tourism market in addition to the local visitor market. However, even though this is meant to apply to both the Parks and the Botanic Gardens with respect to master planning (CCC, 2006b), it is actually only being substantially operationalized in the case of the Botanic Gardens in terms of management operations. Most likely, this is because in terms of space and access it can be more easily commodified as a distinct product. Just as significantly, there are also clear internal drivers in the Management Plan to emphasize the unique dimensions of the Gardens.

The Hagley experience should not be seen in isolation. As noted at the start of the chapter, the urban park, including public botanic gardens, has undergone significant change over time as new sets of values have come along. Arguably, the development of an overt marketing orientation in the case of Hagley Park mirrors similar changes that have occurred in other great parks such as Central Park in New York, Regent's Park in London and Stanley Park in Vancouver, where parks are not just seen as local visitor resources but also as tourist resources. Yet, in the case of Hagley Park, as elsewhere, such a role is also likely to open up new management and marketing issues as new sets of contestation arises over exactly what the purpose of a visitor resource such as a park should be and how that then reflects the need of local users as well as the commercial imperatives of tourism.

References

Archives New Zealand (a). Canterbury Provincial Council, Canterbury Association Reserves Ordinance, Session V, No. 2. 1855. Archives Reference: The Ordinances of the Province of Canterbury, New Zealand, Session 1 to Session XXI, Christchurch 1864.

Archives New Zealand (b). Reproduction of Edward Jollie's 1850 map of the proposed city. Department of Lands and Survey, Christchurch. Historical Maps. Archives Reference: CH 765 item 32.

Archives New Zealand (c). 1851 Letter from WG Brittan, Commissioner of Crown Land, to W. Patrick ordering his removal from Hagley Park, where he has been squatting. Outward letterbook, Canterbury Association Land Office. Archives Reference: CH 290, item 5/1 (154).

Archives New Zealand (d). Early lease agreement for depasturing on Hagley Park and the Christchurch Domain, 20 April 1852. Canterbury Association Archives. Archives Reference: CH 290 item 16/1b.

Archives New Zealand (e). Jones, McGlashan and Coy to Secretary for Public Works, Application for lease to depasture animals and fence grazing area, 24 April 1867.

Archives New Zealand (f). Petition to the Provincial Council, 17 March 1868, objecting to the construction of stockyards in Hagley Park. Papers of the Provincial Council. Archives Reference: CH 287 item CP629e/7.

Archives New Zealand (g). 1962 Master Transportation Plan proposal for motorway through Hagley Park, figures 1 & 2. Archives Reference: CH 134 file 8/3/35 – Reserves – Hagley Park 1962–1970.

Archives of New Zealand (h). Report of the Works and Services Committee on the Harper Ave deviation. Tabled 27/4/1970. Christchurch City Council Archives. Archives Reference: CH 380 No 1 Minute Bk, item 128 folio 61351 p'B' 1970.

Archives New Zealand (i) Christchurch Domains Board 10 April 1931, Draft by laws circa 1931 November 31. Archives Reference: CH 134 file 8/3/35 – Reserves – Hagley Park 1929–1933.

Canterbury Development Corporation, Christchurch Canterbury Tourism and Christchurch City Council (2006). *Draft Christchurch Visitor Strategy*. Canterbury Development Corporation, Christchurch Canterbury Tourism and Christchurch City Council, Christchurch, New Zealand.

CCC – Christchurch City Council (2005). *Contextual Historical Overview – Christchurch City*. Christchurch City Council, Christchurch, New Zealand.

CCC – Christchurch City Council (2006a). *Christchurch Botanic Gardens Management Plan, Draft August 2006*. Christchurch City Council, Christchurch, New Zealand.

CCC – Christchurch City Council (2006b). *Hagley Park/Botanic Gardens Master Plan, Draft August 2006*. Christchurch City Council.

CCC – Christchurch City Council (2006c). *Hagley Park Management Plan, Draft August 2006*. Christchurch City Council.

Conway, H. (1991). *People's Parks: The Design and Development of Victorian Parks in Britain*. Cambridge University Press.

Cowan, J. (1910). *Official Record of the New Zealand International Exhibition of Arts and Industries held in Christchurch, 1906–7: A Descriptive and Historical Account*. Government Printer.

Deverson, T. (2001). Canterbury words: language under the Nor'west arch. *NZWords*, **5**, 5–7.

Hadfield, M. (1985). *A History of British Gardening*. Penguin Books.

Hall C.M. (2004). Parks and recreation. In *World Encyclopedia of Environmental History* (S. Krech III, J. R. McNeill and C. Merchant, eds), pp. 978–982. Routledge.

Hall, C. M. and Page, S. J. (2006). *The Geography of Tourism and Recreation: Space, Place and Environment*, 3rd edn. Routledge.

Mitchell, J. H. (2001). *The Wildest Place on Earth: Italian Gardens and the Invention of Wilderness*. Counterpoint.

Taylor, D. (1999). Central Park as a model for social control: urban parks, social class and leisure behaviour in nineteenth century America. *Journal of Leisure Research*, **31**, 426–477.

The Press (1907). 15 April: 8.

Tritenbach, P. (1987). *Botanic Gardens and Parks in New Zealand: An Illustrated Record*. Excellence Press.

Wilson, W. H. (1989). *The City Beautiful Movement*. John Hopkins University Press.

CHAPTER 19

Theme Park Pricing in a New Century: The Central Florida Market Revisited

Bradley M. Braun and Mark D. Soskin

Aims

The aims of this chapter are to:

- discuss the evolution of the Central Florida theme park industry,
- show how the industry has developed strategies to cope with the maturing of their markets,
- investigate how the Central Florida theme park industry has confronted both demand shocks and growing competition from elsewhere, and
- draw lessons for theme park management in Central Florida and elsewhere.

Introduction

Five years ago, we reported (Braun and Soskin, 2003) that the major Central Florida theme parks had at last achieved the enviable stability that rewards successful price coordination and avoidance of price warfare. Competition among the Disney parks, Universal Studios, Busch Gardens in Tampa, and SeaWorld Florida was relegated to non-price dimensions of advertising, development, and investment in new parks and attractions, as well as price discrimination and bundling plans such as multi-day, multi-park, and season passes. Nevertheless, pricing had become synonymous with collusive price discipline: identical one-day admission prices (or nearly identical, in the case of Busch Gardens) and periodic, simultaneous price rises.

But just when all seemed settled in the world's largest theme park destination, the expansion trend (Milman, 2001) in global tourism and especially theme park travel was detoured by a daunting set of new challenges: a series of terrorist attacks, especially 9/11, depressed demand at air-travel destinations in the short term, as well as imposing permanent airport security, time delays, travel inconveniences, and ticket price premiums. The adverse impact on air travel was especially hard on major global tourism destinations that relied heavily on international visitors. Many international travellers cancelled travel plans to the US, owing in part to the new regulatory restrictions initiated following the destruction of the World Trade Center (Tarlow and Santana, 2002). Continued oil price shocks injected further uncertainties to both auto and air travel.

In continuing with the narrative of previous work on this subject, this chapter investigates how the Central Florida industry confronted impressive competition from Las Vegas and other convention venues, as well as exogenous demand shocks. Simultaneously, theme park managers needed strategies to cope with a maturing industry and a destination region that may have been in decline.

This chapter begins by summarizing and putting into perspective the Central Florida theme park industry as it evolved through to the beginning of 2001. Next, we replicate for comparison purposes the price analysis conducted in our previous research. The relative incidence of price changes and inter-firm pricing patterns will allow us to assess how successful efforts of the theme park industry have been in price stability and collusive price coordination in this four-firm oligopoly. Then, a demand model is fit against the data to estimate the price, cross, and income elasticities and to identify the shifting relationships among the four parks.

Central Florida theme park management in their development stages

In the formative days of the Central Florida theme park industry, the dominant firm, Walt Disney World (WDW), had its way with a competitive fringe of price followers. The competing parks required price discounting to compensate for Disney's financial and name brand advantages. The hypothesis of a dominant firm and an industry without price competition was supported by results of a regression model on prices for WDW and its primary rivals (Braun et al., 1992).

The 1980s evidenced a period of steady growth in attendance, with theme park prices increasing faster than inflation. In the 1980s, WDW's entrance price rose at a compound annual rate of 12.1 per cent. WDW's pricing strategy provided an umbrella for similar price hikes at rival parks. SeaWorld raised prices at an annual average rate of more than 11 per cent. Busch Gardens, hampered by its distance from WDW, was only able to raise prices at an annual rate of 9.5 per cent.

In fact, WDW succeeded in widening the price margin over its rivals through-out the 1980s (see Figure 19.1). Busch Gardens saw its relative price erode the most, from a 10 per cent price gap in 1983 to 30 per cent in 1990. SeaWorld and Cypress Gardens also saw their prices lose ground to WDW. Because this widening price margin occurred even before the external market shocks, the dif-ficulty of matching costly expansions and diversifications by the industry leader must have been the primary cause. Viewed as inferior substitutes for WDW, competing parks tempered price increases. In addition, corporate cash flow problems necessitated an aggressive price strategy to restore market share.

Because of its unique market advantages, WDW was able to retain industry dominance while continuing to command a premium price. The land holdings Disney acquired in the 1960s spatially insulated WDW from subsequent entrants. Its rivals did not match a relentless wave of expansion and diversifica-tion by WDW. Disney invested heavily in new attractions, transportation, shops, hotels, restaurants, clubs, and water parks. Multi-day discount pricing helped to keep visitors at WDW, limiting the residual market available to rivals.

During the 1980s, WDW was able to ignore the individual actions of its rivals. The only way the competitive fringe could attract customers away from WDW was by charging lower prices. WDW was free to fine-tune its prices to maintain optimal profits, consistent with its position as the dom-inant price leader. From 1982 to 1990, Disney raised prices in 20 of the 32 quar-ters. Rival parks had equally frequent price changes, but followed WDW's price increases with a significant lag (Braun *et al.*, 1992).

Changes in Central Florida theme park behaviour in the early 1990s

By the early 1990s, changes in industry structure and market conditions began to exert dramatic effects on pricing behaviour. The lagged response of follower-ship behaviour finally broke down, replaced by pricing strategies resembling parallel behaviour once prevalent in the cigarette, steel, and auto industries.

In Braun and Soskin (1999), we showed that significant transformations in the early 1990s had radically altered the Central Florida theme park industry. It was clear that the days of rapid growth in park attendance were over and the industry entered a mature industry stage characterized by slower attendance growth, a higher proportion of return visitors, and greater competition nation-ally and globally. Furthermore, as happens in all mature markets, consolidation of the industry occurred as the largest rival parks combined under multi-national firm management. Anheuser Busch carried out a series of acquisitions to complete a successful horizontal merger of WDW's three largest rivals (Busch Gardens, SeaWorld, and Cypress Gardens). Busch then mobilized its financial resources, management experience, and park development expertise to match Disney's $10 billion investment in Central Florida.

Meanwhile, a major Disney rival from the Pacific coast, Universal Studios, established a substantial presence in Central Florida. The entry of Universal

Studios was the first major entrant since SeaWorld, 10 years earlier. Universal entered with a replicated set of market-proven attractions from its thriving southern California parent site. Universal also drew upon scale economies to diversify their product mix into high-tech rides. When technical delays threatened its reputation for quality, Universal redoubled its investment. The high-sunk costs demonstrated its commitment to the Central Florida theme park market. In addition, Universal exploited economies of scope derived from complementarities in movies and TV production. The entry of Universal Studios had an immediate effect on local labour markets and theme park prices.

Universal attacked two previously unexploited vulnerabilities of WDW. First, WDW had always enjoyed its strongest appeal among families with younger children. Thus, the under 35-year-old crowd presented a large market niche attracted by high-tech thrill rides and more sophisticated attractions. Secondly, WDW's portfolio had expanded into a wide range of themes, including amusements and rides, water parks, a world's fair, nightclubs, and nature settings. Although this traditional brand proliferation strategy was effective in limiting the market shares of its existing Florida rivals, WDW was late to recognize the dangers from a potential entrant with deep pockets. From a game theory perspective, if a market niche is large enough for only one firm to enjoy economic profits, a pre-emptive strategy of committing large investments irrevocably in that niche provides a credible signal to deter other firms from entry (Dixit, 1980). Disney exploited its regional presence to be the first to open a Central Florida movie themed attraction, Disney–MGM Studios. However, they were too late to forestall Universal's entry. Because of the enormous capital commitments already made, Universal was locked into the Florida market.

Rival entry had occurred before, when WDW underestimated the size of the profitable water parks and nightclub market niches. But with Universal's entry, WDW was forced, for the first time, to play a technological catch-up game against a well-healed rival. As a result, Universal became the only Florida theme park consistently to match WDW's premium pricing strategy, even in the soft market of the early 1990s. Disney's price leader position was clearly being challenged.

Beyond these structural changes, broader market factors may also have affected the Central Florida theme park industry. The industry appeared to be entering the mature phase of its product life cycle, and a consequent levelling of its customer base (Scherer and Ross, 1989).

A maturing tourism industry, like their durable goods counterpart, must obtain an increasing share of business from repeat customers (Braun and Milman, 1994). Attracting repeat business requires potential guests to be convinced that previous visits are inferior substitutes for vacation experiences at the new and improved parks. For this strategy to be effective, new and more exciting rides, attractions, and entire parks must be designed and constructed. For example, Disney opened its Animal Kingdom in 1998, which was closely followed by the opening of Universal's Islands of Adventure. This form of non-price competition involves high-sunk costs as parks race to bring state-of-the-art designs on line. Without a proven market demand, this investment commitment raises the stakes by increasing the chance for a runaway product-proliferation arms race and the possibility of a game-of-ruin, single-victor scenario. It also has the side effect of cannibalizing the customer base. For example, in a study of local visitors to Central Florida theme parks, Milman (2001) could find no relationship between admission price consciousness and the frequency of visits. Throughout the 1980s and 1990s, Central Florida boomed as the world leader in terms of its number of visitors and hotel rooms. As domestic highway visitation peaked, WDW maintained market growth by successfully tapping into an expanding international market. By early 1990, both auto and air arrivals to Florida stagnated as a result of the Gulf War and worldwide recession. At the same time, competition for tourist dollars was expanding into cruises and all-inclusive resorts, both of which Disney later became a major player. Also, competition intensified for WDW's brand of wholesome, 'family-style' vacation. Massive investment by hotels in Las Vegas was focused on merging casino operations with a new version of the theme park model. With changes to industry structure and the weaker market of the 1990s, the pressure on pricing discipline intensified. The pressure was sufficient to elicit more aggressive and independent pricing conduct, thus weakening the leadership–followership behaviour observed in the 1980s.

Three developments in pricing patterns provide evidence that strategic behaviour in the Central Florida theme park industry had changed substantially in the 1990s. The growth rate of park admission prices slowed substantially, prices converged, and the frequency of price changes has fallen. Despite costly upgrades and expansions, the growth in prices slowed dramatically. From 1990 through 1995, the annual average rate of price escalation was less than 7 per cent at each of the major theme parks. At WDW, prices rose only 3 per cent, barely one-fourth that of the previous decade. The result was a steady narrowing of the price gap between Disney and the other parks.

As described by Braun and Soskin (1999), prices were observed nearly to converge by 1993. Universal reached price parity with WDW, and SeaWorld narrowed its price margin to within 5 per cent of WDW. Although Disney responded briefly with an aggressive price cut, it quickly resumed matching Universal's price. It was also noted in the 1999 study that the Central Florida theme park industry experienced a statistically significant increase in price stability following the 1990 opening of Universal Studios, Florida. That paper concluded that WDW and Universal had begun to act as co-market leaders that contemporaneously matched increasingly infrequent price changes. We speculated that the dominant-firm price leadership behaviour of the 1980 had been replaced, perhaps permanently, by a classic case of collusive oligopoly pricing.

Changing behaviour leading into the new century

Upon revisiting the industry later (Braun and Soskin, 2003), the authors confirmed that the coordinated pricing behaviour was clearly continuing into the twenty-first century. In addition, the newer evidence strongly indicates that the Central Florida theme park industry has moved toward an even greater degree of cooperation and inclusiveness among the major parks. Table 19.1 supports the authors' previous research contention that price changes remained at least as rare during the succeeding six years as they had become since the entry of Universal at the beginning of the 1990s. Price adjustments (nearly all of them increases) continued to average only about one in every ten months. This reticence to alter prices is consistent with recognized inter-dependence, while operating under oligopolistic uncertainties (Cecchetti, 1986). While dominant price leaders freely respond to changes in costs or demand, fear of misinterpreted market signals may deter oligopolists from initiating most price changes.

Moreover, price coordination became substantially more successful. Nearly four-fifths of the months from March 1995 through February 2001 witnessed no price changes by any of the four major parks (Table 19.2). This represented

Table 19.1 Prices as or more stable despite shocks and competitive pressure since 2001

Price stability (major Central Florida Theme Park)	Price changes (per cent of months)		
	Jan. 1990– Feb. 1995	Mar. 1995– Feb. 2001	Mar. 2001– Mar. 2007
Disney	13	10	8
Universal Studios	8	10	10
SeaWorld	15	13	10
Busch Gardens	10	8	8
Mean for four major parks	11	10	9

Table 19.2 Major theme parks more successful recently in coordinating price changes

Price change coordination (number of parks)	Relative frequency (per cent of months)		
	Jan. 1990– Feb. 1995	Mar. 1995– Feb. 2001	Mar. 2001– Mar. 2007
No parks changed price	66	79	82
One or two parks changed price	32	12	12
Three or all four parks changed price	2	8	5

a sizable increase over the two-thirds of months experiencing no price changes during the first half of the 1990s. By contrast, industry disharmony or independent behaviour manifested itself in price changes by some parks and not others. We also report a dramatic decline in this type of industry pricing behaviour (Table 19.2). The incidence of only one or two parks changing prices fell from about one-third to one-eighth of the months. Finally, nearly two-thirds of price changes in the later 1990s occurred in concert with price changes by at least two other parks in the same months. As a result, only 8 per cent of the months contained the bulk of all price changes.

As industries move toward stronger collusive behaviour, variable pricing mechanisms often emerge to orchestrate cooperative actions. As already mentioned, one such mechanism is infrequent in price changes. However, market pressures and inflation eventually make price modifications necessary. The question is how to alert rival parks of a price change so as not to cause misunderstandings that could trigger a mutually destructive price war. One common device is to reserve price changes for specific times of the year. The auto industry, for example, raises prices each fall when it launches new models. During the period 1990–1995 (Figure 19.1), price changes occurred at least once in every month except October. But by the second half of the 1990s, the Central Florida theme park industry appears to have settled on a handful of months to alter its prices. While price changes were completely absent in five of the months (February, July through September, and November),

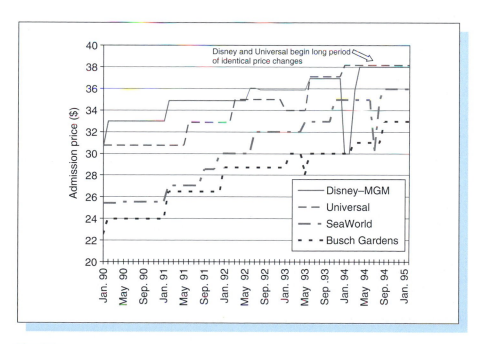

Figure 19.1
Little price coordination after Universal's entry until the middle of the 1990s

January and March became the favourite months for orchestrating broad industry prices hikes.

Price coordination also broadened and became firmly entrenched during the late 1990s. With the exception of the first quarter of 1994, Disney and Universal prices were within 25 cents of each other from June 1993 through February 1995. However, their prices were never identical until they both raised admission prices to $39.22 in March 1995. From that month on, the two parks mimicked one another's prices through five subsequent price hikes (Figure 19.2). Price increases were duplicated the following two months of March to $40.81 in 1996 and $42.14 in 1997. A lockstep ratcheting-up of prices thereafter recalls the heyday of cigarette pricing parallelism during the 1930s.

Some of this price regimentation was extended to include the other two theme park giants in Central Florida. SeaWorld had poured enormous amounts of capital and advertising in an attempt to attain price parity. They narrowed their price to slightly more than $2.00 below Disney and Universal in September 1994. In May 1995, they shaved the price gap to only about $1.25. This gap was maintained for the next 18 months, but with a submissive overture to the pricing regime created by Disney and Universal, SeaWorld chose to raise prices in 1996 and 1997 in the same month that Disney and Universal did. Previous price moves by SeaWorld had all occurred at different times than those of its two biggest rivals. Having matched the timing of their price changes, SeaWorld made its final move by replicating the industry

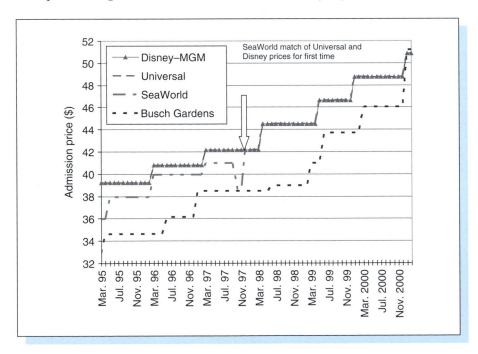

Figure 19.2
Progressively more price coordination through the beginning of the century

leaders in price in December 1997, and again the following April when all three proceeded with a matching price hike. It was clear that a collusive tri-opoly had been established in Central Florida. February 2001 marked the 39th consecutive month of identical pricing by these three theme parks.

Until then, Busch Gardens seemed to be the odd park out, despite owning two other parks in the market. Pricing independence could be anticipated by its relatively remote location from tourists arriving by air into Orlando, combined with access to Florida's distinctive west-coast tourism market. Yet Busch was heavily promoting its Tampa park in the Orlando media and bundling their parks with extended and discounted admission prices. As the convergence and coordination of pricing firmed up among the other three major parks, it was predictable that Busch would not be willing to remain aloof. But Busch Gardens had a larger price gap than SeaWorld to make up. As recently as February 2000, Busch Gardens was still charging $5.00 less than its three main rivals. The following month, a price increase cut this margin to under $3.00. Busch Gardens, which had never timed its price hikes to coincide with the other parks, made sure that its next one did – and virtually duplicated the new price of Disney, Universal, and SeaWorld. Although it was not possible to conclude that a four-firm, collusive oligopoly was now in force, the Central Florida theme park industry definitely operated in a much more orchestrated environment than in the days when Disney did what pleased and left its competitors to scramble for the crumbs.

Over the 1990s, Busch Gardens raised its prices $8.00 more than Disney (an annual increase of 7.4 per cent) in order to reach pricing parity by the beginning of this century. SeaWorld increased prices 6.3 per cent per year on average to make up its $5.00 initial deficiency from the beginning of the 1990s. By comparison, Universal and Disney each averaged a smaller, but still respectable 4.6 per cent annual price increase over that same period. It remains to be seen whether these two Busch-owned parks can generate sufficient visitation rates without discounting. The competitive structure determines whether such a strategy can succeed. A further constraint is the depth of Busch's pockets; the question is whether its pockets are deep enough to maintain investments in attractions and promotions to fend off pressures to cut prices.

The smaller parks still held onto a modest share of the theme park market in Central Florida. The largest of these are Cypress Gardens and the WetN'Wild water park. In the 1990s, Cypress Gardens charged about three-fourths of Disney's admission price, which slipped to under two-thirds by 2001. WetN'Wild prices were even lower, averaging 60 per cent of Disney's. Both of these second-tier parks relied on whole-dollar price hikes, with prices ending in $0.95. As a result of this pricing device, Cypress Gardens and WetN'Wild needed to change prices only about once in a year, as infrequently as their bigger rivals. Two-tiered stable pricing thus extended across the industry. Cypress Gardens was dissuaded from short-term market advantage of cutting prices, for they must be concerned about their smaller rival parks and Disney's new animal-nature theme park, Animal Kingdom. Eventually, Cypress Gardens was unable to keep up with the billion dollar investment budgets of the four majors, and shut down operations for a brief period early in the 2000s. Thus, these intermediate-sized single-themed parks had to content themselves with drawing away tourists from those attractions for day trips at a lower admission price. The lesson, then, is that managers in a concentrated market have less power to use pricing, which means that other strategies must be employed. The appropriate strategy is dictated by the competitive structure.

Changes in pricing behaviour since 2001 and overall demand analysis

As the new century dawned, a healthy, mature industry in Central Florida was rocked by major global economic shocks and powerful outside competition that threatened the pre-eminent position of this king of theme park destinations. The new realities of terrorism prompted restrictive travel regulations and reticence by traditional theme park visitors. Moreover, the trend in declining convention bookings combined with overbuilding by the convention centre hubs of Chicago, Atlanta, and Las Vegas. Speaking of Las Vegas, they emptied their wallets to the tune of billions in new family-friendly, themed hotels in attempts to lure away market share from Disney and Universal, Florida. Despite continued heavy reinvestment by Universal in an adjacent new park and by Disney, SeaWorld, and Universal in new high-tech attractions, marketing, and unprecedented discount ticket plans, substantial changes transformed the Central Florida theme park industry back to a two-firm dominated market.

Besides the two lessons of consolidation and decreased power to use a pricing strategy as indicted by the statistical price analysis, additional insights may be gleaned from performing a demand analysis on the price, cross-price, and income elasticities. That demand analysis is capable of revealing how Central Florida theme parks fit into the overall national and global market for economic bundles of vacation consumption.

The demand analysis was conducted for data over a 13-year period, 1993–2005. All variables (Table 19.3) were deflated by the overall consumer price index (CPI) to constant dollar terms and then converted to natural logs so that the fitted regression coefficients would estimate elasticities. The log-linear model contains the relevant components of a demand function, such as income and the prices of primary substitutes and complements confronting each potential theme park visitor in the market. Specifically, combined attendance at Disney's Central Florida theme parks was regressed on the prices charged by the three theme park competitors, personal disposable incomes per capita and prices of the related goods and services (those being petrol, air travel, and lodging).

Lastly, the model needed to account for sizable but continually shifting tourism seasonality. In the Central Florida theme park market, domestic tourism is higher around holidays, winter 'snow bird' months and vacations travel periods, while international tourism peaks in the late summer and the convention travel season is busiest in the early fall. Therefore, an annually lagged dependent variable (Disney attendance lagged 12 months) was added to the

Table 19.3 Variable definitions and sources for demand analysis regression

Variable	Description
Disney attendance	Disney Florida combined attendance
Disney price	1-day admission USD, deflated to 1982–84 price by US CPI
Busch price	1-day admission USD, deflated to 1982–84 price by US CPI
Universal price	1-day admission USD, deflated to 1982–84 price by US CPI
SeaWorld price	1-day admission USD, deflated to 1982–84 price by US CPI
Per capita disposable income	Real per capita disposable personal income USD (BEA, quarterly)
Petrol price	Petrol of regular USD, deflated to 1982–84 price by US CPI
Airfares	US price index (BLS, monthly) deflated by CPI 1982–84
Lodging prices	US price index (BLS, monthly), deflated by US CPI 1982–84
Disney attendance 1-year lag	12-month lagged dependent variable

model to control for variation in attendance due solely to seasonal factors present during the corresponding month of adjacent years.

The fitted regression equation is the following:

$$
\begin{aligned}
\text{Disney Attendance} = {} & -3.0 - 0.38 \,(\text{Disney price}) + 0.15 \,(\text{Busch price}) \\
& - 1.30 \,(\text{Universal price}) + 0.83 \,(\text{Sea World price}) \\
& + 0.63 \,(\text{Per capita disposable income}) \\
& - 0.12 \,(\text{Petrol price}) - 0.47 \,(\text{Airfares}) \\
& + 0.41 \,(\text{Lodging prices}) \\
& + 0.73 \,(\text{Disney attendance lagged 1-year})
\end{aligned}
$$

All but two variables were significant at the 0.01 level for two-sided tests. The two exceptions were Income, which was significant at the 0.05 level, and Bush Garden prices, which was not significant ($p = 0.29$) (see Table 19.4). The adjusted R^2 was 88.5 per cent.

Table 19.4 Regression results of logarithmic model

Predictor	Elasticity coefficient	Standard error	*t*-ratio	*p*-value
Constant	−3.0	2.2	−1.33	0.19
Disney price	−0.38**	0.12	−3.09	0.002
Busch price	0.15	0.14	1.07	0.29
Universal price	−1.30**	0.22	−5.90	0.000
SeaWorld price	0.83**	0.16	5.21	0.000
Per capital disposable income	0.63**	0.30	2.09	0.038
Petrol price	0.12**	0.04	3.40	0.001
Airfares	−0.47**	0.11	−4.35	0.000
Lodging prices	−0.41**	0.09	4.30	0.000
Disney attendance 1-year lag	0.73**	0.07	10.2	0.000

Note: Standard error = 0.045; Adjusted R^2 = 88.5%.
*Significant at 0.05 level.
**Significant at 0.01 level.

The elasticities for the prices charged by Disney's competitors allow us to determine the relationships among theme parks in the Central Florida area. Coefficient signs and magnitudes for the statistically significant variables in the demand model led to quite dramatic conclusions about the demand conditions confronting this market. First, the price elasticity of 0.38 indicates that Disney park attendance demand is inelastic to its own admission price. That implies that Disney has developed a sufficiently strong market position and brand image to lose only 2 per cent in sales for each price 5 per cent price hike. That puts Disney in the enviable position of knowing its revenues are guaranteed to rise each time it elevates its prices faster than inflation. Knowing that, Universal will usually match the magnitude and timing of Disney price increases (and vice versa) and protect both from market share erosions in the Central Florida theme park industry. Moreover, the strong and continued loyalty to their product insulates them from any substantial reservation cancellation or visitor substitution over to nearby parks.

SeaWorld prices did exercise a significant effect on Disney attendance and the results indicate that a strong substitution relationship exists. The estimated elasticity of 0.83 translates to mean that a 6 per cent increase (above inflation) in

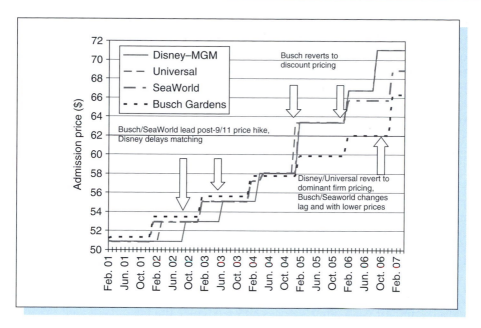

Figure 19.3
Global competition, 9/11 strain coordination and prompt a return to Disney–Universal dominance

SeaWorld's admission price will be associated on average with a 5 per cent rise in Disney attendance, other things being equal. One should note that this result does not necessarily suggest that SeaWorld is somehow the primary focus of tourists and convention visitors. Instead, it is more reasonable to interpret this relationship to take its most common form in visitors substituting more days at Disney parks (thus raising attendance days) if SeaWorld hikes its prices.

By contrast, Busch's other Central Florida major theme park, Busch Gardens, had the only price not significantly related to Disney attendance. Apparently, its weaker brand name and distance from the other three parks (a 90-minute drive west of Orlando in Tampa) combine to make Busch Gardens too weak a substitute to register any significant impact on Disney's gate receipts. This result is consistent with our observations of only intermittent success in trying to match the higher prices at Disney and Universal, or even rarer success to act as a price leader. Evidently, Bush Gardens would require further substantial investment in creating a more diverse and distinctive portfolio of attractions before the typical visitor views it as anything other than an optional side trip. A strong and unique brand image may also be required. For all but 4 of the 13 years (namely, 2001–2004), Busch Gardens prices marched to an independent drummer, and a discount one at that (see Figures 19.1–19.3). One lesson for park managers is that the more distant regional attraction from the centre of tourist activity, the more need to depend on lower prices (Fodness and Milner, 1992).

On the other hand, the analysis indicates that Universal is an unusually powerful complement to Disney. This complementary relationship is a consequence of Universal's much greater appeal to teens and Generation Y (young unmarried), while Disney largely controls the pre-teen and older demographic bookends of the market. Because the two theme parks' mix of attractions are targeted at different age groups, family groups, which commonly contain both types, will want to visit both Universal as well as Disney parks during their stay. The result is that Universal, unlike SeaWorld, acts as a complementary good, which visitors to Central Florida will consume along with Disney parks to obtain a satisfactory theme park experience for all members of the family.

The significant and large magnitude of this cross-price elasticity, −1.30, means that it would require a 5 per cent *cut* (below inflation) in Universal admission price to increase Disney attendance by 6.5 per cent on average, other things being equal. Conversely, if Universal raises its park prices substantially faster than inflation while Disney does not, Disney attendance will suffer on average because potential visitors consider their travel costs based on the combined park admission prices for their entire family. This large, complementary relationship provides another reason for Disney and Universal to closely monitor each other's prices and recognize the benefits of tacit pricing coordination. In the 1990s, Disney and Universal attempted to make substantial inroads in the core attractions of each other's parks, rides, and venues.

The heavy cost and disappointing record of such direct competition apparently caused a *modus vivendi* to evolve between the two price co-leaders. This recognition of mutually superior core competencies (Fodness and Milner, 1992) has generated the observed complementarity. As a consequence, Universal Studios was the first theme park with deep enough pockets and a strong brand name to challenge Disney's dominance in Florida (Braun and Soskin, 1999). Disney was therefore forced to accommodate Universal's market entry in 1990 by allowing the latter to share price leadership. By the mid-1990s, both Universal and Disney were routinely charging identical admission rates and making price changes in unison.

The impact of demographic factors, typically associated with travel demand on theme park demand, is also quite informative. The traditional family focus of Disney theme parks, with their stroller-friendly environs and youth-targeted marketing campaign, still made Disney the most popular destination for families with young children. The lesson here is that major theme parks will thrive as long as there is healthy growth in income of the target market. However, the income elasticity estimate was only 0.63, indicating that Disney theme park visits can no longer be considered a luxury. As real incomes have risen, the appeal to middle-income families for a typical week-long trip to Central Florida theme parks does not rank among luxury travel, such as a winter ski trip in Aspen or a Hawaiian vacation. As with other tourism meccas of previous eras, such as Atlantic City and Saratoga Springs, perhaps Central Florida as a vacation destination has passed its peak. It is also possible that the age of the theme park may be entering a secular decline in the same way world's fairs and expositions lost favour three decades ago.

Florida theme parks are both auto and air destinations, so factors that raise travel costs will adversely impact Disney's attendance. The negative and significant coefficients on airfare and petrol prices (i.e. cross elasticities of -0.47 and -0.12, respectively) support this contention. Specifically, a 10 per cent rise in airfares will translate to a nearly 5 per cent attendance decline at Disney parks. However, it would require a four-fold greater increase in petrol prices, over 40 per cent hike, to achieve the same attendance declines. The smaller sensitivity of auto visitors to petrol price fluctuations is due to the fact that petrol purchases constitute a small portion of highway vacation travel costs. Vehicle depreciation dominates in the cases of sport utility vehicles, recreational vehicles, and luxury touring cars, which is a major fixed cost of this travel market. The lesson here is that theme parks must strive for a diverse transportation mix that is not too dependent on any single mode of arrival. Recent large and erratic petrol price fluctuation and the post-9/11 security fees added to airline prices support the position that parks need to attract a balanced portfolio of travel modes. Fortunately for Central Florida theme parks, they remain one of the most balanced air–auto destinations in the world.

The final component of the model is national lodging prices. The cost of accommodations constitutes a sizable share of family vacation and convention visitor spending. When hotel and motel prices are relatively high, Disney parks have an additional appeal. The cost of lodging in Orlando is among the lowest of any major metropolitan area, so budget-conscious travellers will tend to look more favourably toward visiting WDW. Furthermore, travel surveys consistently report that a large portion of Florida visitors stay with friends and relatives rather than paying for their accommodations. Central Florida's population has passed 3.5 million and grows even larger during peak tourist months when 'snowbirds' return for their annual winter residence in Florida. The seasonal and permanent residents provide a ready supply of alternative free lodging to Disney's theme park visitors. The model lends strong support to the substitute relationship that national lodging price plays. The relatively large positive cross-price elasticity (0.41) implies that a 10 per cent real price increase in average US lodging prices translates into a 4 per cent increase in Disney attendance.

Conclusion

Central Florida's experience provides a number of lessons to other theme park managers. First and foremost, long-established theme parks in mature destinations do not necessarily have to yield to stagnating or declining attendance and discount pricing. The parks owned by Disney and Universal have taken advantage of their strong global brand image, deep pockets, and commitment to continual investment in cutting-edge attractions that address shifting tastes and demographic trends. This combination of aggressive and proactive management has allowed Disney and Universal to recover rapidly from the unprecedented economic shocks to international tourist destinations from counter-terrorism restrictions and price hikes following the World Trade

Center attacks. The best demonstration of their success in this strategy is shown in Figure 19.4, where Disney (and its nearly identically price rival, Universal) were able to raise prices consistently faster that inflation despite stronger global competition, the adverse impact of terrorism on travel, and host of other exogenous factors.

The flip side of this lesson is that major theme parks with less advantageous locations and less aggressive reinvestment strategies, like Busch Gardens in Tampa, are easily susceptible to attendance declines, which eventually force substantial price cuts. It remains a question as to which of these two fates will befall the more distinctively branded and centrally located SeaWorld, the other Busch-owned Central Florida theme park. In the years immediately following 9/11, SeaWorld needed to offer increasingly generous multi-park and multi-day discount ticket plans to continue matching the high admission prices of co-leaders Disney and Universal. In 2006, despite major investments in new attractions, SeaWorld – like its partner Busch Gardens – yielded to reduced demand that forced it to set prices explicitly below the market leaders. Later that year, SeaWorld delayed matching the timing of the leaders' price hike and the price gap increased further at the beginning of 2007 (though still only half the $5 gap of Busch Gardens).

The above conclusions suggest a second lesson for major theme park managers located in long-established destinations. Although it may still be possible that further commitment of capital by Busch management would allow SeaWorld to resume its role among the price leaders, that outcome is by no means certain. Busch management may find greater return on its investment

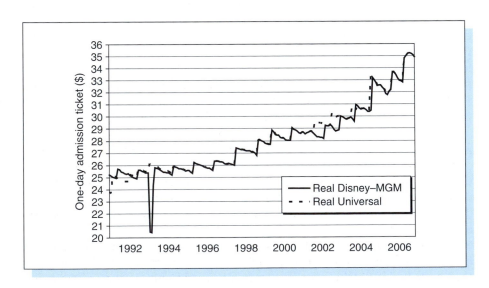

Figure 19.4
Disney–Universal prices constant (1982–84 US$) nearly flat (1.1% annually) through 1998, but rose 3.4% annually thereafter

elsewhere, rather than sinking even more capital in what already may be a saturated market in a global destination that could have past its historical peak.

The third lesson for theme park managers is the strategic effectiveness of 'coopetition', that is, cooperating on shared market interests while maintaining competitive aggressiveness in product development, promotion, and innovative organizational methods. The return of the Central Florida theme park industry to a duopoly price leadership structure may reflect successful division of a destination market among complementary rivals. Disney and Universal act as if they have reached a point of mutual recognition that each enjoys unique core competencies and brand allegiance for distinct portions of the traveller demographics. Consequently, the new century was marked by reduced resources dedicated primarily at their largely unproductive attempts to gain market shares at the expense of the other. Instead, successful price coordination was followed by greater coordination at vanquishing outside threats to their common interests. This serves to protect Central Florida's tourism and convention market from Las Vegas, which was a major competitive challenger. It also serves in restoring Central Florida as an air and auto destination nationally and, in the longer run, globally.

If the Central Florida experience is any guide, managers of theme parks can expect a natural product life cycle to occur in their regional market (Baum, 1998; Karplus and Krakover, 2005). Because attendance is sensitive to both petrol and airfare price changes, it would be wise for managers to build a strong regional customer base that is not reliant on visitors who travel by any single mode of transport. Managers should be supportive of policies that encourage hotel and convention centre development, keeping the price of lodging and bed taxes at a competitive level overall.

References

Baum T. (1998). Taking the exit route: extending the tourism area life cycle model. *Current Issues in Tourism*, **1**, 167–175.

Braun, B. M. and Milman, A. (1994). Demand relations in the Central Florida theme park industry. *Annals of Tourism Research*, **21**, 150–153.

Braun, B. M. and Soskin, M. (1999). Competitive strategies in the Central Florida theme park industry. *Annals of Tourism Research*, **26**, 438–442.

Braun, B. M. and Soskin, M. (2003). Theme park pricing strategies: the case of Central Florida. In *Managing Visitor Attractions: New Directions* (A. Fyall, B. Garrod and A. Leask, eds), pp. 220–235. Elsevier/Butterworth-Heinemann.

Braun, B. M., Soskin, M. and Cernicky, M. (1992). Central Florida theme park pricing: following the mouse. *Annals of Tourism Research*, **19**, 131–136.

Cecchetti, S. (1986). The frequency of price adjustments: a study of the newsstand prices of magazines. *Journal of Econometrics*, **31**, 255–274.

Dixit, A. (1980). The role of investment in entry deterrence. *Economic Journal*, **90**, 95–106.

Fodness, D. D. and Milner, L. M. (1992). A perceptual mapping approach to theme park visitor segmentation. *Tourism Management*, **13**, 95–101.

Karplus, Y. and Krakover S. (2005). Stochastic multivariable approach to modelling tourism area life cycles. *Tourism and Hospitality Research*, **5**, 235–253.

Milman, A. (2001). The future of the theme park and attraction industry: a management perspective. *Journal of Travel Research*, **40**, 139–147.

Scherer, F. M. and Ross, D. (1989). *Industrial Market Structure and Economic Performance*. Houghton Mifflin.

Tarlow, P. and Santana, G. (2002). Providing safety for tourists: a study of a selected sample of tourist destinations in the United States and Brazil. *Journal of Travel Research*, **40**, 424–431.

CHAPTER 20
• • • •

Marketing Visitor Attractions: A Collaborative Approach

Alan Fyall

Aims

This chapter outlines a variety of approaches to the collaborative management and marketing of visitor attractions. Given the increasingly
competitive environment in which many visitor attractions now find
themselves, effective collaboration may make the difference between
success and failure (Fyall and Garrod, 2005). In particular, collaborative
strategies offer a potential solution to problems and challenges too large
or complex for individual attractions to conduct in isolation.
   The specific aims of this chapter are to:

- outline the conditions in the visitor attractions sector which encourage a collaborative approach to management and marketing,
- discuss the advantages and disadvantages of collaboration,
- identify those situations where collaborative strategies are appropriate and desirable,
- introduce a set of guiding principles for effective collaboration, and
- discuss the feasibility and constraints of collaboration with reference
  to a specific case example.

Introduction

Although there are a number of encouraging signs that attendances at many
attractions have increased substantially in recent years, it is clear that there
remains a wide discrepancy between those attractions succeeding and those

that have encountered difficult times. With regard to attendances at attractions in the UK, attraction attendances in England grew by 1 per cent between 2004 and 2005 while they recorded a slight decrease of 0.5 per cent in 2005 (VisitBritain, 2006). Gardens showed the biggest increase in visitor numbers with a jump in attendance of 8 per cent, while many other outdoor and rural attractions also recorded healthy increases, primarily because of the weather. Beyond England, Northern Ireland recorded an increase in attendances of 3 per cent between 2004 and 2005 (Northern Ireland Tourist Board, 2006), while a 1.1 per cent increase was recorded in Wales (Visit Wales, 2006) and a 2.7 per cent increase recorded in Scotland, albeit for the period January–July 2006 (VisitScotland, 2006). Nationwide, the Association of Leading Visitor Attractions (ALVA) report a healthy 2006 all round, although they continue to argue that support for the country's attractions industry is still required if they are going to be able to compete globally (ALVA, 2007).

Despite the above promising trends, however, for most attractions – and most notably for small attractions – competition is tight with very few able to hold their own in the market by working in complete isolation. Although there are many reasons for this, the increasing availability of 'no-frills' flights allowing highly cost-effective travel across Europe remains one of the principal drivers for change. Not only does this enhance the level of competition but it also introduces new regional and overseas competition to local providers, as it can change quite drastically the nature and volume of the origin markets of overseas visitors. In the context of the UK, the influx of visitors from Eastern Europe, Russia, China and India is likely to have a major impact on the future pattern of visitation trends at many attractions, most notably in the major destinations such as London and Edinburgh. However, despite some healthy rises in demand being recorded, the still widely acknowledged oversupply of attractions is likely to ensure that all attractions are set to continue to face a challenging future. Further, with the transformation in the geography and typology of visitor attractions more generally (see endnote; Stevens, 2000), the visitor attractions sector arguably needs to adopt a more strategic approach to managing its activities if it is to have a lasting future. The challenges are considerable. For example:

- although the overall number of visits to attractions in England is encouraging, the average number of visits per attraction is declining,
- competition both from within and outside the visitor attractions sector is intense, with considerable additional pressure on people's leisure time,
- consumer expectations continue to rise,
- funding from Lottery and EU sources continues to stimulate the development of new attractions, while existing, predominantly private-sector attractions struggle to raise funds, and
- privately owned attractions continue to experience the displacement effects of the 'free-admissions' policy to the national museums and galleries.

Not only are these challenges likely to impact on the quality of the visitor experience, they also determine the very long-run survival of existing and new attractions, most evidently those in the private sector. The challenges identified here were initially discussed in much greater depth in the report by the English Tourism Council (now Visit Britain), *Action for Attractions*, which provided an extensive overview of the sector (ETC, 2000). The report outlined a *Framework for Action*, which provided a comprehensive set of strategic objectives and recommendations for the visitor attractions sector in England. Ten key areas were identified for attention. These included market measurement, increasing visitor satisfaction, improving attraction management skills, benchmarking, quality, funding and investment, taxation, development and planning. While these were, and continue to be, highly pertinent issues to the future development of the visitor attractions sector, this chapter focuses on the final 'strategic' area deemed to be of future importance: that of improving cooperation and coordination between attractions. While designed specifically for visitor attractions in England, the objectives and recommendations set out by the former ETC were, and continue to be, equally valid for attractions across the UK, and indeed throughout the world. A study conducted in Scotland outlined a number of recommendations for visitor attractions which were consistent with the findings of the former ETC's report (Fyall *et al.*, 2001). These included the need to:

- Consider the adoption of collaborative marketing strategies with a view to the collective creation, branding and theming of local, regional and national attractions to make best use of limited resources and limited markets, especially in the peripheral areas of the country.
- Investigate the potential for collaborative marketing relationships with other tourism sectors to facilitate the collective creation and development of destinations.
- Work in collaboration with the other sectors of the tourism industry in an attempt to coordinate all-year-round interest in the wider Scottish tourism product to address the problem of 'seasonality'.
- Investigate the viability of joint-ticketing initiatives and marketing consortia membership.

The need to move forward and begin to adopt some of the above recommendations is perhaps best demonstrated by the significant success of attractive discount attraction entry pass schemes that have become commonplace in many destinations across the world. Although a relatively simple concept, collaborative 'discount cards' are a highly effective means of bringing together a whole host of attractions, restaurants and hotels in a truly holistic destination package. While *CityPass* is available in San Francisco, New York, Boston and Philadelphia, among others, *Go Cards* are available in the likes of Orlando, Chicago, Seattle and again, Boston. The *Go Boston Card* includes unlimited free admission to more than 70 attractions, express entry at select attractions, free visitor guides and generous retailing discounts and discounts at many restaurants around the city. Passes can in most cases be purchased through the Internet, telephone or at participating sites while they also facilitate trip pre-planning and the cross-selling of destinations. In the UK, sales of the *Edinburgh*

Pass, which was developed by VisitScotland in partnership with Scottish Enterprise Edinburgh and Lothian and the City of Edinburgh Council has sold over 7500 cards since being launched. Although this is just one example of how attractions can collaborate, it does demonstrate the potential of collective working. This chapter will now explore the benefits and drawbacks to visitor attractions of collaboration more generally.

Advantages and disadvantages of attraction collaboration

Collaboration among visitor attractions can potentially take a number of different forms. For example, attractions can share resources, identify areas of mutual benefit, achieve economies of scale or collectively promote the generic appeal of a 'day out' to visitor attractions. The question underpinning all forms of collaboration, however, is the extent to which attractions can best achieve the potential advantages of collaboration, given the severe reservations that pervade the visitor attractions sector when it comes to undertaking collaborative actions. Within this context, the benefits available to attractions from collaborating with one another include:

- the opportunity for attractions collectively to brand, theme and/or package the visitor attraction product within a geographic area,
- benefits to be derived from the pooling of resources (time, finance, expertise, human resource and training),
- scope to reduce individual risk and uncertainty through the sharing of market information,
- an opportunity to enhance the promotion of attractions and distribute the message through even more complex channels of distribution,
- a chance for attractions to raise their individual profile, launch joint marketing campaigns, conduct and share joint research and partake in attraction-specific forums,
- the occasion to develop more effective 'collective' representation with industry and political bodies, and
- the opportunity to work towards harmonizing the objectives of small-, medium- and large-sized visitor attractions.

Furthermore, both intra- and intersectoral collaboration are likely to bring further benefits, including:

- the creation of a 'vehicle' for the natural congruence of tourism objectives between interdependent partners within tourism destinations, and
- an alternative to uneconomic and inefficient 'free-market' solutions whereby decisions are made that are likely to benefit the wider destination rather than individual attractions in isolation.

Despite the many benefits to be derived from collaboration, however, visitor attractions need to be aware of the drawbacks that can potentially arise from such action. Collaboration between attractions can lead to:

- mutual distrust and bad feeling among attractions with contrasting visitor numbers,
- possible apathy, due to the potential tension between competitive and collaborative forces in the marketplace,
- inertia, owing to the failure or inability of attractions to advance at the same pace,
- unhealthy competition from non-participating 'honey-pot' attractions, and
- conflict between attractions with various ownership backgrounds and objectives.

Likewise, further disadvantages that can be derived from both intra- and inter-sectoral collaboration include:

- broad unease over an apparent loss of control over decision making, with some partners sensing a greater loss of control,
- non-achievement as a consequence of limited time, finance and expertise,
- general scepticism of too many attractions being involved to achieve an adequate outcome, and
- widespread unfamiliarity among attractions, which can involve the switching of resources to more familiar, 'safe' strategies.

In addition to the above, a major study undertaken by Canadian Heritage (2006) identifies some highly significant issues pertaining to the wider collaboration of attractions. Notwithstanding this, in view of the current market environment, the author believes that the advantages of collaboration currently outweigh the disadvantages. However, progress will only be made if strategies are seen to be appropriate and desirable. The following section outlines a variety of strategies with existing examples of collaboration 'good practice', firstly with regard to the development of attractions, and secondly with respect to the management and marketing of visitor attractions.

Collaborative management and marketing of visitor attractions

The visitor attraction product and visitor management strategies

When considering the adoption of collaborative management and marketing strategies, it is imperative to balance collaboration with actions and strategies likely to be conducted in competitive isolation. The first area where collaborative strategies can be adopted is with the visitor attraction product itself and corresponding visitor management strategies. It is unlikely that attractions

335

will collaborate in the search for a differential competitive advantage with regard to their 'core' product offering. In other words, each attraction will display a degree of uniqueness which distinguishes it from competing attractions, locally, regionally, nationally and sometimes even internationally. The example of New Zealand's Leading Attractions (NZLAs) is appropriate here, in that it is comprised of a group of the country's most frequently visited attractions, which for the most part are unique and are located in a number of iconic locations in both the North and South Island. Independently owned and operated by a group of professional and well-established operators, this example of attraction collaboration, although dedicated to delivering the best experience possible to visitors, contributes much to the wider development of the New Zealand destination product. In London, the example of Vinopolis, London's unique Wine Tasting attraction, is distinct in that rather than purely being a museum of wine, it offers retailing and merchandizing opportunities, corporate hospitality and the organization of events (Vinopolis, 2007) and represents a unique and multi-faceted attraction. However, in raising the profile of the South Bank as an alternative destination to the more traditional tourist sites north of the Thames, it can be argued that a collaborative 'domain destination' can succeed. Whether through formal or informal collaborative networks, attractions in the vicinity of Vinopolis, such as Shakespeare's Globe, the South Bank Centre and the Tate Modern Gallery, could develop 'destination' visitor management strategies and 'cannibalization avoidance' strategies. This would help to strengthen the collective appeal of the area, while allowing individual attractions to retain responsibility for their own uniqueness, overall quality and 'core' appeal. In order to establish a critical mass of provision, it is advisable for attractions to work in close collaboration with one another.

Further to the above, the search for standards of quality and attainment of quality assurance marks, most probably from the local tourist board, could also be considered to be an individually competitive target for visitor attractions. For example, the Cornwall Association of Tourist Attractions (CATA) has for over 30 years now brought together attractions across the county to improve the overall quality of the visitor experience. Having grown from seven pioneering attractions to over 40 today, CATA has a rigorous programme of inspection that attractions need to pass before joining, while inspections thereafter are ongoing. A similar and longstanding scheme is that of the Hampshire and Dorset Benchmarking Project, which has the collaborative support of a number of key organizations including Hampshire County Council, the South Eastern Museums Service and the Dorset and New Forest Area Tourism Partnership. Of particular interest is the fact that participating visitor attractions are encouraged to seek help from each other, visit one another's facilities and exchange information face to face; in other words to pursue informal collaboration irrespective of their size, location, ownership or volume of visitors.

One further collaborative strategy is that of 'exhibit leasing'. Although it tends to occur between attractions outside of the local area, it can help to address problems of seasonality and/or contribute to the organization of *ad hoc* special events or exhibitions. Although this approach is only just beginning to be adopted among historic houses and castles in an attempt to 'rejuvenate' and 're-energize' their permanent displays, it is a strategy which has been used for many years among operators of Museums and Galleries Commission (MGC, 1998).

Price setting and revenue generation

The need to strike a balance between collaborative and competitive behaviour is particularly evident when it comes to price setting and the generation of revenue by attractions. Whereas initial price-setting decisions and the setting of revenue targets are most often individual attraction decisions, numerous opportunities exist for collaborative price-banding and joint-ticketing initiatives. These opportunities are, however, highly dependent on the demographic profile of visitors at attractions, visitor dwell time and the complementary nature of attractions. For example, very popular attractions such as Edinburgh Castle are often reluctant to participate in collaborative campaigns unless they are very carefully researched and benefits clear. This was not the case with, for example, the Edinburgh Pass, which the attraction declined to join. Joint-ticketing can lead to reduced time spent by visitors at individual attractions, impair visitor satisfaction and reduce the potential for attractions to earn much-needed secondary spend. One area that presents considerable scope for collaboration is in the formation of retail collectives and buying groups. Large numbers of attractions source supplies from the same caterers, printing companies and merchandize producers as their competitors do, and they frequently promote themselves via the same media. Hence, the enhancement of buying power and the benefits to be derived from economies of scale are a real possibility through collective bargaining and collaborative buying.

Marketing communications, advertising and promotion

Perhaps the area where collaboration can bring the most visible benefits to individual visitor attractions is that of marketing communications, advertising and promotion. Collaborative 'generic' promotional activity, which can encourage people to visit attractions in general, is not only a relatively simple task but also one which is likely to generate a relatively quick and positive response. For example, the outbreak of Foot and Mouth Disease in many rural parts of the UK in 2001, especially in Cumbria and Devon, seriously impacted on visitor numbers to attractions in general. Rather than to confront the challenge in isolation, collaborative marketing campaigns offer participant attractions a bigger campaign budget with the potential to reach a wider audience than could possibly have been achieved in isolation. This can then lead to the collective theming, branding and packaging of groups of attractions with possible additional benefits such as opportunities to develop corporate hospitality and collaborative web campaigns. Both the Whisky Trail and the Castle Trail in Scotland are testimony to the success of this approach. They also represent good examples of developing an enhanced identity for attractions in peripheral locations (Briedenhann and Wickens, 2004; Martin and McBoyle, 2006).

With many attractions drawing visitors from both domestic and overseas markets, a dilemma exists as to how the different campaigns are to be balanced between individual competitive and collective collaborative communication. In many cases, it may be that domestic promotional campaigns are handled on an individual basis whereas more expensive and high-risk marketing campaigns overseas benefit from collaborative strategies. This would certainly be the case for attraction attendance at overseas trade fairs and exhibitions where a number of attractions can be represented under an umbrella or themed brand. The cost of developing educational packs, a very important segment for a large number of visitor attractions, would also be spread across many attractions with limited competitive damage to individual attractions. Explore Edinburgh in Scotland is a collaborative marketing campaign designed to draw attention to Edinburgh's scientific-based attractions (see Explore Edinburgh, 2007). With a heavy promotional remit, the development of a dedicated Internet site and educational material are key objectives of the collaborative strategy for attractions which include Our Dynamic Earth, the Royal Botanic Garden Edinburgh, the Camera Obscura, the National Museums of Scotland and Edinburgh Zoo.

Distribution and booking channels

When it comes to the management of distribution and booking channels, visitor attractions can choose to conduct individual 'peak-season' strategies when there are higher levels of demand and adopt collaborative 'off-season' strategies when visitor numbers are likely to be lower. A collaborative approach on this occasion can broaden awareness of the wider attraction's destination and encourage visitors to visit attractions rather than alternative commercial attractions such as shopping or going to the cinema. Perhaps, the greatest benefit here lies with the potential increased bargaining power and scope of influence of attractions with area and national tourist boards, associated bodies (such as the ALVA, the British Association of Leisure Parks, Piers and Attractions and the Association of Scottish Visitor Attractions) and tour operators, than if they were to act alone. With so many individual attractions, over 4500 in England alone, the balance of power is clearly not with visitor attractions. The collaborative approach recommended by the ETC does therefore offer considerable advantages. It can offer the potential for higher margins; it can serve as the vehicle to engender sectoral harmony, direction and influence and it can help to reduce both fixed and variable operating costs. Leaflet-distribution networks are just one area where cost savings can probably be made. Furthermore, collaborative booking systems can serve as engines of change and bring 'virtual' collaboration into being.

Research and human resource management

Finally, the benefits and opportunities of collaborative marketing and management can be applied to the undertaking of research and the management of human resources. For example, although attractions can individually monitor aspects of quality control and conduct customer tracking studies, more in-depth research programmes are normally either too expensive to undertake or too time consuming for staff to conduct. There is also the issue as to whether day-to-day staff members have the necessary skills and expertise to conduct such specialized research. For many visitor attractions, the human resource is a fundamental component of the success of the visitor experience. Hence, although individual attractions are likely to retain control over recruitment and attraction-specific training, the acquisition of skills of benefit to the entire sector such as languages, customer care and visitor reception skills, may best be delivered on a more economic and quality footing if delivered collaboratively. While this may prove difficult in peripheral locations, there are considerable advantages for attractions in close proximity to each other, particularly in urban locations. With staff difficult to recruit and train, cost-effective collaborative approaches, which can bring benefits to the entire sector, are to be encouraged. With so many attractions relying on volunteer staff, particularly those of a heritage genre, there are also benefits to be derived from an agency approach to recruitment. Not only does this keep fixed recruitment and employment costs down for attractions, it also guarantees a 'flexible' labour supply of suitably skilled individuals for the 'destination domain'. Through informal discussion forums, there are considerable advantages to be gained from the dissemination of good practice, and the bringing together of like-minded commercial and business development oriented individuals, which may be to the benefit of the entire visitor attractions sector.

Collaboration dynamics and effectiveness

Collaboration dynamics

Before adopting any of the collaborative approaches to attraction development, management and marketing proposed in the previous section, it is recommended that operators of visitor attractions consider the likely dynamics of collaboration and the potential effectiveness of collaborative strategies. In evaluating the dynamics of collaboration, it is suggested that operators of visitor attractions consider the motives, membership, mission, structure and desired outcomes of collaboration.

Motives

An understanding of the underlying motives among prospective participants for the adoption of a collaborative approach is important in that an examination of motives frequently:

- highlights past or potential problems,
- gives an indication to collaborative organizational forms,

- can identify key individuals and/or a collaboration convenor,
- exposes outside or internal vested interests, and
- can clarify likely stakeholder groups in the collaboration.

A thorough understanding of the reasons behind the adoption of collaborative strategies is also important in that it identifies whether the strategy has arisen in response to a general trend, to an impetus generated from the public sector or whether it has been activated by private-sector need.

Membership

The nature, scope and spread of participants are important in that they are likely to determine the 'domain culture' of the collaborative form. For example, how representative is the collaboration with regard to public and private attractions, those drawing large or small numbers of visitors and/or those that charge for admission? Likewise, are natural attractions, attractions built specifically for tourism (such as museums, galleries and visitor centres) and those built for other purposes (such as castles and historic houses) represented fairly? In short, are sufficient key attractions included to give the collaboration credibility or the scope to achieve desired outcomes? It is frequently the case that the larger the visitor attraction, the less likely they are to participate in collaborative strategies. This was certainly the case back in the mid-1990s when Alton Towers, the number one theme park in the UK in terms of visitor numbers, decided against participating in the Year of the Roller Coaster campaign, a collaborative promotion between 17 theme and amusement parks across the UK (Gilling, 1994). Reasons given for non-participation included the feeling that the promotion was inappropriate, that Alton Towers have a policy of non-participation in discount schemes with other attractions and, as the market leader, collaboration was deemed unnecessary.

Mission

It is also desirable to identify the strategic direction, mission or sense of purpose of the collaborative form, often via the interpretation of the overall objectives. It is essential to clarify:

- the agreed coverage of the collaboration with respect to its span of influence, functional competencies (such as marketing, training and research) and its geographic coverage (whether it is local, regional, national or even international in its remit),
- that participating members share a collective vision for the future, and
- the extent to which broader benefits, other than purely commercial objectives, exist.

The latter point is a highly topical issue for many museums, galleries and historic houses in their attempt to administer effective social-inclusion strategies to meet the aspirations of central government. More generally, it is necessary to agree the time frame for the collaboration as some participants may view it as a short-term 'quick fix', while others may view it as something with more substance and for the longer term.

Structure and outcomes

It is always necessary to identify the desired or likely structure and the planned or desired outcomes of collaboration. When considering the constitutional structure, the balance of power (be it political or financial) needs to be taken into consideration. This leads on to the issue of financial and strategic decision-making independence within the confines of collaboration and raises the dynamic of interorganizational behaviour. For example, is there likely to be a conflict for attractions wishing to preserve their autonomy of decision making while at the same time participating in collective actions? While perhaps wanting to minimize collaborative dependencies and preserve autonomy, many visitor attractions will become part of collaborative relationships as a necessity to acquire the relevant skills, financial and/or human resources to effectively achieve their individual goals. In addition, is collaboration membership driven by 'networking' opportunities rather than the need to achieve strategic goals? Whatever the structure, it is necessary to minimize self-interest and 'free-riding' tendencies if the wider visitor attractions sector is to benefit to any great degree from collaboration.

There is also the question of the desirability of having a degree of flexibility in the structure, or the extent to which a rigid organizing committee structure is necessary to achieve the desired outputs. Related to this is the need to consider the intrinsic nature of the relationship among collaboration partners. This will encompass participants' degrees of commitment, extent of participation and general interest. Attendance and contributions at meetings, and involvement from key personalities, can all evidence this. The cost of membership, the opportunity cost of non-membership, the desire to avoid duplication and overlap and the donation of subsidies or grants may impact on structure, as might the time scale given to achieve the desired collaborative outcomes.

In all of the above, the ultimate goal is the achievement of collaborative compatibility. It is now therefore necessary to outline those factors which contribute most to long term, mutually beneficial relationships.

Collaboration effectiveness

It is in the individual attractions and collective attractions' interest that whatever form of collaboration is adopted, desired outcomes are achieved and maximum effectiveness is reached. A variety of factors are suggested as integral for the achievement of effective collaborative relationships, as seen in Table 20.1.

Table 20.1 Factors contributing to collaboration effectiveness

- The involvement of key stakeholders
- A chemistry of good interpersonal relations and the development of trust among participants
- A suitable inclusive management style and organizational culture
- Domain similarity and goal compatibility among participants
- Duration and nature of previous relationships among collaborating partners
- Effective contractual conditions and exit barriers
- An equity share arrangement
- The balance of management resources and power
- A well-planned project, carefully chosen partners, balanced structure and subsequent high payout in relation to cost
- Decisive leadership
- Sound administrative support
- A tight focus
- The transparent implementation of policy

Table 20.2 Reasons for collaborative failure

- Lack of clear objectives
- Lack of staff time
- Slow decision-making process
- Changes in personnel
- Lack of new ideas/new initiatives
- Lack of adequate negotiation
- Responsibilities not sufficiently established at the outset
- Lack of capital
- Lack of communication and vacuum of objectives

Source: MGC (1998).

In addition to the above, a major study conducted by the MGC (1998) identified a number of factors which contribute to collaborative failure, as evidenced in Table 20.2.

In reviewing the appropriateness of the above factors, it is understandable that different factors will carry more weight in different forms of collaboration. The following section will now discuss many of the issues discussed above and throughout this chapter in the form of a case study, and will attempt to shed light on the collaborative dynamics and effectiveness of interorganizational collaboration.

Case Study

Rembrandt 400: 1606–2006

Motives

In a country where collaboration between tourism and cultural institutions is not commonplace, the 400th anniversary of Rembrandt's birth served as an ideal catalyst for collaboration among a whole host of attractions and organizations. At the very outset, there was acknowledgement among those taking the initiative that such an event provided a once-in-a-lifetime opportunity to raise the profile of both culture and tourism with the quality of the Rembrandt product, a potentially powerful brand for the broader development of visits to museums and attractions, and, of course, Holland. Although it was recognized at the outset that a collaborative approach was never going to be easy, and that good intentions alone were insufficient for real progress to be made, the opportunity for an innovative year-long celebration of Rembrandt was believed to be too good to ignore.

Membership and structure

Commencing with a meeting in January 2003, the Ministry of Culture and Netherlands Board of Tourism & Conventions (NBTC) encouraged collaboration between parties in Amsterdam and Leiden, Rembrandt's place of birth, to bring together a wide diversity of high-profile stakeholders from culture, tourism and local authorities. At the outset it was deemed desirable for stakeholders to be drawn from all sectors of the tourism industry and beyond. Early on however, it was decided that, whereas in later stages of the process all parties would be invited to participate, in the defining stages only those essential for the ultimate success of the project should be setting the structure and goals. The success in gaining early adoption of the generic idea and building belief among the primary stakeholders resulted in the founding of the Rembrandt 400 Foundation. This high-profile board, which included representatives from the Rembrandthuis, Rijksmuseum, Municipality of Leiden, the NBTC, in addition to private and independent members, was successful in establishing a clear goal. This was to commemorate Rembrandt's 400th birth year by initiating a programme that was internationally appealing, both culturally and touristically (see Rembrandt 400, 2007). The Foundation focused on coordination of the programme and of the international promotion and communication. With Queen Beatrix of the Netherlands herself acting as patron for the year and the generous sponsorship of TNT, Shell, the National and Provincial Governments, the cities of Leiden and Amsterdam and Amsterdam Schipol International Airport, funding was set aside in time to be able to encourage match funding and commitment from other partners.

Mission and desired outcomes

With a year-long programme of events planned across Amsterdam, Leiden and Den Haag the objective set was to attract over 1.5 million visits from 900 000 visitors, with 50 per cent estimated to come from abroad/outside the Netherlands. The direct expenditure target set for Amsterdam and Leiden was in the region of €100 million. Although ambitious, at the same time this was considered to be a realistic target based on an attractive proposal which carried a very clear message. Although all participants were responsible for the contribution of their own museums, all parties shared a collective responsibility for the success of Rembrandt 400. Hence, individual museums were not required to pay anything to the Foundation directly but were expected to finance their own exhibitions and individual promotions. Clearly, the investment of time was significant, while individual attractions were responsible for providing tickets, invitations to openings and individual after-hours receptions for Foundation sponsors. Hence, the funds generated by the Foundation were in addition to those funds provided by the individual participants. With regard to marketing, an incremental approach was adopted, with specific local actions planned for 12 markets. Individual marketing communications strategies were planned for the separate country/market mixes with the campaign launched in November 2004, at the World Travel Market in London, to the value of €4–4.5 million. The quality of exhibitions and events included in the programme clearly had to be of a standard commensurate with the 'once-in-a lifetime' theme and consistent with the quality brand developed for the celebrations. Targeting previous heavy users was central to the campaign, while much focus was attributed to the use of the website (Rembrandt 400, 2007). One of the issues arising from the campaign was a fair distribution of attention between Amsterdam and Leiden. It therefore was primarily presented as an event in the Netherlands mainly taking place in two cities. It was also important that each museum and location felt they were getting equal benefit and profile. There was also the constant issue of being realistic about what could be achieved and maintaining the overall quality and consistency of the proposition. The democratic nature of collaboration was questioned on occasions, in that truly democratic collaborative marketing activity can be both time consuming and wasteful. Other issues arising included the fact that to succeed collaboratively sometimes means keeping a distance from some of the other parties involved. Finally, although the Foundation was able to generate a substantial budget to fund the programme, scale clearly does not guarantee success. That said, it was recognized with Rembrandt 400 that sometimes a certain scale is required for collaboration to be successful.

At the end of the year a considerable amount of success was achieved. For example, the initial €1 million budget generated an additional €3 million of match funding, over 2 million visits to museums were recorded with 69 per cent of all visits generated by foreign tourists and over €150 million of extra spending was generated. In addition, Rembrandt 400 served as the catalyst for new channels of distribution, while it also generated a significant amount of positive international press attention. All in all, it proved to be a highly effective form of collaboration with a number of factors contributing to its success. Rembrandt 400 benefited from a long lead time which more than anything else enabled all the partners to get to know each other very well and allowed trust to be built. From the outset a clear, step-by-step approach was adopted that was transparent vis-à-vis goals, conditions and ambitions, while everyone was left alone to undertake what they did best. Clarification of key themes and criteria for the programme were established while once implemented, interference with the local nature of the content was limited with individual partners left to deliver high-quality exhibitions and events. A collective marketing approach was instituted, with the consistent use of the Rembrandt 400 brand logo as its symbol – partly chosen to overcome different needs and language issues; even if in some instances individual participants forgot to use it.

Recognizing that improvements can always be made, a number of lessons were learned for the future. Clearly, the actual form of collaboration was crucial in providing the appropriate processes and structures both to engage partners and to deliver actual results. One important lesson here was the need to ensure that only those deemed essential for the process to occur have influence while everyone else is communicated with, with all partners invited to contribute afterwards. Overall, it was a much bigger success than was ever anticipated and this in itself highlighted the vacuum post-collaboration in that no legacy was planned as it was always viewed as a one-off event. Clearly, opportunities exist for the future with this somewhat belatedly being recognized with a proposed event in 2056!

Source: Gerben Baaij, Rembrandt 400 Foundation.

Conclusion

Irrespective of attraction type and location, visitor attractions need to be far more sensitive to the future needs of the marketplace if they are going to survive in the longer term. Considerable competition from within and outside of the visitor attractions sector is sufficient to threaten visitor displacement at ever increasing levels. In the UK, with the additional burden of government financial support for 'free-admission' policies and generous awards of Lottery funding to many national museums and galleries, the visitor attractions environment is particularly hostile for smaller attractions which constitute the vast majority of the visitor attractions landscape.

This chapter has outlined a number of collaborative management and marketing strategies which, it is hoped, will encourage attractions to play a much more proactive and participative 'collaborative' role in the creation, development and sustainability of the wider tourist destination, as well as to preserve their individual status. Although endorsing the very positive steps taken by the former ETC in the UK in promoting the launch of a cross-sectoral attractions advisory group, the success of any collaborative strategy is ultimately dependent on attractions collaborating with each other. What is required is a far less proprietary, more holistic approach to the management of individual and potentially 'collaborative' attractions by managers and owners for the benefit of the entire visitor attractions sector. Competing attractions are no longer the threat they once were; they are now the source of future strength and 'collaborative' survival.

References

ALVA – Association of Leading Visitor Attractions (2007). *Visitor Attractions Back on Track Following 2005 London Bombings*. Association of Leading Visitor Attractions. Press Release, Wednesday 21 February 2007.

Briedenhann, J. and Wickens, E. (2004). Tourism routes as a tool for the economic development of rural areas: vibrant hope or impossible dream? *Tourism Management*, **25**, 71–79.

Canadian Heritage (2006). *Getting Together: Collaborative Approaches to Cultural/ Heritage Tourism*. http://www.pch.gc.ca/pc-ch/pubs/tourism/documents/ 2006-04/4_e.cfm.

ETC (2000). *Action for Attractions*. English Tourism Council, London.

Explore Edinburgh (2007). *Explore Edinburgh*. http://www.explore-edinburgh.com.

Fyall, A. and Garrod, B. (2005). *Tourism Marketing: A Collaborative Approach*. Channel View Publications, Clevedon.

Fyall, A., Leask, A. and Garrod, B. (2001). Scottish visitor attractions: a collaborative approach. *International Journal of Tourism Research*, **3**, 211–228.

Gilling, J. (1994). Ticket to ride. *Leisure Management*, **14**, 32–34.

Martin, A. and McBoyle, G. (2006). Scotland's Malt Whisky Trail: management issues in a public–private tourism marketing partnership. *International Journal of Wine Marketing*, **18**, 98–111.

MGC (1998). *Collaboration between Museums*. Museums and Galleries Commission.

Northern Ireland Tourist Board (2006). *Survey of Visitor Attractions Annual Report*. Northern Ireland Tourist Board Research and Evaluation Department, July 2006.

Rembrandt 400 (2007). *Rembrandt 400*. www.rembrandt400.com.

Stevens, T. (2000). The future of visitor attractions. *Travel and Tourism Analyst*, **1**, 61–85.

Vinopolis (2007). Vinopolis. http://www.vinopolis.co.uk.

VisitBritain (2006). *Visitor Attraction Trends England 2005*. VisitBritain, London.

VisitScotland (2006). *2006 Scottish Visitor Attraction Barometer*. Commissioned by VisitScotland.

Visit Wales (2006). *Visits to Tourist Attractions 2005*. Visit Wales, May 2006.

Conclusion

Alan Fyall, Brian Garrod, Anna Leask and Stephen Wanhill

The task set for this book was deliberately a more ambitious one than simply to consider how visitor attractions have been managed in the past and how they might best be managed in the present. The editors wanted to try to look into the future to see what visitor attractions have in store for them. This is not to suggest that there is no value in having a sound understanding of the issues that are important to the management of visitor attractions at the present time. Nor is it to ignore the historical antecedents of the present-day visitor attractions sector, the forces that have shaped the development of the sector and the difficulties it has faced along the way. The present depends in no small part on the past. The structure, conduct, and performance of the visitor attractions sector we see today are all functionally related to the various influences the sector has been exposed to in the past and to how visitor attractions, individually or corporately, have responded to those influences. The current management practices used by the visitor attraction, its management culture, the ways in which its core products are presented to the public, and the ways in which it is marketed are also to some extent rooted in the past. Even so, the editors of the book contend that it is not enough simply to have an appreciation of what has happened in the past and to understand what is happening in the present: the most valuable knowledge we can acquire is knowledge of the future. What are the critical opportunities and challenges that visitor attractions can expect to encounter in the future and, most crucially of all, what can and should the managers of those visitor attractions do about them?

Each chapter in this book has sought to identify particular issues that are likely to be of significance in the management of visitor attractions in the future. Many of these issues are generic to the visitor attractions sector as a whole, while others have greater relevance to some types of attractions in particular geographical contexts and less relevance to others. The purpose of this concluding section of the book is therefore to draw together these issues and to present an overview of the management challenges and opportunities that the authors of the various chapters believe to lie in the future for the visitor attractions sector. This, we believe, will provide the reader with further insights into the management of visitor attractions as the sector proceeds into the twenty-first century.

The changing market for visitor attractions

The major markets for visitor attractions are currently replete with challenges for visitor attractions, and these challenges look set to intensify rather than decrease in the foreseeable future. Changing patterns of leisure, an increasingly crowded attraction marketplace and the impacts of new technology are themes that occur time and again in the various chapters of this book, as they are all anticipated to present serious issues for the visitor attraction sector. In Chapter 1, Leask refers to the work of Stevens, who in the early years of the new millennium forecast difficult times ahead for the visitor attraction sector. For smaller attractions, the major threat is that changes in consumer demand are increasingly rendering their product offerings irrelevant to the needs of the market. The result may be that many of the weaker lights will be extinguished from the visitor attraction map over the coming decade.

New responses to the management and marketing of visitor attractions will need to be identified and engaged with if the sector is to rise successfully to such challenges. These issues are discussed in Chapter 3 by Richards and Wilkes, who review a range of influences that are considered likely to increase and reduce demand for visitor attractions over the next decade, and the necessary operational response to maintain successful positioning in the market place. Meanwhile in Chapter 2, Wanhill explores what constitutes necessary conditions for development success by examining the attraction concept, which he terms the 'imagescape'. Failure at this stage implies that no amount of operational expertise can put matters right. Without substantial re-development of the project and a re-launch, the attraction will be one that struggles to survive from one year to the next: a situation that is commonly found among publicly owned attractions and those belonging to not-for-profit organizations.

Taking a larger platform, in Chapter 4 Wanhill identifies the globalization of themed entertainment attractions market as a potential threat to many existing visitor attractions. With acquisition driving the globalization process rather than organic growth, attractions need to beware of being swallowed up by the emerging breed of multinational giants. The imperative for larger attractions will therefore be to become more innovative with their product offerings, develop a much stronger consumer focus, embrace the need to develop quality and to be prepared for casualties along the way. Braun and Soskin, in Chapter 19, make a similar point in the context of the 'living laboratory' of Florida's theme parks, where market consolidation has led to new relationships emerging between visitor attractions and new pricing strategies being adopted as a result. Attraction managers might anticipate further consolidation, leading to further changes in the strategic environment.

Meanwhile, the markets for different visitor attractions continue to fluctuate. In Chapter 11 Ritchie, Carr, and Cooper explore the various opportunities afforded by the school excursion market, while in Chapter 13, Fox and Edwards examine the changing market for garden attractions. Meanwhile in Chapter 17, Boyd highlights a number of growing markets in respect of heritage visitor attractions, including thanatourism (or 'dark' tourism), attractions based on ordinary people and places, heritage trails and routes, and attractions based on personal heritage, such as those based on genealogy and diasporas.

New management approaches

Many commentators paint what is perhaps a somewhat bleak picture of the future of visitor attractions, in which the large get larger, more multifunctional and more commercialized, driving smaller attractions to the wall. Many chapters in this book are, in contrast, rather more optimistic about what lies ahead, although none is entirely confident of a bright future for all. The sheer variety of imagescapes and the number of attractions suggests that the market as a whole falls into the economist's definition of monopolistic competition. This is a situation in which many firms compete and entry and exit is relatively easy, but each is protected by a differentiated product. In the case of attractions, this product differentiation is often in the form of geographical location. Indeed, unlike commodities, the product offer has to be consumed at the place of production, which highlights the importance of market boundaries or catchment areas. The position usually taken is that even smaller, traditional-style attractions can prosper in a changing market provided that they smarten up their operational procedures, perhaps even adopting new management strategies when existing approaches are deemed no longer helpful or appropriate. The adoption of information technology (IT) is crucial here, for by lowering distribution costs for suppliers and reducing search costs for consumers, via the Internet in particular, market potential is widened. Experience has shown that the IT phenomenon has radically increased the collective market share of niche products and flattened the sales distribution pattern, producing what has been termed by writers in this field as 'the long tail' that allows many more products to sustain themselves in the marketplace.

Where the chapters taking this more positive view differ, perhaps predictably, is on the question of which elements of the management process require reform. In Chapter 16, for example, Watson and McCracken highlight a need for visitor attractions to adopt a more strategic approach to human resource management. After all, if visitor attractions are essentially people-centred activities, improved human resource management is likely to provide a coherent response to the challenges faced by the sector both now and in the near future. In Chapter 10 Garrod offers a sustainability route, arguing that heritage-based visitor attractions in particular should be more seriously concerned with the task of walking the fine line between enhancing the accessibility of the site for current generations and protecting the authenticity of the site in the interests of posterity. The importance of sustainable development thinking is also stressed in Chapter 17 by Boyd in the context of heritage tourism.

On the other hand, Xie and Wall in Chapter 8 take up the torch of authenticity, although in the very different context of visitor attractions based on ethnicity. Central to their argument is that while authenticity may be a multidimensional and slippery concept, it is nevertheless one that those responsible for managing visitor attractions must come to terms with or else risk failure. Meanwhile both Boyd, in Chapter 17, and Fyall, in Chapter 20, stress the importance of marketing in the successful management of the future visitor attraction. Yet even then their emphases are rather different. While Boyd proposes a widening of the marketing approach to include people, programming, and partnership, Fyall highlights the central importance of developing collaborative partnerships in the marketing and promotion efforts of visitor attractions. In Chapter 18, Hall highlights the importance of urban parks as visitor attractions and demonstrates how they can become part of the sense of place of residents in the local community. He goes on to explore how the marketing and management of an attraction can be influenced by wide institutional changes over time.

If there is agreement among the various authors of the chapters of this book, however, it is that new directions in managing visitor attractions must be identified as a matter of urgency. It is clear that existing paradigms do not provide an adequate basis for the visitor attraction sector as we know it to prosper. In the face of increasing competition it is important to take a wider look at the operations of the business through the process of benchmarking. The latter is a systematic way of identifying how your business performs against a given reference point, thus enabling management to assess their functioning against that of their competitors and identifying opportunities for improvement.

Continuing challenges

Various chapters of this book also identify a number of perpetual challenges for the visitor attraction sector: one being the influence of temporal variation. In Chapter 12, for example, Goulding shows that seasonality is a broad and complex phenomenon that goes beyond the immediacy of the market place. He goes on to argue that while there is much that attractions can do to address the effects of seasonality on their operations, many will have to accept that developing a year-round operating period is an unrealistic target. Such attractions should therefore concentrate their efforts on adapting to the seasonal 'down-time' in more innovative ways.

The role of technology is highlighted in a number of the chapters of this book, and it is clear that information and communication technology is set to play an increasingly central role in various management functions, including marketing, promotion, interpretation and education, and visitor management. While this much is agreed, there would appear to remain very real differences on the matter of whether this might be a good or a bad thing. In Chapter 4, for example, Wanhill points out that the most recent radical innovation coming from the 'imagineers' of the giant US theme parks is to combine the physical and virtual world using state-of-the-art technologies. However, the costs associated with such innovations have tended to be immense, so that only parks that are located within their own resort destinations have been able to bear them. This further increases the competitive advantage of global chains over their smaller independent rivals. Earlier, in Chapter 2, Wanhill notes the concerns that have been expressed about the popularization of the attraction imagescape through the use of technology, such that the medium becomes emphasized at the expense of the message. To take the technology route alone is to embark on a fashion cycle that may be unsustainable financially in the longer term. Contrary to the position of some media pundits, Voase presents in Chapter 9 the beneficial view that rather than 'dumbing down' the cultural visitor attraction experience, the use of new technology has enabled the proliferation of knowledge in society more generally. This, in turn, has changed the nature of the visitor experience: rather than to undermine or dilute it, managers of visitor attractions have been able to lower the threshold of engagement of the experiences they offer. As a result, two new breeds of visitors can now be identified: the 'thoughtful' visitor, who is the product of the proliferation of knowledge in the technology-dense postmodern society, and the 'smart' visitor, who is the product of the commodification of that same knowledge. Moscardo and Ballantyne, meanwhile, discuss the 'mindful' visitor in Chapter 14, within their appraisal of the role of interpretation in the success of an attraction.

Many of the chapters in this book note the growing recognition of the sustainability imperative among managers of visitor attractions. In Chapter 10, Garrod argues that sustainability is central to the mission of heritage-based visitor attractions, and therefore that managing visitor impacts on the attraction site should be seen as fundamental to the role of the visitor attraction manager. If today's visitors compromise the very things that they are coming to see, then clearly it will not be possible for future generations to witness these treasures in all their splendour. In some cases, all that may be left is a virtual representation of the artifact in question. In Chapter 7, meanwhile, Robbins and Dickinson highlight the potential for attractions to provide more sustainable alternatives for those travelling to, from, and within tourism destinations. They note the somewhat paradoxical situation wherein attractions that are marketed as sustainable exist in locations where access is largely by car. To date, policies to achieve modal switch have not worked and they report the need to formulate a coherent integrated strategy combining tourism and transport policies on a regional and national level.

In Chapter 5, Prideaux considers the task of creating viable visitor attractions in peripheral areas. He identifies a number of continuing challenges for attractions in such locations, including overcoming lack of accessibility on the part of visitors, coping with competition, and gaining local community support. Certainly it would appear that as the degree of peripherality increases, so the issue of scale becomes more important and the risk of failure increases. He goes on to argue that if the countryside is not to be littered with the wreckage of failed visitor attractions that have been developed using public funds in the name of supporting local communities, funding bodies will need to examine the long-term viability of such attractions much more carefully. Meanwhile there is much that peripheral visitor attractions can do to secure their viability in spite of their location, including encouraging visitors to overcome the effort and inconvenience involved in travelling to out-of-the-way places by providing them with high-quality visitor services and experiences not found in the core.

Finally, it is clear that visitor attractions will continue to be challenged by ever more rapidly changing visitor motivations as we move further into the new millennium. Nowhere is this better illustrated that in the case of spiritual attractions which, as Shackley notes in Chapter 15, have generally been experiencing growing visitor numbers in spite of the increasing secularization of society. One can only speculate as to why this might be the case: perhaps today's visitor is seeking to spend leisure time in holy places as a substitute for personal prayer and worship, or perhaps visiting religious sites represents a new form of pilgrimage. What is clear, however, is that visitor motivations across the visitor attraction sector as a whole are changing rapidly. Yet for the most part they remain seriously under-researched and, as a result, poorly understood.

New drivers of attraction development

A number of the chapters in this book identify the considerable tensions that underlie the management of visitor attractions. This is made clear in Chapter 1, where Leask argues that the multiple stakeholder interests involved in a given visitor attraction, be they related to education, revenue generation or conservation, inevitably lead to management conflicts as visitor attraction managers are pulled between their competing demands. These aspects are largely related to patterns of ownership, as well as the type of attraction. Cultural heritage establishments are the classic examples of not-for-profit organizations where their mission statement, rather than the financial bottom line, has defined the outcomes. The past decade has seen the visitor attractions sector continue to widen and deepen their stakeholder relationships, taking their clients and the local community into their web of stakeholder interests, so that the challenges facing these organizations come in many forms, including changing visitor attitudes and societal needs, increasing public and private competition, the need to find alternative financial resources to public funds, and their involvement in non-pecuniary forms of exchange – time, expertise, and commitment. It might therefore be expected that such management conflicts will intensify in the future. Shackley observes that such conflicts are particularly evident among religious sites, where managers are expected to juggle the opposing interests of worshippers, visitors, the local community, and conservation. It is clear that one of the new drivers of change in the visitor attraction sector in the coming decade will be an increasingly intense interplay between an ever-widening stakeholder-base and therefore the ability of managers to reconcile the different agendas. Meeting the organization's objectives becomes clearer when all the participants are guided by a sound marketing plan, which is based on a strong foundation and makes the most of relationships with management, the board of governors and external stakeholders – sponsors, community volunteers, and visitors.

In Chapter 6, Henderson moves the discussion of visitor attraction development onto a higher level by considering developments in East Asia. Noting that attraction projects are rarely driven by economic forces alone, she shows how in the cases of Hong Kong and Singapore they are employed by national governments and their agencies in exploring, discovering, and expressing various dimensions of their national and cultural identities. Hence, political and social factors are at least as important drivers of visitor attraction development as economic forces. In Hong Kong, the development of visitor attractions has been central in reaffirming the distinctive local culture following the return of the former British colony to China, whereas in Singapore visitor attractions have been used as a means of assisting the social integration of culturally disparate local communities. The two destinations are now responding to the challenges of tourism expansion in the region by pursuing comparable tourism strategies, which are directed at almost identical objectives of pre-eminence as Asian city destinations, through investing in similar types of attractions, namely integrated resorts in the form of Hong Kong Disneyland, and Marina Bay and the island of Sentosa in Singapore. While it might be argued that the exporting of the Disney theme to Hong Kong represents the working of a rather similar global agenda, it is interesting to note that the lessons learned from Disneyland Paris have been used to draw back on some of the more overtly American cultural features of the Disney product in Hong Kong.

Finally, many of the chapters in this book emphasize that collaboration will be increasingly important in the future. Indeed, in Chapter 20 Fyall makes the case that collaboration represents a lifeline for smaller, independent visitor attractions that are threatened by the changes in market conditions referred to earlier in this conclusion. He goes on to point out that the success or otherwise of collaboration lies in how well individual visitor attractions prove willing and able to work with one another through supporting the growth of the visitor economy, so that the 'rising tide lifts everybody'. It is clear that in order to achieve this, individual visitor attractions need to adopt a less proprietary and more holistic approach to management and marketing, viewing competitors not as a market threat but as a source of potential future strength and collaborative survival. This theme is also taken up by Boyd in Chapter 17, who argues that investing in partnerships will be a key factor in determining the success or otherwise of strategies to secure a prosperous future for the visitor attractions sector.

Endnote

Terry Stevens

What does the future have in store for visitor attractions? In considering this question, it is worth reflecting on the unprecedented growth in the number of attractions of all shapes and sizes that have developed in recent decades. In some countries, supply has more than doubled, while in others the development of new attractions has transformed landscapes, rejuvenated destinations and in some cases served to create new identities for cities, regions and even countries. Since the turn of the century, however, the attractions industry has faced intense competition from a wide range of rapidly emerging, innovative leisure and entertainment products to the extent that in many mature tourism destinations, demand for these traditional attractions is actually now in decline. There are real fears for the viability and survival of many of these attractions. At the same time, however, major new players in the industry are responding strongly to changing market demands with the development of an exciting new genre of attractions. Some of these are being built in unusual venues, thus creating very different tourism destinations for the new millennium. These developments will require different forms of management and organizational structures if they are to work, while all attractions will have to respond to the challenges of major external factors affecting demand. These include demographic changes, growing environmental awareness and issues pertaining to 'carbon footprint', security and safety issues, new booking and travel patterns, and factors relating to health, well-being and lifestyle.

In recent years, designers, operators and investors have attempted to reinvent the concept of the visitor attraction in response to the changing patterns of consumer demand. Much of this activity has built upon the pioneering work of Disney with its resort developments in the USA, Japan, France and Hong Kong over the past 40 years, but recent developments break new ground. This includes the emergence of a new geography of destination attraction that emerges from development in association with other sectors of business or tourism; innovation to create a new generation of all-inclusive, multifaceted destination attractions with year-round operation, appealing to different markets at the same time; and the polarization convergence of retailing activity with the entertainment and enjoyment aspects of day trips. The distance between these aspects of the day visit is rapidly eroding and will, no doubt, soon disappear. The result will be that shopping and entertainment will become fully integrated with the visitor attraction. Although the investment appeal of these developments has traditionally been limited, these new trends are likely to lead to fresh sources of funding and finance being introduced to the sector. All these developments result from the changing patterns of leisure behaviour leading to the growth of demand for leisure shopping, eating and drinking and entertainment as essential components of a day trip and holiday trip.

Increasingly, leisure consumers are becoming constrained by complicated lifestyles and are seeking leisure offers that are more in touch with their needs embracing healthier eating, growing interest in activities and requiring a range of experiences. The markets most likely to visit attractions and destination attractions are the more affluent, better-educated, older and more travelled, and markets with greater experience in quality service and facilities, markets more sophisticated in their use of leisure time. In the future, therefore, all attractions must be able to meet successfully a wide range of customer requirements that embrace retail, entertainment, education and fun in a safe, comfortable, high-quality environment. These attractions will increasingly trade in ethical ways, constantly innovate and have clearly identifiable brand values. Most probably they will also have well-articulated corporate social responsibility policies and programmes. However, while these attributes are to be found in abundance in the new generation of destination attractions being specifically designed for this purpose, they are much more difficult to provide in the more traditional visitor attraction context.

The future is likely to remain relatively bright for those signature attractions that are regarded as 'must-see places' on most tourist itineraries. Equally, those attractions that continue to innovate with their product and become market- or customer-focused are more likely to survive. This will necessitate a real commitment to quality, as well as becoming more price competitive and developing multiple sources of revenue. It can be argued, furthermore, that the emerging economies will soon create resident markets with disposable income and aspirational demands for entertainment and enjoyment in unusual settings. These countries will also offer attractive land and property deals to investors. As a result, there is likely to be a burst of interest in the potential to create these new destination attractions in these countries. Both of these trends effectively use the concept of the 'destination attraction' to create new tourism destinations in their own right. Under these conditions, Gunn's original testimony to the power of the attraction as the main energizer of tourism in a region appears to remain true even under these new conditions. If, however, the attraction is to remain the 'lodestone' for tourism the industry must accept this redefinition, be prepared for casualties and adopt new ways of working, as evidenced in this very timely and much-needed second edition.

Index